ORIGIN OF INSPIRATION

Seven Short Essays for Creative People

SAMUEL ADOQUEI

Lectures Given at

The National Academy School of Fine Arts,

New York City, New York

SANKOFA

Readers who are interested in seeing more of the author's artworks are invited to visit:
www.samadoquei.com
or interested in reading books and articles by or of the author
visit www.HowSuccessfulArtistsStudy.com.
Email the publisher at:
unionsquarestudio@earthlink.net

The meaning of the image on the cover is explained at: www.OriginofInspiration.com

Origin of Inspiration is a sequel of the author's first book
How Successful Artists Study published in 2010
by Sam Adoquei, printed by Advanced Litho Printing,
226 9th Avenue South, Great Falls, Montana 59405

This edition of *Origin of Inspiration* is published in 2013
by Sam Adoquei, printed by Advanced Litho Printing,
226 9th Avenue South, Great Falls, Montana 59405

ISBN: 978-0-578-07278-4

Typeset in The United States by Jeff Sangray
Printed and bound by Advanced Litho Printing,
Great Falls, Montana

FURTHER READING
Download articles by and about Mr. Adoquei
For free at: www.OriginofInspiration.com

This book is for my parents
Aunty Adjorkor and Jesse Adoquei
and my dearest Julian Casablancas.

This book, in some ways, is a token of my appreciation to the United States of America. I would like to thank the United States for giving me the greatest of opportunities, platforms, and freedoms. I could never ask for a better opportunity.

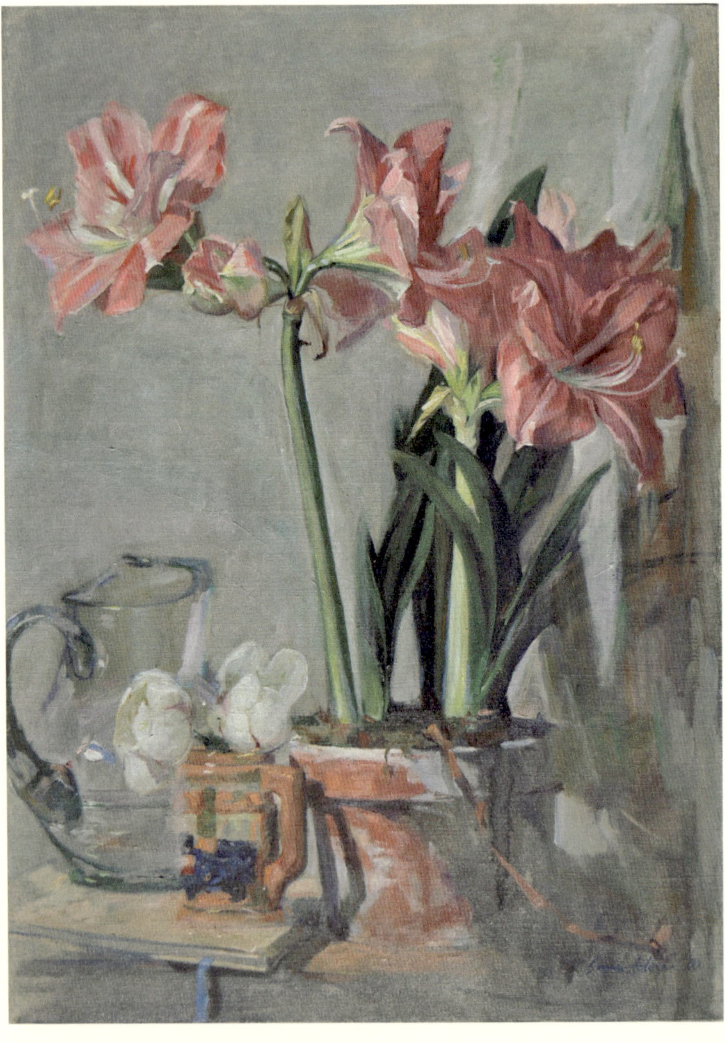

Irises and Peonies, Sam Adoquei

ENJOY IMAGES IN DETAIL download all images for free at: www.OriginofInspiration.com

Table of Contents

FOREWORD

I owe everything to Sam and the ideas he has revealed in this new edition. My life completely changed once I was introduced to him. He taught me how to think about art and eventually how to attack it, making me a living example that his approach is almost fool-proof.

Every artist needs a mentor, and this book is like having Sam, the greatest one you could imagine, all for yourself. Reading it is just like hearing him speak, and hearing him speak is what single-handedly taught me to be the best artist I could be.

He explains things in a simple way, taps into the part of your mind that holds all your passion, and helps you unleash it. People think it's mostly talent which makes you good, but there are actually objective principles that can help you be among the best, or at the least pretty darn good. Sam is able to break it down and lay it out in an attainable strategy, which can be inspiring in and of itself. Even if you don't become the "best" technically, your mastery can still give you an exceedingly high level of fulfillment and confidence.

Sam's message has always been exciting for me to hear because it makes all of your goals and dreams right within your grasp. He teaches you how passion makes practice fun, and how each step, each drawing, each exercise, when done the right way, becomes an everlasting brick towards building greatness, skill and accomplishment.

Still to this day, the teachings and fundamentals in this book continue to guide me on my learning path...

I hope you can take as much from his treasures of wisdom as I have.

Enjoy!

-JC

Julian Casablancas is an American songwriter, singer, musician and frontman of The Strokes.

ACKNOWLEDGEMENTS

This book is only possible because of the experiences and knowledge I have acquired from both my luck and my misfortunes as I have been pursuing art and living life. For this reason, I am very thankful to have the reasoning knowledge to accept that everything that has come my way is good, to have the mind that avoids any sort of resentment due to all unwanted experiences. Looking back, Nature embedded all the lessons I needed and gave me the strength of mind and knowledge to see my challenges and failures as inspirations in disguise. My friends, too, have served as guardian angels in disguise, especially Julian.

In taking on the writing of a book, which is new territory for me, there is nothing more important and challenging than tough questions. And thanks to my students, I have had an abundance of such tough questions. I'd like to recognize and acknowledge the valuable editing experience of my great and kind editor, Martha Crow. Without Martha, the manuscript for this book would still be buried amongst my other hundreds of sheets of manuscript in my files. Martha made this book possible. Thank you, Ann Buenaventura, for all your help with all my books.

In particular, I would also like to thank Nancy Little, and special thanks to Jennifer King for all her help and great editing skills and experience. I also want to express my deep thanks to Mr. Stone and Tom Shea for all they have done for me. Jeanette Christjansen, Usha Sharma, and Karen Haider – thank you all for everything. Thanks also to Willye Malveaux Dent, Cidny Klein, Kenji and Nao Motomatsu and Marilyn and Jay Bould.

Special thanks to Marie-France Siegler of Chataeu de Pecany for her friendship. Daniel Petit, Sylvie Ducrocq-Chevallier, Jean Francois and Annick Chassaigne, Jean-Luc and Emmanuelle Ojeda, Mr. Large, Jim Pattinson, Joyce Petit, Mr. and Mrs. Gilbert Fauchet, Richard and Susan Griffen and Brigitt Autet. Thanks to Bill Cady. Without Bill Cady's help, this book would have stayed a dream.

How to Use This Book

The content/sequence of the book is not in a particular order, it is put together like a buffet: Take, eat or drink what you want at the time you want it.

Note From the Author

Readers who have already read my companion book, *How Successful Artists Study*, may notice some familiar passages borrowed from it and incorporated into this book. The passages may look the same, but there are subtleties in reasoning that differ and new ideas added that you'll find worth exploring further.

PREFACE

Once I was going through my lecture series when a student stopped me with this comment:

"You talk so much about ethics and creativity! I am stuck here with my stupid little painting, and I have no inspiration at all to continue. How can I think about everything you are talking about when I feel like destroying this little painting and going home? I am not inspired. How do creative people get the inspiration to work? Please, I'd like to know." The series of lectures that answered this frustrated question became the foundation of this book. Even though the initial context was art, *Origin of Inspiration* will benefit all creative people—entrepreneurs, musicians, actors, writers, anyone in search for inspiration.

I have always made it a point to search and find answers and solutions to questions or problems my students might have, as long as the question or problem relates to the pursuit of fine arts. If after 30 years of practicing fine art, I can't find answers to a question related to pursuing art, then I have somehow missed some key knowledge. I'm talking about the experience and wisdom one should gain from three decades of teaching in a particular field, not curiosity of the innocent student who is thirsty for knowledge. To me no question is a bad question if I don't know the source of the questions; it is this personal principle that led to searching and finding an answer to a frustrated but honest and genuine question of "how can any creative mind find enduring inspiration to assist their dreams and goals? How can anyone find the source of inspiration? And why do only few artists have enduring inspiration that leads to accomplishing their dreams? The answers to these questions provide the foundation of *Origin of Inspiration*.

Origin of Inspiration is a book for artists, musicians, filmmakers, actors, entrepreneurs, and creative people—anyone who would like to find the enduring inspiration and continuous enthusiasm to support his or her artistic journey.

Instead of believing that inspiration comes only to the chosen few creative people, *Origin of Inspiration* taps into three decades of experience to prove that any creative mind can find enduring inspiration to guide his dreams until he achieve his goals. The book points out how creative minds attuned to a certain purpose and focused on certain goals never run out of inspiration. Drawing upon similar research, the book also proves that it is never too late to find one's own creative path and passion.

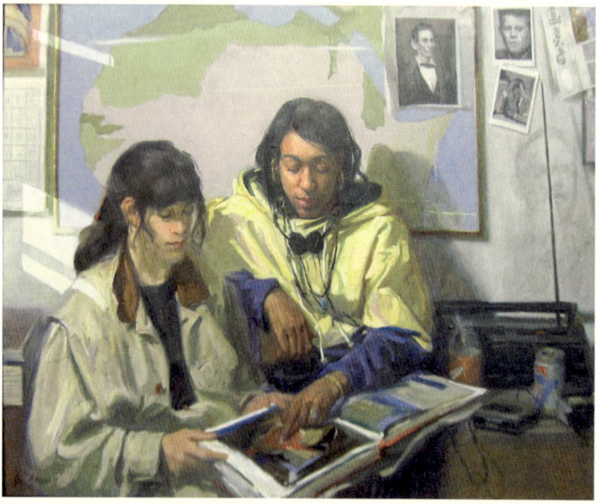

Social Studies, Sam Adoquei

ENJOY IMAGES IN DETAIL download all images for free at: www.OriginofInspiration.com

1 EARLY INSPIRATIONS

Introduction

Art does not change man's nature—profound ideas do. Neither being a highly creative nor a highly skilled artist, nor the use of attention-grabbing techniques, contributes to the noble mission that is life. It is great ideas that make the difference and contribute to the advancement of mankind. Creative visionaries with a purposeful mission to be of some use to humanity always change the status quo for the better.

To be blessed with talent is to be chosen to fulfill your noble duty by developing that talent. We see this in the Old Masters, who were more than just skillful technicians. They were creative professionals following their highest, most noble desire to contribute to the advancement of mankind and to life through their art. The difference between yesterday's Old Masters and the artists of today is in the focus of their efforts and the nobility of their quest.

More than thirty years of experience in helping artists to find their own vision and to follow in the path of the great artists has helped me discover how the Old Masters achieved greatness—what traits and practices they had in common with each other. I have also learned how the artists of today can cultivate their own awareness and their own creative talent in order to improve life and the physical universe. If I want to contribute to the culture that I have become part of I can no longer keep to myself and my students my secret discoveries, theories and ideas about art. This book is my token of appreciation to America and to everyone in America for what they have done to help me pursue my artistic vocation. The following essays, which contain some of my ideas, are partly based on material from my book, "*How Successful Artists Study*."

In these essays, I make certain the traits of the Old Masters accessible to today's artists so that all of us may use our creative minds to make a difference and to leave a lasting legacy. Everyone acquires an advantage from having some kind of map, as well as some ideas, to use for our guidance in the new era. How can we as artists best use our creative talent to encourage and inspire through creating meaningful works of art for all?

I have kept the views discussed in these pages personal. As an educator with years of experience, I have tried to avoid putting forth scholarly views so as not to repeat facts and bore the reader. Almost all of the material in the essays is based on question and answer lectures I gave while teaching. I have expanded them here in hopes of refreshing the reader's thinking with my new and natural artistic thoughts. My ideas are new mainly because I come from a different background than that of my students, a background that holds different views of the role man should play in both his mundane and his sacred environment.

From Abraham Lincoln to Martin Luther King, Jr.

As a child growing up in Ghana, my friends and I were very happy whenever we saw white people. We followed them around and sang songs, songs of thanks to God for creating different people. Almost forty years have passed and I still remember vividly some of those songs. The lyrics offered thanks and praise to God who made it possible for us to see people who had come from across the ocean. The few times that whites passed by our school, the teachers would suspend classes to let us go look at them and wave. When I lived in Italy, the tables were turned. My boss's children followed me to the washroom, curious to see if my skin color would wash off. It was the most wonderful, beautiful and innocent experience.

In America, we have so many rich experiences of differences between people that we no longer see them as gifts. We don't understand that they are what make this country unique and different from any other country in the world, and that they need to be celebrated. The wonderful, beautiful and innocent experiences I had in Ghana and Italy have not only influenced my art but will always be part of my art.

I started my painting "From Lincoln to Martin Luther King" (which was mainly influenced by this childhood experience) more than seven years ago. At the time, I wanted my painting to represent America. In the first version of the painting, I included images of John F. Kennedy and Martin Luther King, Jr. Three years ago, I added Abraham Lincoln. In October 2008, I added Barack Obama because he represents both the celebration of our differences and the unity of our nation. He reminds me of the beauty of innocence. When I first painted this piece, I was advised that the subject could be a bit too political. Seven years later the Historical Society of Washington, D.C., exhibited the painting at The Historical Society of Washington, D.C., Museum.

After thirty years of painting and teaching art, I still don't know if art imitates life or life imitates art. But experience tells me that all meaningful purpose gets rewarded. It is this that inspires me to create art from the universal and timeless subjects that promote peace and love among people.

Samuel Adoquei, 26 August 2008

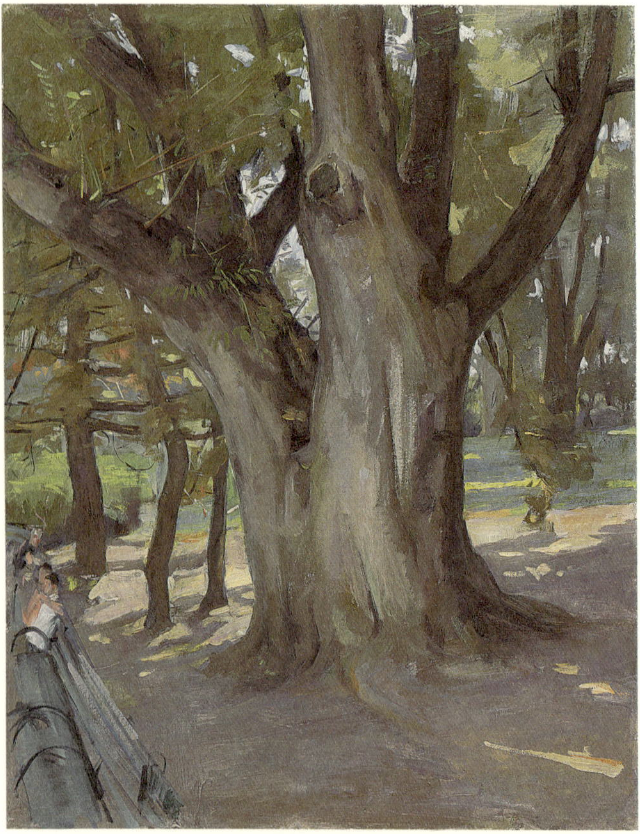

An Old Tree in Central Park, Sam Adoquei

ENJOY IMAGES IN DETAIL download all images for free at: www.OriginofInspiration.com

2 IN PURSUIT OF PASSION

Throughout man's evolution, or progress, few achievements have been accomplished without passion. Great accomplishments are generally produced by those with a passionate love for their field of expertise. Why else would someone with the ability and brains to make millions on Wall Street choose to become a nurse, to make less income and be unknown? Why else would one scientist choose to find a way to put thousands of songs on a small portable device, while another chooses to study how cockroaches multiply? Why else would one young man pursue law to help the underprivileged while another pursues music to entertain? The simple reason is that we humans have a certain innate quest, driven by passion, to fulfill a certain duty. We must feed this inner desire in order to feel worthy of living.

Passion is a reward given to us long before an accomplishment is realized or a duty fulfilled; it is a reward just like others, such as success, money, prizes and recognition. But unlike those rewards that one gets from the finished accomplishment, passion is invisible and intangible. It is cast upon us without our choosing. It comes in the form of a spell from the supreme intelligence. Passion is embedded in our subconscious and protected within us until our duty is finished and every little bit of the reward has been fully enjoyed. We are no match for the spell passion casts upon us. Money gives us the means to afford things. Prizes and recognition give us fame, which is sometimes a certain kind of happiness in society. Only passion gives us a powerful emotion, a supreme strength and the enduring energy to fulfill our duty. It provides a stimulus, giving us hope and courage as well as stamina. The strength, love and joy passion gives us have no limitations. They are what drive us to sacrifice everything in order to achieve that which our passion requires. Passion is like a bribe from the gods, its great enthusiasm enticing us to do a particular work and to enjoy that more than anything else, without thought of the sacrifices and consequences.

As we go about our daily business, there are several signals that lead us to claim this love and boundless enthusiasm known as passion in the service of our duty. All that is needed on our part is to lean toward that duty, to listen to our inner self and look carefully for the clues. Because of the supreme intelligence's ultimate design everyone has an individual passion (a means of automatically contributing to the well-being of the universe). It is the universe's form of division of labor. For the universe to go on forever the seasons should not fail and the books must be balanced at all costs. We must all contribute by fulfilling the particular duty assigned to us. It is for this reason that we cannot accept the theory that some are created with more talent and passion than others. Not finding your own passion and thus fulfilling your duty does not mean that the creator overlooked assigning you your responsibilities and therefore you can just breathe freely. Neither does it mean you have been refused a bliss to follow. The quandary you are in may be due to circumstances beyond your control. Or it might mean you have felt comfortable settling for what life throws at you—perhaps you think that only a certain kind of person deserves to pursue a special purpose and you yourself lost out long ago. However, it is in the interest of the Creator, the architect of the universe, and it is his duty, to see that the universe go on forever. Our natural material world should advance and be preserved.

For that matter, it is in the creator's interest that no one should be left behind without a purposeful life. It is also in his interest that we should have inner strength and love, everlasting joy and happiness. In addition, we should have inspiration, an electrified, charged agenda while we pursue our purposeful life. Without such an innate reward as passion, we will not fulfill our duty well and it will be his creation, our natural material world, that will suffer. So it is our right to have passion as a tool to assist our ambitions. Ambition in a specific field without passion makes work a nine-to-five job. Our passionate ambitions are therefore our special assigned duty. And the joy of living a fulfilling life is to create with a meaningful purpose.

The way to find your own passion is to ask yourself questions about what you like to do, and then narrow the many possibilities down to just a few. Start with your own list of ideas. What did you dream of doing when you were a child or a teenager? Ask your friends, your colleagues and your family what they think you like to do based on their observations of you. You might have 10 lists by the time you're finished. After all the lists have been made, cancel out the ideas you definitely know you don't want to pursue.

You can know those you don't like just because you are a human and it is not part of your genetic makeup to like many fields equally. There will be some things on the list that will hold your interest more than others. And then there will be some that you really wouldn't like to cross out—it is those that you really don't want to cross out that you might want to consider. Narrow the remaining items down to three, five or seven options. Hide the list for a month or two; mark this down on your calendar and resist thinking about the list during this time. When the time is up, without looking at the list, see which idea you remember without too much effort. Follow your heart at the end of the day. If we really and honestly listen to ourselves, more often than not, there is one thing that we prefer to pursue. But for some weird reason we always find excuses why we shouldn't or can't pursue that field. We never ever give that field a try. If you follow your heart, you will not have to go too far to find your own passion.

At this point, if you really want to challenge yourself and pursue happiness, you might want to get out of your existing situation, your comfort zone, and pursue the choice you have selected. Don't imagine that it is by chance you have found your talent, rather see this self-discovery as if it is your calling and nature is on your side. Take this further by acquiring skill, experience and knowledge in the area you have chosen, in order to enjoy both happiness and success in the field of your passion. You are only a dreamer if you follow your passion without skill, experience and knowledge. It is also very frustrating to love a field in which you lack skill and knowledge. The best way to acquire skill, experience and knowledge is to start with a couple of fun workshops in two or three of the choices you have made, then see which area you really like. Then, when you have discovered one you like, follow up and take the whole thing further by taking more workshops, until you decide to take regular classes in the specialty you prefer. If you can see these workshops as an investment in yourself, then it will be the most inexpensive investment you can ever make. Spend two to three years trying different workshops before finally deciding. On an average a couple of years should be sufficient to acquire enough skill, experience and knowledge in any field you have dreamt of to be able to pursue the field professionally. This also proves that between the ages of twenty-eight and sixty-five one still has a chance to find his calling, either professionally or as a hobby.

If, after reading this essay I have written for you (to prove that the creator is not partial in his distribution of talent, passion and inspiration), you don't do anything with this information (these wakeup calls), if you don't take the initiative to find your own talent, passion and inspiration, you have indirectly proven that it is you who has made the conscious choice to be a follower. It is not a choice made by an unfair, unkind or wicked creator or a bad environment. Because of this essay you have been enlightened, directly or indirectly, by the idea of the pursuit of self, talent, passion and inspiration. Whether you find the arguments I have made awakening and take the matter further, asking the right questions to find helpful answers, is left up to you. If you don't give it a try, or attempt any of the suggestions here, you should not be shocked at what the future brings. As Honoré de Balzac said: "An unfulfilled vocation drains the color from a man's entire existence."

The gift of passion is too good a reward to waste. Those who do not claim the reward leave their duty unfulfilled and may well suffer self-guilt and blame strong enough that no other rewards can be enjoyable. Generally, such people just seem bored with life and guilty; this boredom and guilt is a form of punishment from nature for not fulfilling one's responsibility to contribute to the division of labor. Life will not be as enjoyable and rewarding as it is supposed to be. Some great achievements can be accomplished without passion. But it is more inspiring, adventurous, rewarding and worthy of life's journey to achieve life's goals with passion.

Passion is very elusive and intangible; you don't have to worry if you have it or not. The student does not have to worry at all about having it or not. Sometimes the awareness of the passion comes to you slowly over time. The student should not wait for it to show up before acting on his vocation, because there have been many great achievers whose passion came once they were already in the field. You can find your passion by using the method I have described above.

They are other reasons why one does not necessarily need passion at the beginning of their education or training. For instance, statistics show that over two-thirds of all successful people are successful doing something they don't like. Less than one-third of successful people like what they do and only one percent of this one-third is passionate about what they do. Whether this passionate one percent went into their field with innate passion or discovered their passion afterwards is hard to tell. But anything is possible when passionate people have a reason and purpose supported by experience and knowledge. Some people are very good and very successful at what they do but not passionate about it. However, passion alone gives you that overwhelming joy and love that nothing else, no reward, prize or recognition can replace.

Written as a lecture for students at The National Academy School of Fine Arts, November 2008

Surviving 72 Days of Nothingness

How did two men survive a 10-day hike through snowy mountains—without proper gear and with no skiing or mountain climbing experience? Scientists have been unable to answer this question for decades. More than thirty years ago a plane crashed in the Andes, near the border of Argentina and Chile. Searchers, sure that no one could survive under such frigid conditions, gave up the attempt to rescue the plane's 45 passengers after just eight days. Seventy-two days later, the two men who made the trek out directed the Chilean air force to the crash site, where 14 more survivors waited.

Of all the passengers who died during the 72 days of nothingness, only 12 died in the crash; however, another five died soon afterwards from crash injuries. The survivors, some of whom were also injured in the crash, faced freezing weather at high altitudes with little equipment or food. During their long ordeal, four more passengers died from their injuries and eight during an avalanche.

As some of the passengers gathered around the crash site, the two left the shelter and comfort of the wrecked plane and went deeper and higher into the unknown of the snowy mountains. They embarked on their adventure without sufficient food, proper gear or training but with the hope that to die trying is the only option they had at hand. They had only will, hope and determination; they were without any idea of the odds of finding help and without any clue as to when they might find such help, or indeed how they could find help—or even if they could survive. Guided only by their faith, with hope that whatever god they believed in would guide and watch over them, they had come to the conclusion that without action they were facing a death sentence—sooner or later the survivors must all die. Therefore, any way of trying to survive could not be worse than just waiting for death.

With no knowledge of where they were and without any sort of navigation skills, the two climbed one high snowy mountain after another for more than ten days. One said to himself, "My father needs me. I want to take care of him. If I die, he will have no one. I have to find help for my friends. My nineteen-year-old girlfriend will find another man," he thought. That was his answer to how one can be inspired to stay alive.

The second answered: "My mother lost her husband and her daughter. If she loses me too, she will die or go crazy. I cannot afford to die here and now because of my mother. I must live. I will do whatever it takes to survive. I am not going to die here."

These two survived because they took on the noble task of finding help for their friends stranded at the wrecked plane and in order to return to their parents at home. With this kind of sincere and noble intention it is impossible not to have blessings and guidance from the creator of life.

The holocaust survivors had the same inspirational premonitions. Apart from those who died from the inhumane deeds of the Third Reich, most of those who survived, survived because of their faith and their will to continue living. The conditions at hand for them were bad enough that any future could only be hopeful.

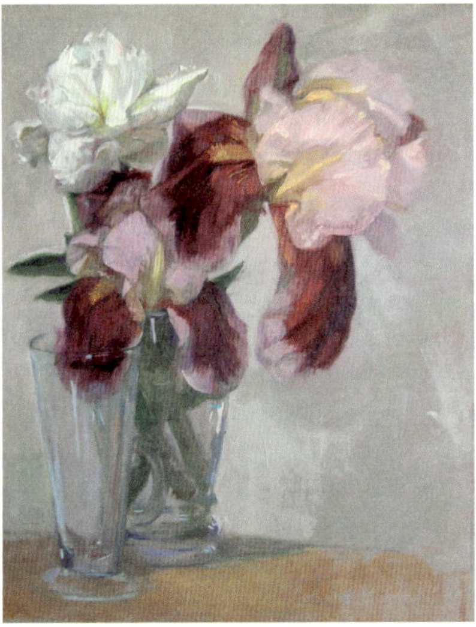

Untitled, Sam Adoquei
ENJOY IMAGES IN DETAIL download all images for free at: www.OriginofInspiration.com

How sincere and noble are our desires to be of use to mankind, they determine if we should sacrifice our existing conditions and find out what we are worth. When we realized that our life has become an invisible whirlpool leading us down hill, and when our existing conditions have pushed us into a corner, with our backs against the wall, the only choice we are left with is to push ahead with all that we have, not knowing when, how and if we will make it, but having faith that some way, somehow... We have come to accept that this is it, now or never.

In moments of silence if we listen carefully to ourselves, our situations, our conditions and our circumstances, they can often be the best source of inspiration, giving us no choice but to push ahead, to sacrifice what we have at hand in order to succeed because our purpose or vision in life will be unattainable if we accept or succumb to our existing conditions. That in which we have engulfed ourselves in—our comfort zone, the level of success that only reminds us of our accomplishments rather than of what we are worth, and what we have achieved, instead of what we can do.

Forward ever, backwards never — Ghanaian motto

The Trashman and Tragedy at Sea

An OFF THE FENCE production:

Again, there was an occasion when I was flipping through the channels at midnight, when I stumbled upon a documentary about a tragedy at sea, a 900-mile sailing trip that led to three people dying while two survived. Even though I had already finished my book "The Origin of Inspiration," I was still very interested to know if it is different at sea, if there are additional things that inspire people to endure, survive and succeed. Because of this desire, I became very curious to watch the documentary. I wanted to know what inspired the two surviving members of the crew.

A young captain (John) hired four young people to help him deliver Trashman, a 58-foot yacht, to Fort Lauderdale, Florida, from Annapolis, Maryland. As Trashman entered an area off the North Carolina Coast known for unpredictable and dangerous weather (the Graveyard of the Atlantic), the winds became dangerous. The high winds quickly sank Trashman, leaving the crew drifting on a rubber dinghy without food or water in a shark-infested area with no sign of rescue. Surrounded and followed by sharks that smelled food, the first casualty of the crew died of wounds sustained aboard the pounded yacht. The two crewmen who died next had become delirious from drinking seawater and went overboard. At the end of the documentary I was shocked when one of the survivors admitted that he was very mad at seeing one of his friends jump into the ocean and get eaten by the sharks. The reason he gave for being mad was not because the friend died but because he didn't stay strong enough to survive. He said that all along he was working hard to make sure he saved everyone, and he had wanted to help the one who jumped into the sea survive so that he could be a hero. To him the whole five days of no food and water was more about staying strong to save his peers. Helping his friends survive inspired him.

"The great and glorious masterpiece of man
is how to live with a purpose." — Montaigne

Tribute to Nature

Those who are open to philosophy, religion and science will agree that all living things are part of a grand plan. Their existence and importance should not be taken for granted, so it is natural for me to record my gratitude for these things in my plein-air paintings. As an example of that gratitude, I related this story in an article in *Plein Air Magazine* in 2005:

When I was asked why I was painting the "ugly" cypress trees in a cemetery in southern France, I replied, "The trees are 70 years old. They have sheltered all of the locals who have been buried here for decades. To spend some time getting to know them, painting them and preserving their images for posterity is not such a bad thing. They deserve the best of any good, honest artist who appreciates and respects them. Who knows? They might give us shelter, too, if we leave before them."

Note: An excerpt from *Plein Air Magazine*.

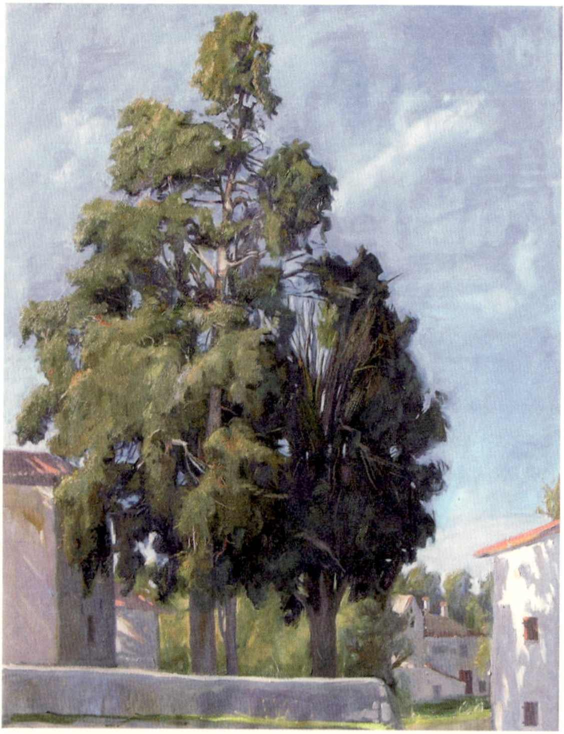

A Family (Tree in Monbos), Sam Adoquei

ENJOY IMAGES IN DETAIL download all images for free at: www.OriginofInspiration.com

3 IN PURSUIT OF INSPIRATION

If your actions inspire others to dream more,
learn more, do more and become more,
you are a leader. — John Quincy Adams

Five qualities are required for great accomplishment: inspiration, passion, talent, skill and vision. Taken as a group, the first three attributes—inspiration, passion and talent—are subjective, abstract and indirect. They are gifts given to us without our asking for them. We receive these gifts simply by virtue of being human, i.e., beings with an innate responsibility to contribute to the universe they have inherited and who should leave the physical world as they found it for those who will follow them. In this way people differ from other living creatures. We have been given all of the necessary components (like large brains) to care about nature. Had the Creator wanted us to just live and enjoy and not contribute, we might have been created like rocks, to do nothing but live forever.

On the earthly level there are humans whose special duty is to provide passion and inspiration, and it is a part they should play. The teachers, gurus, parents and friends who provide inspiration are those who themselves have achieved something beyond common expectations. They know what the rest of us want and they convert that desire into something easy to attain using realistic formulas and solutions. Inspirational people make our difficult dreams seem easy. These gurus have methodical, realistic formulas that when used get tangible results—it is this that makes gurus more human. Spiritual leaders on the other hand make us dream, and provide us with everlasting hopes, dreams and promises, even if we have to wait until after our death for their fulfillment.

An inspired person is someone whom the supreme intelligence has transformed so that he has an obsession to believe, to follow his passion and to act with strong hope and the optimistic view that what he is creating has importance in life and must be created at any cost. While he is thus inspired his mind is in a trance-like or hypnotic mode, so that nothing else matters. Because of the strength of this obsession, inspiration comes in spurts. The state of being transported, so that one strongly hopes and is quite optimistic, cannot persist for long at a single time; the physical part of our being would not be able to cope if it did. It is this state of being transported that great teachers and gurus used to teach effectively because they know that the art of teaching, which I explained thoroughly in my book on how to study effectively, works more powerfully when people are first inspired, that is, transformed so that they are hopeful and optimistic. It is only when a student is in this state of being that the teacher should provide the student with ideas, questions, formulas and solutions for that which the student dreams of and intends to accomplish. Great teachers do not teach if at first they haven't provided the student with inspiration and haven't made difficult problems seem easy to solve or big dreams attainable.

Passion and inspiration are meant to assist dreamers who have realized their uniqueness and feel it is necessary to be useful to mankind and the physical universe. Through having these noble thoughts the talented dreamer with passion and inspiration will have a sort of supreme and inexplicable energy, a kind of supernatural energy not common to the ordinary person of talent who is without a good purpose in life. Those artists whom we think have this kind of energy are those we see as possessed; they are possessed because everything has come together to help them fulfill their purpose in life so that nature's cycle will continue in order for the world to live on. What they do is inexplicable. While we can recognize talent when we see it, we can only imagine that someone has passion or inspiration. Talent solves a particular problem; we can always see the results of talent. By what our friends do around us, we can tell what their talent is but we cannot tell if they are passionate.

"Talent is a gift given to us from the creator of our universe. Talent is a special gift with a specific purpose, directed toward a specific field, and cannot be used in any other way." This theory, why the layman believes (that talent is a special gift given to a person who has all the right and specific attributes that make him eligible to have that particular talent), makes me not believe in the idea that some are born with a special talent for a specific field. No one is born with the talent for dentistry, painting or singing. It is hard to accept an argument that suggests that the talented basket weaver was created for Calcutta while the fashion model was created for Paris or New York. While we are born with a certain innate brain-power (or certain physical attributes) that, when put to use in a certain field, will make us better in that field than in certain other areas, and we will do better in that area than others whose talent lies somewhere else. One can do badly at one discipline, but very well in a different specialization. Time, circumstances, conditions and situations all contribute to the nurturing of talent, passion and inspiration. If someone is given the ability to play football or the violin, then playing football or playing the violin is what that person's talent is. It is what will come easily to that person.

Special gifts are part of nature's division of labor: the one with the gift fills that particular spot. And at the end fulfills his share of responsibilities. This is why artists have a feeling of accomplishment whenever an artwork is finished. Passion and inspiration come automatically when one is working within the field for which he is talented. Everyone has some sort of talent; sometimes one can know what it is immediately and sometimes it will take some time to discover one's talent. One can have talent for doing a certain thing but not necessarily the passion needed to support doing that certain thing. Also one can have desire and passion for a certain thing but not talent for it. When two or three of these gifts click or come together, that's is when one can consider himself lucky for that's when it becomes impossible to fail. Passion can wear out, but not talent.

The last two of the five attributes—technique (or skill) and vision—require development through education, which will allow us to acquire the necessary objective and tangible knowledge. These two attributes, moreover, are much more within our control than inspiration, passion and talent. It is left up to us as individuals to decide what kind of knowledge is compatible with our personal human machine (our genetic makeup), what kind of education we want, how much we can afford, what is suitable and required for what we intend to achieve and how badly we want to achieve it. When technique and vision come together in an artist, that person embarks upon an attainable quest, not a chase after a wishful dream but the pursuit of a tangible reality that will enable the artist to be useful to men and to the universe.

As a young man just graduated from art school in Ghana, I had a burning desire to use my art for the good of the universe. But first I needed more education, so I was inspired to find a way to get enough money to study art in Europe. I took a job in Nigeria, which remains the most horrible job I've ever had. From the work itself to the working conditions to my salary, everything was bad. But the thought of making enough money to get to Italy kept me motivated and enthusiastic. Every day that desire was so strong that I worked almost eighteen hours a day without ever feeling any resentment. Whenever my colleagues complained about the job, all I could think of was the money I was saving and my dream of furthering my education.

I had a similar experience when I finally made it to Italy. I still needed to earn more money, so I worked on a farm from about five in the morning until eight or nine at night. I did not have an innate passion for farming but I had so much inspiration that I consciously developed a love of farming, even though I was an artist. I loved driving the farm tractors, harvesting the vegetables and fruits, and making wine. The best part was having lunch in the fields with seven to ten Italian farmers and learning the language from them.

If our back is not against the wall and we don't create just to survive, then we have to question ourselves regarding the purpose and meaning of our life on earth. What is our talent for? Should our vocation serve ourselves, our community, our town? Or should our vocation serve all the people in every generation. This is a conscious decision artists have to make and they need to hold the answer in their subconscious as they pursue their noble vocation. What are we glad of when we create? Are we glad that our art demonstrates tremendous skills, or are we happy that our art portrays something that is useful to all—that is the question for everyone who want to live a purposeful artistic life (whether creatively or commercially).

At some point the concerned artist will have to confront these questions if he is to have a certain expectation from the world he lives in. Our purpose on earth mainly depends on what our answers are to these questions. I once saw an interview by Charlie Rose with the playwright Harold Pinter, and I was amazed to see how far this legend has had to go to make sure he satisfies his audience and how open he is regarding his concern about what is happening in the world. I was very moved by his sincerity and genuineness.

To have an important reason, such as the thought of accomplishing a goal or a humanitarian purpose worthy of our talents, is the most powerful generator of inspiration for the creative mind. The more important the goal is, the more inspiration one gets from it. This is because good intentions contribute to the universe; because of this the grand architect makes sure he provides abundant fuel free of charge. After all it is in his interest that the great law of the universe take care of itself and those who are in sync with his intentions deserve a free supply of all that he can provide. Have good helpful thoughts toward society, have a cheerful and positive vision, dream of doing good deeds for mankind, use your creative talent in a positive manner. Let your talent help people, and friends and inspiration to handle the task will come more often than you imagine.

One can achieve a lot without any inspiration, as one can without passion. It can seem as if an achievement is coming from inspiration, but often this work comes from such a selfish source that it does not last long. It does not have the same positive spirit for endurance as inspired work does, even when such work looks similar on the surface. Then again, the artist sometimes paints for therapeutic reasons. Sometimes he paints for commercial reasons and sometimes in hopes that the artwork will add to society—to bring joy, comfort, pleasure, hope or inspiration that triggers the thoughtful mind to look at life differently. Sometimes, he paints to unveil the things in nature that man often misses. But an artist whose goal is to do creative work to help mankind is more likely to have inspiration coming to him—certainly, more often than the artist who just creates for the sake of creating. The dreams and creations of an artist do not have to be grand and ambitious to evoke inspiration, they could just be for yourself, for your own therapeutic reasons or for bringing some special thing to a friend. Whatever the intent, if the idea is to take on a task to fulfill a goal, that alone is good enough to trigger inspiration. It is this sense of acting with goodwill, of adding to men's lives that inspires professionals from all fields, from bakers to professors to our leaders.

Our differences, our uniqueness and our specialties are mainly due to the division of labor included in the plan and design of the universe. If the baker chooses baking, then he should cherish baking and do good baking. Only by finding a good purpose for the path he has chosen will he be rewarded with the right fuel—the driving force to do more with enthusiasm. The sportsman should love his sport so that he can play to his fullest talent. Love, gratitude and feeling responsible maintain the inspirations and passion that come to us. It is also the mental acceptance of our duty that will make us whole-heartedly embrace our uniqueness.

Human beings are the only animals that receive inspiration to do something, so it makes a lot of sense that the inspiration is not to be wasted. We cannot wake up each day and feel passion and inspiration and then choose not to act on that inspiration. We are always to use inspiration for the improvement and preservation of life on earth. This is what the Creator asks of us.

Take a moment to think about this scenario: Imagine you have a kingdom of your own. Think of all the living beings in the kingdom—of the delivery boy to the king and queen, from the passionate lawyer trying to protect the innocent to the poor entertainer bringing joy to homes, from the baker feeding the warrior protecting his country to the scientist working sleepless nights to find a cure—Among all these special people in your kingdom are also the do-nothings, the slackers, the opportunists and the selfish. As the Creator does with us, you would recognize those individuals who contribute to the well-being, prosperity and longevity of your kingdom. You would not wait for the good-minded people to ask for inspiration and passion, but rather you would give them all they need. You would richly reward the kind and the generous. To whom will you give inspiration and passion? Who will get more inspiration and passion? And whom will you regularly reward? With these thoughts in mind, how would you reward the artist who creates or performs with only himself in mind?

Inspiration is the driving force that provides natural stimulation and prepares and conditions the mind to work in an emotional state such that nothing can get in the way until a chosen work is done. The difference between the three attributes of inspiration, passion and talent is that talent is part of our being, passion we develop and inspiration comes accordingly. While passion lasts a long time, inspiration comes at intervals and doesn't last as long. It comes and goes according to what the mind is open for and how big a dose the mind can take at a certain time.

The secret of success is to find out what your talent is for and then seek to develop the technical abilities you will need to assist you in acquiring the necessary skills. It is here that the secret of success or the forming of great achievements lies for every noble artist, no matter what their medium is. Passion and inspiration will come automatically to assist your noble vision when you broaden your experience and knowledge to become an expert in your particular field, thus helping to improve the lives of mankind. Believing that what you are creating will bring advancement to man's life will also follow as will hopefulness for the future. Those who benefit from your service, directly or indirectly, will reward you for that which your rare talent has produced and for improving their lives while contributing to the advancement of humankind.

Samuel Adoquei, 26 November 2008

Living Life Purposefully

(This is an excerpt from *How Successful Artists Study, The Street Musician*)

Once on my way home I stopped to watch a street musician, a guitarist. In his open guitar case he displayed coins and dollars so that passersby could throw in their donations. In the case he also had several 8x10 photographs of great guitarists, from Jimi Hendrix and Charlie Christian to Wes Montgomery.

Seeing the lineup of photos of these guitarists, I sensed an opportunity to learn something about guitarists and the art of the guitar, which to me is exactly the same as painting, so I threw in a dollar and then waited until his break.

"Who is Charlie Christian?" I asked.
"Oh my friend, you got to find Charlie Christian, he is your man, the soul man of guitar." After this introduction, I got about three minutes of lecture on Charlie Christian.
"What about Wes Montgomery?" I asked.
"My friend, are you from Africa?"
"Yes I am."
"When you think of Soul, when you think of the spiritual qualities that come out of your music, think of Wes Montgomery," he said, and then he gave me some more minutes of lecture on the evolution of guitar playing from the thirties to the present. All the others came from Wes Montgomery," he said. "Every guitarist came from Wes Montgomery."

By this time, I had missed five subway trains, and was running late in getting to my studio. Still I couldn't help but try to squeeze in one more lesson. So, I did my normal Colombo approach.

"Come on, my friend, Jimi is the man, my hero. The lessons you gave me tell me these guys are all great masters in their own right. But let's face it. Jimi Hendrix is still the man."

"They all have the spirit and the soul, that African Soul. They all lived in different times and brought their different souls and experiences to their music, the soul that young artists are missing today. The soul that made rhythm and blues so effective," he answered.

For a moment I thought to myself: How can this guy know so much, play so well and still perform on the platforms of the New York subway? I couldn't help but behave like Colombo again. I asked, "You are so good that I wish you had a record out. I would like to buy one. Why don't you?"

"It is not all about record deals nor it is about being famous," he said. "It is very pleasing to play and entertain people on the street, when they are coming from work and need some soothing sounds to finish their day. It is nice to just be around and play for them. It makes being a musician a worthwhile life to live. Raw, natural and direct to the people."

I thought the lesson worth more than a buck so I threw in a five-dollar bill, hopped on the train and started to think how I could share this invaluable metaphysical, artistic way of seeing and living a purposeful life with my students.

If the artist sits for a moment and thinks about the reasons for choosing art as a vocation, he will realize that there are several noble reasons why he wants to become an artist: love of nature and love of people and the most noble reasons of all—to make a difference that will improve man's life directly or indirectly—to share what the mind's eye sees and what the artist feels while observing, studying and responding to nature in hopes that his work will better society. The dancer shares inward feelings by the flow of movement through his body, in hopes that people will feel good while watching him. The writer does the same by the use of words and the politician by helping the public. The philosopher serves by asking questions and posing answers that will lead to new ideas. Unfortunately, without good, realistic and solid knowledge and experience in how to solve the technical problems that arise in creating, the artist will not be able to share these beautiful invaluable things with anyone. After all, ideas go through several stages—from conception of a goal to achievement of that goal—before the actual message achieves its purpose.

Noble intention is one of the amazing rewards you get in choosing the field of Art. It is the realization that an artist's creations can make direct or indirect changes in our natural material world. Artists' work can enrich homes, bring inspiration to many and, most of all, artists' creations remind man that they do not live by bread alone. For these reasons, artists with noble intentions never give up their goals of achieving beauty and order, and it is this sort of contribution that has developed our society to its current level. Also the indirect psychological effect is what's fascinating about paintings, the way great paintings can psychologically stimulate our imagination and direct that imagination on to other areas. It is often so indirect that most or no one can pinpoint how a painting has positively added to their growth, yet it is a fact that most of the great minds in western civilization had either direct contact with the arts or came out of an era where the arts were very important. At least now one can claim that the economies of some European countries still depends on art that was created hundreds of years ago. Yet at the time leaders could argue that paintings were not the most practical or direct contribution to society, now imagine taking the arts out of some countries in Europe!

When I left Africa to Europe as a teenager I realized the indirect psychological effect. It became clearer how for some reason the so-called developed and civilized countries were recognizing the importance of their art collecting, encouraging and preserving their art hundreds of years ago. The so-called underdeveloped or third world countries are countries that put importance on other areas of their culture, which were immediate, practical and logical. I also noticed in Europe that other arts, like music, theatre or dancing, have more direct practical and explicable effect on our culture than painting, (music can directly make you laugh smile, think, love, dance go crazy and sometimes cry.) Therefore artists in these areas receive immediate rewards by the whole public more so than painting.

Because one cannot explain these indirect psychological effects on our psyche it makes it very easy for decision makers to make decisions that are more practical, direct and explicable to society and ignore the arts. This is why sometimes one wonders if the layman is aware of this indirect psychological contribution that paintings have on our culture.

All artists of good intention know that great ideas shape the world around them. Imagine the world without noble minds.

(Colombo is a detective in a television series, who acts innocent and ignorant and sometimes stupid in order to find answers for cases he is investigating.)

"This we know: the earth does not belong to man,
man belongs to the earth.
All things are connected like the blood that unites us all.
Man did not weave the web of life, he is merely a strand in it.
Whatever he does to the web, he does to himself."
The Words of Chief Seattle - 1852

divine habits

In silence seek wisdom;
seek the path to where the wise
reveal their intentions,
seek contact with the prophets,
the messengers and the immortals,
Allow their great examples
to form your character.

Seek all the thoughts
that form divine mind
and divine actions.
Seek the divine love and the divine law
in order to be divine.
Seek actions that are harmonious
to the universe/cosmic world.

Seek habits that lead to greatness;
Allow the wise to speak through you
and be the vehicle of their divine intentions.
Beg that all they intended to do
be your life's purpose and dream.
With hope, faith and passion
complete their task.

Let every new day
revive undeveloped thoughts
that ring in your cathedral of ideas,
so that you can bring to life
what the immortals have revealed
to you in silence.

Let all that you do, all that you dream for
and all that you aim for
be inspired by the desire
to be of help to all mankind

In silence let the saints of graciousness
appear before you daily.
Be humble; make yourself available
and let humility, grace and kindness
Oil the bolts and wheels
of the carriage of your mission

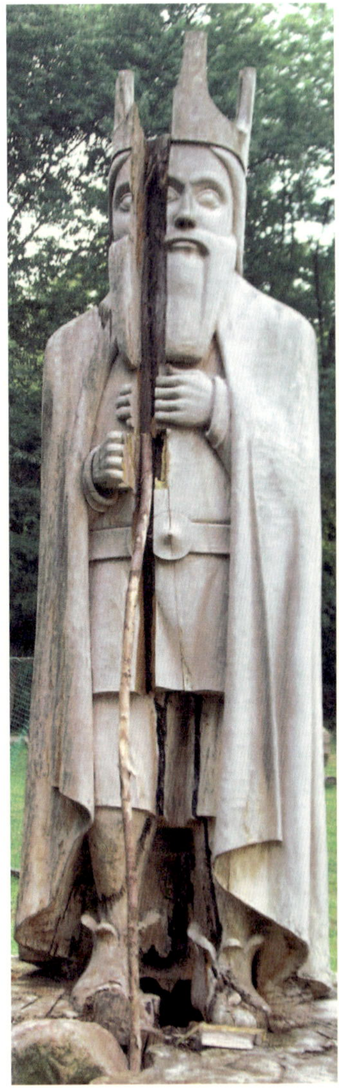

Sculpture by David Svane at Liselund Ny Slot, Món, Denmark

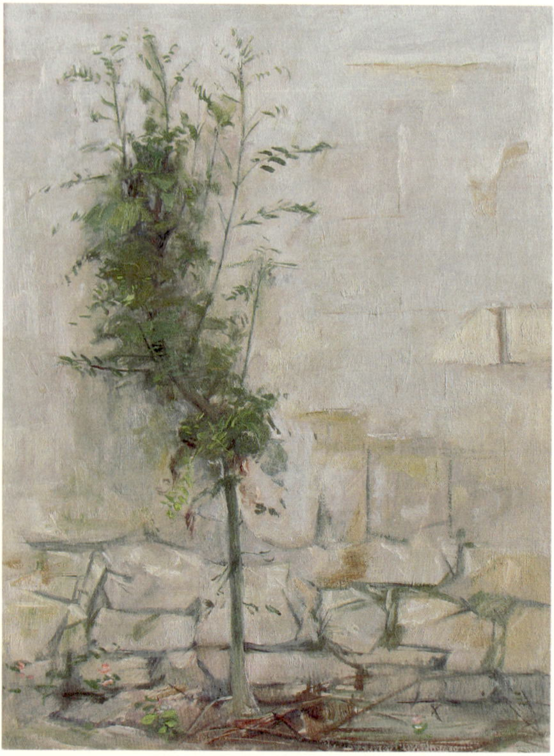

Growing Up in a Concrete Jungle,
(A Young Tree, Chateau de Pecany), Sam Adoquei

ENJOY IMAGES IN DETAIL download all images for free at: www.OriginofInspiration.com

4 FINDING YOUR VISION

The fifth attribute an artist needs in order to be able to accomplish great things is vision. To attain vision, we need the other four qualities (inspiration, passion, talent and skill). Our vision is what makes us unique and special. Literally, vision means an artist's unique way of seeing the world, the special and specific choices the artist makes when observing the world around him. It is also what the artist imagines and sees with his unique mind's eye and brings out by way of his art. Vision is like a lighthouse, it guides the artist to a specific area of nature or life or to a subject that is personal to the artist, one that others might have overlooked. Vision also includes that which the artist's conscience tells him the world ought to be—or what the world is lacking. Vision is that unique and special contribution we bring and add to life; it is that which no one can provide but us. Passion, inspiration, talent and skill all have to come together so that our vision can be achieved.

Two artists standing in front of a landscape scene, or still life subject or a figure in its surroundings, will find inspiration from different parts of the same subject. In a landscape, one artist might choose to paint a view that emphasizes the sky while the other will focus on the vegetation. Vision is what makes life meaningful. The uniqueness and importance of a vision is what makes one artist or scientist's legacy endure more than that of others.

"*The influence of each human being on others in this life is a kind of immortality.*" — John Quincy Adams

Some aspects of vision can be explained but not all. For example, an entrepreneur can explain what he wants to bring to a certain culture. An artist can sometimes explain his ambitions and intentions. But not everything. When Marconi explained that he envisioned sound coming out of wires, he was put in an asylum because he was thought to be going mad. He eventually went on to invent the radio. Leonardo da Vinci faced his own problems with authority when he decided that in order to pursue his vision he should dissect cadavers so that he would better understand the human machine in order to pursue his vision.

In recent years, because of Modern Art (which says that anything goes and everything is art—and if I call myself an artist, therefore I am one), it has become common to have skills and style but no vision, or to have vision but no technical skills. An artist can also have skills and vision, but no style. Of these three essential qualities (skill, style and vision) that serve as the backbone for successful artists, style is the only element an artist can do without, but luckily style comes without the artist making too much effort. Technical skills and vision when improved upon make the pursuit of art very easy and enjoyable; they can maintain the artist's legacy and contribute to life. Artists without these three elements of skill, style and vision are prospects for fifteen minutes of fame. Fifteen minutes of fame results when great things are achieved in a short period of time, and the fifteen minutes represent a moment of recognition of the great vision that the artist has displayed, even though he has not enough skill to create again or to carry out his vision for a longer time. To maintain any sort of fame and greatness for the ages, the experienced artist must create artworks that are unique and have timeless qualities, as well as a meaningful and noble vision.

Noble Vision

What all great successful people have in common is a vision that leads to serving others: from Thomas Edison, who wanted electric lights for every household; to Abraham Lincoln, who wanted freedom for all; to Bill Gates, who at seventeen was already dreaming that every household could have a computer. Matisse wanted people to feel restful while they were enjoying his art. It is this purposeful approach to life that makes life meaningful.

As children most of us think of accomplishing goals that satisfy others. From our twenties to our thirties, we think of ourselves. From our forties to our fifties, acquisition of power, status and prestige becomes our priority. From our fifties to our sixties, our legacies and prosperity dominate our thoughts. After that we start to become concerned about those we will leave behind. Besides this natural way that people think, there are a few individuals who, from day one, think about and envision how they can practice what they do best in a manner that will improve life or add to life. Then, they start living a life that serves others. All their artworks are inspired by these noble thoughts. These are people whose vision is so much in sync with the divine plan of the Universe that they are bound to succeed no matter what their circumstances are.

Whether we create to win awards, get attention, please others or with the intention to let our creations be of use to others is a choice left to the individual artist to make and it's a choice that can also determine or influence how the artist does in our physical universe. But the road to success as proven by every great person, from Mother Teresa, Mahatma Gandhi, Martin Luther King, Jr., Marconi, Thomas Edison, Abraham Lincoln, Leonardo da Vinci and Michelangelo to Bill Gates, is such that no one ever goes wrong and misses out if his dreams and ambitions and his inventions and vision aim to achieve that which men need for their improvement and the advancement of life.

An artist without a vision is like an individual programmed just to live, breath free air, eat and then move on. It is that important vision that we see with our mind's eye and believe in that society cannot live without. The artist with foresight is the one who is responsible for making it possible. Vision encourages us to pursue art and it gives us reasons to live a purposeful life. But without a conscious effort to maintain and focus on our vision, some unimportant thing can sway us from our path and persuade the artist to become something else. And without technical skills to clarify what we think is purposeful and meaningful, the artist can be misunderstood.

On the surface, it might look as if vision is the hardest thing for artists to acquire because so few artists explore visionary ideas. Yet vision is the part of the artist's talent that comes automatically with the artistic DNA. Vision usually develops and changes with age and life experiences, but sometimes it remains the same. In other cases, various conditions can influence an artist's vision and ideas. For example, an artist inspired to work by feelings generated by a war may find his creative vision unchanged as he spends years portraying images that promote peace, while another artist with the same feelings regarding the war might change due to other influences. An artist portraying beauty by painting flowers and other of nature's beautiful things can change with experience and move on to more somber things. Life experiences have more influence on how the artist's vision changes than do biology and gender, etc.

The uniqueness and meaningfulness of one artist's vision is what separates him from other artists. Technical skill clarifies the artist's vision and makes it easy to understand what he is trying to say. Even though it requires some skill to get a message across to its intended target, it does not necessarily require a whole lot of skill to demonstrate that an artist has vision. But it requires skill to make one's vision readily apparent to those who encounter the artwork. No matter how great and grand a vision is, if it is not assisted by good and efficient technical skill, the artwork will not communicate its content as intended. In some cases, the result can be misleading. A writer might have a great vision but without a good command of the language he will have a hard time getting his ideas across.

Style, when taken literally, can come across like vision, yet style and vision are miles apart. Style is like our signature. Style is the way the artist personally uses his materials. Style gives his work a certain special look. An artist can therefore imitate another's style in order to support his vision. It is like this for all creative people, such as writers and musicians as well as various kinds of leaders and politicians.

For the artist to have a unique vision all that the artist has to do is to be as honest as possible. Naturally, it is not as bad to copy another artist's style as it is to copy his vision. Vision is too unique;

it is totally designed for one particular artist. It is what represents and makes that artist. Vision is made up of his beliefs, experiences and ideas, his ups and downs, his temperament, taste, wishes and philosophy. So, to copy another artist's vision is to change your identity and take on that artist's identity. You might want to paint like Monet or Van Gogh but it would not be wise to follow in their footsteps and go to the same spots where they painted and paint the same views they did. Or in writing, you might want to write like Mark Twain but writing about his subjects in 2008 would be odd. On the other hand two artists can stand in front of the same view and be inspired by it and paint it. So two singers can sing about the same subject so long as they are honest and maintain their own identities, they will produce different works.

In order for the artist to find his vision, he should live a life of constantly drawing his inspirations from nature and his life experiences. He should create without too many preconceived notions; he should respond to his inner feelings and observe those parts of nature that he knows are untapped. There are still hidden treasures in nature, awaiting the honest and curious artist. He should select these treasures from the natural world, creating images that he strongly believes are able to represent what his contributions and legacies to society are. He should be very personal in all his creative decisions. He should avoid being influenced in his choice of subject matter. He should be strong enough to withstand criticism and stick with things he finds new and original, especially if he thinks he is the one to discover that new thing. He should be honest and very sincere in his selections of subject, sincere and honest enough that anything apart from what his heart desires won't be worthy enough for his purpose of living the artistic life. He should be practical enough to know that his new ways should correspond to the real world. In the way he treats things, his work should also be unique and meaningful.

It is this noble idea of contribution to society that makes life worthy of living for the artist and makes art the right medium to convey this purpose. The artist should do whatever feels sincere and natural within reason and listen to himself. One cannot be that wrong if one's ideas are coming from nature, experience and knowledge of the field. The experienced artist should cut off all the programmed ideas he has inherited and only do what comes natural to him. Instead of worrying about what to create, he should just create. The artist should just do anything he feels comfortable doing with a thoughtful attitude; sometimes it requires trial and error to find one's own vision. If what the artist envisions comes across as odd, he should remember that odd things are part of man's being, too, and it requires an artist to explore that odd vision in order for it to make sense. If the ideas behind the odd vision make us look at life differently or make us reason differently, then it's a good vision. If, by thus finding a new way of seeing that makes sense, we stumble on ideas that help us improve as a society, then that is good.

Publicity and advertising help increase an artist's reputation, but a noble and meaningful vision is the only achievement and legacy that can help it endure for the ages. Culture changes, like almost everything. But while most things change, great ideas endure. For centuries, unique, meaningful and noble art has been the secret beacon signaling the endurance of our important legacies. Art provides timeless beauty and continuous inspiration for future imagi-

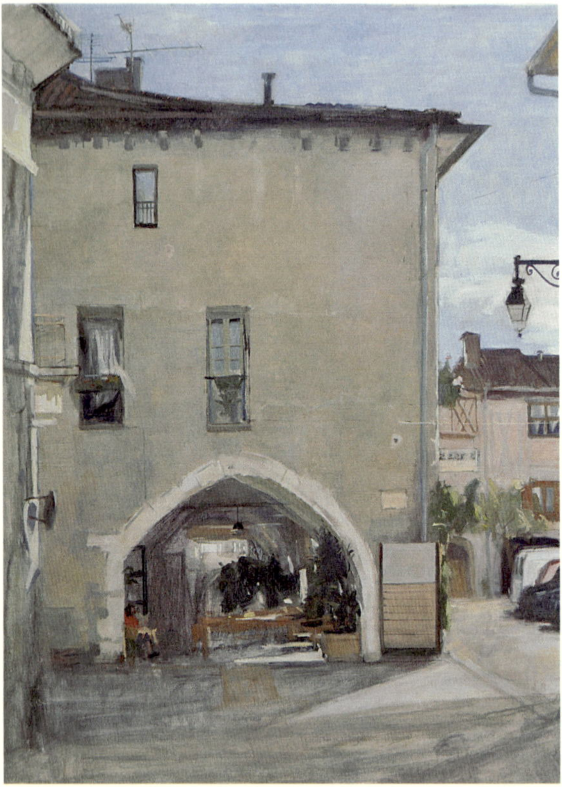

Bastilde of Eymet, (Daniel's Place), France, Sam Adoquei

ENJOY IMAGES IN DETAIL download all images for free at: www.OriginofInspiration.com

nations. Because of this, today's artist must know that what makes great art is nature, tradition and innovation. The artist must create unique and timeless artworks worthy of his important heritage, as well as of posterity, to leave as a legacy. This then becomes the secret law of success and explains how the artist can secure his reputation and legacy.

This is more common and obvious in politics. The political figure, whose vision is to help all men, will endure for a longer time than the politician who just wants to get reelected. The same is true for musicians. The musician whose aim in composing is to provide hope for mankind can do so only if his course in life is sincere and noble. One's vision will not be embraced and accepted all the time. Sometimes it is not accepted until the artist is long gone. For this reason, most artists will need more than one skill. Ideally, all students should learn to be versatile; they should learn the skills and develop the temperament to produce commercial works as well as creative works (your vision). If he is to innovate, the artist will need to learn to experiment. Any artist with such a versatile temperament is likely to have success in his pursuit of a career in the arts.

The student in any artistic field shouldn't worry too much about how to find vision and style because they are part of an artist's being. Vision and style are so embedded in our being that it would take a lot of effort to lose them. If a student lacks these traits now, they will surface eventually if the artist is honest, sincere and true in his work. Skill, technique, experience and knowledge are the top priorities (the first things the student should concentrate on) and style and vision will follow. Style and vision are things the advanced student should pay attention to. Once out of school your style and vision will start to show.

Written as a lecture for students at the National Academy School of Fine Arts.
November 2008

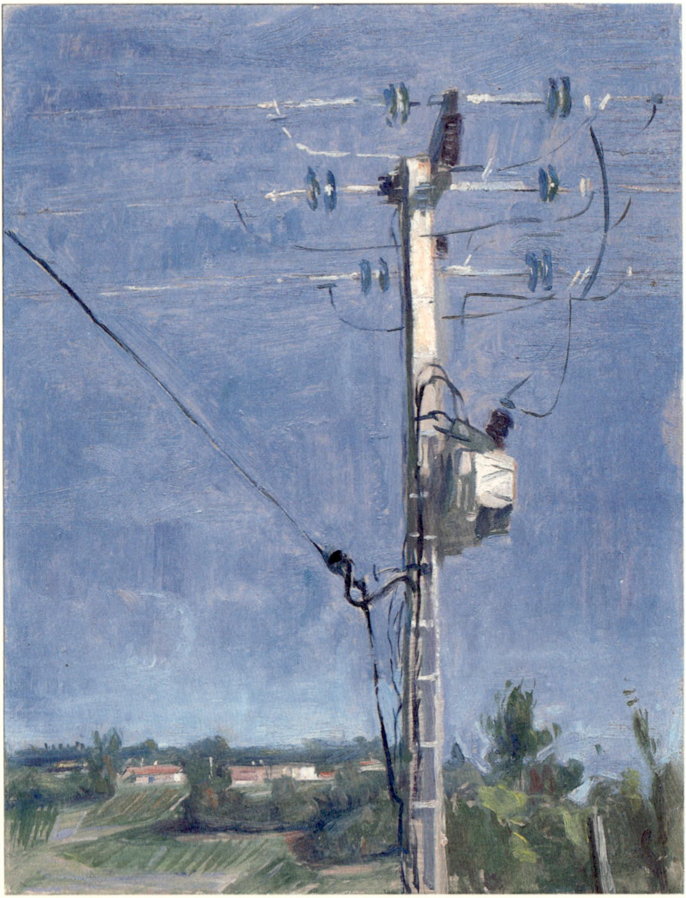

Dinosaurs of Pomport, France, Sam Adoquei

ENJOY IMAGES IN DETAIL download all images for free at: www.OriginofInspiration.com

5 HOW DOES ART BECOME TIMELESS?

Imagine visiting a friend's family home. You walk in, and on the wall in the living room amid several artworks you see a beautiful painting that touches you. In awe, you move closer to see the work better and learn more about it. In amazement you exclaim to your host, "How beautiful and wonderful this artwork is!" Then he tells you the history of the work—inspirational stories dating back through several generations of his family. He goes on to explain the artwork's content. Your love of the painting grows even more after the short history and the explanation.

The opposite scenario is the story of the painting that eventually ends up in the attic or is given or thrown away because of its tasteless, mediocre qualities. In the hope of encouraging creative expression, we as a society have become more accepting and tolerant regarding the quality of works of art than we used to be. Because of this we collect almost everything and hang anything—careless of what the work might represent—and in the process disregarding our own reputation.

Have you ever wondered what it takes to create a good work of art? Or what makes a painting timeless? Why are some artists able to create timeless artworks? The only difference between a common painting and one with intrinsic value is the artist who paints it. Why do some paintings move from homes with all their history to prestigious exhibitions to honored places and to some of the world's best museums while others are cast aside? Basements and attics are full of paintings that were once the "big new thing," but then faded into obscurity. Like the new circus in town, they were as great as the noise and sounds of the drums and trumpets, but now they are silent, reaching no one.

The Three Most Important Types of Art

Within the universal cultures, there are three types of art that always stand the test of time: classical art, traditional masterpieces and timeless art. Only one of these groups is able to appeal to most people for all time.

An artwork is considered a masterpiece or a classical work depending on what is in the painting and what the painting stands for to certain people. Masterpieces and classical works are like the essays or papers written by scholars in various professions for their academic environments, which only those in that particular field can understand. Classical art is only classical to the tradition and society in which it was created, the culture or the society that understands its meaning. It fails to qualify for the timeless art status. The same is true of masterpieces. A masterpiece is only considered so by those who know what qualities it takes to make a masterpiece. Knowledge and experience of a field helps one judge where a work stands. A masterpiece in African art may be rejected by other cultures due to their lack of understanding of what makes it a masterpiece; therefore, the work fails to pass the universal and timeless test. In short, a masterpiece results when all the principles of a certain tradition have been expressed so well that the average practitioner cannot achieve the same high level of results; a masterpiece is a result that is achieved by artists with experience and knowledge beyond the average.

A classic work is one that is typical of a certain tradition. Classic art is based on the manner, style, subject matter and ideas or meaning of a certain tradition; for example, if you copy the style of Rembrandt and paint Dutch subjects from the 12th century, you might not have a masterpiece but the look you achieve can be that of a classic of the Dutch tradition. This is why masterpieces and classical works of art can suffer by being in the wrong place at the wrong time. A visit to any museum basement can attest to this.

Even within the culture or tradition in which the masterpiece was created one might need to be educated in order to know the difference between the ordinary and the masterpiece. Hundreds of people from different backgrounds look at a religious painting—no matter who painted the picture or how great the painting is, each one will respond to the artwork differently. This illustrates how the message and subject of art are very important to the creation of timeless works of art.

A timeless artwork can be a masterpiece, a classic or both, as well as being timeless. But a masterpiece or a classic might not necessarily be universal and timeless. Most great artists' works become classics because within their oeuvre they were able to create timeless artworks. Understanding timeless and universal art does not require special knowledge. There should not be any esoteric meaning behind universal and timeless art.

What Makes Some Art Timeless?

For any artwork to be timeless, its message must be its essential quality. The clarity of the message and how accessible the message is to all will determine how timeless the work is. Timeless art can be broken down into four separate elements: adherence to a tradition, nature, meaningful purpose and artistic sensitivity. These are the inherent traits shared by all great, universal and timeless art.

This does not only apply in the visual fine arts; it applies to all the arts, from the culinary arts to music and moviemaking to literature, playwriting and even to oratorical skills. The reasons why the French croissant has been a classic for hundreds of years are not so different from those that explain why we still like Mozart or Shakespeare. With very few exceptions, classical works and abstract works rarely have the right structural foundation to allow them to stand the test of time. Sometimes the subject matter is too esoteric or the viewpoint too idealistic to be comprehended by those who come in contact with the work. Any work without the above four qualities of tradition, nature, meaningful purpose and artistic sensitivity will suffer the consequences of not being able to last. It is the lack of these qualities that makes the reputation of most extreme artworks so fragile.

In all the arts—film, music, and painting, dancing—and from time immemorial, he taught me, apart from accidental great scientific discoveries that all great achievements come from tradition, innovation and invention. The artist who creates difference just for the sake of being different will survive for some time in an environment where the uncultured and uneducated cannot differentiate hype and transience from timeless. Change for the sake of change is the greatest license for the incompetent. Inexperienced, attention-seeking artists who are incapable of taking advantage of the great creative minds of the past are exploiting the naïve art enthusiast. The sound of the ocean, the color of the sky, the movements and grace of flying birds, the cry of a baby, the aging process; the pain and mourning for a loved one are ongoing cycles of nature. Timeless art, timeless beauty and noble ideas that provide enduring inspirations come from nature, life, tradition, innovation and invention. New for the sake of new, different for the sake of different and change for the sake of change will always occupy, exhaust and drain the energy the creative mind needs for improvement and perfection of all that can be turn into unique and timeless art.

One-hit wonders, 15 minutes of fame and the constant attempt to be the next Picasso are results of talents unable to back great luck with knowledge, experience, vision, hard work and enduring inspiration. Sometimes hubris, too, can steal great luck away. If you find yourself blessed with such great luck, doing some homework to update all that you lack can help you seize opportunities that come your way.

Tradition

It is a mistake to think all great works of art are timeless. It is not the greatness of an artwork that makes it timeless; there have been thousands of works that were great in their time but then became lost in obscurity. For a timeless artwork to be created, the artist should have a knowledge and understanding of the tradition in which he works. A timeless message in an artwork depends on the subconscious and conscious mind of the craftsman—first, his knowledge and understanding of the field; second, how he executes the message; and last, how he delivers the message and makes it accessible. Timeless art must always deliver its message with precision, whether it is a literal message, a psychological one or both. It will always be the responsibility of the artist to have total faith in the delivery of the messages in his works.

If an artwork is to last for ages, the message of the artwork should be clear, accessible and meaningful due to its noble, visionary intentions. And to achieve this goal, the artist needs to have sufficient technical skills and knowledge of his field; it is skill that often separates today's artist from those of the past. Today's artist tends to have ideas and to convince himself that skill is unimportant. Skill is what separates Picasso from most modern artists; he was as skillful as most great traditional artists. He delivers whenever he wishes to do so. As abstract as Picasso's art is, he was able to bounce back and forth between artistic traditions. He had what it takes to make himself understood. Matisse had the same artistic temperament, unlike his contemporaries and his followers, who were guided by his abstract ideas but missed the noble vision that gives a meaningful purpose to art. Art, being noble, requires more than just ideas to produce timeless works. Skill is the art and science of the craft.

Traditional principles are the structure used to hold together the elements of communication in an artwork so that the work and the message are understood properly according to what the artist intended. They are reliable, technical ways of painting and solving technical problems, passed down to us by masters of the field before us. When understood and followed, certain favorable and predictable results can be achieved.

For any artist to have a voice in the arts or to create timeless art, he must understand his craft. Traditionally, artists who understand their craft have tended to express and convey their important messages better. For the professional writer, the parallel would be the standard or universal way of using a particular language. When used, any person educated in that language will understand the message of the writer and likely accept it.

Traditional skills do not hinder creativity nor do they have anything to do with the artist's vision. Their use only demonstrates that the artist is educated in his art and has a knowledge and understanding of the craft. They also mean that any work he creates has qualities similar to those of the masters of the past. The meanings of the painting and its symbols, its elements and its devices deliver messages that can be understood now and for ages to come. Having traditional skills also means that the artist's sense of taste and judgment of quality in the arts are of a high standard, similar to that of the Old Masters. Whatever he creates comes from experience, as well as a knowledgeable and understanding background. This experience and knowledge guide him so that his own works reach the same high standards he advocates. Traditional skills allow a work to be great at the time it is created and enable it to stay great forever.

To create timeless art, a noble and meaningful vision is not enough. The message must have reliable, traditional skills to support its structure in order to make what it says as clear and accessible as possible so that everyone can enjoy and benefit from the meaningful purpose it provides. The way timeless art influences artists of all generations is what separates it from ordinary art; its influence on artists explains why we are drawn to it as well as why it is preserved. It is this that separates timeless paintings from trendy and fashionable artworks.

Nature and the Essence of Life

For the message in a timeless work of art to be meaningful, the subject should be understandable to all human beings. The subject (as well as the content) should reflect nature and the essence of life. The subject should be aimed at both existing generations and at generations yet to come. It should have no cultural, religious or ethnic boundaries. If he wants to reach everyone for all ages, the creative artist can consider any subject as long as it is natural to all men.

As humans we have many things in common, such as emotions and needs. A person of any culture, race, gender or religious group at times of crisis will yearn for comfort, happiness or celebration. The experienced and sensitive artist should first be a student of nature and human behavior. For the artist to understand what makes humans tick, he should understand our natural traits as well as our common likes and dislikes. The artist may capitalize on his understanding of popular culture for his commercial success, but to create timeless works, the artist should pay particular attention to the traits that unite all human beings. He should eschew all passing trends if he wants to think broadmindedly. Great artists, musicians, filmmakers, actors and writers understand this.

The portrait artist, for example, must develop a pleasure in learning about faces and facial expressions. He must understand faces that have timeless looks, timeless expressions and moods that are common to all men. Our facial expressions when we smile are similar to those when we laugh, yet the way the upper class and educated elite in any culture laughs is very different from the way the lower class laughs. In landscape painting, the artist should know the differences among various types of landscape scenery, from the commonplace and the mundane to the heavenly or spiritual.

The figurative artist, too, must learn to understand the kinds of movement, gesture and action that are natural to all humans. Like a movie director dressing his characters, the artist must consider what people wear if he is to touch the natural feelings of everyone. The actor, in order to touch people from all walks of life, must also learn about natural behavior traits, especially those that don't change according to a person's background. The colorist, too, must adopt this approach to studying color. To learn what makes art timeless, be observant of the movements and actions that all humans have in common.

Even though a human figure is a human figure everywhere, it is easy for a painting of a Parisian or a stereotypical Frenchman to be outdated within a short period of time. Not so with a painting of a man or a woman. A man or a woman has universal appeal throughout generations. Even in fashion, there are still certain qualities that are universal and timeless. An artist who is a student of nature and human character should learn to understand what differentiates "a woman" from a Parisian woman or what differentiates "a man" from an American man.

If the artist is not painting special projects, then it is wise for him to keep in mind the differences between that which represents a particular time and a particular people and that which represents all times and all people. He should understand that cultural things will change with time. Again, this is true of all the arts. A playwright might produce a play that might win several awards and touch the hearts of a generation but with time the play might fall out of favor. The musician must learn sounds, lyrics and compositions that are natural and universal. The writer needs to know the way people behave naturally.

In my lectures to students, and through helping collectors understand what timeless art is as well as helping them understand what makes art timeless so they can collect with an informed knowledge, I start off both collectors and students by first teaching them how to recognize what constitutes an ideal subject, what is natural and what is cultural (what is adopted or programmed by education or culture, including style), and what can be timeless. I continue by teaching them the difference between what is classic and what is a masterpiece in the arts and how human beings respond to art. I also teach them what is expected from art, and what are the responsibilities of the noble artist. We study all the art forms, from painting to music to screenwriting, observing those aspects of the work that will endure and those that will suffer obscurity. From that point on, the lessons concentrate on particular writings, certain artworks and certain movies. We also study the humanistic values, humanistic concerns and noble characteristics common in the life of almost all great artists so that they don't think that it is nothing but the choice of the right subject that makes for universal and timeless art. On the contrary, it is the humanistic spirit of the artistic soul that all three elements (humanistic values, humanistic concerns and noble characteristics) stem from. That is what is important. This is based on a simple natural law: We are what we think. As in nature, nothing good comes from a bad source. We finish our lessons by arriving at certain analytical results that make our predictions favorable to our answers. This is the science of the anatomy of timeless art.

Even though some timeless works of art have been achieved through an accidental creative process, the well-informed artist with knowledge of the anatomy of timeless art will be equipped to apply the theory and principles when he encounters a suitable subject. He will know that if his message is to reach and touch a certain audience, then his subject should be made understandable through the devices of technique, substance and clarity of message. An understanding of this theory will help him be a good, communicating creator whose work will touch and inspire for both his time and the future.

The Importance of Artistic Sensitivity

Where the spirit does not work with the hand
There is no art. — Leonardo da Vinci

In my early years in art classes in Ghana, I never understood what he meant when my landscape professor told me that I paint landscape too much like a technician. It took me years to understand the difference between just painting trees, using shades of green, blue and brown, and painting a specific place, a place where people live. It requires the same amount of effort for me to explain to my students not to respond to portraits as if they were depicting vegetables.

For any artwork to possess timeless qualities, the human source the message is coming from must have artistic sensitivity. How well people can relate to a message will depend on how accessible that message is. Tradition, nature (or spiritual significance) and meaningful purpose will not be enough; even a close realistic rendition will not be enough if the mind behind the work does not have that special artistic sensitivity. Artistic sensitivity and an understanding of nature are the qualities that humanize the work so that it becomes timeless.

Artistic sensitivity is like a special built-in radar detector that alerts artists to nature's hidden treasures. This sensitivity highlights the essentials in nature, in life and in the physical world, things the layperson misses although they are all around him. Painting recognizable or universal images with photographic accuracy does not mean the work is going to become timeless; any artist with reasonable technical skills and some experience can tackle a subject familiar to many. There have been thousands of paintings of universal subject matter that gave way to great works of art. As in other professions, we expect honest and sincere professionals to be sensitive toward their field of expertise, but this is not always the case, there are those who care and those who don't care as much. To those who don't care, it is just another day at work. This is the same in the arts. The kind of concern and sensitivity I am describing is what makes the difference between what is put in an artwork and what comes out of the artwork. Such sensitivity demonstrates different artists' levels and the qualities and standards they use to create.

There are higher levels of sensitivities, the professional ones we develop through our life experiences and the curious ones we develop in order to become better artists, to understand and know more about life so that we can become more effective communicators with our artworks.

To have compassion and a sympathetic outlook towards life doesn't always come about because the artist knows more or sees more and has experienced more. But it can occur because the experienced and curious artist wants to learn and understand more. Without understanding the artist can easily be detached from reality; in return, he will lack ideas for his artworks. His works can be out of touch with humanity.

Like other skills, the artist's level of sensitivity depends on how much time and effort he spends in developing it. As there are artists who have been technically more well trained than others, and therefore are better technicians, so too there are artists who have developed more of their sensitivities than others, and therefore are more empathetic and sympathetic. They show more concern towards life, nature and the physical world. The quest for knowledge and improvement is the same for all the arts; nothing men do cannot be taught and what men have been taught men can teach.

It is the artist's innate sensitivity that makes him special and different from other professionals. Society expects the artist to be more compassionate and understanding in order to bring out that which will enlighten, inspire and encourage life in his work. His vocation should not just be art for art's sake.

Where the average person sees an old beat-up shark, the artist sees a symbol of beauty in aging and imagines bringing out those qualities that the shark has sheltered over the ages by means of artistic creation. To the intelligent and sensitive artist, the homeless man lying on the street corner is a symbol that reminds us of what we, as a society, should do to better our living.

Sensitivity comes into play when leaves that appear to the general viewer to be uniformly green are seen by the sensitive artist to be different shades, tones and subtle nuances of green. Without sensitivity, special and important characteristics of nature will be out of our sight and out of reach to the viewing layman. Only the obvious, the average and the common will reveal themselves to the insensitive artist. The endurance of certain works will depend on what the artist has captured with the help of his sensitivity and because of the ideas behind the work.

Should we artists paint what we know, what our mind tells us to see or what our eye tells us? What is the main reason we choose to create from a particular subject? These are questions all artists will have to understand and clarify before they can properly understand nature and become helpful to her. The intelligent and sensitive artist's knowledge and appreciation of nature will determine when to rely on nature, what to extract from her and what should come out of her.

How can the artist see beauty in nature and the world around him, if he has not yet developed that side of his artistic senses? Sensitivity, respect, concern and the love and understanding of nature and the world around us have a lot to do with living a life and vocation that is meaningful and helpful to others. How we share these ideas depends on an artist's experience in the art and science of creating as I have discussed in the section on tradition.

When I was growing up in Ghana, we didn't have apples and grapes. Apples, grapes and most of the Western fruits are now imported and the economy determines what and when certain fruits are imported. I first saw apples and grapes and tasted them when I was in my teens. Yet I was about ten when I started collecting reproductions of still life paintings by Western Old Masters. Before I saw a real apple, a picture of it to me was just a beautiful spherical-shaped fruit. I had no idea of its taste, its attributes and its symbolic meaning. At ten in Ghana, I had no idea what most of the objects were in the reproductions I collected. I collected the reproductions only because of what the artist had sensitively made me feel when looking at them without understanding what the pictures meant. An apple in the West can have various symbolic meanings; for example, to some an apple might suggest a healthy diet while to others an apple is a symbol of New York and to yet others it is just a piece of fruit. Why do we often like a certain painting long before we understand the meaning behind the picture? Or why should we like a painting first and the meaning later becomes an extra gift? How the artist answers this sort of questions will separate the sensitive artist from the insensitive and impersonal artist. And it is his answers that help the work of the intelligent and sensitive artist endure. With his intelligence and sensitivity, he is concerned with the pictorial laws of attraction and knows what grabs and attracts viewers to pictures—he also knows it is necessary to grab and attract the viewer before the artist can impose his message on the viewer. Because of his knowledge of human nature, this artist is able to psychologically use pictorial devices to lure the viewer into enjoying, appreciating and accepting the picture before delivering his message. The intelligent artist with special well-cultured sensitivity, knowing where most mediocre artworks end up, knows that his timeless picture should provide enjoyment, pleasure, timeless beauty and continuous inspiration for future imaginations. So he uses all that he has to help his art.

The difference between the still life painting that will touch people and the still life that will be just another artwork will rely on what the intelligent and sensitive artist sees and brings out of the still life set up before him. Whether a portrait will touch many or it is just a face with accurate features will depend on the mind of the artist.

In the art of rhetoric, the importance is not what the speaker says but what the audience hears, and if the audience wants to listen. Therefore, to be a good communicator the politician or public figure needs to have command over the language, as well as communication skills and people skills. The same is true for the movies, music and writing as it is for painting. The artist cannot rely only on the art and science of creating but he must also have a well-developed personal sensitivity towards nature so that she can reveal more than the eyes can see.

In order for artists to evolve like philosophers and scientists have and accept the world as they have accepted it, artists must understand, accept, enjoy and respect nature. This does not mean that artists should not be concerned with the ugliness of nature and oblivious to unpleasant things, but rather that they must understand everything in order for their positive outlook on nature to help their creations bring hope and beauty to our environment. It is this kind of sensitive outlook that will make artists pay special attention to nature's hidden treasures, so that figures are not just figures with faces but rather unique entities with characteristics that are the best of nature's creation. This essay presents a paradoxical view from the common one of an art student. In my other book on how successful artists study, I explain that while studying art the most important concern of the student should be to acquire skill, knowledge and experience so that later on he can well express his ideas and vision.

Art that becomes timeless exhibits the empathetic feelings that other art lacks. At any time (like our own) when there are extreme differences in style and tradition and many movements, then many things, such as technique, skill, experience, innovation, invention and style will level the field for all artists, but survival and endurance will favor the work of art that many can relate to and depend on for a continuous and timeless source of beauty and inspiration.

Written as a lecture for students at the National Academy School of Fine Arts

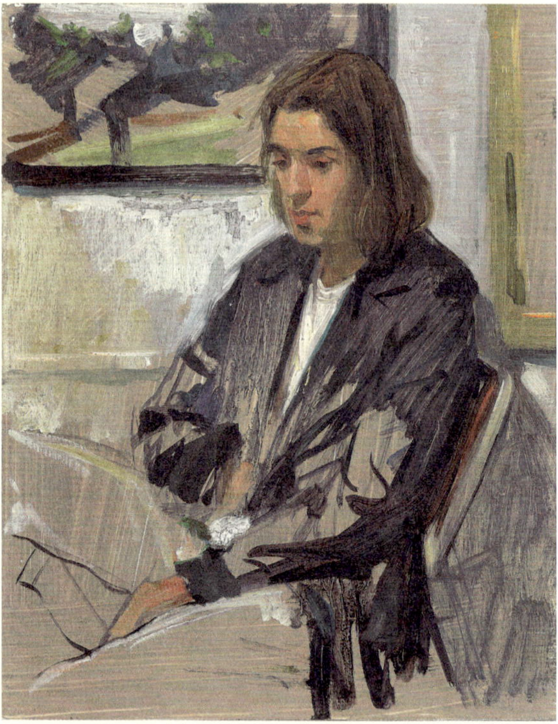

Julian, Sam Adoquei

ENJOY IMAGES IN DETAIL download all images for free at: www.OriginofInspiration.com

6 MEANINGFUL PURPOSE

There are painters who transform the sun
into a yellow spot, but there are others who,
thanks to their art and intelligence,
transform a yellow spot into the sun.
— Pablo Picasso

Why do some artworks inspire us, while other artworks do nothing for us? Why do some artworks inspire most people while others inspire only a few? Why would Homer's Odyssey, the Bhagavad Gita, Boethius's writings and the Western literary classics live on forever? The answer is in that which separates universal and timeless art from decorative works that match the couch but are as invisible as the wall they hang on, a meaningful message.

For a timeless message to be effective, the artist's subject should have a meaningful purpose—delivering either continuous beauty and inspiration or a thought-provoking idea that all can gain from. The message of a timeless painting must be important enough that it will be preserved, so that it lives on to provide its purpose, beauty, inspiration, joy, comfort, happiness, courage or hope to whomever encounters it in the future. The same is true for works in all the other arts, such as music, movies and literature.

A great work of art does not generally come into existence by accident or luck—its meaning, purpose and structure must be thoroughly planned. Living a purposeful life creates meaning in the artist's work so that whomever the work touches is exposed to timeless art.

The reader might well ask, why bother with such metaphysical issues? Why not create without putting too much thought into the process? Imagine if the scientist, the writer, the doctor or the historian were careless about improving mankind's life. Do you know the power of the talent you have been blessed with? And have you thought what the options would have been had you not been blessed with your talent? Have you ever asked yourself why are we here on earth? Who knows, perhaps you would have been assigned a more difficult vocation.

Inspirations From Heroes and Saints

Why can't we remember any of the mythical tales about all the mean gods and wicked heroes? Yet I remember the gods, saints and heroes of ancient classical books. Books like the Bhagavad Gita, Boethius's Consolation of Philosophy and Homer's Odyssey, as well as the modern Western classics will live on. These books were great when they were new and continue to be great. When I left Ghana for Nigeria to start my life as an artist, I brought along with me twelve books, seven of which were Eastern and Western classics. I also brought along two pages of handwritten life instructions given to me by my mentor, my cousin. He was in his late twenties and was very protective, he wanted to make sure I was properly guided. Each of the seven books of classics communicated something special to me (kindness to people, courage, survival and endurance, pursuit of a noble course and living a fulfilling life). The remaining five were art books.

The Eastern and Western classics are full of gods, saints and heroes, all striving against life's odds and overcoming them with perseverance, courage, energy and hope as well as help from some sort of divine energy. Unlike the gods, the saints, gurus and heroes are humanized in creative works. Otherwise, we would find it difficult to accept them, relate to them or look up to them for inspiration and courage. It is the humanization of the subject that makes the supernatural sometimes feel real. And sometimes makes the impossible seem reachable and achievable. The classic writings all contain humanized heroes, saints and gods. The characters in these books are so humanized that the courage and inspiration we get from their endurance in overcoming life's challenges will keep on inspiring readers forever. Because of this we can aspire to their accomplishments. If we too are able to create meaningful works providing timeless inspiration to help others, our work will live on.

Older nations with great classical and mythological stories are among the most developed nations today. This tells us that the contribution of humanized gods, saints and heroes in these nations' books has played a major role in their culture.

Humanize your creative works or whatever you do, and humans from all walks of life will understand and relate to your work easily. On the other hand, depict a superhero that no one can relate to and you will attract a very small audience.

A story or a painting of the truck driver's daughter who became the mayor of a big town will inspire and encourage people for ages. Or the story of the poor neighborhood kid who became a superstar by winning a competition because he took advice from the local barber. These stories will always serve as inspiration. Whether the classics were intentionally written with the specific purpose of helping readers, or were written just as mythological poetry, celestial songs and stories for all times, we do not know. While we may not know the intentions of the authors, we do know that great artworks do not come from lucky and accidental efforts. The works have lived until now, so they must possess some qualities, which, when emulated, will achieve similar results.

What Happened to Picasso's Legacy?

Do not go where the path may lead,
go instead where there is no path
and leave a trail.
— Ralph Waldo Emerson

The age of using artistic materials for personal therapeutic purposes, the selfish age of the me-me-me syndrome, the age of shouting and yelling to draw attention to one's self, the wasteful era of everything and anything goes as art, tagging tricks and cheap art as high art and the era of attention-grabbing tricks for the sake of fifteen minutes of fame is passing quietly and slowly, and will soon be history. It is no longer going to be fashionable or cool to support incompetent and meaningless works of art. Did we take Picasso's talent for granted or did we abuse Picasso's legacy? If we did abuse his legacy, this will not go on forever. The public can now see through the dishonest. Who wants to be choked up, looking at other people's personal problems on museum or gallery walls? Who cares about our selfish me-me-me problems at times when the world needs honest and capable professional artists to contribute the best of their talent? The era of "What can I do with my talent to help?" has arrived or at least is just around the corner. If the Renaissance artists contributed to mankind, why can't we? Learning from and taking advantage of past legacies can guide us.

In times like this, when our political leaders are working hard around the globe to bring peace, hope, courage and timeless inspiration to the relationships among countries, why should we make a special exception for inexperienced artists shouting for attention and fame while taking advantage of the freedom bestowed on good artists. We artists too can live a meaningful, purposeful, fulfilling life. We should not blame the ugliness we foster on society. The role we artists play can contribute and be as helpful as the role we expect our authorities to play for us.

We, the artists who are meant to provide art and teach the importance of beauty, have not yet been able to educate the public to know the difference between beauty and ugliness. How then can we not take some responsibility for the ugliness around us, and try to make things better for the new era? Change has begun to arrive. It's time to make sure artists with good intentions are ready to be taken seriously and to gain back their noble respectful place in culture. We should be ready with our own high standard of art for the new era, in which art patrons and a society that are more informed than ever will be thoughtfully critical and will expect everything from the artists they support—talent, knowledge, skill and experience. Freedom of expression in the new era will level the field for all. This knowledgeable society and its informed patrons will decide who should be responsible for society's creative beauty and inspirations.

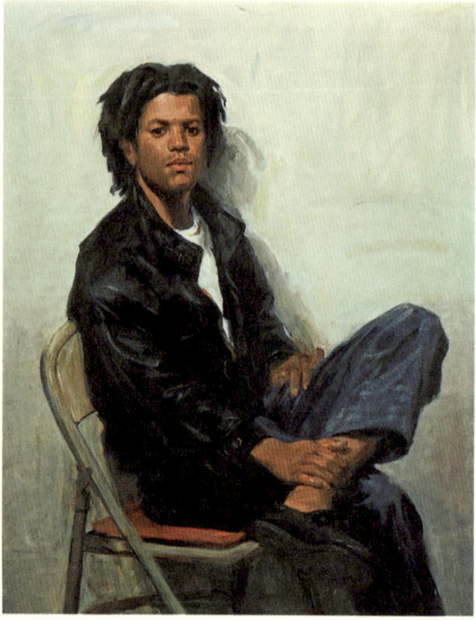

Portrait of My Friend, Sam Adoquei

ENJOY IMAGES IN DETAIL download all images for free at: www.OriginofInspiration.com

Why I Painted Rodney

I met Rodney during my early years in the United States. I was inspired to paint him because we became friends, and also because I had never seen a painting of a young African-American man in dreadlocks on any museum wall. Who knows, maybe one day his portrait will end up in some museum. I painted Rodney through my African idealistic lens. His dreadlocks to me represented a kind of spiritual symbol. I had no idea that in the Eighties dreadlocks in America were not the ideal fashionable look. I was shocked and surprised when the painting won an important international award a year or two later, but was rejected by an African-American organization in Chicago for a prestigious book cover on the premises that a portrait of a black man in dreadlocks is not a good representation of black Americans. When I painted Rodney I painted a handsome and kind, noble, dignified young black man, but the organization that rejected the portrait could not see beyond the dreadlocks. They saw only what they wanted to see and did not bother to ask me what inspired the painting. A couple of years later another publishing company who saw what I saw used the portrait on a book cover for "Literature and Language."

We see life, nature, the universe and people through a certain lens that we have developed. What we see depends on how pure, clean, natural, innocent and transparent that lens is. The beauty we see in others depends only on the effort we make in cleaning and purifying the lens.

Less than 20 years have passed since the painting was rejected for the book cover that I wanted so badly to be on. Since then the symbolism of dreadlocks has changed in America. If my vision of Rodney had been idealized, time would have aged the painting and its beauty would look old-fashioned. Since that time, dreadlocks have appeared everywhere, from Wimbledon to Hollywood, in politics, in the media.

Food for Thought

Why do the works of Shakespeare, Mozart, Leonardo da Vinci, Rubens, Monet and some works of ancient literature still live on after centuries? Why do most movies come and go and only a few become classics? Why do some masters continuously produce masterpieces that become timeless, yet others produce some good works that eventually fade into obscurity? How can the ambitious artist learn from the experiences of those who create the universal and timeless works? To think it is luck that makes some masters produce timeless work while others miss the target is to believe great things happen by accident.

There are formulas to all things that are judged by results, and in our culture concerned with results the intelligent scholar must try and learn the formulas that create those certain successful results so that he can share the knowledge with those who want to achieve similar results in that field. We live in an age when one can no longer let luck, fate and superstition decide the future of his business, his work or his life. Artists will have to approach their vocation with the same attitude if they are to contribute to their world and excel just as professionals in the sciences do or as their predecessors have done. For any institution to do well, it must make sure its people receive the best leadership training in schools that have good records of producing great leaders. Good law schools produce good lawyers; the best business schools produce the best businesspeople. Why is this not also true of the arts?

The artist who wants to produce timeless works of art must learn that which makes art timeless. Any subject natural to all men is what the creative artist has to consider if he has the desire to reach generations to come. He should take into consideration what has taken me more than 30 years of professional artistic life to discover: no great achievements happen by accident, although on the surface it might appear that way. With this theory of timeless art, the serious artist can at least take into consideration the role tradition, meaning and subject play in the arts.

Greatness: The subject, the tools, or the artist?

I recently saw a movie by one of America's famous directors. I went with five of my mentees — two of them are filmmakers, one a musician, and the others painters. We saw the movie because I was planning to give a lecture on Greatness: The subject, the medium, or the artist?

After the film, the two moviemakers claimed that the director did not have enough material to make a great movie because the protagonist is a great American historical hero and nothing greater could be done in a film — and it was the director's fault to take on the project. They reason that some subjects should be left alone. The fine artists thought the acting was very good but the movie was mediocre for a famous director. The musicians didn't think it was good.

It is here where I asked what amount the subject, the tools, or the artists contribute to greatness?

So you have studied and learned everything there is to learn in your field, you know every word in the dictionary, you have the best and most expensive camera and can afford anything, you have the most gifted voice, you can travel to wherever the story or the subject is, and you can afford the best tools for any subject you decide to tackle. What next? These are advantages that make the execution of a vision easier, but they do not guarantee greatness. It is a relief to shift blames on to your tools or your subject and never find the extraordinary within the ordinary. An artist without a cultured vision doesn't see greatness in nature, and therefore doesn't gravitate to subjects that have timeless and greatness qualities and values; instead, he imposes and gravitates to that which is familiar to all.

It is here that our unique vision plays a major part in the creative process. What extraordinary things do you bring out in ordinary subjects, common places, and regular people? In my coaching classes, I set up a situation where it becomes the artist's duty to find the extraordinary and greatness hidden beneath common places. The unique vision we bring to our subject is what matters, it is that unique vision the artist has to develop— not what the subject is. It is only when the mind is cultured by mentoring, coaching or guidance that it can see and extract greatness out of anything. Any other access is an advantage that makes the execution easier.

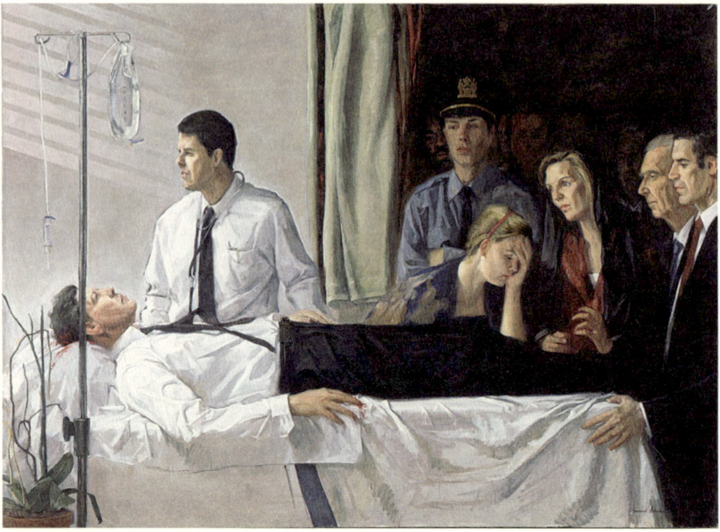

John F. Kennedy, Sam Adoquei

7 INSPIRATIONS IN DISGUISE

There was a time when "The Conciliation of Philosophy" by Boethius was as popular a book as the Bible. From a very early age this privileged young man not only had accomplished more than the average, but he also had the best of everything. While still in his twenties, his whole life suggested that he would easily gain any goals he aimed for. Groomed to be the ideal successful man, Boethius became a member of the senate while still in his twenties. Coming from a high-society background, he believed that the only ambition worthy of a scholar of high birth was to translate, harmonize and bring together the works of the greatest philosophers, Plato and Aristotle. Boethius was unable to accomplish his ambition because he was wrongly accused of treason by a jealous member of the senate and sentenced to death by torture.

While in prison awaiting execution, Boethius found the inspiration to transform himself from a privileged and over-accomplished young man into a wise one, capable of making sense of life and death as well as the cruel and ugly side of mankind. Boethius used that inspiration to write the book that in its time and for a millennium afterward was as popular as the Bible. This and similar stories teach us that what one does with what life offers us is everything. Even though things may go against our desires, by rational reasoning and putting things in perspective, we can develop the mental powers to choose the desired state we want to be in, and to use that state to do something that in return will benefit us.

Unusual Places for Inspiration

What do you do when you don't know where or how to look for inspiration? What do you do when you don't know there could be an inspiration waiting for you? What do you do when you don't know there is an inspiration coming to you? How can you be inspired if you don't know you are staring into or sitting in that which should inspire you? What do you do when you don't know you are living in an inspirational environment? Before continuing reading, I would like the reader to take a moment to give these questions some thought.

"People spend their lifetime climbing the ladder of success, only to find out the ladder has been on the wrong wall." — Joseph Campbell

The source of inspiration, or the origin of inspiration, does not send signals to reveal itself to the hero within us to wake us up, to tell us that the moment to be inspired has come. Rather the hero within us awakes now that the time has come to act, to wake up, to survive and do something—to prove that bad conditions will not force us to surrender to an unwanted fate. Happiness, sadness, contentment, freedom and peace are the same as inspiration. They can be found in unusual places and they only reveal themselves to those ready to grasp the truth. Many times we wait or go around searching for inspiration. We expect inspiration to walk in announcing itself via a bold noisy entry, giving us a prior warning: I am inspiration and I want you to take advantage of me. I will stay until you notice me. This is like the athlete who prefers to be behind so that he can use the psychology of the underdog—coming from behind—as a motivation to play hard. This is not inspiration.

How can conditions be worse than the death sentence Boethius faced? What condition can be so bad that one cannot find the peace within oneself to reason and keep going in order to find answers to life's journey? "Every fortune is a good fortune," said Boethius. Imagine an accused man writing this down and thanking nature for the enlightenment he has gained.

Maybe if we take a moment to put things in perspective we will be able to see that our existing condition is a detour, an experience that is leading us to find that which lies waiting for us… Can a bad profession, an unwanted piece of luck or an accidental decision or choice cause us to fail?

Why haven't we awakened the hero within, what are we waiting for? More suffering or do we expect a signal? Maybe this moment is it; the status quo might be the writing on the wall that is telling us we should do something.

Life's Detours

I wonder if I were to ask you, the reader, why all of a sudden you have become aware that your condition is not worthy of the life you want to live? Why all of a sudden you want to change in order to do more, to achieve more to live a more fulfilling life? Or if you know why you have read these chapters to reach this point? Chances are, you will say, you have been waiting until now or you have realized things should no longer be the way they are when in essence you have forgotten that everything so far has been part of a journey or a path that should bring you here to this particular place. Take a moment and think carefully about everything, your complete life journey since birth, a journey that you may not have had control over, but the only journey you have been on, the only trip that has taught you all that you know and brought you here to this moment.

Did you choose your race and gender? Did you choose your parents? Or did you choose the city and country you were born in? Can you think of any other reason why you have come to this conclusion (that your life needs to change) besides this life journey? Any reason you might think of will need strong philosophical reasoning, support and argument to make its case. And what if I make the point that the journey that has brought you here was a journey to provide you with the necessary tools so that you would be equipped for the journey ahead and that every turn in the previous journey that you did not expect was a sort of detour—or a blessing in disguise—added to the trip for you to learn from. Whether good or bad, whether you like it or not, everything is meant to help you reach this junction.

If for a moment we think carefully about our present condition, situation or experiences, we will realize that we may have not achieved what we deserve because we have not paid attention to all the signals around us that are supposed to encourage and force us to do something towards altering our situation. We have been missing all the blessings in disguise because we are too busy denying the existence of things we dislike, things we think ought not to exist, conditions we don't think we deserve.

Circumstances do not make people
but reveal the true hidden self. — James Allen.

If it is true that time and circumstances do not make us, but instead reveal our true selves, then I think the greatest life lessons we can ever receive are through the true-life experience we have gained. It is through this natural experience, whether good or bad, that we are able to realize and awaken our healthy double, which has tagged along with us waiting for the right moment, wanting the best for us.

We should be thankful and feel blessed for the knowledge and experience we have gained. It is because of this existing experience that we are able to envision the happiness and bargain for the life we deserve that lies waiting for us. It is better to accept all our past hardships with a constructive attitude since they have not left us with the mental and physical destruction that would deprive us of our will to dream or to wish for that which is our mission and purpose in life is. Rather everything so far has helped clarify that which we realize is our true calling.

Blessings in Disguise

You might want one thing, but while you are busy pursuing that thing other opportunities can be waiting or passing you by. Often we are so fixated on that which we think we want that we don't see all the Blessings in Disguise. That is, until we realize that whatever we are doing and whatever our condition, it is mainly the experiences we have had that will lead us to finding our goals and purpose in life. We all find our calling at different times; some will find it very early in life, some after continuous failure and others after several changes of direction.

Many will never find their calling at all, others just drift from one thing to another, tag along and stay with the flow. The purpose of life is to learn new things, gain new experiences, gather more knowledge and wisdom so that one will be better prepared and equipped for the trip ahead. Experience, knowledge and wisdom are often embedded in certain life situations, often in unexpected places. We miss these hidden inspirational lessons because we expect that which should inspire our life lessons to come from a certain ideal place. We expect inspiration to look and feel a certain way and to expose itself when we are ready. In most cases, circumstances brought about by nature are meant to bring out the best in us.

After you discover your calling, chances are that even though you have gotten the necessary inspiration to move on, you won't rejoice and realize that you have escaped from a bad reality and will soon enter a new and better life. Thinking this way will make you blame things on some of the misfortunes of the past without realizing that it has been those misfortunes that have led you to this destination. Whatever has happened so far to get us to realize what we really desire has been neither good nor bad luck, neither failure nor success. Failure in your past has not been punishment and success has not been reward. Even though it might not seem so to you, in the bigger picture everything has happened for your own good in order for you to enable you to acquire the necessary knowledge to pursue that which will bring you a purposeful continuation, leading to a desired ending. Often it is only at the end that you realize the reason why things went the way they did.

Detours in Western Culture

Horatio Alger, a Harvard graduate, wanted to become a great poet but ended up becoming America's most successful and famous writer of *From Rags to Riches* stories that changed so many lives.

One of the greatest Roman emperors was not known for bringing peace by conquering empires. His fame and importance do not rest on the battles he won and the armies he conquered, but rather on his writings about living the perfect life in accordance with nature. Marcus Aurelius wrote *Meditations* in his quiet moments when resting from battle.

Marcus Aurelius was a warrior and an army general who defended his nation and won several wars, conquering empires. One would think such a man would be famous for writing a book on war strategies; instead, he became the most famous Roman Emperor because of his private humble thoughts, his diary published as *Meditations*, which gave suggestions on living in accordance to the laws of the universe. Though he never intended to publish his work, over thousands of years it has shown the way to finding inner peace for lives everywhere.

The Sistine Chapel, not his sculptures, will forever keep Michelangelo's reputation in the history books. Yet Michelangelo in the beginning refused to accept the commission to paint the Sistine Chapel because he did not think of himself as a painter. "Painting is for women," he told Leonardo da Vinci. Leonardo, on the other hand, had to find solutions to scientific problems so he could get painting commissions.

Joseph Campbell, a respected academic mythologist and one of the greatest storytellers who ever lived, is the co-author of *The Power of Myth*. Campbell returned from Europe to the United States just a few weeks before the Wall Street crash and was unemployed for the next five years. This experience served Campbell as a natural detour. He rented a small shack and spent the five years reading in search of knowledge. It became his quest to find the key to all mythologies. Through this experience Campbell became one of the greatest mythologists who ever lived. "People spend their lifetime climbing the ladder of success, only to find out the ladder has been on the wrong wall," he said. It may be that the right wall is the one you are looking at while standing on your ladder.

Even though I had had a lot of experience as a professional artist before coming to the United States, I was no match for the challenges I faced when I was hired to teach at New York's National Academy of Design School of Fine Arts. When I started teaching, my first challenge was my command over the English language. My speaking skills were very poor and teaching the science of art requires constant discussions and explanations.

My second disadvantage was that I came from Africa, where I had started teaching at the early age of 15. Because of this I didn't fit the stereotypical idea of a great master teacher a Westerner might easily trust with their art education.

Third, I had left Ghana when I was 15 and migrated from one place to the other before coming to the United States, so I was inexperienced in everything except art and survival. In the West, art in some cases is learned by people of talent who don't care too much about survival skills. At the end of the day the worst that might happen is that the government will help you—this meant that all the survival skills I could teach artists were unnecessary.

Fourth, I had no understanding of Western culture. The leadership and management experience that had helped me in Ghana and Nigeria as a 15-year-old managing a studio of six billboard artists was incompatible with New York's art institutions. In addition, some of my early students consisted of professionals, such as the retired president of one of the country's prominent institutions, as well as lawyers, doctors, professors and others undertaking career and life transitions. This meant that for me to survive and pursue the Western traditional manner of artistic vocation and teaching, I would have to quickly learn to understand my students and to be understood by them as well as to learn everything there is to learn for an outsider. My professional experience, what I knew about teaching and how I could paint were not necessary for me; I needed to learn new skills so that I could understand the culture and people before I could teach in these circumstances. It is at this moment I realized I should get some greasy and sticky crayons, pencils, brushes, erasers and T-squares and rulers to design or touch-up my blueprint and prototype. To survive in my new environment, the archetype I had brought from Ghana needs some tweaking.

I made it a point to spend my leisure time learning everything about my new country. It was this transformation that occurred during my detour that has brought me to this point of being able to write and apply all that I have learned to help the creative people I meet. Looking back at all the challenges at the Academy, they have formed a great detour, a source of inspiration necessary for someone so foreign.

A very good artist friend of mine told me a story of how she once went to a school to register for music lessons, but the elevator stopped on the wrong floor. It was a floor with painting studios. She stayed for a while, came back a couple of times to visit, and then ended up registering for drawing and painting classes instead of music lessons. I too had a similar experience. Six months into my accounting exams, I was one-and-a-half hours late for my school bus. An older friend of mine was on the bus I took. He was going to the art academy. Out of curiosity I played hooky from my accounting classes to join my friend and see what art classes are all about. I think you know what became of me since then.

Guarantors of Inspiration

To aim and focus on a goal, to believe in that which your mind's eye sees and to have tunnel vision so that nothing can distract you from attaining your aim are the greatest guarantors of success in all ambitious tasks.

After that, you need the ability to reason and to develop a strategy that will allow you to see every chance and opportunity that is embedded in the existing situation that might otherwise pass you by, so you can act on them. Reasoning about a situation with the eye of a general helps you achieve that which leads to a fulfilling and happy ending. Reaching and achieving a great goal is one thing and reaching a desired happy ending that makes life worthy of living is another thing. Despite all the different roads we take in life, at the end of the day we want our journeys to lead us to the desired happy ending, worthy of our short visit on earth. It is this that makes great strategists and generals weigh the end reward over existing gains.

Coming from Africa and being in a Western profession, my life has been constantly changing, not by wish but by condition. With each new change, I have had to alter my game plan and my strategy to suit the new conditions, to create new tactics and to accept new experiences and make the best of things or to find the best of each new circumstance and experience. Looking back, I wouldn't have thought I had the natural experience and knowledge to write my first book. Neither would I have expected to be known as a teacher, artist and author of the #1 Best Seller *How Successful Artists Study*.

By desire and wish Pablo Picasso wanted to become as great as history's great traditional artists, but by condition, experience and open-mindedness, he became a genius by means of what he adopted and took advantage of. By wish and desire we get what we think we want or deserve, but by nature, condition, experience and open-mindedness, we metamorphose into our real hidden selves, what we really are. By wish and desire, Picasso wanted to become like other past old masters, but by condition, nature and experience everyone now wants to become Picasso.

What wish and desire have arranged for us, and what nature, conditions, experience and open-mindedness hide from us, it is here that caution should always be observed. Our true worth and aspirations, our dreams and our calling are all woven into our daily conditions and experiences. All we have to do is to make the conscious decision to be aware of the possible danger of not accepting any condition we don't like. Not liking a situation, a condition or an experience reminds me of the king who would not allow a messenger into his kingdom because the messenger did not look or behave properly, so because of the outward appearance of the messenger the king missed out on the message. The Grand History Book of Happiness is littered with millions of pages of unhappy disappointed individuals who refused to see all the blessings that came to them in disguised form. They were so fixated on their expectations, demands, desires and wishes that they couldn't see the blessings in disguise awaiting their attention.

Every Fortune Is a Good Fortune

One of the most successful landscapes I ever painted came to me in the form of a blessing in disguise. I was driving through Bar Harbor in Maine on my way to painting a commissioned work when I saw an amazing scene, the kind of ideal painterly subject that often brings out the best of everything I know about art. At first I was disappointed and upset about not having the time to paint and not being prepared to paint. So I stopped my car and made some notes and recorded the time of the scene, did some sketches and then quickly went to my hotel and prepared a large canvas to use the following day at the same time.

Because I am a realist, I prefer being in nature and recording her in person so I always start my landscape paintings on location.

I came the following day about two hours before the time I had noted down and set up all my materials and waited for the scene to happen. It was like a sport for me, I was geared up, psyched up and ready to go. Five minutes before the time arrived, I picked up my brushes, meditated for a moment and then took a deep breath, possessed and ready to start. Just when I was about to put my brush on the canvas, I overheard a mother saying, "Tommy, he's an artist, go and show him your drawings." I pretended I didn't hear her. And I said to myself, "Not now, please God, not now. Please God, this scene is my kind of subject, the kind that guarantees my success and provides my bread and butter."

Knowing myself, I realized that I would never have the guts to say no to any enthusiastic talented artist, most of all a kid, so I kept my cool and concentrated on my canvas in hopes that the mother would get the message. But before I could put down my first stroke of color I saw the kid standing in my blind spot, looking up at me with his crayons in his left hand, raising his drawing pad. By the time I finished going through his book and encouraging him, more than 30 minutes had passed. My scene was gone. "Tommy, we have to go, Daddy is waiting for us," said the mother. Tommy left with my scene and left me standing like a penguin, dressed in the perfect attire, prepared and ready for the occasion, but with nowhere to go and nothing to do. I sat on a rock, feeling wasted and defeated and thinking that Tommy's mother had taken advantage of me, discouraged but not bitter because I had always lived a life constantly envisioning any situation and comparing it with the worst possible scenario.

I sat there quietly thinking, throwing some rocks into the ocean, when all of a sudden the scene, the view, the look of my subject became different. Something very beautiful—a wonderful and perfect representation of Maine that I had never, ever seen before. So beautiful I could not help but re-psyche myself and paint like a mad, crazed, artist possessed. I looked up, prayed and thanked God, asking him for the energy and mind to capture the new subject. The resulting painting has brought me more commissions and more recognition than any other. So ever since that day I have forever kept advocating the idea of staying aware of detours in life.

Intentional Detours

As much as a sharp focus on an idea can lead to achieving a goal, sometimes it is not a bad idea to make an intentional detour. This allows you to be alert to things that happen that you have never noticed. You will never know what you might discover, what you might learn or where unknown roads might take you, unless you try these intentional detours.

Last December I was evicted from my apartment and was given a month to move out. I remember my last day of packing. I went home with a list of about 25 things to do, from cleaning and emptying my closet to enjoying the last steak in my fridge. I had to do everything and be sure to finish my list sometime between 6 p.m. and 1 a.m. Around 7 all the stress hit me. "Why in my late forties don't I have a place I can call my own?"

Depression took over. At one point, my emotions started to break down, and before I knew it, I was sitting doing nothing, not knowing whom to blame. I took a moment to relax and then asked myself what would be the worst thing that could happen to me if I didn't finish my list? My eviction, after all, had happened only because the property was sold and the new owner wanted to tear the building down and build something new and not because I had failed to secure a shelter. At that moment, I decided to take an accidental, detour, to do something different from what I was doing. I stopped everything, took a deep breath and sat down.

At that moment, my eyes fell on an old dusty calendar I had thrown away a couple of days before. It was a five-year-old promotional calendar with a diary sent to me by one of my portrait agents, but I had never opened the calendar and it had been sitting behind my fridge unused in its envelope. Just for fun, I decided to take it out of the garbage bag and read the days and months. Just read for no particular purpose, just to do something different for the sake of creating an accidental and unintentional detour. I started flipping through the months. As I flipped through I realized each month was represented by a famous person's quote and a short description of his achievements. As I went through I saw the quote: "True heroism is not the urge to surpass all others at whatever cost, but the urge to serve others at whatever cost." —Arthur Ashe.

On another month's page I saw a little bio of Horatio Alger. I went on to read everything in the calendar. Equipped with these inspirational stories of great achievers, I stopped everything, sat on my bed and wrote this chapter you are now reading.

Yielding Is Not Defeat

The stoic philosophy teaches us that only through submission to the laws of the universe can one find true happiness. If taken literally, one might think that going with the flow is the only way to Nirvana. Why complain when you are defenseless in a situation or an event that you have no control over? Instead; yield, reason and understand, find your equilibrium and your inner strength; you might be in a natural detour or staring directly into the eyes of inspiration in disguise yet refusing to yield in order to acquire knowledge. Learn from the situation. Think about how you can use whatever lessons there are to assist you in your search for happiness. So long as you don't surrender but strategically yield, you will be in control of the means of finding a way out. Yielding is not being defeated. Yielding when cornered is the ideal strategic move of generals who have a grand overview of the bigger picture.

We constantly encounter all sorts of setbacks, such as deaths, loss of work and sickness. There will always be detours in our lives, the only problem is that they come unannounced with uncertain dates for their departure. And until they leave they will not tell us why they have come. It is we who have to accept, understand and acknowledge their existence, and yield in order to reason so that we can use the lessons these detours bring. These detours are always blessing in disguise but it is left to us to determine and find their hidden gifts. We might not like the setbacks because we expect our life to keep on moving forward all the time; according to how we have scripted it in our minds; because of this we don't see setbacks as life yielding in order to find its proper course. Yielding to those who are in control of the powers of their faculties sometimes is a form of going with the flow. It also means putting your whole faculties in a psychological position where you are enlighten and motivated by the existing situation.

Going with the Flow

When I was growing up one of the leading causes of death among children in my city was the sudden change of currents at our beaches. I have seen my schoolmates and neighborhood people die. Even though as children my friends and I didn't know how to swim, one of the dangerous games we dared our friends and ourselves to play was seeing who could enter a strong current and then get back out. Some of the currents were not as dangerous as others but to us the thrill of getting out after we were worn out and exhausted was worth everything. I have been drowned twice, once I was lucky to get out exhausted and drunk with seawater, the other time I was not so lucky. It was not during a game of dare but by mistake I entered a dangerous current. Until today the only thing I remember from that near-death experience is the tumbling, the swallowing of seawater and the CPR given me by my uncle.

The concept of going with the flow is similar to that of swimming. When swept down by a dangerous underwater current, trying to swim against the current, no matter how experienced or strong the swimmer, is a waste of energy that can lead to drowning. Experienced swimmers stay patient, calm and alert while in the current and wait for the right moment to make the move to swim out. They allow the current to take control because sooner or later the current will release them in a place that is safer. Inexperienced swimmers, on the other hand, fight with every breath until their energy gives out and then they die of exhaustion because they have not enough energy left when released in a safer area. In the mind of a person in control of self, going with the flow means, "Calm down, relax, yield, think, reason, plan and wait, because sooner or later everything will manifest itself, and it will all make sense that can be of use to you." Wasting one's energy in complaining and not acknowledging and accepting, forces us not to relax, yield, think, reason, and plan. Rather, we sleepwalk through our experience.

Submitting and accepting an undesirable situation does not mean giving up, surrendering and accepting defeat. It means accepting and understanding that there is a reason and purpose why things are happening the way they are, and that what is happening is happening for a reason favorable to the journey we are making. It is easier to accept, yield, reason and make good use of what is happening than to fight against something we have no control over. The opposite reaction of not accepting is more self-defeating because one is in the situation in any case.

How Have You Arrived Here?

How have you reached this place? To reach a point where you can expect more from yourself is the great awakening that most don't have and that they envy. Some sleepwalk through life and never ask, never attempt to do something about what they are going through that they detest so much. Maybe they detest their lives because the status quo needs to change or maybe because their journey needs new challenges. Perhaps the realization has come to them that contributing to the world around them is the way they want to live. Or simply because life so far has not given them what they think they deserve. Or perhaps they have not asked for and pursued that which they honestly deserve.

Whatever has brought you to where you are may not appear fair, and it is not going to seem right. Neither would it be true if you blamed life, or mistakes in your past, for never not having achieved your share of what you deserve. Apart from natural accidents, we cannot blame problems in the future on past setbacks. Everything that has happened is part of the reason why the road ahead will be clearer. Everything in the past has been a detour leading to where you want to go. Your head full of recorded information, ideas and experiences, your wise mind and your demanding double has this function at the same time because *the yearning to fulfill our potential has always been human nature.* —Ralph Waldo Emerson

Don't Mock Nature (Food for Thought)

Nature is not a bad politician from a small town who does not see the bigger picture and does not know who he is supposed to represent. Responsibility is not handed to a friend or a family member. Don't pretend all your creations and intentions are for improving humanity and then turn back and use that opportunity to scheme and make profits at whatever cost to others. Do not, in the pursuit of gain, produce harmful creations that bring you profit but harm people. In doing this, you will get the profit but not get the necessary reward that you require. In pursuit of inspiration, nature stays from start to reward with the sincere mind, the honest, and the kind. Don't mock nature by praying for success, putting on the image and facade of a servant of nature, telling everyone how much you want your creations to help mankind, improve lives and wish everyone well, but behind the scenes it is all a facade to be concerned with fame, glory and all the superficial rewards. Don't pray for success and make believe nature is on your side because you are praying and doing the right thing while going around taking advantage of people. Nature is not a narrow-minded leader.

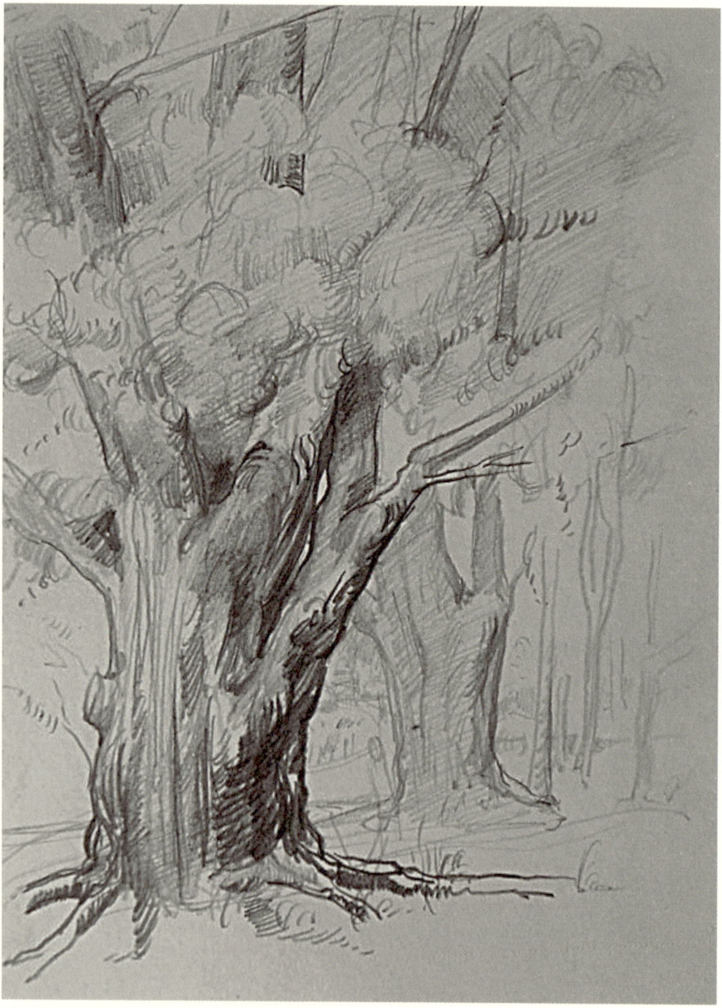

An Old Tree in Central Park, Sam Adoquei

ENJOY IMAGES IN DETAIL download all images for free at: www.OriginofInspiration.com

GROW YOUR DREAM

"Your time is limited; so don't waste it living someone else's life. Don't be trapped by dogma – which is living with the results of other people's thinking." — Steve Jobs

Notes from the Sage of My Teenage Years

I started my artistic profession at a very early age, when Nigeria's economy was flourishing, oil was booming and life was good. At weddings, funeral ceremonies and big parties, the rich showered dancers, brides and musicians with big nara bills (Nigerian currency).

Ghana, on the other hand, had run out of steam. Famine, constant coups, corruption and inflation had brought the country to her knees, and Ghana was on a downward spiral with nothing to hang on to. Conditions could not have been worse. During this time, young Ghanaians migrated to wherever they could find work, and Nigeria ended up with almost all the Ghanaian immigrants. Like all nouveau-rich and unprepared countries, Nigeria did not know how to use the immigrants to her benefit, so they dwelled on all the negativities and blamed the immigrants for all of their political, social and economic problems. Because of this, crime set the tone for this period, and immigrants received the worst treatment imaginable. You could barely make a 30-mile trip across Lagos without seeing a dead body on a side street.

It was during this time that I went to Nigeria as a stepping-stone to Europe. I was 15, the youngest among the Ghanaians who had come to hustle.

This was the era of Fela Anikulapo Kuti, the greatest musician Africa has ever produced. The most enigmatic artist I had ever seen, Fela was a force, a thunder. Politicians considered him a menace to society, but for Nigerians he fought against the regime of corruption and injustice.

Fela's shrine, Kalakuta, was about 10 blocks away from where I lived. I was too young to understand his political message, but my love for music led me to understand his greatness. His rhythm, melody, suspense and musical composition are still a major influence on my art, and my desire to be of service to man has roots in him as well. Although his approach to fighting for freedom, fighting for the poor, fighting for those who could not defend themselves is very different from mine, he is always at the back of my mind, asking me to do more, to contribute, to share and to inspire those I come in contact with. He always seems to be telling me to help those I believe need my help. For this I owe a lot to Fela, and also to Bob Marley, whose music and beliefs were introduced to me by the Ghanaian hustlers I mingled with for protection in Lagos.

With hindsight I learned that our friends who had no goals or dreams got stuck in Lagos, and those who where lucky enough to survive where repatriated back to Ghana. The few of us who dreamed and established goals were able to leave Lagos and go to Europe, where we educated ourselves and changed our lives.

It was during this period in Nigeria that I started working as a professional artist, and I met the sage Chief Okumola at my first job, at an advertising/sign shop. Chief Okumola gave me the wisdom and clear map that I needed for my life's journey. We became friends, because he lived next door to my workshop and he liked art, so he came by regularly to hang out and talk while I painted my billboards. I entertained his visits because I often worked alone in a big studio for 12-18 hours, with my helpers only coming after 3 or 4 in the afternoon.

Chief Okumola called me Oga Kekre, "Little Boss," and I called him "Chief." I liked him and we got along because he reminded me of my grandfather, who had passed away when I was in primary school. I was my grandfather's favorite; I sat hours with him every day after school and he told me story after story My grandfather couldn't walk and spent his days in a wheelchair. From cleaning to buying tobacco and alcohol and lighting his pipe, I was the only kid who served him. I didn't run away from whatever he needed. I loved every moment of being around him and listening to his stories.

Like my grandfather, Chief Okumola was not very popular with the kids, so I made myself available for all his needs. Because of him I started working on the weekends. I preferred to be in his company listening to his wise stories than being back in the dangerous ghettoes where we were living. I was young and alone in a hostile place, and it felt safe to work.

During these weekends I learned from Chief Okumola about how to achieve one's dreams. He knew how dangerous Nigeria was and he was worried about my future, but I wasn't aware of his concerns. I was learning all I needed to learn about life from his stories and advice, and making money while I worked. For me, life was very good, until one day the table turned. On this particular day, instead of him talking and me listening all day long, he threw questions at me as if he had spotted a weakness in my life's plan. As if looking at a map, every route he pointed to led to a dead end. It felt like concentrated artillery bombarding my life goals blueprint. Every missile he shot targeted the weakest spot of my defense. I thought I had designed beautiful and perfect routes with no faults.

The conversations continued the next day. The two-day barrage brought to my realization that I was naïve about life and relying too much on wishful thinking, luck and God to make things happen. There was more to life than just hoping for magic to happen. You can't just pray, hope and wait. Chief Okumola constantly advised me to pray, prepare, hope and act upon a certain plan. Empowered by this realization, I strategized how to launch my own barrage against him in our next meeting.

It was a weekend of questions on dreams, goals and aspirations. I wanted to know everything. I launched my own barrages back at him, threw in question after question. One idea I learned straight from start was that young people avoided him because they were not happy with his honest approach to extracting out their best. They did not appreciate his constructive criticism.

My artillery was no match for him. With logic and philosophy he answered almost all my life questions; those he couldn't, he told me to let the search for answers consume my daily thoughts. What do you think Kekre Oga? he always asked. What do you think, Kekre Oga?

These encounters with my sage—the discussions, conversations, stories and lessons I learned and the advice and ideas he gave me—are the source of this dream essay. One main reason for this dream essay is "*Origin of Inspiration*," the first edition of this book, which is about how we find enduring inspiration to help us stay strong when pursuing life's mission and goals, even in the face of bumpy roads. Naturally, great dreams and great ideas play hide-and-seek or catch-me-if-you-can in our minds. The dream essay is about how you, the dreamer, can find and catch a great dream, cage it in your mind's prison, interrogate it until the dream becomes a reality. It is meant to help you follow your own path in life so you can arrive at your destiny safely.

Dreams and Goals – The Source of Dreams

Nature offers us three alternatives to live in a world designed to evolve and advance. It gives us the will to choose how we want to live. It gives others the advantage to choose for us. It chooses for us but helps us maintain our free will and freedom of mind to make decisions and choices along the way. Beyond these choices nature reminds us constantly that life is fragile, short and no one lives on the stage forever and no one can play all the roles. So we must choose the roll we desire and play it well. When we decide to dream, misfortunes and blessings put some at an advantage or disadvantage right from the beginning. While most are handicapped by conditions, situations or lack of wisdom and will, others push until things bend into their favor and they tag along. Then there are a few whose dream allows them to live life as they desired. This essay addresses why it is important to dream, what kind of dream to take on, where and when to dream and how to choose the

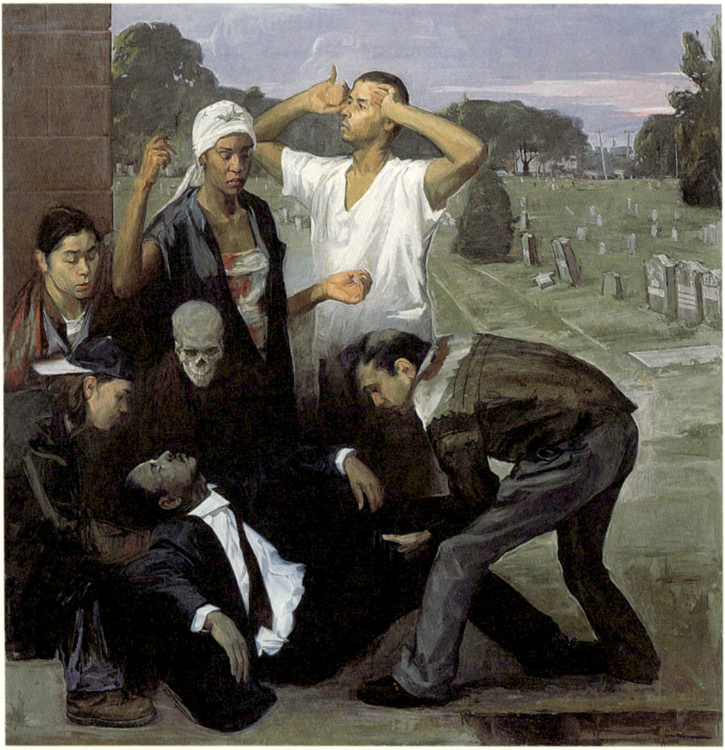

The Legacy of Dr. Martin Luther King (tryptic), Sam Adoquei

ENJOY ALL 3 PANELS IN DETAIL download all images for free at: www.OriginofInspiration.com

right dream. It helps provide the right mindset, the required life preparations and the awareness that it is not by magic that some achieve great dreams. A bit of strategy can help you simplify your mind in order to move smoothly toward salvation with a plan that tells you how to find, choose and achieve your dream. It helps those who dare to dream approach their goals so that they have no choice but to achieve their dreams.

This is an essay about the dreams we pursue—our goals, our aspirations and the great things we hope to achieve in life. Since nature offers us the greatest and most diverse choice of dreams, how can a dreamer choose a desired dream, guard and nourish it until it becomes reality, then use the rewards to do noble deeds? Dreams are formless, shapeless, wandering entities, searching for visionaries to seize and bring them to life. Dreams provide inspiration and bring our wishful desires to life. They make the future ever hopeful. The most potent psychological state of mind is believing that tomorrow will be better than today—it changes all that needs improvement in mankind. Purposeful dreamers are makers of new life on earth; dreamers see wonders awaiting. Visionaries and dreamers are special humans who see the hidden ingredients and opportunities needed for advancement of our universe. Purposeful dreamers are alchemists who transform ideas and dreams into reality and bring to life invisible opportunities.

Because the purpose of life is not just to eat and drink, breathe free air, populate the world and die, then it is clear that nature has planted in our mind an unavoidable desire to pursue our dream in order to fulfill our purposeful life. We are doomed and suffer a life of mediocrity and unfulfilled self-worth if we let go of our dreams; we fall in the hands of others who see us as nothing more than machines, workhorses or cattle in need of direction, and they use us for what they think we are worth. For this reason, we have no other choice than to find our dream and pursue it with passion. Timidity, or the fear of failure or vanity, leave only a few strong visionaries to dream big, take chances and pursue their chosen dream. Because of this fear, many choose to play a lesser role in life. They forget that the price and consequences of not pursuing a dream is more costly and painful, and they go through life day-dreaming, never taking advantage of their own self-worth.

While fame and greatness don't necessarily guarantee that you will achieve your goals, the dream alone can guarantee you fame and greatness and all that you wish to become. When a dream dies, it goes with the music. The dance stops, the inspirational spirit lingers, the questions of why must life go on begin to attack your self-worth, and discontentment with life attracts depression. Because of this, to have an enjoyable, happy and fulfilled life, we must find the right purposeful life, then follow our dream passionately in order to achieve our aims.

Karma Virtues

It is here that I like to plead with today's youth: Focus on your priorities; let your dream for great causes become the thoughts that dominate your being. Be aware of vices incompatible with your great dream. Don't let vices bend you to look downwards. When accomplishments, great looks, wealth and power drive you to look down on those less privileged, think again; it is hubris in disguise boosting up your ego so that it can have some smiles at your expense. It is virtues testing your humility. If you let your guard down and allow your vices to get the best of you, if temptation beats you into submission, it is because you lost track of your developing self-discipline and abandoned the noble aim that once dominated your desire to acquire continued growth so that you can improve the world. As a youth, you believe you can do anything. Don't let pressure cause you to lose that powerful and fearless mind. Don't let the rewards of instant gratification conceal the hidden price tags from you. If vices keep prevailing in the choices you make, you are trading your greatest potential for failure in disguise. If depression cloaks and masks you, if depression takes charge of your mood and daily actions, you have failed the warrior in you and allowed transient defeat a place to stay in your kingdom.

If temptation persuades you to take the fast road, think twice, retreat, be patient and let go of the pull. With cultivated virtues, all in life comes with a cheaper price tag, with no fine print or hidden fees.

Machiavellian ideas may convince you that it is a dog-eat-dog world, destroy or be destroyed, do others in before they do you in, succeed at all cause. Machiavellian advice may cause you to be deceptive, divide and conquer, take power and maintain it at all cost because the end justifies the means. But please tell Machiavelli: It is that filthy, selfish way of thinking, that cruel, insecure mind, that ended his life in misery, untrustworthy, alone and friendless in a small village. Please tell Machiavelli that you will succeed with virtues.

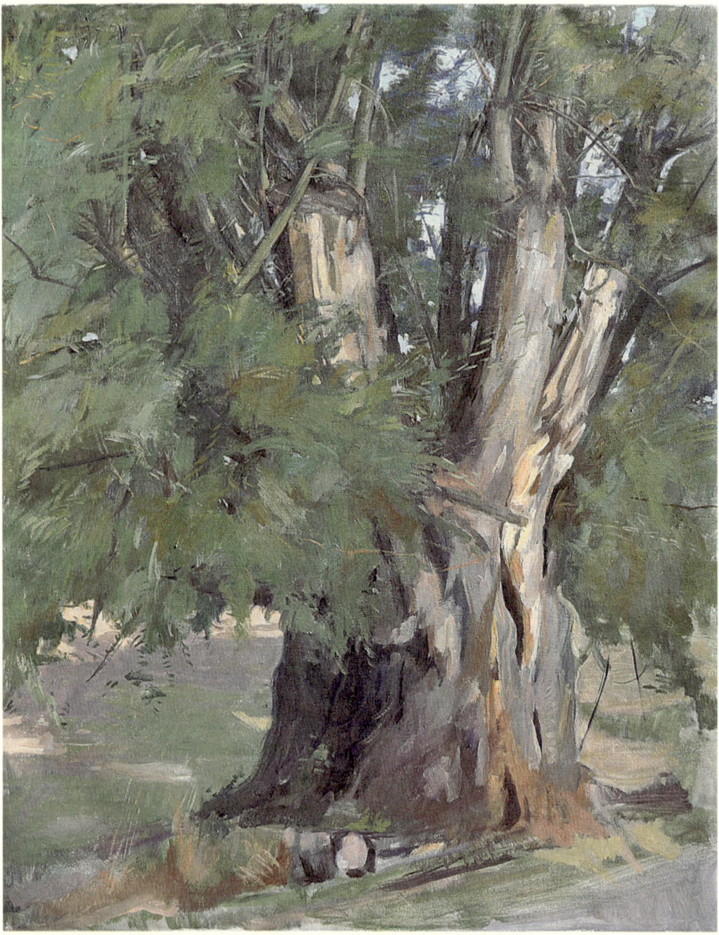

The Tree, Sam Adoquei

ENJOY IMAGES IN DETAIL download all images for free at: www.OriginofInspiration.com

Wage war against vices and dishonest thoughts, or they will bring hidden and costly damages at a time you least expect. If time makes you panic and the desire to get ahead quickly keeps dangling in front of you, remember that you are not in a rat race or a competition. The epic journey of your life is also a unique psychological reward, with several hidden benefits.

Like virtues, these cultivated habits become invisible protectors that radiate around us wherever we go. Long before and after our interaction with people, they remain on our behalf, defending our character and intentions. Without these cultivated virtues, everything in life comes with a higher price tag. Like guardian angels, our virtues remain behind the scenes, ensuring that people understand our real and noble intentions. Virtues succeed where crafted words and creative acting can't.

"Life is one big road with lots of signs, So when you riding through the ruts, don't you complicate your mind." — Bob Marley

Shields for the Dreamer's Conquest

How fun could it be to wake up at 4 or 5 a.m. on a cold, breezy morning and jump on the back of an open truck to harvest tomatoes 45 minutes away? To find enjoyment from this chilling experience, I turned the ordeal into a fun and competitive experience among the group of Moroccan, African and European students who had come to Napoli to make some extra cash. At the end of the day, the one who harvested the most boxes of tomatoes was awarded three bottles of wine. The winner earned respect and was celebrated as a hero. Losers hoped for the chance to win the next day. Camaraderie, friendly competition and the hope of winning the following day inspired me to move past the misery and pain of being a laborer despite my artistic dreams. It helped me to welcome every morning.

The "I hate my job and this is not what I am meant to do" attitude defeats dreamers who lack positive attitude and insight about all the detours humans make through life's journey. In such situations it is the positive and peaceful attitude you have cultivated that helps transform tough conditions into graceful life detours.

It would be nice to have a chauffeur who drives us comfortably wherever we want to go. If you find that the express train you are waiting for is broken or running late, wouldn't it be wise to take the local train or accept whichever transportation is available and enjoy the ride? Take the time to go through some notes on your life's plan without disturbing the peace of others. In reality, you will do many jobs that you might not like, and it is the cultivated positive attitude you have developed that will calm you down to think far ahead and go through such tasks gracefully.

Conditions, situations and places determine what to dream for. Thus, we dream because we know it is achievable. Because of this, condition, situation and place are the first ingredients the dreamer must consider. This does not mean the dreamer must limit himself with what is at hand; rather, the sky is the limit. Everything is attainable because the mind's eye sees all the unseen possibilities.

The second, but most important, factor is the dreamer himself; the sole captain of the conquest, the decision maker, the vehicle, the general and the warrior. The dreamer must have the virtues, skills and stamina to survive all circumstances, hunt, catch and keep the dream, to maintain it until it becomes reality and then use it to help others in need.

Third is the more complex, unpredictable world you have no control over. The ever-changing yet changeless, incomprehensible world that permits the existence of all opposites and favors the virtuous, the self-controlled, the courageous who follows his mission, task, duty and purposeful life. The world that does not owe human explanations as to why things are the way they are. The world that requires wisdom to understand. Because of this, the dreamer must be mindful of life's challenges and traps; he cannot drift aimlessly and play "Eeny, meeny, miny, moe" when making important life choices.

"The accurate knowledge of what has happened will be useful, because, according to human probability, similar things will happen again."
— Thucydides

The Sacred Oath

"In the long run, men hit only what they aim at. Therefore, though they should fail immediately, they had better aim at something high."
— Henry David Thoreau

Once I was at a restaurant with two friends. The waiter gave us the menu and went through the normal routine of telling us the special of the day, the combinations we could have and the special orders the chef could make. After all these unlimited choices I wasn't too sure, so I ordered the catch of the day and asked if I could have pasta with tomato sauce as a side dish instead of the mashed potatoes. My friend knew exactly what he wanted, so he ordered his yummy, greasy, rich penne alla vodka with some chunks of salmon. My friend's friend also wasn't sure, so he asked us for suggestions. I told him just to combine some recognized dishes, but he insisted we choose. After the waiter came back and forth twice, my confused philosopher asked the waiter to choose anything for him, with restrictions of things he is allergic to. In order to avoid blame, the smart waiter brought in the chef/owner of the restaurant. My friend was very happy to have the grand chef himself attending to him. After a few suggestions, my friend asked the chef to surprise him. (As the cook turned around, he said in a low tone in a slang French: "This guy is lucky I don't serve raw monkey brains.") Of course my adventurer got a dish he didn't like.

Without set goals, you will be at the mercy of everyone, from family members, friends and colleagues to strangers who will decide what they think is good for you. Whether your snails or frog legs are leftovers or your filet mignon is overcooked, you will be at the mercy of a kind chef or profit-driven chef.

To avoid false dreams, we must know ourselves well enough to choose our dreams wisely. Dreams attract people with strong convictions; bold and assertive people who can catch them, keep them, provide security and commit to them until they trust that they have found the right partner.

It is at this realization that the marriage vow is made between the dreamer and the dream—the Sacred Oath: for better, for worse, for richer, for poorer, in sickness and in health, until death do us part. After this vow, you have promised to follow your dream, and you must keep your promise. As in life, remembering the sacred oath you promised to your dream and keeping the future in perspective help you to know how much and how hard you must invest on keeping the dream alive. Unlike so many humans, after the vow you shouldn't cheat or develop interests in other dreams; in doing so, your dream, too, will start looking for a stable heart, a more secure home and loving surroundings.

The dues of being successful at something or achieving a dream are the same, but a dream is more grand and rewarding than just being successful at something. You can choose to become successful at the restaurant business after 25 years in a different business, but you can't be a successful boxer, musician or artist and, after 25 years, succeed in football. On the other hand, you can choose to be in all sorts of businesses in order to eventually pursue a political career.

Whether we are confused and cannot choose a partner, or too selfish to choose one and deal with the conditions it brings, depends on our awareness of the consequences our choices bring. In the end there are different ways you can take to reaching nirvana so long as you don't forget the golden rule of navigation: If going right, stay right, and make sure all turns lead in the right direction.

Everyone running everywhere with no one getting anywhere is the dilemma of the confused and undisciplined mind. When we try to sample everything greed entices us with, we are deprived of the special joy and wisdom of knowing one thing well. The impatient and greedy dreamer forgets his vows and chases more partners than he has energy and time to commit himself to. He forgets that a dream in search of an assertive, decisive man runs away from the unfocussed, disloyal and dishonest partner. Perseverance, commitment, trustworthiness and loyalty are the most sexy, attractive, irresistible virtues and qualities that charm the best of dreams. Cultivate these virtues and you will see the most beautiful dream of your choice following you and begging to be taken away.

Food for Thought

In some advanced, old cultures you don't have to be totally or madly in love before marrying. To these cultures, romantic love is not the only important path to a successful marriage. These cultures believe that if you focus and work hard enough on a relationship, if you do all the right things, more often than not love will follow.

You might not have the perfect dream, but the ideal dream suitable for your life's journey. Ronald Reagan took acting and later became a great president. Bill Gates went from computers to philanthropy. In modern times, modeling, acting and music have become a stepping stone for many people to do great things. Nelson Mandela went from prisoner to president. Do you know Mark Twain started out as a train driver? As an author, Steven King has sold hundreds of millions books, but do you know what he did before becoming a successful writer?

Advice from the Wiseman of my Teenage Years

Do not get trapped in the pendulum of life unless the thrill of swinging up and down excites you, my sage often advises me. To achieve your dreams, you must let reason, discipline, the will to focus and faith help you become self-reliant. (Reason means the mind analyzing and making unprejudiced choices.) By reasoning, you will find solutions for your questions, discipline yourself to obey your plans and have faith in what reason has chosen for you. Reason allows Hope the freedom to stay, and all negative thoughts fade away when Hope comes in. Hope never quits. Hope's stubborn nature and I-won't-quit attitude are why true dreamers must reason sincerely.

You must know and master yourself; you must know your strengths, your weaknesses and your needs. Always look at the patterns of the past so that you can best decide for today and predict or imagine what will work tomorrow. When our human desires and greed face temptations from other beautiful dreams, and when we turn our life's mission into a religious task. It is the strong faith we have in our chosen dream that will shield us from dreams that might seem attainable but incompatible to our life's journey.

With reason and a little intelligence you can understand nature and life, and be able to achieve anything you want. Reason breaks all impossible tasks down into understandable, doable and solvable puzzles. These are a few of the kernels of advice from the Wiseman of my teenage years. It was he who advised me to find quiet times to communicate directly with nature's messengers. "What have I done to deserve this fate? and "What should I do to better things?" and "What is the best thing to do now?" are questions you ask yourself in quiet times in hopes of being answered by a guardian angel, or by the better, double you. You asked yourself these questions because you expect your double—who you think has different knowledge, different insight and different intelligence—will have answers. You wouldn't have asked yourself such questions if you didn't think you had the answers. The Wiseman also advised me to habitually ponder what my duty and purpose in life is, and to spend some time meditating and concentrating to find answers for that question. He believes engaging one's self with such questions helps avoid junk and superficial thoughts. These are ideas that have transformed some of my mentees into national stars, some to "A" students, some to find their dreams and many to find their happy path. I hope the reader gets as much from reading this dream chapter as I got from my sage.

It is only by developing a habit of honest and constant reasoning that we arrive at the true questions that jolt us into finding the correct answers for our journey. With reason, all is possible. Without reason, we approach life in small, discriminative parts and therefore the whole picture eludes us. How did I get myself into this situation? Why me? What have I done to deserve this? These are classic questions that can only be answered by reasoning. Whether you fight to claim what you believe belongs to you, or protect what you already have; whether you fight because your back is against the wall, whether you exploit the weak or defend the weak—it is reason and discipline that will help you choose the noble and just conscious fight.

In the end, mentors, gurus, books, life lessons and experiences can help us make the right decisions, find the great ideas, implement the perfect plan and choose the right order and most effective method that leads to a new and better path—but it is our disciplined mind that helps us to religiously obey, follow and execute our well-designed plan. Who will provide continuous motivation for meeting your responsibilities and focusing on the important things? No One Else But You— the NOEBY Attitude. Who will regularly check your tank so your engine does not run out of fuel in the middle of nowhere? No one else but you. When you feel like a little dose will take you farther and higher, will you be able to avoid the temptation and say no, I will do without the influence? Who will make you the obedient servant of your dream's plan? No one else but you. When your ego, pride and honor are cornered and your courage and ambition are being harassed, who will remind you to stay calm and focus on the bigger picture? Patience of mind, endurance of will, calmness and serenity are habits and attitudes only the NOEBY Attitude can cultivate.

Our dreams do not elude us because they are too big, or too hard to achieve, but because we spend our short life sampling all the dreams thrown at us to entice us. The I-can-do-everything, Superman mentality and I-can-have-it-all attitude overwhelms our untrained willpower, forcing us to believe we must have everything. To have free will, nature provides us with abundance, but it is left to us to be cautious of how the selfish and the greedy suffer disappointment, exhaustion and failure from the confusion of having too many choices.

Only a few people with strong willpower are able to obey their orders and focus on the certain task that leads to the chosen goal.

Are you focusing on developing your willpower so that it can focus on only the important choices nature throws at you? To have a strong mind that avoids all temptations, are you training yourself to smile when greed approaches with offers so convincing only a few can resist?

A self-disciplined mind, faith and conviction differentiate the successful dreamer from the wishful thinker. Self-discipline is a sacred gift of mental power; it is the armor against vices in disguise. Faith is derived from the reasoned assurance that there is no other way but the chosen path. Only by discipline can your tactics be strategically applied for the desired results. How is your spiritual strength? How strong is your faith in the gods that protect you spiritually? How respectful are you of your spiritual beliefs that you are willing not to impose your human understandings of spiritual laws onto others? You should be willing to make your gods proud of you by asking them to guide, protect and help you achieve your dream so that you can be of help to society, the universe and the advancement of humanity.

Blessed are those who show their faith through their contribution to advancement and love of humanity and evolution of the universe, for they shall find enduring inspiration to help them achieve eternal happiness, and their name will be praised forever.

Stop for a moment and imagine in your mind's eye the reward so real and waiting for you to grab it. What should be the first thing you do to begin your life's conquest to receive the reward? This was the question thrown at me by my old Wiseman. I hope the reader will pause for a moment and ponder the question: What are you doing, or what are you going to do, to make your dream reality? Even though nothing in life is certain, this awareness alone helps put a dreamer's journey in perspective.

Because our life's journey consists of adventures, dangers and trials, you must first transform yourself into an unconquerable being. You must develop fortitude, self-control and moral courage in order to transform yourself into a self-contained entity fit to endure all of life's earthly challenges. First, have knowledge of self (strengths, weaknesses and needs); second, have knowledge of nature (people skills), wisdom and awareness to understand the game of life and foresight to maintain enduring inspiration. Because you will spend most of your life among humans, will you attempt to acquire people skills? Third, develop the habit to maintain continued growth.

The Dreamer's Conquest

Life's complexities, challenges and crises demand that the dreamer's mindset should be like that of a general, because in real life over-excitement, passionate ideas, wishful thinking and superstition can replace reality. Great generals cultivate survival skills and enduring will. Like computers, calmness and serenity of mind are instincts they activate to handle and neutralize unexpected, inharmonious and incompatible forces. Because of these instincts, successful generals have the ability to shield themselves from all sorts of obstacles. They know the warrior who must survive, will survive. With a forward ever, backward never "never say die" attitude, they adopt and adapt easily.

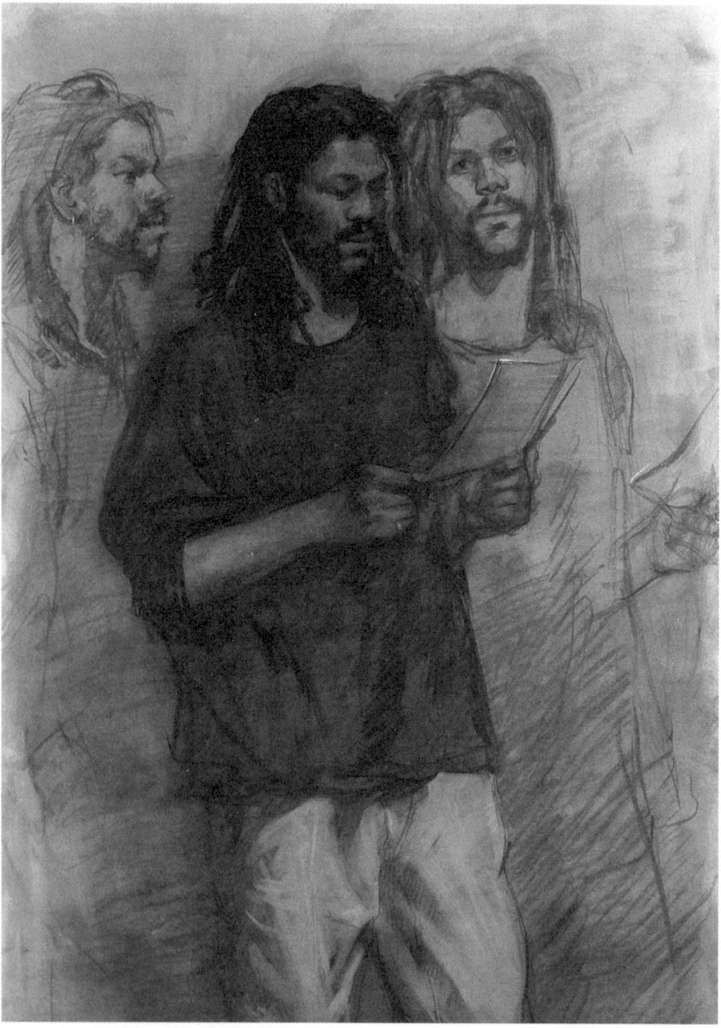

An Actor Rehearsing, Sam Adoquei

Some important traits generals have in common are: 1) they research when they take on assignments, 2) they pay attention to planning and execution, 3) they have a strategic approach to all missions and 4) they make and seize opportunities. Ethics, courage, confident discipline and enthusiasm are also common habits among generals.

My mentor advises: Human beings, when pushed and cornered against an obstacle with no way out, will learn new skills to survive. Whatever you do, if it is what you love, if it is what you want and if it is what is important to you, then you must be able to find time to invest four to seven hours a day, three to four days a week and three to five years to gather all-important tools of that field to help you succeed.

The pursuit of a dream is very simple: Keep your eyes on the goal at all cost. Have a plan you can change or improve on. Make sure all decisions eventually lead to achieving your dream. Cultivate virtues that bring good karma. Master the art of self-development and self-control. In the aftermath of all dangerous tornados, earthquakes and accidents, you cry a little, comb your hair, button up your shirt, put on some shoes and shift yourself into a new gear. Conceal the pain, put on a smile and start your new life with new determination, always maintaining the forward ever backward never attitude.

Journey from Denmark

In a recent visit to Denmark I went on a bird-watching trip on an island called Mon, where certain birds flock at the end of each summer. For days, at a certain time, the birds flew back and forth, diving and swinging around like orchestrated ballet dancers. The perfect rhythmic movements despite their multitudes were the most beautiful, coordinated wonder of nature.

I asked one of the natives why these birds migrate here. They come to eat the special, big mosquitoes from this place, and it is also the training ground for migrating birds. They come purposely to eat the mosquitoes and to grow fat, then train daily before their epic journey to Africa. So they are not dancing, swinging and flying around enjoying their lives? I asked. Not at all; this is not dancing, it is heavy-duty, disciplined training, and among the flocks are leaders, watch guides and trainers performing their duty. I opened my mouth to ask how they know when and how to train, how fat they should grow, the distance of the journey ahead and when to start the trip to beat the wicked Nordic weather. What instinct, force or intelligent or invisible guide helps these birds to know all the right things to do, and then repeat the same drilling process year after year? Just before I asked the question, I remembered an African proverb: "God wipes out the fleas on animals without tails." In this kingdom of the birds, anyone that dares not to train will not survive the coming winter, and those without the will and courage do not dare the trip. I couldn't help but imagine how by instinct, experience and wisdom, everyone in the flock plays their part for the success of all.

Who will be left behind, and who will make it back next season? The fate of those too old or too young and other invisible realities of nature, those whose fate will be left in the hands of predators and the hunters in Africa awaiting the arrival of the flock and praying for a great hunting season, are left to nature to determine. Birth, death and unavoidable realities are left to nature to decide. For now and now only, the most important thing for the birds is to focus on the task at hand: eating big mosquitoes and growing fat, staying disciplined to follow the drilling routine in hopes of avoiding exhaustion, starvation, errors in navigation and the wicked, icy Scandinavian winter.

Like all great achievements, the dreamer must have one goal and only one goal in mind and all efforts will be channeled toward attaining that dream. Through different paths, different applications and different tactics, all energy is directed and aimed at achieving the goal.

Humans face the same fate, but sometimes by forgetting what is important in their pursuit, they choose an inharmonious direction; they avoid responsibilities toward life and nature. In return, the societies and groups we invent suffer the fate and consequences of going against the natural laws of our advancing world: Together we stand, divided we fall.

We don't have a bird's instinct, but with a purposeful dream we gain the inspiration and endurance to achieve our life's mission successfully. We are guided by both instincts and wisdom learned from history, traditions and life. For this reason, the importance of taking advantage of our intelligence, knowledge, experiences,

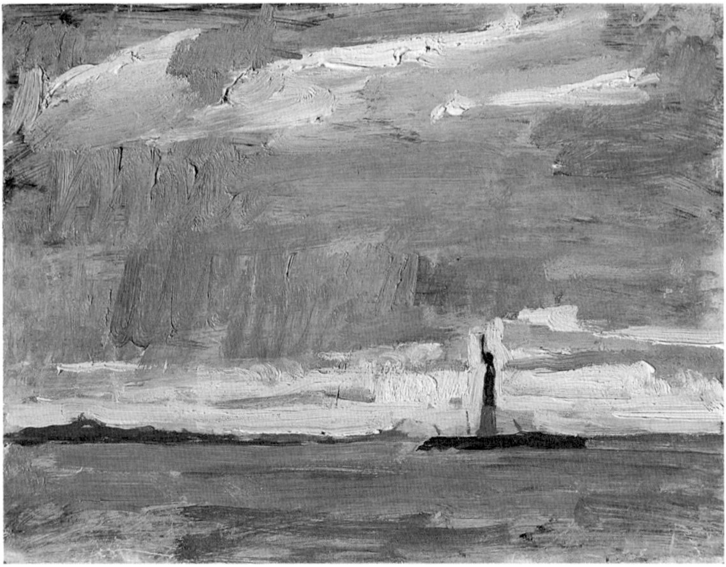

Statue of Liberty, oil on panel, Sam Adoquei

ENJOY IMAGES IN DETAIL download all images for free at: www.OriginofInspiration.com

history, traditions and nature are what the dreamer must concentrate on.

A dreamer's life is like an epic story from ancient times, one adventure after another, from birth to death. But for us, everything is real, there is no supernatural intervention. Fights, battles and wars are trials we must experience in order to mature and complete our chosen mission. Before a dreamer takes on his mission, he must be mindful of the task ahead. Unlike in Greek mythology, where the hero is punished severely for mistakes, in real life we have chances, choices and the opportunity to try until we get things right.

Like the birds we, too, have such a strong instinct to pursue our goals and gain our reward that the failures and trials we encounter are nothing compared to living a life without a dream. To help us achieve our dreams we have been given a coconut designed to make, gather, contain, preserve and produce the juice needed to help us find solutions to life's problems. We have everything we need to lead us to a successful ending. Thus the dreamer's first task is to seek knowledge, experience and wisdom for guidance before taking on the conquest.

These writings contain the knowledge and wisdom from my meetings with the Sage of my teenage years, the man who made sure I understand that we are all mortal creatures and that our time on earth is short, and we must do our best to be useful to all. He taught me to be hungry for wisdom, to never be fanatic in my beliefs, but rather to approach all things in life with a philosophical outlook. He taught me to use philosophy as a way of reasoning to find answers to life's questions and to live as rational creatures, rather than using philosophy as an accumulation or body of knowledge to be used in arguments or be worn as ornaments or badges of learning.

Stories and questions in this essay are designed to trigger ideas to make you, the dreamer, develop a habit of constant pondering. Is there more to life than just living? What is one task I must tackle now to prepare me for life? What am I destined to do? Do my daily actions lead to a fulfilled journey?

My Wiseman made me understand that, to succeed, dreamers must know the advancing world rests on five pillars: science, philosophy, politics, religion and commerce—all of which contribute their equal share to help our advancing world evolve. Extreme beliefs, extreme adherence to creeds, anything extreme is incompatible to the supreme law of our advancing and evolving universe. All opposites are created to help us engage and explore in order to find the beauty and enjoyment our bountiful universe offers.

This essay is not advocating intense and over-zealous cautiousness; fear of failing can kill great ideas. You can almost always analyze everything to death, and at the end kill great ideas.

"Everyone has a plan, until they get punched in the face." — Mike Tyson

The aim here is to help dreamers be mindful of their journey, and to be aware that any sort of homework is an advantage. In short, the hero takes on a purposeful mission; he plans and prepares, then takes on the conquest. If well prepared, his success comes with wisdom gained from the journey; then he uses the reward to help our evolving and advancing universe.

Great achievers have certain pragmatic habits: They are mindful of life's journey, they have disciplined minds, they ponder ideas and reason through tough situations, they acquire cultivated virtues. If these habits are taken into consideration, the dreamer will avoid most of the hidden costs in our harsh human life. The price of not pursuing a dream is as costly as the price of pursuing a dream, so it is in the interest of the dreamer to choose well.

Some dreamers have big dreams, stamina, energy, zeal, willpower and a big heart. With extreme enthusiasm and excitement they jump into pursuits and hope for the best. As a mentor, a teacher and an artist, I have seen too many hearts broken unnecessarily due to a weak approach to pursuing a dream. It would be hypocritical and uncivil not to share my teacher's wisdom. It is this moral duty that inspired this essay.

Nature's Messenger

When you achieve your dream, remember: You have been metamorphosed into a selfless messenger, a member of messengers of immortality. Your real mission to help our evolving world has just begun. You have become the provider of abundance, the messenger with moral obligation to bring good news. To safeguard your dream from vices incompatible with your noble deeds, you must sincerely link your purpose to great causes. It is the great and sincere things you do with your achievements that matter to the saints of posterity. Your selfless acts of charity are what immortality rewards and preserves.

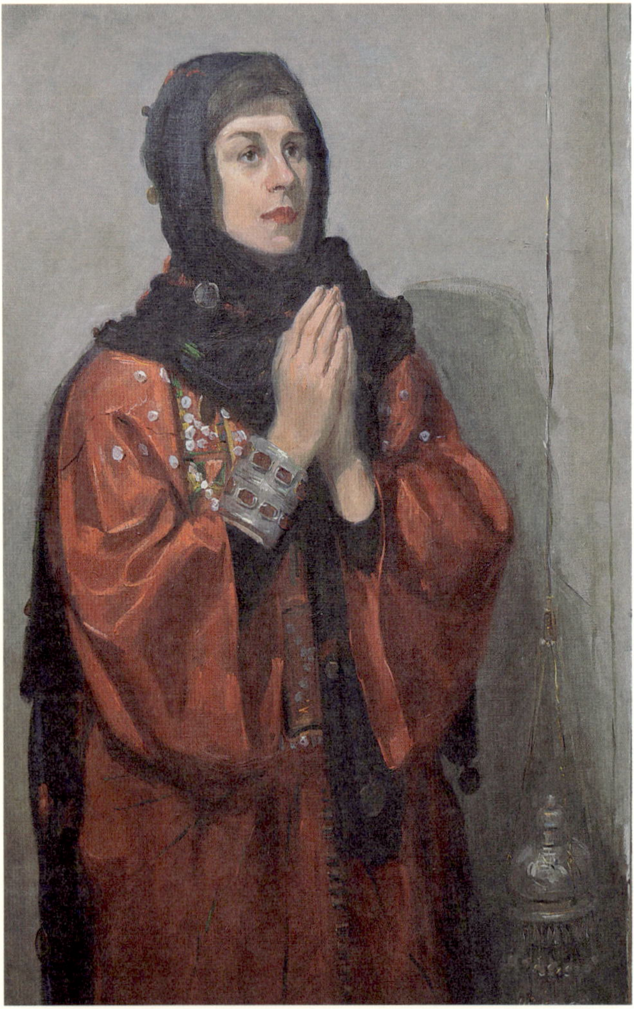

Prayers, Sam Adoquei

MEDITATION WITH GOD'S MESSENGERS

Sometimes when I'm in solitude and can't consult my books, I try to imagine how my first mentor would have helped me reason through problems. It was during one of these moments of consolation that the following conversation occurred with him. He is no longer with us.

During one of my meditational and contemplative moments, my mentor, Mr. Adjeman, appeared in my imagination.

"How are you doing, Mr. Adjeman?" I asked.

And he responded:

> I have come to you because you came to look for me when you were visiting home. I am sorry to have left without any notice. There are so many people I would have liked to say farewell to, to have the opportunity to mend some bridges, to thank some great people, but the calling came unannounced. My maker believed my mission with humans was finished and he sent for me to return home. I pleaded to stay a bit longer in order to enjoy some things I acquired on earth, but no, the time has come to move on. Nothing is important anymore and I must return; my mission, my task, my purpose are accomplished. It has been 17 years since I left and this is the first time I have the freedom to visit old friends and share my insights between immortal and mortal.
>
> I didn't answer your calls because I know your inquisitive

mind, your curiosity, your constant consultation of books and your imagination will lead you to find solutions for life's questions. Everything you need is hidden in pages and in nature. With reason and discipline, keep questioning life the way you used to in class, and all will be well. I lived in the underworld en route to my eternal destination. My persuasion to live in the same town where my heroes live was accepted, so I live near several great people. Here everyone who makes it to this point is the same. I saw Plato, Euripides and so many others who are always questioning and looking for answers to mankind's problems. I ran into Leonardo the other day, and Michelangelo, Frans Halls and all the artists I asked you to study and read about. They live a few miles away. Jimi Hendrix, Ali Farka Toure and Mozart also live nearby. This weekend I will visit Peaceville, where Gandhi and Luther live. I can't wait to see how they are in person. Visiting their neighborhood brings me lots of joy. I like visiting them every now and then because their surroundings inspire and teach me how I can be a better mentor. It is not so clear to me yet because I am new here, but I think I will be sent back in a different image for a different task in a different place. So far I am enjoying the great minds and their ideas.

In our last conversation you asked questions about everything. As you know, I was a teacher whose mission was to prepare the young for the future, and your metaphysical questions had gotten a bit too complex for me, so let me give you to my neighbor. She is a nice person whose job was to help people find answers so they could help themselves. Her name is Ajena, and we call her the Queen Mother of Reasoning. She believes all problems can be solved by logic and reason. I will hand over the phone so you can talk directly to her.

The Queen Mother of Reasoning began to speak:

Hi Sam. I have visited you several times; How is your mission going? I saw that you bought some books on ancient Rome and ancient Greece. I wish you had bought T.E. Lawrence's *Seven Pillars of Wisdom*.

"How do you know what I bought?" I asked.

I am the Queen Mother of Reason. Don't forget, all practical, pragmatic and logical people have to come to me. Lincoln came here several times. Socrates spends his time conversing with us. We were watching you and wondering how best you could understand today's life, and we decided reading about the past will help you to understand what is going on today.

At first we wanted to let you go through some life experiences, but we decided you have seen enough and that books will be easy for you. Don't forget to read Seneca and Cicero.

Do you remember, before you wrote your books, about five years ago you spent the whole summer at the Dordogne in France just reasoning back and forth? It was I who engaged you and asked all the necessary questions. You are a very curious man, always searching for more effective ways to help those who come to you for answers.

I am pressed for time, but let me tell you a short story before I leave. I will continue to visit with you whenever necessary. Yesterday, while on my way to engage in conversation with some people arguing over religious issues in a small land in the Middle East, I stopped by a place where I have been invited to reason with the attendees. There were about 1,500 people and they were all looking for magic elixirs to instantly cure their life problems.

They were there because some of the messengers I sent to help have turned everything into business, and they charge tremendous fees and use crafted words and acting skills to communicate. They make the message so complicated and so spiritual. I hope, when dealing with those in need, you maintain your honesty, sincerity and respect, and don't take advantage of those facing misfortune.

What surprised me was that everyone in the audience had personal requirements. No one accepted that everything is designed for the greater good—for themselves and for the universe—or that everything in life makes sense with time. Everyone wanted magic provided according to their checklists. They expected their dreams to be fulfilled how and when they wanted. I was shocked and decided to leave and head toward my real assignment. It was only when someone accused my master of a trumped-up charge that I decided to set the record straight before leaving.

Someone asked, "Why were evildoers created? Why did nature create all that is bad?" Without reason, everything is bad under the circumstances we choose to judge nature on. But with time, nature has proven that everything happens for our own good and for the greater good of the universe. When picking and choosing from nature's actions, some things seem right and some seem wrong. But to nature, all things are necessary, good and beautiful, and must happen for the universe to go on. It is incomprehensible for humans to explain the magical dynamics of nature, the existence of the opposite and the suffering of the innocent. And it is unfair to judge harshly or blame what you don't comprehend without reasoning or without asking for wisdom to understand.

I think it is selfish of men to judge nature in parts, in circumstances and in moments, while forgetting how everything is in harmony for the advancement of the universe.

Just imagine, the universe has been around for billions of years before human arrival, and it will continue billions of years after you depart. The length and depth of it is incomprehensible to humans with their short lives. You were not there in the beginning when plans of the universe were made so that the world continues to evolve and advance, yet you are quick to criticize the maker.

"Have you ever wondered why there is snow and extreme cold while others have the most severe dry temperatures man can endure?" I asked.

Do you know how many begged and prayed around the clock for wealth and power, then became destructive because they asked for what they want, not what they need, without paying attention to the divine intention and natural order of things. They forget that everything is in accordance to harmony of the universe.

Those who blame nature whenever there are natural disasters never live to see how necessary those disasters were to future lives, and how those disasters make room for lives yet to come.

“Let’s reason for a moment,” I answered. “What is bad?” I asked.

War, diseases, bad people. Have you bothered to learn or understand why things are the way they are? Have you bothered to ask for wisdom to understand? Do you know that if you judge life by the hours you get different results than if you judge it by days? If you judge it by months you get different results than if you judge life by years and decades? It was better 50 years ago than it was 100 years ago, and better 25 years ago than 50 years ago. It is better today than it was 25 years ago, and it is going to be better tomorrow than it is today. Do you think humans learn because of the terrible earthquakes, accidents, life experiences and disasters? After disappointments and cries they go straight back to their normal ways. They walk around behaving like supermen, never, ever asking for wisdom to understand and comprehend the wonders of nature.

“Humans entangle themselves too much in the small picture and miss the bigger frame that holds the image together,” I answered. “It is all for the greater good. Whenever you are in doubt, please ponder the idea that ever since creation, Time, the father and soothsayer of all things, has never been wrong with his continuous predictions that everything has been for the greater good for man, his universe and his future. Natural laws and man made laws might put some lives at a disadvantage straight from start, but at the end it is all for the greater good and all will balance itself," I added.

Nature has no reason to be impartial. To nature, everyone gains at the end. It might not be the same time, the same place or the same circumstances, but all will gain. The universe is organized to evolve and advance as a whole, not to serve an individual's personal needs. It is funny how humans can easily question the Maker's actions and results. Yes, I know, sometimes evildoers prosper while the good-natured human suffers, but it is the lack of human knowledge and understanding that make me wonder if humans think nature inflicts pain, then enjoys watching them suffer.

You know what you want, but do you know what you need? I asked you these questions because many people come to ask me for things. Many ask for one thing when in reality they want something else. They throw away what I sent them, not realizing that *the gods don't send what we want, when we want, according to our checklist.* I don't keep gift-wrap, labels and boxes around me in order to beautifully wrap your gift, box it, label it and send a prior message for you to expect your package. So many have thrown away their dreams and sometimes never claim their fortunes because they were too busy watching others open up their packages or chasing dreams that belong to others. So many souls in crossroads come to me in search of the way, of freedom, of understanding and inner peace, and when I show them the safest ways to captain their own ship to salvation, they almost always end up surrendering their souls to others who promise them a magic pill. Magical wonders of life are felt, not seen.

Once I took some time to reason with a 48-year-old friend who kept asking me for the opportunity to make 250G. I asked him what he wanted to do with 250G, and he said he wanted a house. I thought it was a considerable and important request. For fun I asked him why a house, and he said at his age he needed the security of a home. Again, I thought it was a mature and appropriate request, so I felt proud not having to deal with all those who waste my time for the sake of acquisition and power. As I have grown to like this individual, I asked him why he wanted the security of a home. He said that whenever he is at a gathering or with friends he feels incompetent because society judges people based on their homes, fancy cars and wealth.

Since I am the one to bring the dream, I decided to ask more questions to ensure I would get his request right. I asked, "So you want 250G because you want a home, and you want a home because you want security, because security provides you with accomplishment and confidence? Accomplishment provides self-esteem when you are with others. Why is self-esteem so important to you?" He answered that self-esteem clears all his troubles and gives him a peaceful and tranquil mind, and that he is more productive and happy when he has peace and tranquility. If that is the case, and all you need is peace and tranquility, why didn't you ask straight away for peace and tranquility? It would have been easier and less hassle. He didn't think it could be achieved without the material attachments.

Almost always I find people are not the best judges of what is good for them. You need to look to history to search for the hows and whys of life. You need advice, discipline and education to be the best judge for yourself. To choose well and decide properly, you must know yourself. I looked into the crowd, randomly pointed to a few of them and said it baffles me how some humans spend time reading so much that is irrelevant to their life. They ignore all the troubles the wise men of antiquity went through in order to leave us that rich legacy. Have you read carefully the writings and ideas of Russian literature? Have you read carefully the writings and ideas of Benjamin Franklin? Do you know that the stores that sell the books you buy are the same stores that sell books with the writings and ideas of my children, prophets and messengers?

Wisdom of the Ages

Sages, Messengers and Divine Teachers

In the book of the Mahabharata verses, in the Bhagavad-Gita poem that I inspired a poet in ancient India to write, I gave wisdom and answers to anyone confronted with difficulties in making life's tough decisions. In the Book of Job you have all you need to cope when misfortunes and constant hardship ruffle you. In the Book of Job I gave solutions to how to maintain a clear mental strength when you know you have done everything right but all is being taken away from you; I gave the willpower to stay strong and undefeated without losing faith. People ignore all the wisdom and secrets hidden in these books because my lessons are not sensational enough and are not offered according to your standard. The only mind that human beings have for helping themselves make their short life's journey a successful, adventurous experience is the only mind they don't spend enough time improving upon. I sent my prophets, Isaiah and Jeremiah and others, to help humanity, but people would rather read junk news than pay attention to their own development.

Humans spend their leisure time reading shallow, vain things, then blame me for not preparing them for the life I have created for them. They throw away the love and wisdom of antiquity and, instead of desire for wisdom, they occupy their coconut with undrinkable juice. I wish they would let their thoughts be consumed by finding answers to that which brings them happiness. I gave human the choice of open mindedness so that by the help of Reason they can spot wisdom hidden in unfamiliar places, but they block out, shut off and deny the entrance of that which they judge through the screens of their rigid beliefs. With humans' quick persecution of my creations unfamiliar to them they make me look and seem like a mean, bloodthirsty creator; on my behalf they do all sort of cruelties against themselves.

I have given humans every necessary reason to believe that loving thyself, loving thy neighbor, tolerance, loving all my creations and the quest for unity are the roads that will lead them to enjoying the glories of the world and achieving peace, harmony and salvation. By the process of birth, life and death, I made them aware that all are mortals participating in this grand theatrical universe, that your time will come and you too shall move on. Your immortality depends on how all benefits from your performance.

Everything around you is the proof of my existence and that the natural order of the cosmos exists for the greater good of mankind. Birth, life and death (how things come into life, how they live and how they depart); the ocean, the stars, the rainbow, the seasons, and you humans with all the things you see as faults and complain about, all these are the testimonies of my existence. The silly tricks and gimmicks you call magic and believe, trust, and sometimes worship because of their instant gratification come and go but nature's constant evolution and all my creations live on.

I embedded so much inspiration, enlightenment, encouragement, joy and happiness into life experience. I cannot come to everyone with every cry or call; I do not perform magic for people to whom I have given the free will and power to choose their happiness and destiny. That's why I created talents to record the wisdom of all ages to assist humans. Wisdom seekers of the past have left all that humans need. I have informed many that serenity, calmness of mind and happiness come from within, yet humans look outside for happiness.

A man is a blueprint or a prototype of his past until he writes or designs a new one. Which heroes are you using as archetypes for your life's journey? Which template are you following? Which dreamer's blueprint do you have hanging on the walls of your minds eyes rest on? What are the last five books you have invested in? Who is your mentor and what is the last conversation you have had with him or her? I hope the reader revisits these questions every now and then, because whichever behavior and habits you are encouraging is what will form your tomorrow.

The seeds to help you become greater than yourself are hidden and awaiting those who are searching. There is no human or earthly problem that I have no answers for, and there is nothing humans can't achieve with discipline, will and power. You can get anything you want: happiness, wealth, love, health and power. By just focusing and doing a little research, you can achieve anything in life, but humans disapprove of the ways I package wisdom and knowledge and treasures. Humans never take advantage of the talents I created and inspired to put the answers in writing. They fall for temptation, greed, glory and instant gratification.

For your life's journey, I have sent to you all the help and secrets you need through the writings of the wise men and sages of the ages. From time immemorial, many of my children, messengers, prophets and saints have left a pool of wisdom: Confucius, Jesus, Mohammed, Buddha, Moses and many, many more came to show you the way. I created talented teachers like Socrates, Confucius and Plato. For accessibility I have among you parents, teachers, friends and elders you can have as mentors, I inspired businessmen to make all that you need available but of course they don't fit into the profile you expect. They come from all walks of life. Wisdom and knowledge are around you in abundance, in common places and within reach, but you must adjust your antennas, clean your lenses and ears and improve your smelling sense in order to notice them.

Parable of the Lost Keys

Many people misplace their keys in their house and lock themselves inside. Lacking calmness and serenity, their emotions take over and in panic, frustration and confusion they exhaust their mind, then call for outside help. They never realize the key to freedom is within reach.

For hope, courage and guidance, for inner strength, vision and fortitude to guide your earthly life, for humility and spiritual discipline to accept the mysteries of that which you don't understand, I have sent you the best of my messengers. My children and messengers have come from all corners of the world. Consult them all at your leisure. In meditation, concentration and in solitude, reason with them all, talk to them, question them to help you understand the way. Ponder their message and ask them for wisdom, knowledge and guidance so that with your free will, power and vision, your wishes and purpose can be accomplished easily. I hope with the wisdom you gain in dialogue with my messengers, prophets and children that you will understand nature so that you will be courageous, just and fair in your dealings with others. This is the best I can do for humans in possession of their free will.

Because of conditions and situations I provided different ways, approaches and methods to cultivate virtues. Through learning, concentration, rituals and meditations human can cultivate the virtues they need

I have rewarded immortality, greatness and salvation to all those who listened and followed the examples and advice of wise men.

I give inner peace; strength, self-reliance and happiness and to the magnanimous whose purposeful life improved the world. So far I have been constant by keeping my promises; I have always rewarded the deserving with eternal glory.

Sacred Order of Nature

You must understand, the natural order of the universe is formless, inexplicable and incomprehensible to humans, yet it is part of the equation that ensures life is balanced, harmonious and advancing. Because of this truth, humans must not leave out the role nature plays in the evolution of life. Nature's unpredictability is predictable and constant: the sacred, the divine and the mundane. The unseen laws of nature are as important as the laws that govern our physical universe. What is concealed and what is revealed work perpetually in our favor. For these and many more daily miracles we must believe that our decisions and actions are not the only force that governs and determines our lives and future; nature should always be an important equation to the choices, actions and decisions we make. Believe this simple truth and all in life will make sense. Believe this as a natural law and serenity, calmness, peace and happiness will come to you.

For this reason Samuel, I think you have been too harsh and brutal on Niccolo Machiavelli, 1469-1527 in your previous pages. It was nature that gave him the inspiration to write his book *The Prince*. He was doing his duty, and playing his role in life. Telling it like it is—the true nature of power-hungry leaders. The wicked always find means and reasons to justify their deeds. He needed to share his insight to help his leaders help secure his country. It is the disguised, mean minded and cruel individual who you must blame. Machiavelli wrote several different books, and he believed that was the only way he could contribute to his nation, and it is the individual who has taken Machiavelli's ideas in pieces, the individual who already has a cruel mind and cruel intentions and uses Machiavelli's insights to execute bad deeds. It could be *The Prince* was written so that humans can spot cruel, ruthless leaders who will do anything to gain power. The fact that those who take advantage of his insights end up being hated, despised and lonely is enough warning to the insecure individual who will break all moral codes to acquire power. From the wise men of antiquity to modern times, nature has produced leadership and political messengers so anyone who wants to be good and has good intentions to lead successfully can find the right ways to lead effectively. Leadership legacies of Confucius, Abraham Lincoln, Tao's principles await the good, virtuous leader to investigate.

You know, Sam, I have been assigned to many missions on earth. When I was assigned to painting like you are doing now, I encountered a story I would like to share with you.

The Story

One day I was painting in Central Park and was intensely involved in my work when a guy about 25 years old came over and stood closer than normal. He was a bit rude and not concerned about me, and he was looking very deeply at the painting. At that moment I didn't have my normal guts to ask him to back off. After a minute

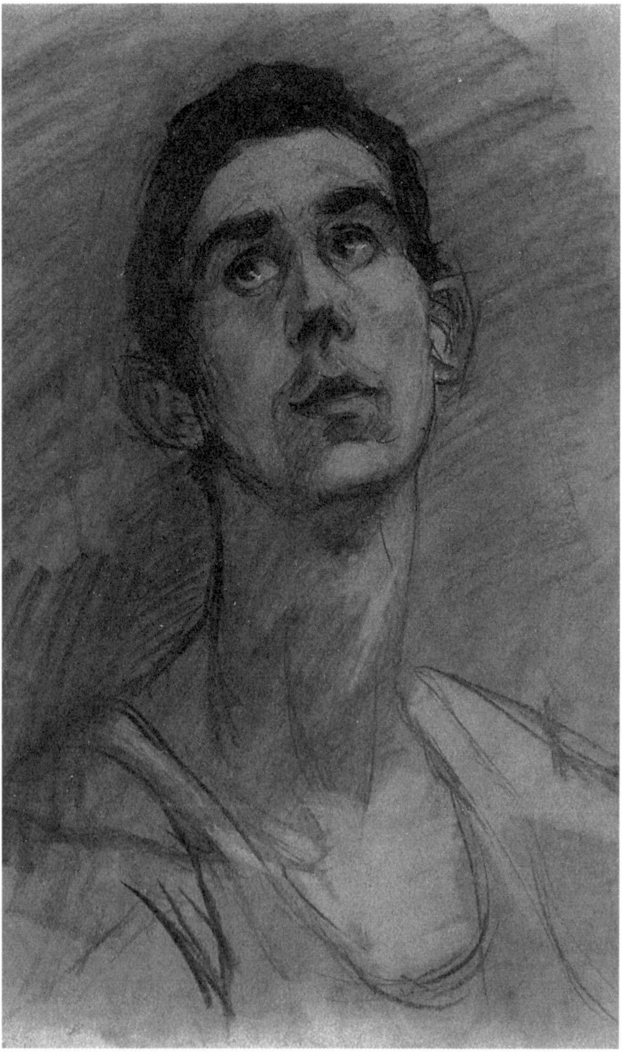

Untitled, Sam Adoquei

or so he exclaimed, "Wow, your colors are beautiful!" then he went on using the most amazing words to describe in detail how beautiful the colors were. All my defenses, agitation and anger went away, then he asked the most detailed, innocent and sincere questions about the colors on the canvas: What colors did I mix, why did I mix, what am I seeing, how do I know that the colors will work, can you please show me the colors you used?

During the encounter a girl was standing near him but it did not dawn on me that they were together until the girl said, "Let's go, Tom." He thanked me, hugged me and expressed the most sincere, genuine and honest appreciation I have ever received from an art enthusiast. He left with the girl, holding her hand. As they got about 10-15 feet away, the girl returned and apologized for the interruption. "I apologize, Mister," she said. "Tom's excitement was rude. Please forgive him." I said it was no problem at all.

She went on to tell me, "About three months ago doctors found out that Tom will gradually lose his eyesight and there is nothing to do. He is experiencing a gradual loss, and it has worsened since last month. Since he realized he has a couple of months to go, he feeds on pictorial images and digests the world around him with such an appreciation. His appetite for visual pleasure is admirable. The pleasure of looking and the joy of living by watching and observing occupy our time; I am taking him to see one of the best clowns in the city. Please forgive him."

– Sam Adoquei-26th August 2012

Readers interested in how to find a mentor might want to read an essay on mentors in my book for artists, *How Successful Artists Study*.

All work without play makes Jack a dull boy

Even though we are always warned to eat healthy food in order to live well, it is not a bad idea every now and then to enjoy a wonderful spicy, salty meal; this is the yin and yang of life. If it seems in these essays as if creative people should live a strictly disciplined life of nothing but purposeful quest, then the reader has missed the point. Void and action, seriousness yet having fun, are all part of nature's balancing plan for the human who wants to have meaning in his life and achieve fulfillment. There is time to explore, time to learn, time to play and have fun, time to experiment and time to create as all artists do.

All these pursuits are equally important if balanced. These essays are ideas to help and guide the reader so that he will be well equipped and ready should he want to dream of achieving his vision.

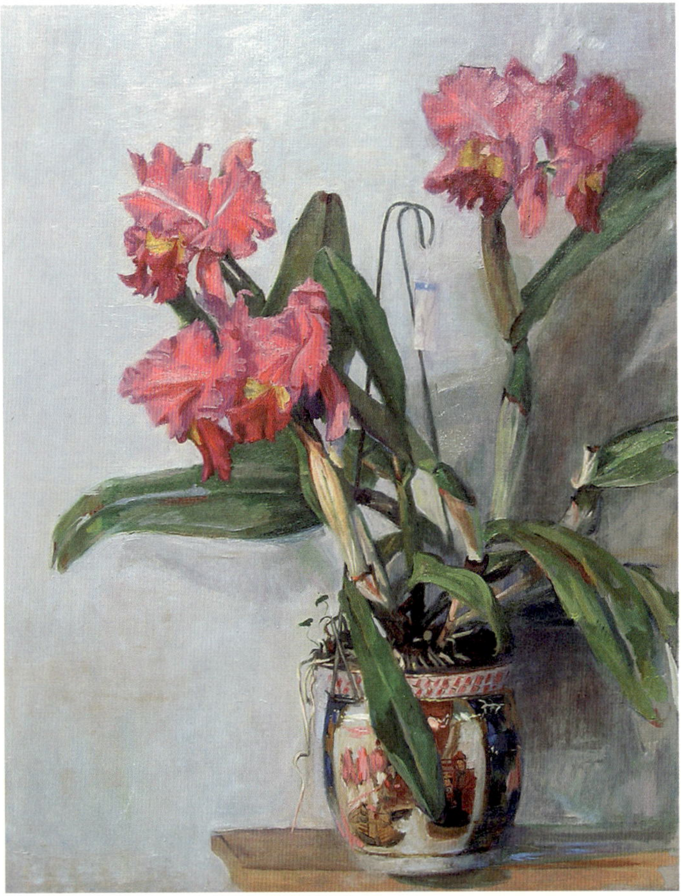

A Gift, Sam Adoquei

ENJOY IMAGES IN DETAIL download all images for free at: www.OriginofInspiration.com

How Successful Artists Study

WRITTEN BY SAMUEL ADOQUEI

#1 Bestseller
STRAND BOOKS

★★★★★ FIVE STARS
ART TIMES May/ June 2010 ART TIMES

2012 Best Book for Art Students
STRAND BOOKS

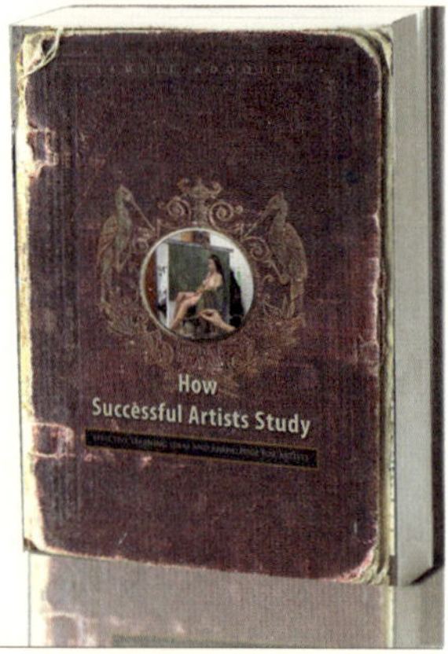

The pursuit of art is hard, tough sometimes, discouraging.
Yet there are a handful of artists among us who—without even trying very hard—succeed and enjoy fame against all obstacles.

What is it that pushes few artists to fame and success while many just tag along and struggle?

If you ever wish to help an artist friend grow his/her talent, if you ever wish artistic success to a friend. If you ever wish your friend continued growth. If you want to help your friend attract galleries of his choice. This is it, the ideal gift to help transform your friend's talent into a rewarding passion.

How Successful Artists Study is brainstorming with a mentor, it is written to help prevent risky hurdles and show you the directions you must take if you desire to follow the footsteps of the few elite successful artists. Any page in the book provides the decisions, choices, strategies, and the help to turn your talent and passion into a rewarding journey.

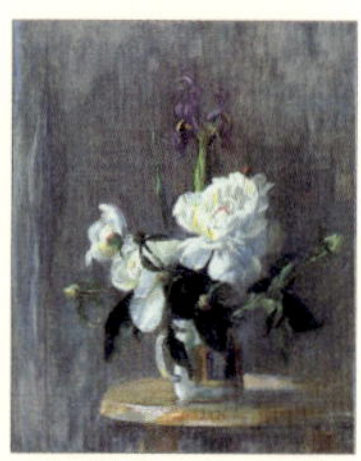

How Successful Artists Study is a mentor and a guide combined in one book. It is packed with information you can't get from art books, magazines, workshops or art schools. It is a comprehensive guide written to help talents at crossroads change their current reality.

Read the book's description at:
www.HowSuccessfulArtistsStudy.com

or visit **www.Amazon.com** to take advantage of the Special Promotional Price of $29.50 A great gift for a loved one.

THE EXPLORER RACE AND J[illegible]US

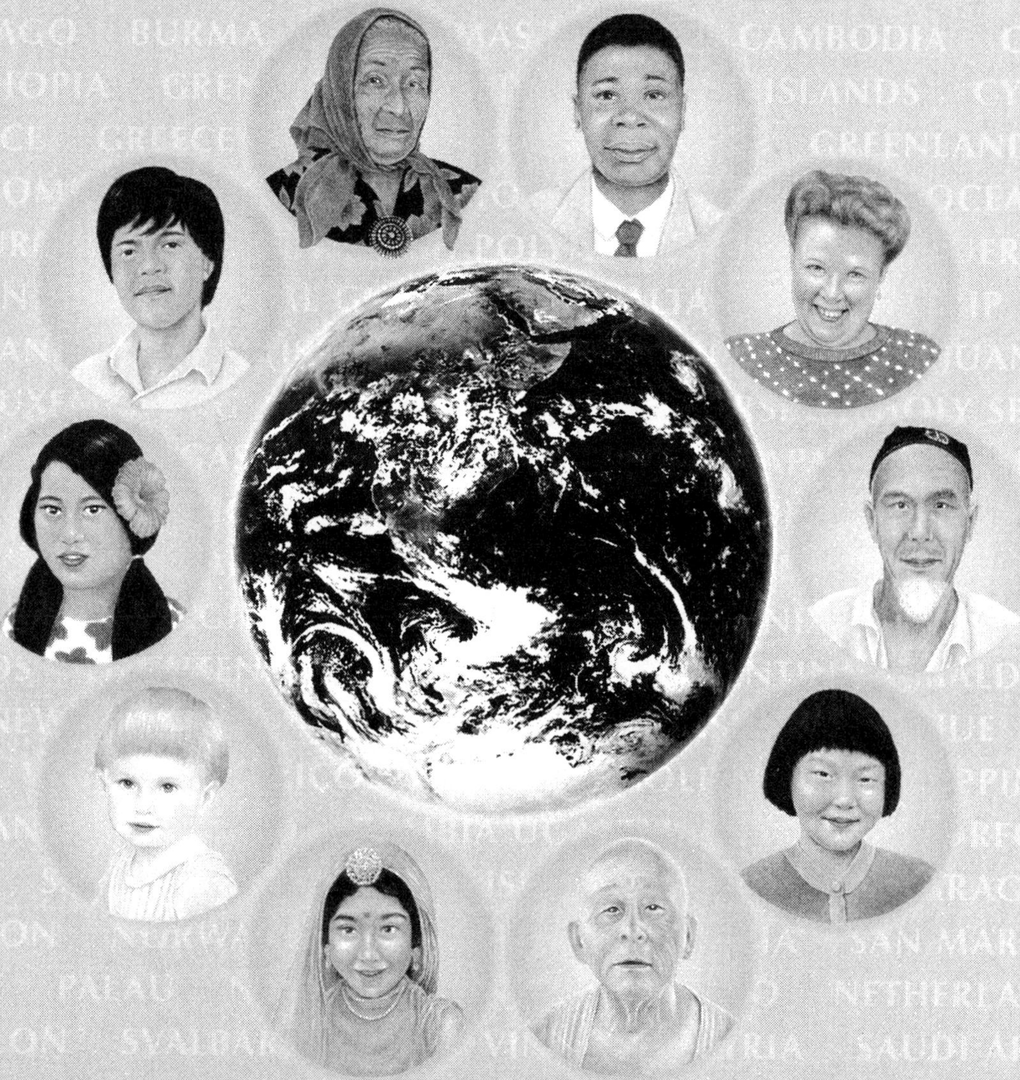

through ROBERT SHAPIRO

THE EXPLORER RACE AND JESUS

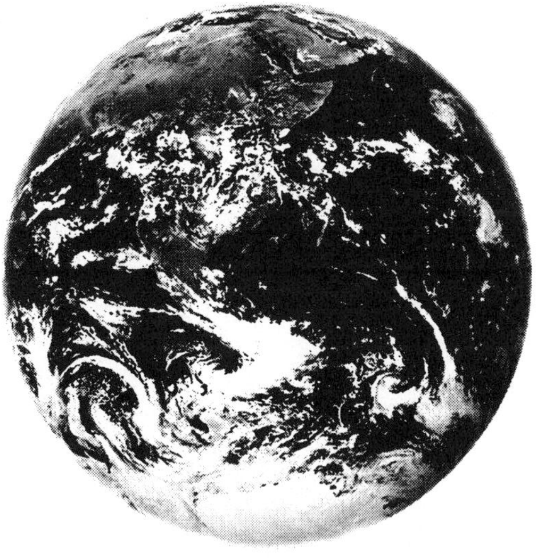

THROUGH ROBERT SHAPIRO

LIGHT Technology PUBLISHING

Cover Illustrated by Michael Tyree

ISBN 1-891824-14-7

Published by

Light Technology Publishing
P.O. Box 3540
Flagstaff, AZ 86003
1-800-450-0985
e-mail: publishing@lighttechnology.com
www.lighttechnology.com

Printed by

Sedona Color Graphics
PRINTING SPECIALISTS
2020 Contractors Road
Sedona, AZ 86336

Other Books by Robert Shapiro

The Explorer Race Series

1 · *The Explorer Race*
2 · *ETs and the Explorer Race*
3 · *Explorer Race: Origins and the Next 50 Years*
4 · *Explorer Race: Creator and Friends of the Creator*
5 · *Explorer Race and Particle Personalities*
6 · *Explorer Race and Beyond*
7 · *Explorer Race and the Council of Creators*
8 · *Explorer Race and Isis*
9 · *Explorer Race and Jesus*
10 · *Explorer Race and Lost Civilizations*
(available 2002)
11 · *Explorer Race: ET Visitors Speak*
12 · *Explorer Race: Techniques for Generating Safety*
13 · *Explorer Race: The Ultimate UFO Book*
(available 2002)

The Material Mastery Series

Shamanic Secrets for Material Mastery
Shamanic Secrets for Physical Mastery
(available 2002)
Shamanic Secrets for Spiritual Mastery
(available 2002)

The Sedona Vortex Guidebook
(with other channels)

Shining the Light Series

Shining the Light
Shining the Light II: The Battle Continues
Shining the Light III: Humanity Gets a Second Chance
Shining the Light IV: Humanity's Greatest Challenge
Shining the Light V: Humanity Is Going to Make It!
Shining the Light VI: The End of What Was . . .

Autobiography

Robert Shapiro: The Man who Moves Hurricanes
Training of an American Shaman
(available 2002)

Contents

Introduction

I am the core being who was known as Yesua . . . let's say Jesus, for simplicity's sake. I am a friend of Qua, (see Appendix) whom you have heard from recently and who has more to say in the future.

I'd like to say to the one, greetings. I am well, and I know you are also, beyond your current trials and tribulations. I salute you for your efforts to improve and broaden the spectrum of mankind and to change history onto a more educational and benevolent path.

It is a challenge to change the course of history, because nothing is easy. When history is fixed—when one can predict the future with authority—then it is possible to engage and maintain stability, yet it is also likely that growth will be minimized. Since it is the intention of the Explorer Race experiment to maximize growth in stages for all life, it is my intention to explain my small part in it.

You have noticed sometimes how difficult it is to change a core behavior of your own and, of course, how difficult it is to change the way things are done—countries, societies and so on. And yet the effort is so worth it, as you say. The capacity to change and to become comfortable with flexibility has been greatly expanded by your work to date. It will not get easier in the near future, but in the longer range it will. In terms of your years, you will notice that it won't get any harder, and that is helpful. It will maintain its current level of challenge for at least another seven years, then the burden will be gradually removed.

What will happen is precisely this: Even though the expansion caused by the Explorer Race is in the future, the effort or work involved in changing the tide of future history will be gradually picked up by other beings in Love's Creation and beyond. For a long time beings have waited to see if you could really do this on your own. Because you have managed to maintain the gradual, yet increasing energy for change and growth, you have won many beings over, and they have instituted a plan to gradually begin to support your work toward change. You won't feel what they're doing for about seven years, but they have begun.

In about seven years you will feel that what you do for yourself and others has become easier. Then it will get easier from that point on. It doesn't mean it will suddenly become simple overnight, but you won't feel like you're pushing a heavy box upstairs anymore. You'll feel that the hill you're pushing the box up has flattened out somewhat and that there are other hands pushing. You'll still have to push, but not so hard. And within five years after that, you'll feel like you're pushing on a flat surface and with many hands; you can even rest sometimes.

I wanted to tell you this because those of you who've been reading these books one after the other have noticed the accumulation of the wisdom, of the stories, really of the broad spectrum of what all human beings are doing, and I feel it is time for some encouragement and support. That's why I want to give it to you in this introduction.

In this book I will make an effort to speak of who I really am, where I'm from, what I'm doing now, why I went to Earth, what I hope to accomplish, what I really did accomplish and perhaps other things. I want to try to explain why things happened, why people did this or that during my lifetime. I will try to fill in details. The reason I won't try to explain their motivation is that if it is necessary and considered useful, *they* might be able to contribute on their own. This would allow greater understanding not only of the motivation of these beings, but of who they are now and in their totality, which might be interesting. As a result, we can get a more complete picture.

You know, most of you have had previous lives. There are a few of you just starting out, but most of you have had previous lives. Some of you have had lives where there's drama, not all of you. I do not hold you responsible for what any life has done in the past. It was something to learn, something to do, there were mistakes to make and things to discover about oneself. One of the greatest challenges for all beings, as they take on more responsibility for the creation of their own life and the lives and worlds of others in time, is to let go of judgment.

Judgment has become the authoritative cousin of discernment. And while discernment is valuable, useful and a foundation of wisdom, judgment in its authoritarian stance is more involved with what is *right.* It is not so much involved with what is wrong, though it is often applied to that. Yet you'll discover in your personal voyage of awakening—and yes, discovery—that what is right is different for each individual and what is wrong is often very flexible.

We know that hurting ourselves or hurting others is wrong. Yet because one must *learn* that it is wrong and *why* it's wrong—not just because someone says it is, but because of its consequences, often felt long and well into the future—schools such as you are in now on Earth are unavoidably necessary. Conscience is not based on the words of others, but on the wisdom gleaned from personal experience. To the extent that conscience can be taught as a philosophy, it is useful and worthy, yet sometimes only experience can teach. I want to tell you that grave misdeeds will be healed and that terrible happenings will be undone, yet there will be a reservoir of knowledge and wisdom so that consequences of misdeeds can always be understood.

It will not be a reservoir to be experienced by the vulnerable or the fragile; it will be a course of advanced studies available to those either in Creator School or to those approaching their own version of Creator School or perhaps to those who have completed Creator School in order to understand the full meaning of their accomplishment.

So know that whatever suffering you experience or cause others to experience will in time be healed, the lessons will be learned well and your conscience will be embraced, because it is of your own creation. I cannot tell you how important that is. It is good to teach values and principles, yet some things must be learned from personal experience.

Enjoy this book and it will unfold gradually for you. I will say good night.

Yesua/Jesus/or as I am referred to in this book, That Man
April 17, 1998

Note to the Readers

I have been asked to clarify the Aramaic name by which I was called in my life two thousand years ago. In my time, if asked, the first time I would say, "I am Yesua Ben Joseph," although the pronunciation would have been Yesua Ben *Yosef.* If a friend introduced me, he would say, "This is Yesua Ben Yosef." After that, when people talked to me, they would simply call me Yesua. Yeshua is used by a second party, meaning others would refer to me that way. But when spoken to in the intimate or by friends–and I tried to help everybody feel that way with me–they would most often call me Yesua.

An analogy in your time would be your use of Mrs., Miss, Ms, Mr. The usage has to do with politeness and tense. The *h* is used as a means of being formal, a formal address, but it is not used in the flow of conversation. If they are talking about me and I am not there, then they would call me Yeshua. If I am there, they call me Yesua.

Aramaic is a language that preceded what you call in your time the Hebrew language. Hebrew was an attempt to formalize language so that it could be reproduced precisely and with formal clarity in print. Aramaic has its own script, but as a language of the people it has many sayings, you would say colloquialisms, that mean different things in different places and at different times. You can see why the formal language of Hebrew was needed.

Yeshua, the man we call Jesus,
through Robert Shapiro,
10 April 2001

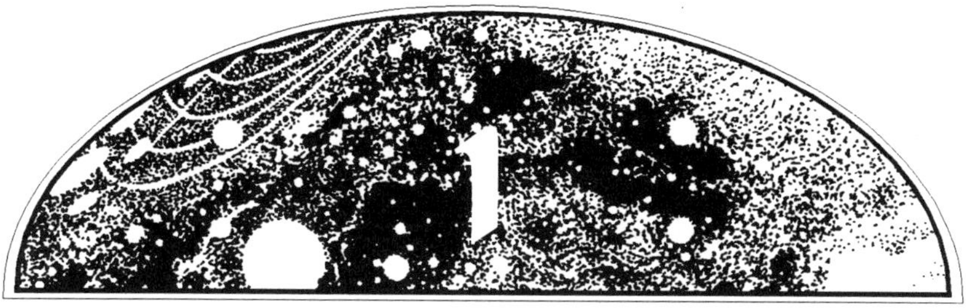

Jesus' Core Being, His People and the Interest of Four of Them in the Earth

Jesus

April 21, 1998

I am, as you say, the core personality of that being known on this Earth as Jesus. I'd like to talk initially a little bit about who I really am and where I'm from and what I do. We'll expand on all of this later on in the book.

From Binary to Individual Beings

I was first aware, cognizant of myself as a binary being, a dual being, you might say. Not exactly like a Siamese twin, as you have in the physical, but to keep it simple, if you were to take two gingerbread men (or women) cookies and superimpose one over the other—not directly over, but slightly offset—that's how I used to be. That's how most of the people where I live used to be.

In recent times (to me, recent times are measured in billions of experiential years), we started moving and we were, as you would now perceive us, individuals. Our council is made up of everyone in this place where I live. Although not everybody comments all the time, we're all on the council; we don't have representatives. Our council had no explanation for this quite radical change in our demonstrated selves. We had always been dual, and it was quite strange to find oneself becoming singular.

The transition to singularity, or what you would perceive as individuality, took awhile—in terms of experiential years, perhaps a billion years. Yet, as we are immortals, that's not so very long. It happened slowly enough that we could realize something was happening, but not so fast that we would be traumatized by it. When some of us started becoming actual individuals, there was a considerable discussion over the idea. Was something wrong? Had something artificial stimulated this? The consensus at that time was that there was nothing artificial, that it was normal and to be expected.

Now, as the process went on and more and more of our people became individuals, we were very curious about the process. At first we considered it a phenomenon, then gradually, as individual personalities, we realized that we were, in fact, still intact on the personality level. We hadn't lost anything when our duality, our other self, split off. Each became the totality of our former selves. It wasn't the kind of separation you experience as man and woman; it was more of a completed duplication (one might say that), although we had always been this dual kind of being.

As we considered what this was suggesting, the consensus developed that this was the process of creating individuality from something else. Thus our society, which had been largely set up to accommodate dual beings, had to make quite significant changes to accommodate individual beings, which we had all become. We considered that for some time, then decided that this was not an accident. We were not conscious, of course, of anybody stimulating it, but it was not an accident and it meant something.

When we were going through these different changes, where a society built up in every way for dual beings suddenly had to accommodate singular beings, we felt, as a result of our experience, that it was positive, that nothing had been lost and that to some extent something had been gained. So we decided that if other societies wished to experience it, this would be a good system.

Individuality: Threads of Potential

Since it is our job (what we do here) to create threads of potential, I'll call them, and release them in all directions to be utilized by creators and/or enlightened individuals anywhere, we felt that we would release the threads of individuality, which we did. Then we felt that there was more to it; perhaps it ought to be coded with individuality as a growth system. We released that.

Then others said, "What about individuality as a growth system that includes all beings?" We had to consider that for a while and discuss it. Many of our people wanted to know if there should be any limits on all beings or whether it should be open—inclusive of all beings everywhere, including beings we weren't aware of. We decided that if the codification was built in and released in all directions so that it would have to be a benevolent experience (if not immediately, at least ultimately), it would be all right. That was the thread of the Explorer Race.

The Growth-Based Universe

I might add that from what I have seen, some aspects—not the totality in terms of what you've heard—of the Explorer Race are taking place in other mass creations. For instance, in one universe I know of, a creator is establishing the universe for beings who are exclusively interested in growth, not really anything else. As far as I can tell, this universe is based largely on the thread we sent out, since the universe will be peopled with individuals. Most likely at some point when the Explorer Race (as discussed in previous volumes) becomes a creator on its own and eventually moves up in dimensions after creating a replacement, one of the first places you will go is to this universe having to do with growth. As a creator, you are going to have a very high priority and good feeling about growth because of your ultimate purpose. And when you visit this universe, as a creator, you will probably discover many other ways for growth.

This is likely to become, then, a very meaningful place for you. When you begin to create your own universe, not just take over this one, you will utilize your accumulated experiences here, and half the motivation behind your new creation will be from your visit to the place that is exclusively growth-oriented. In my understanding, then, you might say (although it is not totally accurate) that the creator involved in this growth universe is really laying out the foundation—the welcome mat, if you would—for you to be able to find it easily. Because that universe is growth and you will be growth, in the larger sense your future agenda is actually being laid out by what this creator is doing.

I wanted to mention that to you so that you could see that the threads we create here ultimately have a purpose and intent even though we do not make them so structured. Rather, we send them out, not unlike you might send out a loose idea or a possible suggestion to others.

In Becoming Individuals, We Discovered Friends

When I became my individual self, I began to understand something that you all, on your planet where you are now, understand very well: As a dual being connected to all other dual beings on our place of existence, I felt a total sense of family with all of our fellow beings. With a sense of individuality, being individual, I still felt family, but I discovered friends, as others did in our creation.

When we were as a dual being (some of our members still say *complete* being, although that's not quite accurate from my perception), we felt family; it was a total bond, a total trust, a total continuity of us all. As individuals, we still have that bond, but as individuals we have the opportunity to explore friendship, what you might call intimate kinship. Not intimate in the same ways you have, but the kind of thing where you would do something with someone. Before, every time we did something it would be with everyone, and we also codified that into the strands we sent out. So we continued to send out energy to any creator who picked up a strand of our continuing experience, offering (not demanding, of course) to that creator the opportunity to integrate what we had learned.

When this experience of friends sort of took us by storm and everybody was doing it and having a wonderful time discovering friendship, there was quite an upswing in interest in those Explorer Race threads, because here was something new and different (to us then—and this is billions and billions of experiential years ago!). There was not exactly enough separation to create the necessity for friends, because the separation wasn't there, but with individuality and singularity come more variety. When there is so much variety, there is a sense of reassurance when one finds someone or spends time with someone who is similar. When we sent this out, the whole concept of moving beyond the total bondedness toward individuals with bondedness and friends, it became very popular very fast. I don't think we can take credit for inventing it, but we might take a little credit for discovering it by having it happen to us and by sharing it. Credit, of course, is not what it's about.

My Home and My Brief Earth Visit

This place (readers of the Explorer Race books know what I mean) is beyond Love's Creation, beyond all the creations associated with the Love beings. It is, as far as I know, a beginning and an end in its own right. We all believe in this place. It is a complete consensus; it is part of our awareness, and we're certain that there is more. We are certain partly because of the physical evidence that we as individuals did not consciously stimulate this change from duality to singularity. This suggests that somebody else did. Also, we have no capacity to imagine experiential limits. Theoretically, even if there wasn't more, because of our concept, bedrock to our philosophy, there has to be more because of what we absolutely believe. So this is not only reassuring, but also, I feel, self-perpetuating.

I have been in this place all my life except for the brief (in terms of years, a *very* brief) amount of time in which I went to the Earth to experience the greater impact of individuality. This is the initial reason I went. Because all our people in our place of existence are very interested now in individuality, of course I wanted to personally experience individuality as a life experience [laughs]. As a life experience, individuality, though it has its downside, as you like to say, also has a profound upside, in the sense that it allows the immortal personality (your personalities are also immortal) to experience life simultaneously as a participant and an outsider. Individuals, if they are not conscious of their total being, will have many opportunities here on Earth to feel like outsiders; yet the larger you is always connected to all life, and you are aware of this in most places other than this profound school you find yourself in.

Since I came here to experience individuality, one of the first things that was attractive to me, even though I always remembered who I was, was the necessity not only for loved ones and family but, as I grew a little older, the actual requirement for friends. Let's say you have a particularly good friend; you will be included while others will be doing what they're doing with their friends. So you are simultaneously included and excluded, although many times you don't care if you're excluded because you're not interested in doing what those other people are doing.

A Way to Understand Growth

I want to tell you that this experience of being included and excluded at the same moment is unique to this place. It forces growth because the inclusion feels so wonderful, whereas your sense of choice and of your [different] opportunities require exclusion to some extent. These two forces, from what I've seen, are what stimulate growth. Not only is the obvious present—"I want but I can't have"—but also "I have and I don't need." So what is happening on this world, when I visited it and now, is in many cases duality. Here you have the complete circle. You have the experience in many ways of male/female, young/old, rich/poor and so on—of duality. You can't actually get away from duality. So from our perception where we exist, you on Earth now are living monuments to duality while you experiment with individuality, which in your case stimulates significant growth.

When I came here, then, that was my great interest. Is it possible to experience growth that is benevolent for yourself and others, should they wish to participate though they are not required? That is why, when I had the opportunity to share my philosophy as I grew up, I wished to share it in such a way as to make it available for those who wished to participate, yet not exclude others who didn't.

When I shared my philosophy, I made certain that it would require growth—that it would offer benevolence and at the same time be demanding. It is a philosophy that's demanding. Understanding the culture and the religions of the time, those religions were also fairly demanding. It did not come to pass then, though it will in your time, perhaps (or a little bit longer, seventy-five or more years from now). I think it will become as I envisioned it, which is a mystical philosophy that incorporates the mystical, embraces individuality and duality, is both as inclusive and as exclusive as people want and allows for others to join and if they prefer, to do other things as much as they want.

My original purpose was, yes, to create a benevolent mystical tradition, but my personal purpose was to understand growth through the necessary tension of individuality and duality.

When you first got this idea, was it shortly before you came here, or had you had the idea a long time? How did you get permission to come here?

It didn't really require permission at the time, because many of us in my place of existence decided that it would be good to go someplace and see if we could either experiment (which is not our way, because an experiment involves too much control) or observe individuality in some form. Most went energetically. I was allowed to go physically, because physicality as compared to the spirit self is, to an extent, duality. Most did not want to even consider going physically, so I didn't have to stand in line. Most went energetically, but we all left at the same time.

The idea of my coming to Earth physically was perfectly acceptable to my fellow beings as long as I abridged what I would say. Being fully conscious, I could do that. Also, as anyone who's a teacher or in any kind of service knows, very often what you do with others is less involved with yourself than with them. So the needs of those you are serving will tend to guide you in terms of what you say and do. I let that occur for me. In that way, I didn't have to remain eternally vigilant that I would say something that could be considered an alteration of the basic existence here.

Is that what you mean by saying that you had to abridge your words?

I would have to if there weren't individuals with specific needs. But almost always I was interacting with individuals with needs. They wanted to know, they wanted to understand—or, as many people experienced, they needed my help for something: "Help us, we're doing this." Then you help, and afterward you all eat and drink together and tell stories. It's no different in your time.

So you were allowed by your peers. But what about Love and all the way down into this creation? Was there any interaction with Love because you were going to put something into the experiment that would change it?

Well, you have to remember that my original purpose for coming was to study. Because of that and because beings who are studying are allowed to come and go freely, that was my open-door policy. The fact that I was going to share a mystical tradition that was a little (only a little) before its time was tolerated, from Love's point of view. From that point of view, it was a long shot. She felt that the people needed more time; while I agreed with her, I felt that I'd like to put some seeds down. I never felt that what I was doing was any more than putting seeds down that would grow, perhaps bringing benevolent results sooner rather than later. In this way it was not controlling but, from my perception, augmenting.

Love's Permission: Communicating with Your Creator

Love felt that she could live with that, and as a result I was allowed to do these things. Your Creator was simply interested, not only because we are peers (I don't want to make this sound too grandiose, because your Creator is essentially shy), but your Creator was . . . not exactly proud, but wanted to see what I felt about Its application of individuality in the world in which you now live.

So during my first five or six years on the planet, when I wasn't interacting with my mother and father and others around me, I was in pretty constant communication with the Creator of this universe, who wanted to experience every nuance of my experience. After all, it was not normal that a fully conscious being would be born here in the usual way and experience things and be able to report on things in the way your Creator naturally communicates. So your Creator was very interested.

At the same time, what I shared with your Creator passed up the line, as you like to say, to my friends in my place of existence.

They were aware of what you were doing at all times.

They were aware of what I was doing insofar as that was an aspect of my communication with the Creator of this universe. When I got back, they became aware of more, because there are things other than individuality and duality. So [chuckles] . . .

. . . you have a friend here.

I have a companion here.

Is our Creator aware that you and your fellow beings created the Loves?

Yes, and the threads.

He knows that.

Yes. He knows this, and that, I think, is perhaps why we see eye to eye and also why your Creator is interested in my feedback. You understand, when my people created the Loves, we did not create everything inside the Loves; we created only the Loves. It would be as if you created the skin of the apple but not the meat. I just want to make that clear.

So you created the Loves, but then the Loves on their own volition then created what was in their creation.

Yes.

Following the Thread

Did they follow threads?

It was available to them if they wished to. I think perhaps because of our experience of individuality and duality, this is only one of the stimulants in this creation for Love and for what she supported in coming to be with the Explorer Race. I think she was most interested in the aspect of benevolent change or growth for all beings. That was the theme she used to support such a system.

But you put out this open-ended thread. Our Creator says it has a whole scenario in it; how did that change? You put it out in a very broad way, so how did it get so specific by the time our Creator . . .

By the time your Creator got to it, it had already been infused significantly by Love. She had added more. If you drew a picture of a Morse code signal, dots and dashes, she filled in some of the dashes and added more dots. So by the time it got to your Creator, it was already a little clearer in its theme. We provided the foundation and, with her particular interests, she added some of the superstructure.

But did your people or this Love know of the incredible expansion that would result from this experiment?

No one could be absolutely certain. For a long time no one really understood the totality of the impact, nor did anyone really understand for a long time the ultimate effect, which would be to change everything benevolently and create more for everything and everyone benevolently.

It's one thing to consider it as a philosophical idea or a theory; it's another thing to look into the future and see how it turns out—which a lot of different beings have done, including beings who live in the future and look into the past and so on. While what occurs is still unwritten in the larger sense, some of it is possible to see. And we've had a long time to study it, to consider it—to see it, as it were. I don't think anyone really realized the wide-reaching impact of it.

It's incredible.

One might very easily become involved with the idea that the average human being will have a bigger brain and a greater love capacity in the heart, greater sensitivity and so on, yet at the same time the average being in all of creation will have a greater capacity in all the benevolent ways that exist for them. And because of our experience going from duality to individuality and discovering that we were not less, but more; not only will everybody become more, but there will be more to become after that! Once *more* is stimulated, it becomes an ever-increasing capacity, as much as I've been able to see. It's as if the pot never goes empty, and even becomes bigger on its own! Thus more is stimulated, and because of the editorial policy of benevolence, it can only be a good thing for all beings.

My Friend Qua

Are you from the same time line as Qua? You said he's from a million years in the future.

I am not, but I still know Qua and he is my friend. I have been to that future in . . . it's hard to describe, but Qua has situated itself (himself/herself) in the future in order to understand how things develop. When you go into any future, you can't understand how things turn out. You can only understand better how things develop. As you go into that future and stop on whatever time line you're on, things don't develop exactly along that time line because as they become more, everything becomes more! So things change, they become more; more is added. If you go back on that time line and then come forward on the same time line, things are different! You can only get a sense of how things are.

So you might say, yes, Qua and I are in the same time. The larger Qua is here where I am at this time, but part of himself is in that future so that he can understand fully the impact of not only what I tried to do, but all the flavors that fed back into what I tried to do. In any event, it gradually becomes, I believe, what Love's original intent was. This is completely established about four hundred years from now in your time, but it begins to happen very soon. Even now there are Christian churches that have begun to openly embrace the mystical. In the beginning of what has come to be known as Christianity, for the first few hundred years the gatherings (not churches) were very mystical, much more so than now. Some of that was lost for a time, but it will return.

Earth Creatures Assist Humans

One thing that will support that return is a greater connection between human beings and all other living beings on the Earth, not only those who are present with you now, but those who have existed in the past. When I refer to living beings, I'm not only talking about your ancestors, but also four-legged beings, many-legged beings, winged beings and finned beings—all of these. As this connection becomes more solid, then a lot of relaxation goes on in the human being, because the human being will realize that it is not as necessary as they thought to do everything. Even many great mystics who exist in your time now have a greater sense of urgency because even though they know they're not isolated and that there are others like them out there, they still feel that there is more for them to do than they can do, and this sometimes tires people out.

Because what you call the animals are doing so much, there's not as much to do as you think. An individual ant or spider will perform and create energetically in a single twenty-four-hour period as much benevolent energy as a prayer group or a meditation circle might produce in ten minutes at the deepest level of their work together. That is why all these different individuals doing all these things all the time are much more unified in their multiples than is apparent.

That is amazing! I don't think humans understand that, or that it's been talked about or taught.

Teaching People to Connect to the Creatures around Them

It's my intent to remind you of these things. When I came to Earth in that life, I spoke a lot about the life around the people. A lot of the people I spoke to were dissatisfied and, not unlike your time, their world was not what they needed it to be. They wanted something more or different, just like now, and they needed it. If they couldn't at that time have something more or different, I would teach them how by connecting with other types of beings. I taught them how to blend with the birds so that they could feel themselves in flight, or with the fish so they could feel total harmony. There is no being as much in harmony with its total surroundings as the average fish. I would teach them how to feel like the animals they would raise, when those animals were vigorous, so that they would understand what the animals needed from them if they could provide it.

Sometimes they need to have their own space, in the case of sheep or goats or whatever creatures. For a long time the shepherd would be too close to the animals, wanting to protect them. But after a while they realized they could stand off at a distance and connect to the animals. For instance, as the shepherd got twenty or thirty feet away, then a hundred feet away and maybe sat on some rocks, as he moved away from them he would feel the animals actually relaxing. Sometimes there would be more than one shepherd, or there might be different ways of interacting with the animals.

I taught this not only to expand the people's experience of their world, but also so that they could understand that the animals were really part of them, that most of the urges of animal beings have direct parallels in the human world. For the sake of human beings, most of the mystical traditions of the average animal have paralleled the needs in the human being. So if you could connect with these animals in benevolent ways for yourself and the animal, you might find yourself dreaming or feeling nurtured or encouraged to do more spiritual, benevolent things for yourself, your family, your tribe and your people, because these spiritual practices are so integrated into the animal world.

Are you on a time line that relates to ours? In your world, is it two thousand years ago that you were here?

My Seeds Have Sprouted and Grown

No, I am not on that time line now. I came into that time line because I wanted to plant those seeds. I must say that even though everything didn't turn out exactly the way I would have liked, those seeds have sprouted and grown. I did not, after all, create on my own these spiritual practices I'm talking about; others had already been to Earth and were practicing these things all over the Earth. But in that part of the world at that time, people were not practicing those things very much. Some people in more ancient religions that were more involved with phenomena—the seasons, the Sun, the Moon, the stars—were a little bit more on the track of what I was teaching. The people I was trying to reach were not the people who were already on that track, but the people who had wandered off the track, who were involved in conflict either to suppress others or to try to liberate themselves, and I wanted to give both groups exposure to the broader philosophy. I think it helped.

If you think about it, the dominant force in the region at the time was Rome, and I can assure you that the Roman Empire did not consider in those days the idea of equality and benevolence to be its watchwords. Yet look how they've embraced it! It is really quite an astonishing thing. I am sure you could cite many faults with the Catholic Church, yet one of its basic tenets is equality as far as one parishioner to another is concerned. Even though the church has a hierarchical structure, they'll get over it. But a lot of the things I was trying to teach are there, and Rome embraced it. If you had been living in those times, they would be absolutely the last people on Earth you would have considered to so fully embrace such a philosophy.

I have heard it argued that they usurped it to use for their own means, but that is only partially true. Ultimately the basic tenets of the religion are very closely connected to what I was teaching, in the broad sense. I, of course, wasn't teaching hierarchical things, but a lot of the philosophy is there.

I am not saying that one religion is better than another; I am just saying that it has not been such a failure as you might think. And since my intention was to plant seeds, I would have to say they have sprouted, though they are not yet done growing.

They haven't flowered yet, right?

Perhaps not. But they are getting sturdy and strong, and when they do flower, it will be a fragrance to enjoy and a sight to behold.

And you'll be here then?

I've always been here; I've always watched.

The Return of Jesus, Buddha and Others

Yes, I know that. Will you come back in a way that we can see you?

I'll send some part of myself in a way that people will have some idea at first who I might be. But in order for the philosophy I will be sharing to do any good at all, I will have to ask others who have been here and who are now recognized as great teachers, and more who will be recognized this way in the future, to come with me so that what we are doing . . .

Who?

. . . oh, Buddha, for example, so that what we are doing will not be misunderstood. It is to be seen as an international training for all races and nationalities (although by that time nationality won't be as much a factor), representing men, women, children, older people. No exclusions.

You and Buddha, that's pretty fantastic! Who else?

Think of anybody that you've heard of related to profound philosophies that have had great impact, anybody.

Is Buddha or any of these other teachers from your place?

Buddha was. As I said, many of the things I was teaching were not new to the planet; they were just new to that area at that time. After all, Buddha's intent was fairly similar. He wanted to put down seeds that would be right for that area geographically, seeds that could support that area, and they have flowered very well. They've sprouted and flowered!

Buddha, Mohammed and I, from the Same Source

Who else came from your place and started a religion or philosophy?

You name names and I will confirm or say no. For instance, Martin Luther did not come from this place. I mention him because of Qua's friendship with him.

Lao-tzu?

No, but he has been a welcome guest on many occasions, being a profound and influential teacher. From his philosophy, he would rather have been an unknown influential teacher; that is perhaps to his great benefit.

For instance, the founder of Islam was from my place. He came here and was very successful in terms of integrating philosophies. If you read the Koran, you will find that a great deal of it has to do with equality, benevolence and other good things.

This is amazing. You're saying that several of you came and sort of touched in at different times and places on the planet to seed this . . .

To seed benevolent principles under the guise of different geographic and nationalistic (at that time) cultures. The basic tenets of the philosophies are very similar. That is why people often say all religions are the same. Even though they're not, a lot of the basic factors are very similar, if not the same.

This is only certain people who were involved with religions that profoundly impacted what we can call the modern world, the last seven or eight thousand years.

Was Buddha conscious while he was here, as you were?

Buddha was not conscious all the time. He decided to remain as an individual Earth person for quite a bit of his life because he felt that a being could not fully understand Earth individuality if he were conscious all the time. I honored that. I feel that he was more conscious than the average person when he was a young man. But as soon as he started teaching his philosophy and becoming more focused and, for those who knew him in those days, more obviously happy and cheerful, he was remembering who he was. Toward the end of his life he remembered, which is why he was so quick to laugh, but when he was a younger man, he was serious, like other men of his time.

How do you feel about that issue? Do you feel you got the full benefit of individuality by remaining conscious?

If I had it to do over again, I might have chosen to live a different life while I was a young man, to be only an Earth person in consciousness, not unlike Buddha. But in terms of what I did, I am not dissatisfied. I can see that what Buddha did has great validity, but I'm satisfied with what I did. If he did it, then I have experienced it also.

Because you are all connected?

Yes.

Some of our metaphysical philosophies say that you had lived lives before and after the life of Jesus; that's not true, then? You lived only that one life on Earth?

I'd have to say that it wasn't exactly true, no. That is the only incarnation, as you understand it to be, that I have experienced on Earth.

Touching Other Humans' Lives

Did you touch into or walk into or share or create other bodies that influenced or impacted us?

No one you would know.

You did it before or after?

I touched into before and after. Many of my fellow beings will touch into someone here and there. We might spend a little time with them, support their saying or doing benevolent things for themselves and others. It is not always that, but perhaps people will say sometimes, "He is showing . . ." and then they use words associated with their religion, showing some aspect of God by doing that. In some way they might say that by way of an acknowledgment and blessing and to perhaps encourage the children.

Are there any lives you touched into where you felt you learned more or gained something, or was it all to help?

I learned something by touching into Florence Nightingale. Considering the circumstances she was working under, I learned that even if one does not greatly impact the overall suffering one exists in, the individual that one serves becomes a part of oneself during that service. So there is that individuality/duality. I touched into her for a time, learning that in a physical way instead of just experiencing it as a bedrock philosophy.

The Meaning of "Christ"

The term "Christ"—where did that come from?

It's just a word. It has many different meanings, but the idea originally was to indicate a level of awareness within an individual. That's the original intention.

It means opening the heart and the heart chakra, but what does it mean related to you?

It became what it is now, a godlike quality. I don't care for that definition because it fosters separation. But it was originally created to be something to live up to, to emulate—and it was possible to emulate it. It was originally a descriptive word, whereas now it has become, as you say, a noun.

The idea that has been put forward is that you were "overshadowed" by the Christ.

Is that totally in error, or is it correct?

It depends on how you look at it. If you look at it politically, you might say that it's so, because a few hundred years after my having been on Earth, I was turned into what amounts to a political figure in order to establish a hierarchical church. So you might say it's true in a way. But when I was living here, I would not say that that was so.

My intention in coming here was accomplished. I planted seeds. It wasn't just to see if we could make it happen right then. It was also to explore other experiences of individuality and duality, which I learned something from. So I feel I have gained as well as provided, and it is my intention to provide more in the future. Right now it is through these words and the occasional picture. Ultimately, it is to return to be amongst you, to walk with you hand in hand, to support you, to assist you and to help you help others of your own kind to be the best of benevolence that you can comfortably accommodate. Good night.

2

Jesus' Life on Earth

Jesus
April 23, 1998

When everyone has to come through the veil of ignorance, how did you manage to maintain your sense of who you were when you were born?

How to Remember Your Identity from Birth

It is not so difficult. Everything is the same physically, but when the soul enters the body, instead of coming in through the usual passage, it finds a window in time and entirely bypasses that usual route. As long as it is a benevolent place you come from (you know, not just anybody can do this) and you feel it is proper, then you go through this window in time, not unlike what people use to travel from planet to planet or galaxy to galaxy. By that routing, you enter the physical body that you will be born into rather than the usual method. In this way you retain all you have been and all that you are, and you can consciously absorb all that will happen to you on the multilevels of your being.

It is not unlike when one departs the physical body and has a guide and so on. The usual method is when a guide or teacher, a benevolent spirit, takes you to the beginning of the veils and, not unlike holding a person's hand, guides you along a very specific pathway through the veils. Every time you go through a veil you shed some part of your immortal self. You could come straight through, but if you did that and entered the body before it was born, if something happened that dissatisfied you, you would easily be able to find your way back. So a circuitous route is taken so that you can't find your way back without being guided.

That's why sometimes people think they are prisoners here. But it is understood that this is sometimes a hard place to be, and in order to finish out what you came here to do, it's best that you need help to go back home, as you say.

Choosing Parents and Birthplace

How did you choose the parents you were born to?

Well, it was mutual. They wanted somebody special; of course, *all* parents want somebody special, but both of them had strong feelings about circumstances in life. They had what you call good hearts. They felt it was important that people not only be kind to each other if possible, but that they try to help each other. In other words, they were fairly enlightened beings. Neither one of them was at all comfortable with the idea of separating groups of people unless there was a very good reason, such as when the groups didn't get along. But they didn't believe in any kind of hierarchical systems. They were modern thinkers for their time. They wanted to have children, and prayed to have children, who would support their cause and perhaps go on to teach about these things through the belief system they had. That was the predisposition on their part.

For my part, it was easy to choose them because I had to go to that *exact* place. It wasn't random in the sense that if not them, then someone else, because they *wanted* someone like me. Let me put it like this: I had a geographical landing zone, let's call it, that was about a five-mile radius from where I was physically born. The physical place was important as well as the parents, because the physical place itself even then, as some physical places still do in your time, had a very precise energy. The energy was resonant and receptive to the doorway I was coming through. It was what I would call more of a moving portal, but it was very specific to that place. So there was that as well.

Then it was also vitally important that I be born someplace where animals were present. This would mean either out on the land amongst the animals or someplace where animals were kept. Animals, you know, are absolutely pure of heart; they're not devious. What they seem to be, they always are. Pure-hearted beings needed to be present, and animals are the most easily available pure-hearted beings. Human beings can sometimes be pure-hearted, but animals are always pure-hearted. That was also important.

You needed this because of who you are, or to stay conscious?

In order that the energy I brought with me would not be too much for my mother, who birthed me, when I entered my physical body I was able to maintain the energy inside my mother. But as I was being born, that energy started to radiate, and as it came through her, it would have been too much for her or the human beings present if there had not been beings pure of heart present to absorb the excess energy. That's why animals needed to be there; they absorbed the excess energy.

You could usually control it so it didn't radiate, but during the birth time you couldn't.

It wasn't so much control; it was that I was using it for other things. But when the birth process was going on, I had to relax any usage of anything because the birth process is so specific. Because I had to completely relax, the energy radiated to its maximum, but the animals completely absorbed it all.

The Essene Connection

It is believed that Mary and Joseph belonged to a group called the Essenes. Is that true?

They didn't belong to it, but they were students. The Essenes were not really people who married and had children. It was more like a university, a place where people went and studied and considered and tried and practiced and experimented, all these things. A contemporary comparison would be a university even though it wasn't that in their times, but that's as close as you can get. My parents weren't actually Essenes, or else they wouldn't have been husband and wife and parents. But they were interested in it because the Essenes were studying and researching and practicing the infusion of the practical mystical.

You see, there is *mystical*, which is absolutely infinite. *Practical* mystical defines the mystical according to the time and place it is used; for example, mystical traditions on Jupiter may be useless on Earth.

The Essenes believed in the practical mystical, and they had knowledge and wisdom of the mystical from other places, but they were essentially sifting, trying things. They would try out on Earth all the mystical of the day that they absorbed or heard of or were inspired by to see if it fit. They were really guiding the practical mystical of their time and geographic place.

How did they gain the knowledge from other places?

The same way people do now, from inspiration or from people—travelers coming to stop and talk with them for a while, bringing the mystical traditions of their religion or philosophy or people.

Oh, other places on the planet.

Other places on the planet and the occasional traveler from the stars. But mostly it was that or inspiration, not unlike the process that is happening here (channeling).

My Timing, What I Hoped to Accomplish

You've mentioned the geographic site and the need for clear parents; what about the time? What told you to choose that particular time?

It was an important time because people were restless and needed a change, as is true today. Not just because some people were suppressed, but the people who were doing the suppressing or colonization, as you call it, were also restless and wanted a change. It was like a window, an opening, an opportunity that could possibly have worked in the way I wished it to work at that time. It didn't, but [chuckles] it was perhaps worth planting the seeds.

Say more specifically how you wanted it to work out. What was your plan?

It wasn't really a plan. I was hoping that the mystical traditions on the practical level would be embraced by all peoples of the time, and if you embrace the practical mystical, you will inevitably see that your enemy is your friend and that everyone is not only equal, but special and unique, all these good things. That's specifically what I was hoping for. What happened in fact is that seeds took root with various individuals and sprouted in different ways. For a few hundred years after my passing the practical mystical was very popular and was really moving under its own steam, as you say [chuckles]. But it had to go underground once the political realities of the structure of organized religion started having an influence. The times were polarized more to the masculine, and the practical mystical is always polarized feminine.

To choose that time, you had the ability to look before and after it.

A Critical Point in History

Yes; I also thought that it was important, even if it didn't work, to plant that energy there and support it at that time. If I hadn't gone or no one else had gone and everything remained exactly the same, things might have gotten a little worse. There was so much volatility between different groups of peoples that it might have turned into a warring situation. This was a vulnerable time in this planet's history (this planet as a being), and the planet could have decided to eliminate people.

So this was much more important than seeding; this is incredibly important.

Well, I knew I wasn't alone. Even if religions weren't starting, there were special things going on all over the Earth—special sacred things happening, sacred energies being introduced from beings all over. Of course, it was being done to support and sustain human beings so that they would feel more benevolent, at least to a degree, and so that Mother Earth would also feel more benevolent, meaning that she might think there was hope for you. This is all she needs to think in order to keep from eliminating you.

You and your place of existence were seeing that if you didn't step in, the Explorer Race, the culmination of this whole Love's Creation, might not make it.

That's right.

It was that serious?

The Infusion of Energy into the Common People

That serious. Others knew about it; that's why I said other things were going on elsewhere. But because of that particular place, I felt that it needed that infusion of energy. But the energy couldn't be infused briefly, like sending some energy to a place for a moment. It had to have duration, which required no less than thirty-two years. It could be more than that, but it could be no less than thirty-two years. I had to be in and around that general area until I could train others to pass on that energy, then perhaps go elsewhere.

I knew that the Essenes would ultimately have to go completely underground. A lot of what they wrote and did in their real traditions would be lost at least temporarily, so I knew that there was no great point in trying to train *them* to do it. The only thing to do was to try and train people who would at least have offspring, children who would likely—at least their descendants—be in that general area for a while. So that's what I did. That's why I went around to different groups of people, regardless of what practicing religion they were, to be with them and find perhaps one amongst this group or two amongst that group and teach them things. I'm not talking about the apostles here; I'm just talking about the students. The main thing I would teach them, aside from sharing philosophies and so on, would be how to connect to that benevolent energy from my place of existence, which feels very good to a human being . . .

I know, I can feel it.

. . . and just radiate it, just let it flow through them, that's all. It would feel good to them, and I would say, "It will feel good to you and those around you, and it will be benevolent for those you never even meet." If I felt that these persons were likely to wish to do this and carry on this tradition, then I would share that with them. I did that with about a hundred different students. Eventually that was the foundational, really almost singular teaching, that happened with the . . . I am shy to call them apostles; rather, they're woman assistants. "Apostles" is really not a term we used then; they were more what you would call students or assistants.

The women who were close to me learned that, but not all the men who were close to me could learn. Sometimes you might want to learn something, but you just don't have the capacity. So with the men I tended to talk more—thoughts, words. With the women it was more radiating energy. So between what the women did and the students, the energy is being maintained even today in the descendants.

So there's been a constant mother-to-child or parent-to-child teaching for over 2000 years?

Yes. Sometimes it is conscious, sometimes it isn't. Sometimes a family dies out or things come to an end, but counting the original 120 or so, today in your time there are about 89.

Wonderful! All over the world?

Not all over the world. Alas, there is nobody in that area anymore.

And that area needs it.

Very much.

Radiate Energy

How can you teach someone to radiate energy like you do?

Well, for starters, you find out if they're loving and dedicated, so at least there's a common bond of basic shared philosophy. Then you allow the energy to flow through you until they can feel it in themselves. When they feel it often enough, they tend to feel it even before you get there. Let's say we were going to meet and talk; before I got there, I would not be radiating energy to them, but they would be feeling it because they knew I was coming. Eventually they would be feeling it themselves.

The more they're exposed to it, the more they're likely to allow it to be with them, because it feels good, and after a while they become conditioned to the energy. They enjoy it, it's a good experience. It's benevolent for them and those around them, so they just integrate it as part of their existence. Then, of course, should they have children, the children will be exposed to that energy. It will be normal for the children, and the children will radiate that energy because it's associated with their parents. The parents might tell them, they might not. In time it might be lost. The main thing is, as long as the energy is there, it doesn't have to be explained.

How many of the eighty-nine are conscious of what they're doing?

Only about four, sometimes five. But that's all right, they don't have to be conscious of it. It doesn't make it better if you're conscious of it. There's no improvement to be conscious; it's the same whether you're unconscious about it or conscious. It doesn't make any difference. The ones who are conscious of it are those who have studied philosophical or spiritual or religious training and have experienced other energies. Others have commented that they experience an energy from them, so they discovered that it is something they are doing. That's why they're conscious of it.

The Childhood Years

I see. Born on this planet during that time of no technology, what were you feeling, what were some of your early experiences? How did you put yourself in a human baby?

Like every baby, I discovered my world. The only difference is that past the age of sixteen months to two years, I was still conscious. Most babies are conscious until they're at least about fifteen, sixteen months old; then it begins to fade very slowly. In those days, by the time you were five or six years old you were not particularly conscious anymore. So in the beginning it wasn't much different from a normal baby.

But wasn't it highly interesting to start learning how to work the body and do things?

It was intriguing to communicate only with sound, and of course in those days people were much more sensitive to the feelings they would pick up from the baby. "Oh, I think it's this" or "I think it's that." Of course, traditions were different in those days, as they are still in many places in your contemporary world, so when babies were born they were in the constant care of mothers or fathers. There wasn't a separate place where babies were put, such as baby having its own room, as you find nowadays. As a result, there was more constant learning and love and all of this. I was no different, really, from any baby.

When did you allow your true nature to show through and when did people begin to realize you were different?

I was about eight-years-old. I started doing things with my father. I would talk about things, using words and phrases that a child of that age couldn't possibly know, speaking wisdoms to him that were secret wisdoms of the times, of the Essenes and others. It was kind of fun. That's when my father discovered that I was different.

You did this deliberately?

Yes, certainly; I wanted him to know, and I wanted my mother to know. Before that I think she knew that I was different, because with mothers and children, feelings and eye contact and touch are the first primary communication. This is not to say that mothers don't use words, but words even then were more important to fathers than they were to mothers. So I think my mother knew it all along.

Because she could feel all this inside.

Yes, and when things were being talked about, she'd notice what I was doing with my eyes. She could tell I was *there.*

What do you want to say about growing up?

There have been lots of different tales told, but . . .

How many of them have come from you?

Some of them have; some of them have been partly clear and others have been more clear. I don't want to say, because I don't want anybody's feelings to be hurt.

When did you allow yourself to start teaching?

I was about nine. I started talking to the other children. When you're nine years old, you really know which children you relate to and which ones you don't. There were several of the children I spoke to, said things to or did things with, and that's when I began. We begin with the children, of course, because it's not normal for adults to listen to a child. So other than talking to my parents, I had children available.

Both in your family and relatives and friends and . . .

Yes. Those that were, as you say, around.

Did any of these children grow up to become your students?

No. Fortunately, they all went on to teach other things in other places, so that spread it around a bit. In those days people moved around a bit, not so much because they were free, but because you couldn't count on resources—water, food and so on—being in one place all the time.

What you taught them wasn't disseminated as your teaching.

Which is fine—better, actually. It created a structure for them to build their future philosophy on so that the philosophy coming from teachers and relatives and so on could be more spiritually sound and heart-centered. As you know, if you *read* philosophy, it will very often be blindly biased according to whoever is writing. The events of the time and so on influence the author. So if you give someone a solid, heart-centered, spirit-oriented foundation, regardless of what they hear, they will fit those pieces into that foundation if they are compatible, and what isn't compatible will be discarded.

Like a beautiful love filter.

Yes, well said.

There are stories that you had to leave and go to Egypt as a twelve-year-old or something. Are they true?

Had to go? I traveled some, but I can't say that I *had* to go. Of course, when I was a youngster I went through the usual traditions and customs of the religion/philosophy I was a part of.

Which was the Jewish religion?

What is today called the Jewish religion, yes.

What was it called then?

Oh, I think it was not given a name so much at that time or any other time. People would say, "This is what we believe," and "we" would be you and your people. There wouldn't be a name hung on it.

What were your people called?

No, no. Nowadays in your time, everything has a name. If it doesn't have a name, there's no place for it in society. Think about it. In those days you didn't have to have a name in order to have a place in society, so very often groups of people would just call themselves "the people." They wouldn't say, "We are this" or that. The Romans, for instance, did not call themselves Caesarites, although they believed that Caesar was a living god. They called themselves Romans—that's where they were from, that's what they represented. Rome was an identity.

So did you take an identity, then—the Nazarene?

No. All these things you hear about me were other people's description. Even today they might, in your time, say that someone is from such a place: "He's from Texas, so we'll call him Tex."

Was it difficult being so different? Did people respect you, or think you were odd?

It wasn't difficult because I was conscious. For people who aren't fully conscious, it's terribly difficult, but because I was conscious, I was not dependent on my life of the moment for my self-esteem. Even if I was considered to be extremely different because I was in different places at different times with different people, it didn't upset me in the slightest.

Teaching by Questions

So you traveled. The stories say you went to study, but you really went to teach when you traveled, right?

I went to teach and sometimes I would listen, because it is polite, you understand. Sometimes I would teach as a student, which is unique. You know that one?

No.

When you teach as a student, you listen to the teacher talk for a while, then you ask a question either because you're inspired or because, if you're conscious, you know the teacher is either in rhythm with the teaching or speaking from inspiration, but you also know that the teacher himself or herself does not know the answer. But because he is speaking from inspiration and connected to all he believes in, the answer flows through him and he learns at the same time he is teaching the others. Because it happens in that way, they remember it. It's exciting, it's wonderful; they remember it.

It's a technique that many people use today. If you want someone to learn something that they have the capacity to learn through inspiration and what I call the discovery process, you ask them something that they discover by answering. It's very useful.

Did you go all over the planet? There are stories to that effect. I don't know how true they are.

Bilocating

It's like this: When you are conscious, you can be in more than one place at once. I wasn't always conscious of being at different places all over the planet, but sometimes in my travels people would tell me they had seen me here or there or heard about me here or there, and I would say, "Oh." Then I would think about it and remember that a part of me was there. It's like remembering a dream. I'm mentioning it to you in this way very purposely, because even today in your time almost every human being bilocates at least once in life, and very often more than once. Someone will see you someplace; you just won't be conscious of being there. But you will be there and you won't remember it.

In your case today, because you may not be that conscious, if someone tells you about it, you will either deny it or have no understanding. If you believe them, you will just be baffled by the whole experience. The reason I'm saying that is that it tells you something. Do you understand what it tells you?

We act from a larger part of our being, even though under the veil we're not aware of it.

Yes. You have the capability to do these things and there is the *necessity* to do them, because sometimes your unique spiritual abilities are needed someplace and only you can do it. You're not conscious enough, perhaps, to do those things, so a portion of you goes to that place and does the things you can do that represent your potential on Earth, but it may also represent things you have done before or will do in the future. Then that part of you will disappear, yet it actually returns to you. But to the casual observer it would seem to disappear.

The most likely scenario for you to remember it at all would be as a vague dream. You might say, "I had an odd dream last night," to your friend. "I felt like I was walking around the scene of some disaster—I wasn't sure whether it was an earthquake or train wreck or plane crash. I remember that there were people getting up and leaving, but there were also some people walking around; they didn't know where to go. And I remember that I was helping to guide these people to where they needed to go. Isn't that a funny dream?" But in reality you might very well have been there.

Helping spirits.

Helping the disincarnate spirits move on. But it isn't just that. That is a spiritual thing, an otherworldly thing that happens on this world. But it might be something else entirely. There are infinite examples; I will pick one out at random. Perhaps you are a wonderful swimmer; maybe you were a lifeguard when you were younger, and you are getting older and are not as spry as you once were. You have a dream, and in the dream all you can remember when you wake up is swimming in the water and pulling a heavy weight behind you. You're not even sure if it was a person or a log or what. Someone may have been floundering out in the water, perhaps in the ocean or a lake, but that person had a future—things he was going to do, things she was going to contribute—but there was no human being around to rescue the person. So whoever is the most uniquely qualified—not just the best swimmer, but the person who would be most comfortable for the drowning person to be with—would go to the rescue. Perhaps he knew them in another life (something, any connection), but there's some perfect connection.

You think you're asleep, and you *are* asleep for all intents and purposes, but a portion of you is actually present there. Let's say you're in your sixties, but the portion of you that goes there and rescues the person is young and vigorous. The drowning person would say, "I was going down, and my life was flashing in front of my eyes. I thought it was the end, that I was going to die. Then suddenly a strong arm was around me and towing me. I caught only a flash; it was a young person, very vigorous and strong, and he had red hair." And when he wakes up in the hospital, the authorities check and nobody like that was around him. Some people say, "It's a miracle!" and other people say, "Who knows how he got to shore? But he's going to get better, and that's all we care about."

[Laughs.] So every person on Earth does that at least once, you say.

Prisons

At least once, and many people do it many times. Another place that people bilocate to a lot is prisons. Very often your loved one who is in prison, for instance, or someplace where he doesn't have as much freedom as he normally has, such as in the military.

Perhaps he's overseas and wants to see you but can't, or he's on a ship, someplace where he's not exactly imprisoned but can't come and see you, so you might go to be with him for a moment. He might be a Navy man at sea who has a wonderful dream. He dreamt of his wife and they were making love. Afterward they visited with the children and watched them play, the neighbors came over and they had dinner, then they went to bed and made love again. "What a wonderful dream!" say you, the dreamer, the Navy man waking up. "Wow, that felt so real!" It gives you this wonderful, loving feeling, and you float on that for a few days. You can get by on that; it's like food. And it's real; it happens at the dream level.

Then of course there are other things that really happen. I mention prisons because people are stuck there. Even the people who work there are stuck there, and very often someone goes there. If you talk to some of the people who've been in prisons for a while, if you get to be friends, they'll tell you some of the strange things—as they call them—that happen. A prisoner who had died a long time ago suddenly shows up, tells someone something he needs to know in order to get along better, and then is gone. The person who gets that information casually mentions it to somebody else, and they say, "That's not possible; that person died five years ago." That happens in prisons a lot because these people are stuck there and need help. Sometimes they need nurturing, friendship, guidance; very often it happens in dreams, but sometimes it's physical.

It interests me that even though you were conscious; you weren't aware of your other aspects appearing somewhere else.

Well, you see, the advantage of being conscious is that you don't have to pay attention to it. When you are unconscious, of *course* you don't pay attention. When you are conscious, you *can* pay attention, but you don't have to. You have the choice.

Is it distracting?

Conscious Bilocation

It isn't distracting, but you have to concentrate more. When you are with someone or teaching someone, you want to give them your full attention, but if you are doing other things—say, in 300 other places at the same time—you can't give the person your full attention. Maybe you can give him 98 percent, but you want to give him your full attention so there isn't a moment when he might question or have a sense of doubt because he doesn't feel you present.

The master teacher is fully present with the student when the student is there. That's why the master teacher doesn't usually spend all his time with the student, because master teachers need to lie down and rest, too. But when the student is there, the teacher is totally present with him. And the student knows that he not only needs to learn and pay attention, but that the teacher cares about him and expects him to be fully present as well. Much more is done in those moments than in a large class environment where you may or may not feel like you wish to be present at all.

Qua said something interesting, that he took a lot of effort not to become close or intimate or have anyone really like him or depend or pull on him [see the upcoming book,* ET Visitors to Earth Speak*]. You've got the whole planet pulling on you, right? How does that feel? You're someplace around the planet even now . . .

You have to remember something. The planet that is pulling on me is pulling on a mythical me. It is not pulling on the real me. Very few people on the planet have much knowledge of the real me, and because I am in the place of my existence, if everybody on the planet (to say nothing of everybody in *this* sphere of existence) pulled on me when I'm in my place of existence, it still wouldn't drain me. It drains me only if I am that person they are pulling on. But because the person they think of as me is largely mythical, it doesn't drain my energy.

But you do interact with many beings all the time on this planet.

Yes, but as myself! The clearest descriptions of those interacting with me would be people in hospitals or people having near-death experiences who say, "Jesus was there, and I felt this overwhelming love, this unconditional love." You and your readers have heard this.

Yes, absolutely.

That is the clearest description of me, of how I really am. And for these people I am really present; I don't arrive with books of learning and tell them they must read these things and know them to get to heaven.

The Mythological Written History

So everything we know about you at this moment we could say is a myth, a story.

Yes, everything you know about me up to this point in time has been rooted in stories in order to keep it alive. Of course, in the old days there wasn't a printing press around every corner, and people didn't even think of writing these things down in symbols in that part of the world. It was all by word of mouth, as you say. So it's not surprising that my life as I lived it on Earth became largely mythological; a great deal of it was simply (not malevolently) made up, because it sounded better.

I'll give you an example. I was known sometimes to visit the criminal classes, because being a criminal in those days—a robber or something like that—wasn't always a reflection on your character. It might be because your people were considered outcasts; you were not given anything, you were excluded from society, and the only thing you could do was be a criminal to survive and feed your children.

So I would sometimes go to visit them. As people know today, so it was then: The only way they would come to trust you is if you would become one of them. It wasn't just that I went and spoke to them and broke bread with them; I would *become* one of them. I wouldn't hurt anyone, but I might participate in a robbery. You might say that's not possible, but if the people deserved what I had to teach them, then I would have to be considered a peer so I could speak eye to eye with them. I would urge them to not be any more violent than they had to be, but I would not talk down to them. The only way to communicate with people in a way they trust is to feel that you are speaking to an equal. So I lived with them; I was one of them.

I might add [chuckles], since irony is so appreciated: Considering the crimes I was involved in, one might rationally say that my execution was . . . not necessarily justified, but people were executed regularly for the crimes I had participated in in those days. If the authorities had known I had participated in them, they wouldn't have gone through all the political stuff they went through for an execution. They would've just said, "Oh, he's a thief. Execute him." I feel that is an amusing irony.

When the people involved in the execution at the time died and went through the veils, we laughed about it. You know, after this is over, *you'll* laugh about things—not because you're laughing at others' suffering, but in the larger picture it's all very amusing. So we laughed about it.

How much of what people are taught today about you is true? Any of it?

About one-hundredth of one percent. That might be an exaggeration; it might be a little less than that. What I'd rather say is what is true rather than what isn't.

Understand that this wasn't done malevolently; sometimes I was made more grandiose (which is the opposite of what I attempted to do) so that people would, as the teachers of the time believed, respect me more. Because the teachers were trying to perpetuate my core philosophy, they felt, "If the people respect this being and if we make a god out of him, then maybe they'll emulate some of these things that are good." So they stripped my basic philosophy down to its core principles. Although the core principles do not completely survive today, a lot of them do, a lot of the core ethics of Christian churches—not all the words, not all their preaching and condemning and all this other business, but basic words: equality, love, cherishing. I talked about that. I didn't talk about things like condemning, damning and judging. I never talked about any of that.

I walked out of church at age eleven when they talked about being born in sin, conceived in sin.

Let me say this: The idea of saying that a human being could be born in sin would mean that *I* was born in sin. I would never say that. The fact that such things were taught has more to do with politics than with anything I ever taught.

Decommissioning the Feminine

Because people would need the church authorities, the preachers and the popes to get them out of it, to save them.

The reason they created that hierarchical system was for their very survival. Remember the historical things going on at the time, which were major struggles between religions and the idea of a masculine deity versus a feminine deity. It was war, so they made a lot of accommodations, as you might say, in order to perpetuate things. It's a curiosity in this country [the U.S.] that wars are still going on, though they really originated in the old days in England. The idea of women being lesser beings was promoted through the decommissioning, one might say, of the feminine, so as to keep the feminine servile. That was a direct reaction to those who, at that time in ancient England and other places, were promoting the feminine god. But you scholars and others who have studied these things know about this. A lot of it is political and understandable—if not justifiable, at least understandable. To me, justifiable refers to justice, not logic.

The Romans and the Jews

That's certainly important, yes. There's a story I have heard a lot, that the people you belonged to saw you as a king on Earth and rallied around you because they thought you would lead your people to some higher civilization as a material king. Was that true?

Some people hoped I would do that, yes. But of course that was the polar opposite of what I wanted to do. It was a fleeting hope that didn't linger, but people talked about it later, and of course it turned into a story. It was never a great issue with the Romans that I was competing with them for allegiance; they knew I wasn't. As a matter of fact, as far as they were concerned, they really didn't care about me. As far as they were concerned, this was an issue that didn't have anything to do with them at all.

How did they see it?

They thought it was local politics; they weren't interested.

They really didn't have anything to do with it, but the local government . . .

Well, they were a colonizing force, a force to be reckoned with, yet they weren't interested in converting the people of the time and place to praising Caesar. They didn't care. They didn't think that the people who lived there *deserved* to think of Caesar as their god. In other words, they weren't trying to convert anybody to their way.

They just wanted to collect the taxes.

Yes; they were there to make money and to get what they could out of the place. They weren't trying to save or convert anybody [chuckles]. They weren't really interested; it was something they would just as soon not have been involved in. Not because they represented authority; they could be manipulated, and they were. Authority can often be manipulated to be authoritarian.

Which then causes people to rebel against them?

No. If you cannot legally kill somebody, find someone who can, and encourage that person to do it for whatever politically expedient means might be available. It is ironic, you know, that Jewish people are blamed [laughs]. That was completely fictional. If there was ever anything fictional, that was it. The Jewish people (as you call them; or as they called themselves, "the people") wanted me to be returned. They said, "Give us back our rabbi!" And the Romans said, "We don't want him; take him!" But there were others who were concerned. It wasn't the hierarchy of the people, it was not the religion of the time—it wasn't them.

Behind the Scenes

There were others who said, "He could be a loose cannon, unpredictable; we don't know what he's going to do. He's talking about equality, he wants people to love each other. We can't have that." It didn't have anything to do with the Jewish people; it didn't have anything to do with the Romans. It was, as always, the people *behind* the scenes. I'm not going to talk about it too much, because why substitute one group for another to be blamed?

Are you talking about a secret government of the time?

No, it was people behind the scenes; no different in your time, really.

You would upset the status quo and interfere with business, right?

That's as good a way as any to put it. It was a good many years later, about six or seven hundred years later, that it was turned to say that the Jews wanted Barabbas and another—that's total myth. They would say, "So give us back our rabbi!" That would have been the term. "Give us back our teacher!" And the Romans would say, "Take him!"

Is this when you were alive or afterward when they wanted your body?

When they were talking things over publicly and the Romans were saying to me, "Because we're not really involved in this, can't you just work it out amongst yourselves? Why do you have to say these things that upset these people? If you keep these people happy, then we'll intercede on your behalf and make sure you're safe. Then you'll be protected and you can go on teaching." But you know, I had to teach what I was teaching; that's what I came here to do. They said, "Well, if you can't change, then we can't protect you."

My Life Span

Did you choose a particular span of years to do that? You said you had to be here thirty-two years.

I had to be here thirty-two years, and I decided, Well, I'll be here thirty-two years. Any more, then that's fine; but I have to be here at least that long. So I was planning on thirty-two years, and it turned out to be thirty-three.

So that part is accurate. What about your birth date, using the numbers we use now?

Using the calendar you have today, it was right around 3 September. But the reason they used 25 December is that it correlated at the time (I'm not going to tell you everything; you readers can look it up) with other religions. It was politically expedient to use that date. But I was born around 3 September. I think there might even be people alive today who have written that. It was written down; it was hard to read, but I think it can be figured out. It's not so terribly important, though, is it really, when I was born?

Was the year correct?

You mean the year zero? [Chuckles.]

The year zero, yes. How many people on this planet have had the calendar changed to reflect their birth date? That's pretty awesome, eh?

Yes; I wish it hadn't happened.

So you died in what we call A.D. 33—that part is accurate?

Oh, I had to go through physical death, or I wouldn't understand why there was fear of it. During the time of my physical death I suspended, for a time, my being totally conscious. If you're totally conscious going through a physical death, there's absolutely no fear and pain doesn't bother you. The moment the pain comes up, you just exit right away. So I wondered, how can I have complete understanding of what is going on here? (In my youth I had jumped off a cliff to die at the bottom just to see what it was like to die, but I was conscious when I did that. Then I reassembled myself and went on with my life.)

But this was important because I had to understand what it was like to die as an *unconscious* person; so I did. Granted, there were moments when I was present there and my basic personality was there. It was not exactly like a normal person's death, but similar. I had to go through that. You can't learn compassion by studying; you learn compassion by living.

Returning through Bilocation

After that, did you reassemble your body and travel around the planet, or did you leave?

I left for a short time and then I returned. I didn't return physically; I kept returning as that bilocating being. For a while I stayed near the planet and bilocated in various places. Sometimes I would be there for quite a while. That's where you get the multiple variations of my after-death existence. I went all over. That's why you get stories, and sometimes the stories seem to conflict—a person who might be interpreted to be me was in China and elsewhere at the same time. That's been confusing for historians, but that's how it's done.

Do you accumulate all these bilocational experiences into part of your wisdom?

Oh, yes. Yes.

So you were not conscious at the time, but later . . .

I *could* be conscious at the time, but I would usually choose not to be so I could give my full attention to whatever I was doing and wherever I was doing it. If I were bilocating somewhere, I would be giving my full attention there, and I wouldn't be conscious of the other places where I was so that I could give the full attention to whatever I was doing *there*. If there were times when I was conscious of my other locations elsewhere, then *all* my locations were conscious in those moments, too.

The Lazarus Incident

That's awesome! There's one other story that Zoosh told. He said that when you went to raise Lazarus from the dead, the Creator interceded. You were just going to see what you could do, but it was the Creator who actually brought the being back to life. What is your version of that?

That's right, that's true.

And that made your life more difficult.

Made it more difficult, yes, because then people everywhere were saying, "Oh, he's not a normal human being. We can't be like him. He's special, he's different; how could we ever be like him?" Then they could say: "Look! See! He's a god." Then other people would say,

"Well, no; we have healers, we can do that sometimes." I hoped that that would prevail, but it didn't.

Did the Creator ask your permission, or did He just do it?

Just did it. It was up to Him, yes? It was His creation; He could do what He wished.

And do you know why He did it?

No, I didn't ask Him to justify it.

But He never did it again.

Oh, I couldn't say; you'd have to ask Him.

Oh, I mean through you.

No, not again through me. He didn't do it for *me*, you know.

Why did He do it, then?

He didn't do it for the man who was dead, either. He did it for the man's family. It was an act of kindness.

But that was interfering.

Yes, but creators can be kind sometimes even if it is interfering.

But it made your mission more difficult, I'm saying.

It did; but you have to understand that while He was allowing me to do what I was doing, it wasn't exactly in His timing, the way He saw things happening. He wasn't trying to interfere with what I was doing, but He was going to do what He was going to do. It just so happened that our intentions crossed at that point. He was going to bring that person back to life anyway, even if I hadn't been there for that family. I just happened to be there in that moment.

What you were saying then was, "What I do, you can do," and that made it . . .

Made it more difficult.

The Disciples

So how did you choose what the stories call the disciples? You said you taught them conceptually rather than from the feeling level.

Yes. I taught the women from the feeling level. Of course, a lot of the women didn't need to be taught; they were already connected with that energy because a lot of them were healers or mystics, you know.

There are no stories about the women leaders, the women apostles, the women anything.

There were for a long time, but when the Church (as it came to be known) was in a battle for its life, as it saw it, with those who were in allegiance to the Goddess, that's when a lot of that was permanently changed (meaning for a while in your time). That's why you don't know about it. It's not that there aren't writings now, as well as things people have written down on their own. There are some ancient writings that talk about them, but it's just not within the church hierarchy, it's not taught. The legacy you're living has to do with ancient politics.

Will writings come out shortly or in the near future that tell the truth about this time?

A lot of writings have come out, but for them to be widely believed and accepted will require religious leaders who believe them, saying, "Yes, this is certainly true."

In your time, was finding women healers who were sensitive to training perfectly normal?

It was easy, that's right. And it was easier to find women healers and mystics than it was to find men, because in most groups of people there would be at least one woman—usually women—who could do these things. That was the easy part. Finding the men was a little more difficult, because then I had to talk to them. It was philosophy and thought and interaction and teaching; in other words, following the traditions of the time in their philosophies. You know, a lot has been said that these men were all from that group of people [Jews], but they weren't all, as you say, Jewish people. Some of them were other things.

What kind of people?

Some of them were from what is now called Islam. In the early days Islam wasn't as widely practiced as it is now, but even then it was practiced quite a bit. It was really a very advanced religion for its time because it touched on everything. That religion was about justice, and it's actually still about that; it just isn't being practiced in the way it was originally intended. It is being practiced by most people that way, but some people are usurping it for other purposes. But you know, that's politics; it doesn't have anything to do with the religion.

Some of the men didn't have a religion or a philosophy; they were just existing the best they could. But my criteria, as you asked, were, did they respond well to my basic philosophy? Did we have a heart connection, did we feel good with each other? It was not unlike the way it is today, when a teacher might pick an apprentice—or an apprentice, for that matter, might pick a teacher: Was there enough agreement and interest in what I was trying to teach that they would want to walk away from their life and come with me? And, most important, *could* they walk away from their life? If they were married and settled and had a family and children, I wouldn't approach them. It's not that I didn't want them; some of the best potentials were people like that, but it would have been outrageous, so I didn't.

I encouraged only people who could to come with me. That's why they were mostly young; they hadn't settled down yet, they didn't have families. Or in the case of some of the women, they were older, their children had grown up and they could come with me for a while. But it was more a revolving group with the women, because they would sometimes come with me for a while, then they would have to go back to their people. So the women came and went, whereas the men, when they joined, would usually be permanent.

So are all the stories we've heard about the disciples also just stories?

Most of that is myth. But they were a lot better than they're portrayed in the Bible. A lot of them were really wonderful: warmhearted, generous, kind, brave, courageous—all kinds of wonderful words. But because of that story of their denying me and so on—that didn't happen, by the way; they were never asked. No one came up to them and said, "Do you know this man?" and all this. That never happened.

So there was no Judas?

There was a person who wanted me to be more authoritarian, but he didn't sell me out for thirty pieces of silver. That didn't happen.

Is there any point in saying what did happen?

I mainly want to say who these people were, not who they weren't.

People Waiting to Be Saved

You've got millions, billions . . . how many people on this planet right now are waiting for you to save them?

Well, they're waiting for *someone* to save them, but that's really to their detriment, isn't it? The whole idea of being saved is a detriment.

Of course, but it's everywhere!

It's pervasive, isn't it?

You have really affected this planet!

Yes; that's perhaps why the Creator was less than enthusiastic about my coming. But He said, "Okay, try it. If it works, wonderful; if it doesn't, then okay." The Creator basically said that. We didn't have this conversation, but this is what it meant: "I'm going to do what I'm going to do, and you can come and do what you want to do. But I'm still going to do what I'm going to do." That was the gist of the agreement.

But did He understand the urgency that if you could not bring this energy to the planet, humans might not survive? Did He understand that?

Yes.

What was His plan?

You'll have to ask Him. I'll give you this: I think He was thinking that you'd just move to another planet. But ask Him.

Move to another planet? Oh, my god! Mother Earth is so much a part of this, in

my understanding. She came here from Sirius to this space. Is that not true?

It certainly would seem to be so.

The Pleasure of Laughter

What gave you the most pleasure during the time you were in the physical body of Jesus?

Laughing. I think laughing was the most pleasure. And telling stories and listening to stories, seeing the children laugh and play—*being* a child laughing and playing. And simple things, simple pleasures, the same pleasures that people like today: being a child, loving and being loved by your parents; having children, raising them (at least for a while) and all those things people like to do.

When you go back to your place of existence, has anyone else there experienced this?

Not that I know of, although one might say that to some extent Mohammed and Buddha have experienced youth and childhood and all this. You'll have to ask them. But not many others there, just those few. Of course, they're interested. They can feel what I've experienced, but of course it's not the same.

Do you have a sense of mission as a result of this? You really care about what's happening here.

I really care, yes. I don't think I'd call it a mission; I care just as much today as I did then.

Is there anything you'd do differently?

If I had it to do over again? Well, it might shock you, but if I had it to do over again, I would probably come and be just an obscure person, not get caught up in the whole big business of it. Just be a quiet carpenter, shepherd, farmer, something like that, and enjoy all the parts of being an Earth person and maybe do a little quiet teaching. But I'd go away, not become well-known—lurking behind the scenes, as it were.

Jesus' Return

The Explorer Race lesson is consequences, so you are feeling at this time and well into the future the consequences of what happened here, right? Are you intermingled or somehow entangled with the Explorer Race?

I wouldn't say that, no.

What would you say?

I don't feel that. I care about you; I don't feel like I did something and now I have to live with the consequences. I'm not part of the Explorer Race.

As you said, it doesn't bother you, but does part of you get pulled close to the planet because your face and your story, even though it's a story, are in so many hearts and lives?

No, because it's not about me. If it were about me, it would.

Ah! Because they are looking at a man who died on the cross, and these stories . . .

It's a myth.

Then what is it? There's an energy there that we call Jesus. What are they tying into, then? Is it just a myth that doesn't pull on you?

It doesn't drain me, it doesn't pull on me, no. It's part of your separation from your god-selves. If it were about me and about my life, I would be closer to you, more involved. But because it isn't about me, I feel almost no identification with it. I don't turn my back on you, but because this isn't about me, I'm not called.

Yet you are coming back in a body, right? Will it be in seventy-five years or when we reach a certain point of evolution, a certain point of opening or a frequency or what?

It might be in seventy-five years, it might be in four hundred years; it depends.

Is it when we reach a certain level of opening?

Yes.

Is there a number on the dimensional scale that Zoosh talks about that you are looking for?

I'm looking for 3.59.

Aha! So 3.59 could be between seventy-five and four hundred years, more or less.

Give a little, take a little.

[Laughs.] All right, I see.

I think that's enough for tonight, all right?

Yes, absolutely. I am so pleased that you are talking to me. We should have a scholar here, someone who's . . .

You know, it's an advantage that we don't, because we'd get caught up in . . . yes, there would be some wonderful questions, but at least half the questions would be about precise things that didn't have to do with me anyway. Any scholar can only study what's known and written in any time.

What survives, yes.

That's right, so even the most educated scholar might be educated in the myth. He might ask me questions that I would reply to, saying, "I didn't do that; it didn't have anything to do with me." And I might not have any great interest in answering those questions.

You're so patient; thank you so much.

Good night.

3

Jesus' Home World, Their Love Creations and the Four Who Visited Earth

Jesus

April 25, 1998

I'd like to open with a little discussion about my place of existence.

Wonderful! I know it makes you laugh to name everything, but is there some combination of syllables that would identify you rather than the core personality you once lived as Jesus?

I'll think about it.

The Place Where I Exist

The place where I exist is a very benevolent, gentle place, as are most places other than where you are, because you are in a very intense school. We must be careful what we think where I exist. Why, you might ask. Consider that for a moment. Because we are all so open to each other, we cannot afford to have thoughts that would be damaging to our other members. This, of course, would not normally come up because we are benevolent beings. Yet those of us like Qua and myself, who are to some extent history buffs, must be very careful. That is why sometimes Qua and I, and occasionally someone else of our people, will step away from the place of our existence in order to fully experience what we've experienced in other places.

The place of my existence is filled with beings who have but one primary function, and that is to create. If we are not careful about what we think, feel and experience in this place, these things that Qua and I have seen and done could affect what the others are doing. Think about it. If you were working someplace where everybody was very carefully making some product and there was some distraction, things might get changed accidentally, though you might not notice it right away. But because what my people are doing involves creation, even if they don't notice it, somebody else will experience the consequences because the threads keep going out all the time to support various creators and their work and, in some cases, individuals.

You have a comparison: Like a computer virus, they won't see it right away and they might not feel it right away because it'll be such a small effect of the greater thread. Yet it will show up at some point and they won't understand: "Where did this come from? What happened?"

So Qua and I are careful, as all historians must be. Your friend Zoosh is very careful what he says to you and to others through you, because if he were less careful, the right thing could be said at the wrong time—or worse. All parents understand this, because there are things you say to a child and things you don't say. If you say some things to a child that the child is not ready to hear or should never be exposed to, the child will be affected, and there's no going back. You can't go back and unsay those things; they've been said. Having been a child, perhaps you all have such experiences of regrets and wishes that things had been different. These experiences are quite universal, because they are experiences in the school and in the testing ground of consequences, which is, as you know, what Earth is about at this time for you all.

I mention this because this place of existence I'm in is so unique. I'm very fond of it. We don't have buildings as you think of them because we don't need shelter. We don't consume food because we are self-sustaining. Without going through everything, if you were to observe it, it's not unlike looking at water, although it is a place where the predominant theme is gold and white light—perhaps more gold than white light, which is readily perceivable. You would see the surface in any place where you might look, but you wouldn't see all that's behind the surface, not unlike when you look at water: You see the surface, but you don't always see the bottom and the fish and the plants in the water and so on. This is intended so that those who do see us in fact or in vision (which is another form of fact) are not overwhelmed by our entirety, but rather see only what they need to see in order to understand about us, at least initially.

You are very much like that; you show just a little bit to people when you meet them so they have some understanding of who and what you are, but you don't show them everything until you get to know them better.

I use that as an example because I'm not going to tell you everything about the place I exist in until I get to know you all better. That's why we might do another book at some point. When I've known you better and when you've perhaps sent in some questions or indicated some themes you'd like me to talk about and explore for you, then I'll know you better and I'll tell you more.

What We Look Like

Let's just start with the look of your place of existence. Do you maintain shapes, like a hundred feet tall or two feet tall, from our perspective? Do you flow and change shape or what?

Pencil, paper? This is a rough example [draws]. Two people, yes?

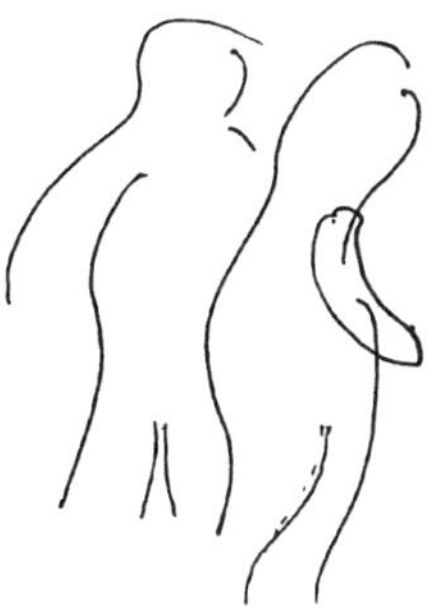

That is Qua [points to each figure] and me also—historians who go places. That's one person.

I misunderstood! I thought everyone in your place became individuals.

Perhaps you didn't misunderstand. The people in my place prefer this binary . . . see, the separation was temporary so that we would understand individuality, but once we understood it, then we returned to our normal state of being.

I didn't understand that.

This is not so unusual; for you it is very simple and similar also. You live a life here, you learn things here, then you return to your normal state of being. So you do not always look like a human being, not like the human being you look like. You learn what you need to learn, then you return to your normal state of being, which for you all is basically a spot of light. If you go from humanoid body directly to another humanoid body, then you might stay in a humanoid lightbody. But after you get through the veils completely, you are basically a spot of light. You are not a humanoid spot of light; you are a spot of light.

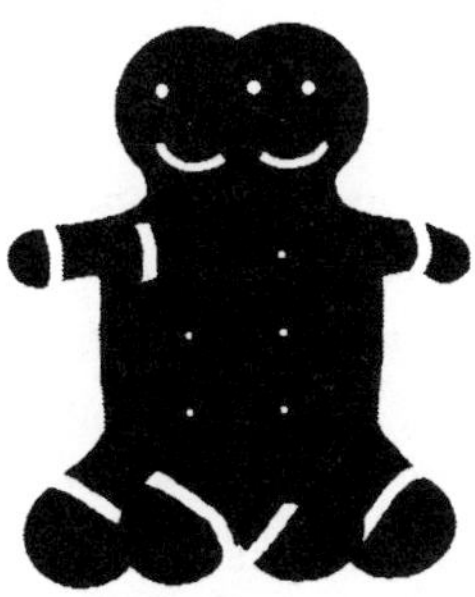

I'm glad you made that clear because I thought everyone on your planet separated permanently.

This drawing is obviously someone in motion—gingerbread person, all right? And then superimpose another one like this.

Two of everything, but sort of joined.

Of course we don't have to look that way, but this is a perfect example of how we are all so connected and why Qua and I do what I said.

When I'm talking to you (you being a humanoid), then my body looks like this—humanoid, what I call a binary humanoid lightbody. And everybody else in my immediate environment looks that way, too.

Really?

Yes, because we are all so closely knit, and the longer I talk to you, the more it spreads. If I talk to you steadily for many years (that's not going to happen), eventually everybody in my place of existence would look like that. Even though they wouldn't feel any different—they would still be themselves—they would look like that.

Say, for instance, that Qua is talking to someone on another planet where they look different; then everybody around Qua would begin to look like that! We are so united that what one does gradually affects everybody. We're not *trying* to affect them; it just happens. That is not uncommon in a totally harmonic civilization. That is why many civilizations are so cautious about contact with you. They know that when their astronauts return home, even if they don't like what they saw, they'll still bring back what they saw in thoughts and pictures, and it will affect others.

Well, that's what's going to happen, so get ready, you guys!

Yes, but it will happen in a slower way. It's intended to happen gently, and it will.

So you separated and became individuals.

For a time, until we understood individuality.

As a frame of reference, how long did this take?

Oh, maybe a million experiential years.

Then what happened?

Then we gradually returned to our normal state of being, just as you do when you pass through the veils. It is simple for you to be in your normal state of being, which is a point of light. I can show you—this is what you all look like normally [draws]. Picture this as light. You're about that big, spherically.

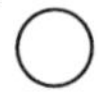

A little spherical point of light, eh?

Yes. That's appropriate, because if you were any bigger, there wouldn't be room for everybody.

This is fascinating. You separated into two, then the other being became an individual and did what it wanted to do. Then you found each other?

Within the harmony of our existence, yes. We didn't have to find each other; remember that as you pass through the veils (my analogy for death), you don't *find* your point of light; you become it gradually. You don't go out, as a spirit, and meet your point of light and join it; you *become* your point of light. Like that, we didn't have to find anybody; we naturally gravitated, as you say, to that person. It would be impossible to blend with someone other than yourself because you would immediately feel that sense of difference—not an incompatibility, but a sense of difference. When you blend with a portion of yourself, you feel it exactly as you; you don't feel any different.

But you did have different experiences during the time of individuality.

Oh, certainly; that's so we could learn and be compassionate toward you, of course.

The point was to be compassionate toward humans?

Eliminating Personal Agendas

The point was really to be patient and compassionate. It is typical for beings who are in a totally harmonious civilization to keep a distance between themselves and those in a disharmonious situation. Yet for people like Qua and myself, who came to be amongst you (and Qua is still doing this sometimes, I think) it was necessary to have no personal agenda. This I have learned, by the way; I didn't think of that at the time when I went in the form of the being you know as Jesus. I did not think of it then, but since then I have considered it. I might add that the reason Qua and I are such good friends is that Qua has suggested to me that having a personal agenda—even if it is the most benevolent—necessarily colors in some way who you are, what you do and how you do it with others.

Oh, absolutely! We all have personal agendas.

Yes. I've spoken to Qua at length about coming back—we discussed that last time—so when I come back with the others, it is absolutely essential that we have no personal agendas, that we just come back and serve your needs without trying to teach anything you don't ask about.

That's very difficult to do.

I've had time to think about that, and I've decided that's exactly right; otherwise we could just repeat my experience. Qua is a wise being, with perhaps a little more understanding of the responsibilities of a historian.

[Laughs.] Yes, he was very clear about not being attached, connected, associated with us so that no one would miss him or call on him or anything.

Yes, he's very respectful of individual needs of beings in your place of existence. That's why he'll do things with groups. He's particularly fond of going to parks with his church group, I think; they go to parks.

But he was quite careful to also say that the reason for it was so that beings wouldn't pull on his energy or cause him to remain near the Earth when he left.

Yes, but also, of course, so they wouldn't miss him. Let's say you are missing someone, for good cause. You will invariably miss opportunities in your life because you are distracted by that. Things might happen that you would normally notice, but because you are missing someone you don't notice them. This happens to you all the time, but he didn't want to add to that. He felt it would not be appropriate.

Individual Golden Light

You were binary, then suddenly you were individual, and you didn't cause it.

We didn't cause it.

That assumes that someone did, but you don't know who?

It certainly assumes that; I do not know who, no. I do not think that anybody else in my place of existence knows, but it is possible. I'm thinking about it now, and I think there is another individual who does know. This being is on the other side of my place of existence, and perhaps at some point we could hear from that being.

Qua said that he doesn't know who created him; he had always been. But Isis said that your beings created constants, ***beings who would always be constant.***

That makes sense.

What I've learned from talking to beings about you is that gold light implies prior experience, so gold light must come from someplace.

We seem to generate it; that I've noticed. And gold light, not unlike other forms of light that has an effect . . . to me, white light is more like food; it is unconditional love, but it is also that which nurtures. Other light does something; I think that the white light nurtures us. You could say that it feeds us, and from that feeding is produced gold light. I have seen this as a functional effect.

Does it stay within your place of existence, or does it go out to feed some other level?

It stays within our place of existence, with the possible exception of when threads are sent out, in which case different forms of light are encoded in the thread so that the thread will be noticed.

Our 360-Some Love Creations

There are so many interesting things here. Right now all we know about is the creations that you and your fellow beings created. We call them flavors of love or different versions of love, one of which created this vast experimental creation for the purpose, I understand, of creating the Explorer Race.

Yes.

Have you beings created other creations besides these different Loves?

No, only this, because we felt that they were vast enough and had the capacity to grow bigger on their own. We also felt that were we to be too involved as creators ourselves, we could not serve the creators who are truly the ones we intend to serve. In a way, you could say that we're really creating receptacles for these love creations, which start out like an empty tennis ball, if you would, but much bigger, of course. And these receptacles are biased to the extent that they are factors of love.

Name them; we only know this one and one called Harmony. What are the different biases?

I can't name them all, but I'll name a few: one is Tone; one is Rhythm (pulse isn't quite it, rhythm is more like it). One is kind of visual—you've seen joints, where things come together at a joint?

Yes.

It's like that.

For the purpose of . . .

. . . anything in that theme.

A joint, a connection . . .

. . . where things come together. I can only tell you the ones that make sense to you, so I'm skipping a lot. One is like an engine, an engine of creation. All that happens inside it is the creation of energy that supports creators, from the greatest to the smallest. There's another one I could call Focus. The last one I will call Youth.

How many Love factors are there? Can you give a rough idea?

Oh, about 360; the others, are too obscure for you to even grasp.

Well, I guess we've got enough book material for the next few years [laughs]. As a group, you created these consciously.

Oh, yes, and we created them in such a way that they are essentially autonomous. Thus we do not have to serve them. They are spheres, if I can use that term (sometimes they're not spherical), meaning a sphere of influence. Because they are a core or a facet of Love, they don't need much looking after; they can generate for themselves. In this way we can serve the needs of Creator. But we created this so that there would be something to start with, at least in our part of existence. I have no reason to assume that there aren't other vast arrays of creation potential in other places. This place of my existence and all the space (if I can call it that) where all these 360-some dimensions—sometimes 361, sometimes up to 363 (depending on how you count them, because once you get past the thirty-fourth or thirty-fifth dimension, I tend to not count those) . . . this whole space is what I'm aware of. I do not know if there is more, but my assumption is that there is. Nevertheless, this is our . . .

. . . playground [laughs]. So how long had you been conscious as beings? You were binary when you got the idea to create these, so where did the concept of the threads come from?

Wait, one question at a time. I can only give it to you by comparison, because years are useless at this point. I will say, in terms of the length of our existence—and this is very relative, since we have always existed—but to give you some kind of numerological comparison, it is only in the last one hundred thousandth of our existence that we created these things.

So what did you do all the time before that?

Existed and did other things, most of which would not relate to anything understandable here.

Okay, but you gathered vast experience—could you say that?

Yes, I like the way you said that. We gathered vast experience; that's nicely said.

Sending out the Threads

Once you created the Loves, then you started sending the threads to support and advise the creators?

We started that a little bit before. We sent them out. We didn't see anything out there, but we had no reason to assume there wasn't, so we started sending threads out. If I must put years on it, then I will just say that in terms of the existence of all of these Loves, that time, times one and a half before their creation, we were starting to send these threads out. I suppose one might say that it was a desire to become aware of what was happening that certainly influenced us to create these Loves. In this way we would be able to have some cognition of our impact or influence and so on. Yet I can see all the threads we sent out before that, and they're still going somewhere.

[Laughs.] None of them ever made contact with anything?

No, I think some of them did make contact, but I can't see where they are. All the ones we've sent out are still going except two; two of them have stopped. I think that nothing has been created yet, but someone must be considering creating something because they're not moving anymore.

Excellent! That's something to look into later. So the Loves were in existence for this very, very long time of creating. Then this one Love we're in said, "There's no change, no growth. We need to create something." Or did you come up with that idea?

No, they're autonomous. That being decided that something needed to be changed, and we didn't say no. We said, "Well, we have created this being in the most benevolent way, and if this being wishes to change something, then fine."

Dangerous Negativity on Earth and a Helping Response

So everything got created. Then we come to the present time minus 2000 years, and this planet was not going to make it because of the extreme negativity, which would not only have impacted the Explorer Race, but the negative Sirians.

It's an interesting thing that in those days there weren't as many people as there are in your time. Even so, Mother Earth wasn't ready for it, because there was too much conflict, control, suppression and manipulation and not enough love and tenderness. It was perhaps because in those times the polarized masculine principle was very dominant. It wasn't the only thing happening on Earth, but it was dominant and it was spreading. And Mother Earth, being primarily a feminine being, could not accommodate it.

Now the most important question of all: In your incredibly, vast place of existence, with all these beings who think alike, why you? You came to save this planet and the people.

Well, I wouldn't say they all think alike. They're all individuals up to a point, but we are all affected by what others of our kind think and consider. However, we do not have a group mind.

I didn't realize there was that much individuality there.

Oh yes, there is individuality, but I told you the precautions that must be taken.

Yes. But you chose to do something about it. Why?

Well, perhaps I was a bit impetuous, but I felt it was worth the effort, and I knew that other efforts were going on at the same time by other spiritual beings on other parts of the Earth. Things had been done before I got there, but I felt that there was still such a serious risk of human existence being eliminated from Mother Earth's surface that I just felt I had to. I couldn't turn my back on it. I am fond of you all, and I felt that I had to do something. So I did what I did; if I had it to do over, I would have done it differently, but [laughs] . . .

But you would still do it.

But I would still do it, yes.

Because the important thing, you said, was to anchor the energy.

Yes; I had to do *something*, I had to put down the seeds. I do not regret it, but I would have been more innocuous if I were able to do it over.

Less passionately . . . what?

Less involved as a public figure and much, much more behind the scenes. As you know, even in your time what is done behind the scenes is usually infinitely more influential.

You wanted to experience death, and you so loved this world and the people that you gave yourself to them?

What it is, is that I so loved the people of the Earth that I needed to understand the fear of death. That's why I suspended briefly the bulk (not all) of my consciousness during my death experience—so that I could completely understand.

Why do we get this quote, then? Is that part of the politics that implied a hierarchy?

Yes, because that would suggest . . . just think about it: If I was His only begotten son, then what are all the other sons? Are they not also sons and daughters of the Creator? Of course they are.

But it put you above them so that we could not attain what you did. That was the political move, right?

That was political, yes. It was what I would call a well-intended error, and those who did it now understand it was a mistake. But those political battles often happen; things are said in the moment to preserve what you believe, then sometimes you have to live with the consequences.

Going up the Line

Did you come alone, or with other spirits?

I'd have to say that I came on my own. No one comes on their own, of course; you always have other spirits who come with you. For everyone who is born, their guides come with them through the veils and so on, so I can't really say that I came alone, but . . .

So even as a conscious being, you had guides while you were in the physical?

Yes. I wanted to experience the human experience as much as I could, so when guides said, "Do you want us to come with you?", I said, "This is what you do for the average being, yes?" And they said, "Oh, yes, and we will come with you if you wish it." They were polite, and I said, "Yes, please; I want that."

But they didn't need to do for you what they do for us behind the veil?

Correct, yes; I didn't have to take a circuitous course through the veils so that later I wouldn't leave.

Every being I've talked to up until now has always had the ability, when they didn't know something, to turn around and ask. You and Qua are the first ones who do not routinely go up the line to ask somebody.

No, we do not. If we need something, we feel first into our own people to see if they have it. If it is necessary, what they have will be passed through our people to us as an individual rather than our having to connect to the other one and so on.

So you've never had a problem that you couldn't solve from information or knowledge within your own group?

Well, we aren't often questioned. This questioning process that we are doing together here is unusual. Creators come and ask about this or that, or occasionally individuals come, and we can answer. If I cannot answer to the satisfaction of the inquirer, then others will chime in or the inquirer will go someplace and ask others. But this circumstance is different, because you are not only an individual with curiosities, but you are the representative of the reader.

Why do we need this process? You're perfectly capable of talking for book after book after book about fascinating things.

Because as a representative of the reader, you represent the needs of the reader, and these needs must be fulfilled as a priority over and above what *I* might think you need to know at this time. Your actual needs, then, are served.

I think that places too much stress on my limited understanding. Do that, but also feel free to say what interests you.

I'll bring it up if there seems to be an opening to do so.

The Beings Who Have Come Here

You are still interested in the Earth and you plan to come back, and Qua is also sort of in and out here. What about the other two, Buddha and Mohammed? Are they back in your place of existence?

Yes.

They're not interacting here?

No, but they will come.

Yes, they'll come with you. How are all of you changed by this experience? You're different from the other beings now, aren't you?

We're different, but because we are blended together, the differences have to some degree influenced the others, but not so much as to disrupt their creative work cycle.

We're different in that we've had the shared mutual experience of living amongst human beings and serving their needs in the best way we knew how at the time. To be unique where we exist is an accepted factor, but to have an elite or an exceptional group does not serve our beings in this place of existence. So we do not pal around (this term might be from the forties or fifties) so much.

So you don't spend a lot of time or have a lot of social interaction or conversation with Buddha and Mohammed.

No, but then we don't have social interaction and conversation with anybody, really. Our communication is more . . .

Felt.

Felt, yes; nicely said. We don't have any extra time with each other; we just have our entire felt experience. Of course, when we return to the Earth in the future we will have perhaps more focus in individual experience together.

Creating the Threads and the Loves

You say you work; how do you create these threads? Do groups get together? Does someone come up with an idea and it's sort of communicated to all? How does the process work?

We are primarily taken as a unit, a feeling being. One could describe our entire population by saying, "*They* are a feeling *being*." Yet it is our capacity to feel that stimulates the thread. We do not sit down and think about it and discuss what would be good; we *feel*. It is possible that we are feeling something associated with a need somewhere. Then the thread (and I'm using the term "thread" because that's the established term now) is created slowly and lovingly of compressed light, not compressed too far, just enough so that it maintains a body integrity and also what I would call creation factors. It would be like an artist creating a sculpture without looking at it: simply putting your hands in the clay with your eyes closed and allowing your hands to move around entirely on the basis of your feelings, without any directed intention.

That's how it's done. When the thread is completed, there is no more feeling to add anything to it. They sit there for a little time, and if there is no more feeling to add anything, then it is lovingly launched.

But you said you created it to satisfy a need.

A *felt* need.

A felt need, but all those eons before you created the Loves, was there was no one for you to feel?

There was nothing we could perceive, but since we felt a need, the feelings we were getting to send these things out would be either future needs or what I mentioned to you, an extrapolation, something beyond what we are able to know. And that's where these things are going—to that beyond place we don't know about. So it is an act of faith, which is really the story of our entire existence. Our entire existence is based on faith in each other and faith in what we feel and hence what we do.

That is incredible! To satisfy the needs of those you'll never know. Most people want a more personal response. That is an incredibly loving and, as you say, trusting process.

People where you are want a more personal or immediate response because you don't have the conscious connection to all that you are. When you have that (and you can be connected to many things), that immortality can be trusted to inform you, or for you to become informed, should you wish to advocate that knowledge for yourself at some point when it becomes what it will. But because you feel mortal and you feel that your time is limited, you desire more instantaneous results.

Patience, Compassion and Intentional Benevolence

You said something very interesting: You felt the purpose for your becoming individual rather than binary was to learn patience and compassion toward humans?

Yes, because it is so easy for people, even people like myself, to become impatient with human beings—not as individuals, but as . . . let's call it the human collective experience over thousands of years. It's very easy to get impatient when you do not see any evidence of an evolution of some benevolent intended purpose over many thousands of years. It's easy to get impatient; that's why it is necessary to live in the circumstances that human beings live in so you can understand the concept on a practical-experience level of limits. We cannot understand limits on a practical experiential level, but Qua and myself and Buddha and Mohammed have all experienced limits as human beings, and therefore we are much more compassionate and patient with human beings. That energy, those feelings, have now blended quite well with the rest of us here as far as I am able to tell.

That's interesting, too! What you four beings have experienced, as you said, has radiated into all of you, into your one being.

To some extent—the feelings, not the details. Therefore all the beings here now are patient and compassionate and do not grow impatient even when no shred of evidence supports your evolution to toward the *intentionally* benevolent.

You see, for you to be *unintentionally* benevolent (without trying to be) is your natural state of being; but in order to be benevolent in this world where you experience mortality, you must be *intentionally* benevolent in order to be so. It has to be a conscious act. You can be supplied with a great deal of your immortal benevolence once you consciously strive to be that way, but the consciousness must be there. Otherwise you can have all this benevolence waiting to flow into you, but without a way to express it because no intentions are there; therefore it does not flow in. If it did, it would be interfering.

Why the Interest in Humanity?

Here you are, the creators of 360-some Loves—vast, incredible beyond our com-

prehension—yet you are focused on one little tiny microscopic part of this little tiny creation, on the human race. Why?

I understand; I am speaking for my people. We are focused on you because you are so unlike us in this moment; you are so unlike *you* in this moment. Because of that, we have great compassion for you and your experience. All that I and all the others who have experienced mortality as humans can do is just imagine what it would be like to be cut off from our totality. I get a lonely feeling immediately. Because we not only appreciate what you're doing, what you're contributing—and yes, what you're sacrificing—we are devoted to your moment-to-moment existence in supporting you through this Herculean challenge of existence.

So it's not just because of what you *will* do; it's because of the *conditions* in which you exist to learn what you must learn. And what you must learn you can learn only in these exact conditions. If people on your planet do not consciously choose benevolence, then we will have to wait until you do. The conscious choice is required because everyone, without exception, has more benevolence waiting for you from all your other incarnations and beings and friends and guides and loved ones than you could possibly apply. But by choosing consciously to do so, you then create the exact timing that states, "This is the moment." We have great faith in your collective choice of timing.

If I were to say, "This is the right moment"—which I did [chuckles]—I would be interfering with this choice. If, on the other hand, I were to say, "I have faith in your collective choice," then I will be able to give and do what I can until that occurs.

Your collective choice will not take place in an instant, where everybody chooses. Collective means that some people choose and some people don't, but eventually, in at least one moment, everyone will be synchronously choosing that. It is that moment we have faith in. Because you are all striving toward this great consciousness, that moment will coincide with the exact, precise timing of future events and be the optimum moment for that choice. That's why we have faith in you; that's why we pay attention to you, because we have faith that that optimum moment is entirely keyed into the future outcome of all you are doing and all that will be done as a result of what you are doing. To put it simply, we have decided to wait until that happens.

What will occur when that moment of consciously choosing benevolence happens for all of us?

Then you will begin to move forward quickly in the dimensional shift.

The Seed Beings of the Explorer Race

At what point in this Creator's creation did you begin to actually pay attention to the Explorer Race? And do you call it the Explorer Race?

I think it's a fun term, the Explorer Race. I, and I think my fellow historians started paying attention when you, as the seed or core beings of the Explorer Race [see *The Explorer Race and Beyond*], started your journey toward this place where you would ultimately meet your Creator, whom you would work with.

Where did we come from? No one has told us up to this point. Where do you see us coming from?

I can't tell you where all your individual factors came from, but . . .

There were three to start with, the two companions and then the Storyteller.

I believe that two of you came from different facets of Love creations and one from someplace else.

Do you know where that someplace else is?

It seems to go past the point of my vision.

Is that the Storyteller?

Yes, which makes sense, because stories are the root of creation. They are also the result of creation.

We talked to the seed beings . . .

It would be good to talk to the Storyteller at some point, who will undoubtedly answer most of your questions with stories.

Ah, that's good. If we do that in the future, we have a much wider map of the infinite to deal with.

Yes, there are more keys on your piano.

[Laughs.] Good. So you began watching the three seeds or roots or core beings and then you understood the significance.

Yes.

Because you had originally created the idea, even though Love focused on it. Do you see it that way, that you had created the original thread that started it all?

We had done that, yes.

When the Suffering Started

When the negative feelings and the suffering started, how did you react then? What were your thoughts?

We were compassionate, perhaps not as much as we are now. We were not surprised. If you cut beings off from the totality of their being, they are going to have to learn everything all over again, at least the basics. No one was surprised. We pulled back a bit so we wouldn't be affected by it. It would have been surprising had anything else occurred. To be clearer, it would have been surprising if that had *not* occurred.

In your awareness, then, this has never been done before, where beings cut themselves off from their totality?

Not for such a length of time or where that condition would perpetuate for so long—in this case, not for an individual but for a group over years, or where it would be an accepted planetary theme to be cut off, at least as a human Explorer Race member. (One is not cut off if one is a cat person.)

A Cat's Role

For the sake of the reader, the cat that is nearby [Tiger] knows all its previous existences completely and has a pretty good idea about future existences. It can receive advice and even consult and give advice to others on his lineage. In the case of cat, lineage would not be considered blood lineage, but all cats everywhere.

And from this great depth of wisdom he still goes out to fight the neighboring tomcat.

But he is on Earth! He must live in ways that cats live on Earth; he must accept it even though it is not in his personality. His immortal personality is very peaceful; he's the philosopher. That's why he likes all this [the channeling sessions], kind of checks in once in a while. It is required that he do things Earth-style, meaning that very often what cats do in their fighting (as you say, being territorial) is primarily intended to be lessons for human beings. What all animals do to each other that is violent all has to do with lessons for human beings. It is not in their nature to be violent to each other. I am ruling out, of course, eating necessities and such; but to be abstractly violent—for a cat to go out and kill a bird—it is not in their actual personalities to do that. But being here on Earth with human beings, they must do things, accept them and even embrace them as having something to do with what they're trying to teach or show human beings. And sometimes they're not aware of it.

When a cat kills a bird, what is it trying to teach a human being?

Most individual cats don't know why, but they accept it as something they must do in order to be here. On other planets, if they looked like they look here (they don't usually), they would be amongst the birds and there would be no problem. But here it is often about reminding human beings; it depends on which human beings are nearby. These lessons are usually done for individuals; they're not what I would call collective lessons.

To take an example (not from this cat—I don't want to invade his privacy—but a cat a few houses down), a cat killed a bird not too long ago because a dog needed to see it. This was so the dog could have the pictures of it and go into the house and be around the people. The people never saw the cat do that; they had no idea. The dog is so beloved in their household that the people would be more likely to pick up the event or the feelings associated with it from the dog than from the cat. I'm not going to say what their lesson was because they might read this someday.

How interesting! As the suffering really intensified, not only on this planet but on the planet of the negative Sirians—due to the policy of noninterference, you couldn't do anything, right? You just had to watch it?

We had to assume that it was all part of something you were doing. Why would we interfere with something you were doing? In our consciousness, our beliefs, yes, we believe that even if you are unconscious of your total being, your total being is conscious of you—and you are still connected to that total being even though it is primarily a one-way connection, at least while you are awake, anyway. When you are asleep it becomes two-way; you communicate to your total beings, they communicate to you and so on. But while you are awake it is different. We could not conceive that your total beings would allow such a thing to occur unless there was some good reason for it, so why would we even consider interfering?

That's an act of faith! [Laughs.]

Faith is the core resonance of our being. If people live entirely in harmony and do everything because of feelings, faith must be their bedrock foundation.

My Return

Your total focus is not on humans, so when you went back after being an encapsulated human, even though consciously, did your life change?

I took my time to get back so that I could let go of some things. Qua came partway to meet me and we experienced things together. Being resilient in his exposure to different beings, the exchange would not be harmful for Qua; therefore it allowed me to have a companion in my travel to my place. We took our time.

Where did you go?

Oh, we just traveled slowly. We didn't go for a rest stop someplace; we just traveled slowly and I experienced things—some of which were uncomfortable, some of which were wonderful—and Qua would resonate them for me. We're getting into areas now that may not be readily understandable.

That's all right, we can stretch.

It wasn't a conversation as you understand it; our communication was a resonance-to-resonance and resonance-from-resonance experience.

In our terminology, did that help you release things you wanted to release and integrate what you wanted to keep? Something like that?

Something like that, so that when I got back to our place of existence I would not be brimming with the experience.

As it was, you were still fairly full of it and radiating it, right?

I was not so full of it [chuckles] that I would radiate to the others.

But that was the goal.

Yes. Qua and I both released excess feelings before we got back so that no one would be distracted from what they were doing.

But then you resumed your existence.

Slowly. I gave myself time to just be.

Even now, do you think differently? Is there anything different in your life because of this experience?

I am more patient.

Is it true you married Mary Magdalene? In another session I'd like to go a little more into your life here . . .

Oh yes, certainly.

. . . and talk about Mary.

Yes, and the women, too.

Individuality and Curiosity

So everybody is individual in your place of existence, in the sense that different people see and know different things.

The best analogy is this: Think of all the different notes in a symphony. All the notes are unique, yet when they are played together in harmony (and we live in harmony), they are a beautiful composition.

You say you don't take time socially; you only learn from each other what you need to know at a given time, right?

We are not ignorant. We know each other thoroughly, so we don't go to the coffee shop and talk. The only reason that Qua and I do things together, and sometimes Mohammed and I, is that when either one of us or the others need to experience something, we radiate something, have it radiated back and perhaps release something that would not be good for the whole. I don't consider this socializing so much as assisting each other.

What I was getting at was that different beings have had different experiences that are uniquely theirs . . .

Yes.

. . . so there is an almost unlimited amount you can learn from each other—if you

desire it or if you need to? There are things that different beings know. How can I say this?

Let me say this. A piccolo and a flute are cousins, wouldn't you say?

Yes.

They do not need to emulate each other because they already complement each other. Even though their experience is different, they still function the same way: with air. So you might say that their experience or what they know is different, yet it is complementary. So must a piccolo completely understand a flute in order to play in harmony with it?

No, it's just that someone with curiosity wants to know if . . .

Curiosity is as strong as it is here because of the veils; but when there are no veils, though curiosity is present, it is just not urgent.

I see. You are all unique. Let's say that a creator or some being comes for counseling—you said that Lao-tzu once came to talk to you all. Where did he come from? One of the Loves?

No.

We're getting lots of things from someplace else here.

Someplace else, yes. I think your Lao-tzu is really a creator who manifested as a person, but not from our place. He didn't come from our place of existence.

Where did he come from?

You'll have to discuss that with him.

Okay. Let's say a creator comes for counseling; how does it choose whom to talk to? You say they don't talk, but . . .

They approach our place of existence with their needs, and even before they get to our actual place of existence, their needs are already being fed by feelings responding to their needs. When our feelings radiate to them, they are then inspired or just know what they will do. So communication, then, is based entirely on the feeling level. It is not unlike having a conversation with a teacher, then thinking about it and perhaps dreaming at night. Maybe two weeks later, for example, you're certain the answer is there. It's because of the conversation with the teacher, if not directly, then indirectly. The teacher said something that caused you to think of something else and so on.

The Council of Creators and Love's Creation deal with creators, but none of them even mentioned you, so they seem to get their guidance from Love itself.

Yes.

So is it mostly the Love creators, then, who come to you?

Anybody might come. Sometimes they come from other places, sometimes they come from different aspects of Love. We have not met everyone, have you?

If they come from places other than the Love creations, is there a feeling connection to where they're from?

We don't need to know that.

Ah, that's the key.

Why do we need to know that? It would be like needing to know why we are creating the threads. I will tell you this: There is a question that drives the human race that we do not experience. What is that question?

Why?

That's it! We don't need to know why; we already know why. When something is working for you, *why* is not the question. *What* might be the question, or *when, where*—all of these things—but *why*, no.

All right, I understand.

It's like asking a bird why it flies.

[Chuckles.] That's good. What would you like to say now?

That's enough; I think I was sufficiently philosophical, ending with a conundrum and amusement.

You are delightful.

Thank you.

4

The "Facts" of Jesus' Life Here, His Future Return

Zoosh and Jesus

April 28, 1998

Zoosh: Greetings.

I'll make a brief comment on the book. And that's that the being who is the core of the one known as Jesus is having and experiencing the long view of Earth and its circumstances these days, though he can encompass only the short view for his time on Earth. What is typical to beings, no matter how broad they may be, is that in order to understand and communicate about anything they've experienced or might experience, they require some personal connection. He has a personal connection with that time when he was here and he'll have a personal connection with the time when he returns, but in terms of his comments on contemporary things, he can comment only from a distance. Understanding that would be a great benefit for the reader.

I'll say good evening and let that being step in.

Jesus: All right, good evening. What shall we discuss tonight?

The "Facts" of the Jesus Story

What about some of the things that are called facts? Were you born through the normal Earth process?

Yes.

There was no special virgin birth or artificial insemination by ETs or anything like that?

No. It was important to come through woman the way all Earth people do, otherwise I could not in any way identify with Earth life. It is typically assumed that if an individual such as myself has some capacity to comment on things, every experience can be fully understood, even without having been lived. But in my experience and in the experience of those whose wisdom I respect, the best way to understand and to connect with those you are most interested in—as I was interested in the Explorer Race, the people here—is to experience to the best of your capacity what they experience. So it was essential for me to be born in the typical fashion. I believe that in later years, *not at the time*, that [story] was added in order to make that being seem more wonderful. I'm referring to the being known as Jesus. But it was not claimed at the time.

How old were Joseph and Mary when you were born?

Oh, they were typical of the time. I think he was in his early twenties and she was about seventeen. That was typical for the time; one must remember that people didn't live as long then. After all, you could catch something that today wouldn't require much more than an aspirin or some cough syrup—and that would be the end then.

What about the stories about Mary's mother and the special circumstances and the angels coming. Was Mary born normally?

Mary of the Magdalene or the mother?

The mother.

She was born in the normal circumstance.

So even those stories are not true.

Well, I wouldn't say they weren't true. Let's just say that some may have been visions of the time, but I'd say that for the most part a lot of this has to do with either visions or, in the case of "miracles," some of these were added later to underscore the value of what that being had to say. You can have the greatest philosophies in your time, but they are lost in the thunder of words from every direction. In those times, philosophy—how to live and so on—was a luxury.

People didn't stand on the street corner and say, "Repent! The end is near!" They were spending most of their time trying, as they say, to keep body and soul together, to provide for their families and survive as best they could. In those times, philosophy was a luxury. The people who could consider or ponder the value of philosophy, not unlike today, have the time to do so. So philosophy was not the available thing in those days. One did not have the time for it unless one was very wealthy, which was not common. What I am saying is this: It is not surprising, then, that people would have to create miracles, impossibilities associated with a being, in order to stop people in their tracks and say, "Look! Pay attention, this is important!" A virgin birth might get someone's attention. He never claimed it—excuse me for saying "he." Should I say "I"?

"He" is fine.

He never claimed it, never. He never said anything like that, never said that he was God, never said that he was the son of God—never. In the tradition into which he was born it would have been grounds for . . . well, not punishment so much, but he would have been considered mad, insane, and it would have been an instantaneous reason to have paid no attention.

These stories are around many ancient avatars. It's as if they took old stories and attached it to Jesus' life.

That's an astute comment on your part, because these old stories all say one thing, and that's that somebody greater than you is here to help you pay attention. That's it. But it is, in my experience and certainly in the experience of others who have guided me, to note only that often the most valuable things to understand are those that fit in your life. That's why Jesus made a point to speak in parables. That was true; he would tell stories. People liked stories then and they like stories now. He would tell a story typical of the time, then he would solve it within the context of the philosophy that was being promoted. It's pretty much the same today. If you were to meet him in those times, you'd say, "a wise man worth knowing," period, no more.

What was his physical appearance?

Not untypical to the people in the area—who, of course, were out in the sun all the time—his skin was fairly dark. It certainly wasn't blond and fair; one could not walk about in the desert [chuckles] or outside all the time, as any blond, fair person knows, and be safe in those conditions. He was Middle Eastern in his appearance; he had a beard, naturally.

About how tall?

Oh, perhaps about five foot three, something like that—not very tall, but not untypical to the time. People were shorter then.

We printed a cover for the magazine some years ago [April 1994] showing Jesus as blond or redheaded, you know, fair, tall . . .

No. It doesn't take too much stretch of an imagination to imagine where that image came from.

Northern Europe! [Laughs.]

Yes. If you take someone as your god, you like the idea that they might have some resemblance to you. But I would say, not to put too fine a point on it, that his skin was fairly dark. To describe his appearance, I suppose he would have looked Arabic, as you might say, but with darker skin. If you have seen a picture of Bedouins, he looked not unlike that. Thin, naturally; you didn't see people very often who were other than thin back in those days. And not a bad-looking person. Longer hair, of course—everybody had that.

The Shroud

What about the Shroud of Turin, which is currently in* Time *magazine—the burial cloth he was buried in?

He wasn't buried in that.

The carbon-14 dating is to about 1300.

I will support the scientists on that one.

It has nothing to do with Jesus.

No. It is associated with a being of great wisdom and all of that, but it has nothing to do with that being. I don't know much about it, but you could ask Zoosh. Yes, I will definitely support science there. If you look at the features, they don't fit for the time and place. The features are actually more European.

Yes. I have a picture of it. There seems to be something magic about the shroud, because it's like a negative photographic image. We'll find out what it really is. You say asking Zoosh would be the best way?

Or anybody else. I would ask for the best person who can talk about it. I'd say that it is perhaps enigmatic, but it's simply not associated with that being at that time. Perhaps this is why the church is not claiming that it is; they have never claimed that in recent years. In times gone by, they might have allowed that belief to be fostered and encouraged, but they haven't done much to encourage it in recent times.

The Messiah Idea; John the Baptist

Look at the tradition of the peoples then—not just the Jewish peoples, but all the peoples of the time, possibly ruling out the Romans, since their messiah had already come (though I'm using "messiah" in their terms, their caesar). They didn't think of him as a messiah. Their leader was with them, so they weren't waiting for anybody else. But it was typical at the time to be waiting for someone to, if not rescue you, at least explain life to you. So people, just as they do today, were consistently saying, "Someone is coming, and he'll be here any time." It wasn't much different. I think you'll find that so-called John the Baptist is more of a composite of people.

Do you know of what people?

A general composite.

Of many people who were out there saying, "He is going to come"?

Yes. "He's going to come and he's going to explain everything to us" and all the things that people wanted at that time. Nowadays people will say, "Repent, because he's coming," but that is a distortion, that repent part.

All these lovely stories that have someone cutting off John the Baptist's head are . . .

I wouldn't call it a lovely story, but I know what you mean. It is, as they say politely in academic circles, unprovable. That's a nice way to put it. I'm not here really to say this isn't so and that isn't so. I'm here rather to say that in those times it was hard to get people's attention about important things that needed to be said and understood. And the best way to do it was to *create* facts, a tapestry in a story. I'd rather say that three to five different people said, "He's coming" and so on. But the story, "They cut off his head and put it on a tray"—no, all that came later.

Well, humans are imaginative people; that's one of our qualities, right? [Laughs.]

Yes, and it is part of being adaptive to the imaginative. And because human beings are adaptive to a wide range of conditions—just look at the planet—being imaginative is an advantage. And really, to know the so-called "facts" of the situation, what really happened, is significantly less important.

Look around your world today. Some things are good, very good, but many things need to be improved before we start worrying about the "facts" of any situation. People need to be clothed and fed and have good work to do that they like or is interesting or intriguing or, for some, challenging, if that's what they like. I don't have to tell you that many things need to be resolved, and the facts are perhaps not as critical.

So if people change the story, I am not upset with that. I grant that there were some changes in later years that corrupted the whole point. But in your time this also happens, where something will occur as a fact, yet to hear it being told by this one or that one, it is hard to imagine what the truth is, what really happened. Ultimately, people have to decide for themselves, and it is best to do so on the basis of who they are in the most benevolent way.

So you grew up and became what your people called a rabbi? You were an initiate or anointed one or . . .

Teacher and Carpenter

They didn't say *rabbi;* that was added later as a term to give consistency. More likely they would say *teacher.*

So you were a teacher. But were you trained and made your living as a carpenter because they didn't really pay the teacher?

Oh, I see. Yes, a carpenter—a good job, honest work then as now. But I might add, we didn't have nails like you have now—very impressive.

[Laughs.] Have you seen the electric saws and electric screwdrivers?

Too fast for me. I like the slow massaging of the wood. But things have picked up apace since that time.

Am I right that they didn't pay the teacher and you did that as an avocation, but you had to support yourself otherwise?

Money, as you understand it, as a medium of exchange, was not so common in general in those days. You traded or bartered for what you needed, or more likely you would do some work for someone and they would give you something you needed. Or they would provide you that thing you needed for a while if they had enough of it, or if they couldn't, then one of their relatives would. In that way everybody got what they needed and everyone was taken care of—a good system still in practice today in many places.

As a teacher, you didn't collect donations or offerings or anything, so you mostly had to support yourself, right?

No more or less than anybody else in that time. But yes, in terms of teaching, if the teacher is saying things of interest, someone else might provide the food if they have enough and if they are interested in what you are saying. But it wasn't that they would give money for the teaching and then you'd go to the store and buy what you needed. Money was useless to the average person; you couldn't do anything with it.

It existed in rarified circles, but it had almost no use for the average man or woman. What could you do with it? You couldn't eat it.

Tell me about being a master teacher. Where does it start? At your place of existence where you are creators, you know everything . . .

Please, not to say we know everything. We know what we know, but "everything" is a lot. Let's just say we know what we know, and we might *seem* like we know everything, but we really don't.

Life before Earth

What other training did you have before you came to Earth? Can you talk about that? Because that's your real interest and your real value.

For a long time before I came to Earth, I was watching what some of my fellow beings were doing on other planets in other places, working with other people. I'll grant that I might have jumped to a conclusion that was not accurate in terms of being on the Earth, because most of my fellow beings were working with civilizations that were benevolent, not self-conflicted. As a result, the smallest amount of advice or guidance was necessary in order to provide the direction or just a nuance of direction. I was particularly interested in how to communicate to different individuals.

Other beings from your place or existence, then, are going out to teach and share their wisdom with other planets in different Loves' creations?

Yes, we teach and share very many of the Loves' creations. In some cases there is a desire by whoever the creator is to not have any outside influences, so of course no one goes there, but for the most part teachers are generally welcome. If you think about being in such an environment as I am, where my fellow beings are very often teachers, the assumption within the context of my environment is that teachers are welcome. I don't want to say I'm raised with this, because we have always been. But before my experience on Earth, my assumption and belief was that teachers are welcome, and to the extent that I had observed what others of my people had done going out to other places, the less and more subtly the teachers work with the people, the better. But coming to such a place as this, I knew that I would often have to be more than just subtle.

But you had looked at Buddha, because Mohammed hadn't come yet.

I had looked at various teachers who had come, regardless of their source, and realized that in order to have any kind of impact that was worthy of you, it would be necessary to be more than subtle because the influences on your society and your individual life were more than subtle.

So you watched; even on this planet you watched.

I watched the teachers and I thought, What I am seeing is good, but I am going someplace where people have not developed much of a university kind of structure. Even in Buddha's time, Buddha wanted to bring the wisdom he was developing to everyone, and until he gave up on that and was comfortable that it would get out in its own time, he was frustrated about it. I felt exactly the same way as Buddha; I wanted to bring it to everyone. But since there was no establishment, no great university, it was not possible. I had to walk about to where the people were, talk to them and often help them with their work so that I would not just be talking to them while they were working (a great way to be shooed away).

Learning How to Teach on Earth

So a lot of my understanding of the application of master teaching came in my young years when I was learning about the society, if I might call it that, of the time.

During your years as Jesus?

Yes. It wasn't until I became about thirteen years old, and around that time a young man of that religion was considered to be put in the position where he would be making his choices about life, to the extent that he had choices. And after the religious ceremony where you became a man in the eyes of that religion . . .

Was it called bar mitzvah then?

That is one way to describe it, yes. It was then assumed that you would either take over what your father was doing at some point or learn a trade and then help the family and whoever else you could help in the process. The main thing is, you had to make a decision. You really started your life when you were thirteen, aside from what you had been doing at home. It was during this time that I decided I wanted to be a working teacher, that I would have a trade, a skill I had been learning. Ever since I was a youngster of about nine or ten, I had been taught carpentry. I wanted to do that, but I also wanted to teach. My teacher—the master, as he would be called—who taught me carpentry said that he thought this was good, because people needed a carpenter.

Even then, just as today, people like to watch carpenters work, because skilled labor is an art in its own right; people like to watch it. And when they did, if you could do your labor in a skilled way and talk, you would already have their attention! [Laughs.]

So my carpentry teacher told me that he supported my ideas. He was one of the people in the beginning who encouraged others to come and listen. My teacher said, "The people will be there for you to talk to because they are watching you or they are interested. Sometimes you will be talking to the children, because they have the time, or to the very old or whoever is available where you are working. But if the people have heard all you have to say and you need to go to other places, then we will go and work there. But we must do the work," my teacher said, "because if we do not do the work, people will not have a reason to listen to you."

So I learned very early on that one of the best ways to get someone's attention about philosophy was to be doing something that interested them, and then you could do philosophy.

This teacher sounds wonderful! You learned from him, like you'd go to class—instead of or as well as from your father?

Yes, and even today there are teachers who have apprentices and who are able to pass on wisdom, what is called a working person's wisdom, I think. This kind of training was invaluable to me. I learned later on that it was one thing to stand up in front of people and give them a talk they would listen to. They would compare it to what they already knew, as people do. But if you were working with the people—let's say you were all working together on something and you would say something or sing something, then everybody would start singing that song—you were doing something together *and* you were also doing the philosophy. In my experience, that works much better because you already have a common ground. It is essential to create common ground; that's what I learned in my early years, and that is what has benefited me and, I believe, what I have passed on to my fellow beings in my place of existence.

Before my experience, a lot of the beings who went out would arrive in ways that were subtle, but they would talk to people. They would sometimes pick out one person and talk to that person, letting that person pass on the wisdom in any way he felt was appropriate. Sometime after Mohammed and Buddha and I had this experience (we all had a fairly common experience that way), my people gradually changed so that they would go out, as they do now, and establish a kinship with the people present and do things together, then pass on their philosophy.

When We Return in the Future

And when we all come back in the future, we're not going to arrive to save everybody. We're going to arrive and blend in, then talk about things or sing about things.

And then you can go on national television and reach everybody!

In days to come, television won't exist anymore; it will have been recognized to have been an unhealthy phenomenon. But there *will* be mass communication; it will just be more benevolent.

With pictures?

It will be something more involving. Right now television is the authority and talks to you as if you were a child, yes? But in the future mass communications will be a heart-to-heart experience.

How wonderful! This planet was your practice run, right? I mean, you hadn't gone to other planets?

I wasn't thinking of it that way, but looking back on it from the context of our conversation, you could say that. Yes, I learned a lot—significantly more knowledge from having had the personal experience of being human than I might ever have learned just standing off at a distance observing. One can observe and learn things, but as you know, when you *do* things, you learn more.

How Humans Develop Creator Skills

Yes, if you didn't have the personal experience of being human and living your lives, you would probably make a dismal creator, if you don't mind my saying so. It is just part of the evolution of creators that creators must become more than what they were created from. They don't have to be grander or smarter or more loving, but they must develop skills and approaches that are broader on the basis of their experiences, not unlike children do compared to their parents. They may not have all the parents' skills, but they develop certain things in greater depth than the parents did, based on who they are, their talents and so on. Creators are exactly the same.

So you as the Explorer Race would make poor creators if you were simply attempting to reproduce what your Creator is. You would not have the motivation of your Creator, nor would you have all the wisdom gleaned from your experience on a personal level of knowing—as you like to say—what it's like and what to do about it.

Creators must have personal experience to be the most heart-centered, benevolent and, for what you will be doing, flexible creators. Many creators are heart-centered and benevolent, but flexibility is not always a creator trait. *Flexibility always comes with personal experience.*

And you define flexibility as the ability to change in the moment or to live in the moment or to respond to various things?

All that and more: to be able to let go of your vision, for instance, no matter how grand it is and how attached you were to bringing that exact thing into fruition.

Learning to Go with the Flow

If things seem to be moving in another direction, you don't put your iron hand down in front of your people and say, "No! Sit up straight and chew forty-six times, because I like it!" You say, "Okay, you can slouch down a little bit, and you don't have to chew so much."

Go with the flow.

You have to allow the water to seek its own path. If you make a concrete channel for it and force it to go in the way you *will* it to go, it might go that way for a while, but eventually it'll find its way out—usually at an inconvenient time for you.

Yes, under the concrete. So two thousand years ago you left here with this wonderful experience. Are you still dealing with that or processing it, or have you found someplace else to teach since then?

No, I haven't gone someplace to teach, though one might wonder why. I've been considering it. That's a lot of it; I've been considering it because I'm still in the planning stages—within the context of time, you understand—preparing for my return. And I'm considering, the best I can, how I will act and react. Yet because of the flexibility I gained from being human for that time, I am not rigidly planning anything. Things could be different, so I'm allowing for flexibility.

For instance (this is an example), I am prepared for the experience to take anywhere from twenty to eighty years to accomplish—and if it takes eighty-five years, okay.

What will you be attempting to accomplish?

Helping People Find Common Ground

Mostly to help people find their common ground . . . well, they will have done a lot of that before I come . . . and enjoy their differences and work together in a universal chorus, with everyone receiving the same acknowledgment of their value. This is a lot, but the people will be well on their way toward that when we get there. Then, of course we will help the people to integrate the value of their experience here while embracing their larger selves. That is the tough part, because you will have, as people say today, street smarts that don't necessarily fit into the broader context of yourself. So people will have to decide what to use, what to adapt (remember, adaptability is one of the main things you're learning here) and what to let go of. That might take time, and I'm prepared to invest that time.

Say more about the street smarts that we need to drop or change our concepts of.

You don't need to do it now, but hundreds of years in the future it may not be necessary to be quickly reactive to something that appears to be even a minor thread. In the future you won't need a police force as you know it now. You might have a governing body; I'm not talking about a government here, I'm talking about what the police will evolve into, something that might be called, in various languages, a governing body, meaning those who help to solve disputes.

Connect to Others and Flow

Minor things like, for instance, now and even then you might be more reactive to people. For instance, now a person might be reactive to other people going down the street. "Which is the safest route, and do those people look safe or not?" That will be a greater level of threat in the future. It would be more like, "How are people moving up ahead so that I can move through the crowd in the most benevolent way without bumping people and without being bumped?" That would be considered street smarts of the future.

But instead of thinking about that in your greater selves, which is what you'll be becoming more of (and it's my job to help you do that in the most graceful way), I will be teaching you how to be sufficiently connected to everybody else so that you don't have to think about it and it becomes a matter of, as you say, flow—how one white cell flows through the red cells without thinking where it's going to go. A flow.

When you talked about your job, this is your self-created job.

Yes, I am not being sent. In large part what I just described is not dissimilar to what you might experience at the end of a natural life cycle, when you might go through the veils with your guide. For the first few moments—or what you might call days, in terms of experiential time—you are reminded gently of what is Earth wisdom and what is spirit wisdom, as you are spirit. It is rather like that.

Going to Fourth Dimension with New Human Beings

So you're coming when we get to 3.59. I've asked, probably a thousand times, but I don't know that I've ever gotten a clear answer: When we go into the fourth dimension, will we go in the etheric body, not in the physical body? Or in one of our other bodies? Do we have to actually drop the physical, or does the physical simply become lighter and of a higher frequency?

Closer to what you just said. Because you are doing it while you're alive, it has to be a gradual change, but to you it will not seem like that. You won't see yourself turn into light, none of that. You'll just be physical. If someone were standing away or visiting from somewhere, they would see your dimension shift, but you won't see it so much. You will notice, however, that the environment or the circumstances of living have improved.

Is it an actual shift, like a one-two-three shift to fourth dimension?

No, it has to be gradual. Think about it.

To live through it.

Yes, it has to be *very* gradual.

You came to seed energy to save the planet. Your next step is to help us expand into . . . you could say lightbodies, but as you say, it's gradual.

Because you won't be seeing yourself doing that, I can't really say that you're expanding into your lightbodies.

We're bringing the light into the physical bodies?

No. I want to be precise, but it's more that . . . you could say expanding. That's all right; but that would be perceptible only if you were, as I say, standing outside the phenomenon watching it. But for you, as beings who will live through it—and this takes several hundred years, so it's three or four generations from now—when these people get to be about the age you are, they will be so different from your current generation that if you were to visit them, you wouldn't know them. You'd feel like you were in the wrong place, that it was the wrong planet—not just because technology had changed, not just because philosophy had evolved, but because things would seem not quite . . . you can't quite grab it, you understand. It's hard to describe something entirely different within the context of one thing.

Will the beings who are on the planet now mostly be the reincarnated beings four generations from now?

No, none of them. There is no one living on the planet today who, when the planet locks into 4.0, will be present—none, not a single one.

Why?

Because, interestingly enough, everybody on the planet today has chosen to be here *in this time*. *This* is the time that excites them, just like those beings three or four generations in the future will be there because that's the time that excites *them*, in terms of their transformation, but other times don't. Once you've had the privilege of experiencing this in this time you've chosen, you will be very satisfied with it. From what I have seen, just looking forward, there is not a single soul on the planet today who will be present in any form when precisely 4.0 is reached, with the possible exception of those who are visiting as observers.

Will these books still be here then?

Books in general will be different then; there probably won't be paper. After all, when you think about the way paper is made, it is destructive to life forms. But there will be information available. Initially it'll be encoded into stone, but eventually when people fully integrate the idea that stone has its own rhythm, the wisdom will be encoded into what I would call eternal accessibility. It's hard to describe because it is not mechanical technology.

Will the words you're saying now be available to those beings?

Yes, just as engineering concepts in building a structural bridge in the twenties will be available, though it will be studied as archaic technology. Bridges then will be made of other stuff.

That's interesting. They've sort of lured us (you know—the carrot) up to this point with the idea that we were going to experience this new stage.

Someone has told you this?

Well, they've never said it quite as succinctly as you have.

Human Interests in 4D

Let's say this happens in four hundred years of experiential time. Do you think that something else might get your attention between then and now?

It's possible.

What do you mean, it's possible? Of *course* it will happen! Everyone will be doing other things they are interested in. If anyone wants to come and see or hear about it, they will; visits will be possible, but more likely from a distance so as not to interfere, not unlike today. Viewing things at a distance does not interfere as long as the distance is great enough.

As you say, it's not like being there.

But the people who *are* there will be the ones who have chosen to be there in that time, yet they will be a portion of the Explorer Race. They will engage the experience and you will be able to access it as part of the Explorer Race—if you are a part.

Well, most beings on the planet right now are, aren't they?

Yes.

Will you interact with the negative Sirians at any time as a teacher?

Probably not. They will need teachers who are (I like this term) rough and ready. They will need teachers who are at least adventurous and rugged, and I have done enough of that, thank you. So I think not. But there are many others who are happy to do so.

Buddha's Approach

Buddha came before you. Did he come knowing that certain energies had to be anchored, or was that just your perception? Did he come to teach the Explorer Race generally and give it truth, or to anchor energies to serve the planet?

I think Buddha was thinking in terms of how to integrate a philosophy in such a way as to be available to be studied and considered in the future. Buddha did not consider that written words had the potential to integrate a philosophy. He felt that the only way the philosophy could be integrated was to have a group of people who had done so and would continue to initiate others. Ultimately he decided that all those things would be useful, and that a sense of humor, which is one of the traits that support the benevolence of any philosophy, would be the most critical. To the extent that a philosophy cannot laugh at itself and its circumstances in life, its early demise is guaranteed.

Well, you have a good sense of humor. I'm not too sure it got into the Christian religion.

Choose What Feels Good

But you know, the interesting thing is that people still have hearts, just like they did when I was here, and they know what fits in their hearts and what doesn't. They can read the Christian Bible, and they can feel what feels good to them and what doesn't. Before too long people all over the world will be able to pick from this religion and that religion, and say, "These things feel good; these other things don't. We're going to gradually let go of these other things and nurture these good-feeling things in ourselves and our children." That is how universal philosophies get born. It's all in the feeling; if it feels good and has good stories, if it fits into life and is practical wisdom, if you can laugh and sing about it, then it might last. But if it forces you to deny who you are, what you are and what you might ever become and creates an authoritarian regime, it will be fleeting at best.

Christian religions that survive will do the former, not the latter. And as Christianity becomes refeminized (because it started out feminine), it will last. And those aspects of the Christian religion that cannot give up their authoritarianism—the need to be right—won't last. Just like any religion or philosophy, if it needs to be right and cannot laugh it off and say, "Well, maybe we can look at it another way," it won't last, that's all.

You know, that's really a given in the affairs of all human beings and who and what they are and what they do. In the larger sense, it's a given in every place I've been or seen—if it feels good, if it works, if people like it, if it supports you and nurtures you and improves your life and the lives of those around you and those yet to come, and if it is benevolent and heart-centered, the chances are it will last.

You learned an awful lot from observing, as much as you can from observing, because you observed many of your fellow beings who were on other planets. You learned about those societies and how they thought. You learned a lot from that, right?

Yes, I learned a lot. It was very helpful. But ultimately I learned the most by being here and feeling what human beings felt and by experiencing the great joys and the great sorrows. There's nothing like experience to have not only compassion, but to truly have understanding.

There's one thing I need to clarify. You trained the women to bring the energy whose purpose was to make Mother Earth feel good enough that she wouldn't remove the negative humans, right? It was to reinforce her love energy?

It was to balance.

Those beings who are doing it today who don't know they're doing it, are they reinforcing love energy from a soul level?

Feminine Energy: Motions That Create Balance

Oh, yes. And of course many animals do it, too. For example, there are certain motions that create balance. In the Native American tradition, this motion [moves arm] . . . you will have to describe it . . .

It's like the movement of a snake or of a winding river.

Yes. This motion tends to mean balance. Why, you might ask yourself? If you look at the way a fish moves through water, that is the way. That motion creates balance. Though I would not want it to happen, if there were no wild fish, free fish swimming through the waters, balance would be much, much more difficult to maintain. Just the motion of these free beings swimming through the water creates a great deal of balance. That's why in my times there were other benevolent beings working with the sea creatures and the freshwater creatures, encouraging them to multiply and be plentiful. It was not only for those times, but more so for the times in the future when the circumstances to support their lives would be less benevolent, when they would need a great many of their fellow beings to not only have a benevolent society for themselves, but also as a side effect to create balance simply by *being*.

Say more about balance. Is that electromagnetic or emotional, a balance within Mother Earth or within humans?

Masculine/Feminine Balance

Balance between what you do (the masculine) and what you feel (the feminine). Balance is not always, as you say, fifty-fifty; sometimes the most benevolent balance is felt as thirty percent masculine, seventy percent feminine. At other times, in times of great action and need, it might be the opposite. So balance does not always and only mean equal balance; one must never assume that. Balance will be *the best balance of the moment for whoever needs it, in whatever context and time they are doing whatever they are doing.*

When the fish, for instance, and human beings are broadcasting an energy of balance, it will be within a wide enough range so that different people doing different things can utilize that support. Balance, then, is like an energy that comes up from below to support you. That is why in many traditions, Earth is pictured as balance, because you, with your legs, balance on the Earth. If there were no Earth here, you would be fumbling about in space trying to catch your balance.

Warmth in the Chest

I think you said there was an overabundance of masculine energy, so you trained women to send feminine energy, receptive energy?

Not to send, but to experience it. When you are experiencing the benevolent feminine energy, which Speaks of Many Truths and others have discussed, it's this warmth in your chest that is love and so on in that part of your body. When you are experiencing it, it is like a meditation. You are simply doing it; it is not words, it is not mental—it is felt, this great love. It naturally broadcasts, and when more than one is doing it, especially in a given place, it magnifies to a greater degree than the number of people who are there. And with this magnification it tends to broadcast to where it is needed. Sometimes, if it is needed at a great distance, other elements will bring it there. If you are on the sea, as the water evaporates it will take it up into the sky and perhaps come down in the form of rain affected by that balance and love. If you are in a windy place, perhaps the wind will pick it up and take it. I recognize that these are shamanic principles, but they fit here.

Well, no one group has a claim on shamanic principles; that's planetary.

"Shamanic" really means honoring what is and working within what is in the most benevolent way for all beings—that's all it means.

I know, but it's been sort of usurped by people talking about native peoples, I think.

Depending on where you live, native people are different. If you are in Russia, the native peoples might be in the north; if you are in other countries, the native people might be out in the jungle. It just depends. City people will sometimes expect native people to have great wisdom. They might have great wisdom within the context of their people; on the other hand, they might not be able to solve a higher chemistry problem on the chalkboard, though they may be able to solve it in the practical world.

Does this energy need to be continually radiated until you come back, until we get to that frequency point? Or will it continue after that?

The more that people are experiencing the energies that have been taught, with the heat, the more benevolent life will come to be in general. That is why it is such an important thing to learn if it is something they would like to do. It feels good and is benevolent for others. One does not *send* it out; one feels it and it projects outward on its own. If one *sends* it out, one is literally rejecting it. Love must first and foremost be embraced, and *then* it radiates.

If one does not embrace love and expects to provide it for others, one cannot expect it to embrace others without being embraced by the lover.

That's beautiful, and I think it needs to be said. Many healers seem to feel that they're sending it out, yet their own lives aren't balanced.

I will just say this: Life is its own reward; it is intended to be lived and savored to the best of your ability. It is not the end, it is a step along the way. Yet at the end of your physical life you will often have an opportunity to go over your wisdom. Try to pass it on if it is something that has actually improved the quality of your life and is heart-centered and benevolent. If it is something that has just made you cynical or bitter, know that it will fall away as you pass through the veils, and it is unnecessary to pass it on to others. Good night.

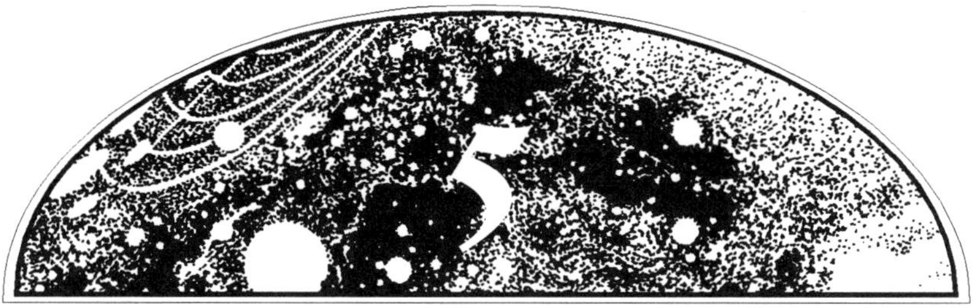

The Teachings and Travels

Jesus

April 30, 1998

Greetings. Well, what would you like to talk about this evening?

I would like to know exactly what you taught your people 2000 years ago. You taught them mystical teachings. Can you talk to the readers as if they were some of your students? There's nothing secret that you can't say now, is there?

Not too much; some of it wouldn't relate to people nowadays, so I'd skip over that. I suggest that the reader look at the next Explorer Race book, because some of what I taught is in it.

***The shaman book* [Shamanic Secrets for Material Mastery, 1999]?**

Shamanic Teaching

Yes. This kind of teaching is not something I initiated, but it is comfortable to people, especially people who live off the land and for whom topographic sites—mountains and so on—might be some significant part of their day-to-day lives. I'd start off by referring the reader to that book. Then I'd say this, pretending I was talking to a group: "First, understand how to live together harmoniously—husband and wife and children, parents, grandparents occasionally, and all the others we might meet in our village or settlement, to say nothing of those who pass by from other places that are strange or unknown to us. In order for us to get along with each other, we have to have many common threads. Some are already present without our doing anything: we all must eat, sleep and have shelter and other things you all know about.

"But sometimes common threads can be celebrated and initiated within all of us at once. You all know when there are visitors you are happy to see; you welcome them and share what food you have, and sometimes they bring their own food and share it with you. And very often, after prayers and food, they will sing songs. If the strangers don't know our songs, we will teach them. If we don't know *their* songs, they will teach us. This gives us common threads, things we share, and we hear about their travels, their land and their people or where they have been; we hear about their adventures. Some of us wish we could go and see these strange and wonderful places; others are satisfied to hear the story and feel thankful to have a wonderful place to live in where we are cherished and appreciated for who we are and what we do.

"Now, I want to tell you that there are other things we can do to feel united, each and every one of us. One of the things is the heat in the chest [see inset]." After people practice that together, I would say, "Now savor all of you together. We have information that comes to us by a traveler that there is some unrest far from here, and there have been some raids on villages. How will we know which way to go to be safe?" (They would build on that heat in the chest.) Then I would say, "We'll pick one of your number, or two or three, who can feel the heat in their chest most easily, most comfortably. Have them stand up and, as if they were in a circle, let them point in different directions. They would stand in places in our village where they can't see each other. We have an elder near them, and the person who is pointing in different directions will notice in which direction they feel the greatest heat. Afterward there might be several directions felt by the indi-

"The Heat in the Chest"

- Practice feeling love as heat in the chest. (You can use your hands over your chest to help focus energy.)
- When you can hold this warmth, add the feeling (not visualization) of gold light.
- Keep practicing back and forth until you can feel both at the same time, and hold it for at least 10 or 15 minutes.
- When you are focused in the heart and can feel the heat or the love or both, I'd like you to simply say out loud (it's a bit challenging, but you can do it), "I give all beings permission to be of love, to be fed, clothed, healed and comforted."

This is alchemy, and can transform any discomfort that arises within you. You will feel ecstatic. It is the closest feeling to the Creator energy that you are.

(For the full exercise and commentary, see page 383 in *Shining the Light IV* and chapter 25 in *Shining the Light V*.)

viduals. Then the elders will get together, compare the directions and find where there is the most agreement. That's the direction we will all go to escape the invaders, bringing our animals, our tents, our property and our families."

That was general teaching, but when you got to the women you taught to handle the energy, did that start with the heat in the chest, too?

Almost everything does, because it is the most profound evidence of physical love between the physical self, all that is around you on Earth—meaning other people, other plants, animals, stone, rain, everything. You can have an interaction of heat with all these different things and feel greater heat as a result. It is also a connection to spirit. One can focus on one's concept of God, and if that concept is a loving, benevolent God, one will feel greater warmth within that context. One might most easily do this through some natural object, maybe a mountain. Ask the mountain to represent God's love and interact; at another time, just for fun, ask the mountain to be itself and interact, then notice which time there is the most heat.

This is the basis of what I taught the women. Most of them knew the heat already; they knew that because they were chosen on the basis of their shamanic abilities, either practicing healers or visionaries or something like that. Most of them already knew that, but if they didn't, they were shown it.

Once they had experienced it, I would focus on some energy of benevolence and sit in the center of the circle. They would close their eyes and feel that warmth, then connect with each other by holding each others' hands or looking at each other, feeling greater warmth.

When they got that warmth of the love as strong as it could be, I would bring in some energy associated with that loving energy, possibly connected to this tribe's or that tribe's source energy from this or that planet, and they would meld with that. Then they could simply broadcast this energy for specific groups of people, because different groups might identify more with a specific heat or love energy than others.

Everyone will identify comfortably with that warmth and heat, but some might identify even more comfortably if that warmth and heat is infused with the source of their tribal origin—a planet, for instance, or a place, even a time. So there would be the foundational feeling, then the secondary feeling.

That foundational feeling was the energy of balance—or was that something you added to it?

The foundational feeling was simply the heat—no different than you're being trained to feel today.

And that radiated balance, then.

Remember, it wasn't their job to radiate so much, just to feel it. It radiated on its own. That's very important, because if it is consciously radiated, do you know what happens? It becomes willful. If you consciously radiate it at someone or something, then you are doing that because you want them to change, and even if you want them to become more benevolent for their own sake, it is a willful desire. But if you feel it, it naturally radiates, and it seeks its own level in any who happen to pass by or who are downstream, as it were, from the radiation. An individual can then take it in or not as they choose, but they are not being manipulated by having it sent *to* them.

I understand.

That is a very fine but critically important point.

It's almost interfering if you send it . . .

No "almost" about it.

There were also deeper, more profound things you taught the women?

Many of them, as I've said already, knew things. I would teach certain things such as invisibility—not meaning invisibility to the point where you wouldn't be able to see yourself, but invisibility to the point where others would not see you if they were threatening you, for instance, or if you needed to go somewhere for some benevolent purpose. I think Robert did a workshop on that not long ago, at least in terms of my time, and it was exactly the same, no different. I'm not prepared to say on these pages how it is done; maybe some other time. Ask Speaks of Many Truths. It will be up to him to choose; maybe book three in the Shaman series.

Since the women were trained in various techniques and methods of healing and nurturing, did you learn something from them?

You have to remember, I was conscious.

Teaching the Men through Language

What about your male apprentices?

With them I was more inclined to talk. They were set up for it because of the religions and philosophies of the time, which encouraged men to speak about issues in their daily life as they related to their religion or philosophy. So I was more inclined to give the men more of the intellectual side of things rather than the applied side, which I was working on with the women.

What were some of the things you would discuss, that you told stories about or taught them?

Things that would come up, such as a man feeling guilty because he found his brother's wife attractive. Even though he had done nothing about it, he would feel guilty or shy or ashamed because he felt urgently attracted to her sometimes and would want to know what to do to avoid it. Or things that come up all the time that ministers of today must answer—no different.

Occasionally one would have a question that would be more cosmic. Cosmic questions always came, with few exceptions, from people who were out under the night sky, such as watching over animals or perhaps out on the perimeter guarding the village, if there was a settlement. No matter how well you're guarding, there's always time to look up in the sky, and people would see things—a light, a streak, occasionally an identifiable ship—and they would say, "Teacher! What was that?" Or they would say, "Founder!" Usually they would say something along the lines of "Teacher!"—that wasn't the word, but it meant that.

And I would tell them what it really was. I would not protect them because I thought they couldn't accept it. People in those days were much more inclined to believe what they saw, smelled and heard, to believe their senses. Today in your now time, people are less inclined to believe their senses because people have given their allegiance to external voices of authority. But in those days, just as today, there are many places on your planet where people believe their senses first and words second.

I would say, "This is a vehicle." Someone would say, "Teacher! I saw this bright light in the sky, and it came down close and I could see. It looked like there were people inside, but they didn't look exactly like us. At first I was frightened, then all of a sudden I felt this very warm glow, not unlike what you teach the women, and it felt good! I have felt that warm glow from the women, and I know this is the same warm glow. So I thought, These people must be like us even though they don't look like us. Then they left. Who are they? Where are they from?"

See, it's an innocent question asked on the basis of what was seen and felt. And I would reply, "Oh, these people are from such-and-such a planet. They were flying here; they have flying ships, and they can come from other planets." And they would say, "Where? Where is the planet?" Almost always these talks would take place at night, because that's when people have moments to talk. So I would say, "Come outside." We would all go outside and I would point in the general direction or to a star, and say, "There! They come from there!" I wouldn't say they came from this solar system and all of that; there's no point in that. Give them the evidence of their eyes.

"When you see that star in the future, you will say, 'Oh, these friendly people came from there!' Maybe they'll come back someday and visit you." Told simply but honestly. And there wasn't a single person who would say, "No, it's not true," because such experiences had been heard about and were more frequent in those days. There was, after all, no threat for such ships to come. If the visitors felt that those who were observing them felt comfortable with it or might be open to feeling comfortable, they would reveal themselves.

So I would speak to them about these things. Sometimes it would make them feel good about what the women were learning and they would say, "Teacher, show us what you show the women." Then I would teach them how to feel the heat. Sometimes some of them would be able to get it right away and sometimes it would take others longer, but they would get it eventually.

Recording the Teachings

Were any of those things you taught written down at the time you told them or shortly after?

No. Books as you know them today were unknown then. No, what they had was stories.

All verbal?

Yes, it was all verbal, or sometimes it was in song, because it's easier to remember a story if you sing about it. Even today, you know, sometimes you can't get a song out of your head, but it's not always easy to keep a thought in your head. So they would sometimes do that. But none of it was written down, not one word.

So when those who put the Bible together are accused of removing some of your teaching, it wasn't very startling.

Not really. You have to understand that when things were written down later, they were written down on the basis of recollections or stories or even songs handed down to individuals based on recollections of previous individuals. But at the time nothing was written down. You have to remember that I was just one person, one philosopher-teacher. There were many philosopher-teachers, and some of them had positions of greater leadership. But even then, words weren't written down as you have them today.

Much later these things were written down. Different people wrote down different things, not only because they remembered them differently or it was told to them differently by their relatives, but because many of them had different experiences—some were at one talk, others were at another. So when they did come to condensing what is now known as the Bible, it was a huge amount of information. They picked not only what they felt was relevant to their people at that time, but also what was, understandably, politically expedient for them. They (those who were writing those things down and making a biblical text) were, after all, creating something that, from their perspective, needed to be more than a government, something that would influence governments and live forever.

So things you said about lights in the sky and this planet or that planet did not make it into the Bible.

Even though some of that is written down, "Someone said that someone said that someone said that he talked about this and that," it didn't have any relevance to the political and social times, and there was no serious consideration to include it. However, it was saved initially for the study of scholars. Eventually the Church hierarchy—having very studiously (and, I might add, tediously) reproduced these writings over the years on numerous occasions—will make them available to future scholars and perhaps ultimately the public. Because books obviously didn't last, scribes would reproduce them very carefully. They would be checked, I might add, then somebody else would check them; they would be checked by two or three people to make sure it was exactly the same as the original. So it was very scrupulously reproduced.

The Lesson Plan

Before you came, had you set up your lesson plan?

Yes, that's a nice way to put it. I had set up my lesson plan to make it general so that it would be possible for just about anybody to learn certain things, and it would be specific only to individuals or groups of individuals, also known as tribes or extended families, as another way. Calling them tribes is perhaps a bit of a stretch; extended families might be more accurate.

So yes, I had a lesson plan that allowed me to follow fairly carefully what I intended to do. Of course, I had to adapt it to the circumstances.

So you had the ability to look over the immediate history of the people you were going to live among.

Yes.

You knew their level of evolution, what they'd been taught and the references to their . . .

Yes, and I was able to adapt what I needed to say to a greater or lesser degree, in terms of the teaching I wanted to share, on the basis of what they could most easily assimilate and what would support them and be good for them to improve their lives. Not doctrine, but actual assistance.

Who had taught them? All we know is that these are the people Moses brought out of Egypt.

I think you are confusing something. You are making the assumption that the people I taught were all of what is now called the Jewish religion. That is not so.

Who Jesus Taught

Who did you teach?

There were people of that group that I taught and was allowed to teach, sometimes encouraged to teach [the Jewish people], but I would certainly be open to teaching any groups, other peoples of the region, such as Bedouins, now sometimes referred to as Arabs. Though it's kind of a concocted word, it's still a good word. In those days, people wouldn't call themselves one thing; they would be "the people," or "the people of." It would be something like "the people of the stars," "people of the sand" and so on. I like that better because it's more to the point of who they are.

They called themselves "people of the stars"?

They might call themselves "the people of the stars" if their stories all had to do with the stars. If it was where they came from or if people from the stars came to them or if they would be going to the stars someday, then they would call themselves "the people of the stars," in the language of the time. Or if they were "the people of the sand," it might have to do with traveling on the sand or a sacred relationship with the sand itself. For instance, there were people of that time who could, if they didn't know what to do about something, reach down and put their hand on the sand and feel from the sand what they were to do. They had a sacred relationship with the sand, not unlike shamanic individuals of today in your time who might have a sacred relationship with a crystal or a feather, for example.

Teaching across the Planet

How much did you travel around? In how wide an area did you travel?

Within the context of my *physical* travels, I traveled around an area not much more than ninety to one hundred miles one way or the other. But when I was reproducing my body and going to other places, of course I would create a body and garments that would allow me to blend into the other places. If the body I was creating needed to communicate with people in China, for example, I would obviously be in a body that looked like a Chinese person because I wanted to be able to be accommodated as one of their own. That's the only way to do it, you understand, so that you do not put people off and so they do not feel that you are a stranger.

That you're one of them.

One of them, yes. If I went to the north country, places where there was snow, I would reproduce a body for the visit that would look like one of the people, or at least a person they might see who passed through regularly, so that they would be reasonably relaxed.

Did you pretty much go all over the planet?

Yes, all over the planet.

How would you choose precisely where to go?

Sometimes I'd go to places that had already established philosophies that were working well, where the society had an established hierarchy. "Working well" means that people knew who they were, what was expected of them, what they would receive and so on. Not necessarily was there equality or fraternity or brotherhood, but there was some kind of established society. Allowing for that time, this was found more often in the East, where societies had had time to develop and were relatively undisturbed by outsiders.

So I would go to such places and communicate with the learned individuals of the time. Sometimes I would teach as a student. Other times I would make comments, if comments were allowed, and once I had made a comment, the learned individuals would give *their* comments. It was all done in a very friendly manner, with respect on both sides, in this way oftentimes initiating a chain of thought that hadn't been considered. Sometimes it had a political context, meaning the equality of man, for example. Other times it was a heart-centered experience, meaning the wisdom and love of woman. Sometimes it was other practical things—animals, crops and so on.

So all societies, civilizations, religions and philosophies on the planet are in some way influenced by what you did.

Yes, but in some cases it is a minor influence, because they already had a fairly advanced civilization for one reason or another. Some native peoples had an advanced civilization, a sacred relationship with the plants and animals and stone and the elements and so on. If their society was working benevolently, I would just visit. I wouldn't offer any teaching at all unless I told a story that would complement their stories. If they liked it well enough, they would include it with their stories, initially saying, "This is the story of our friend" or "our brother who came to visit." Eventually it became *their* story, which was fine, always leaving you with a moral, but always being entertaining, sometimes lighthearted and sometimes even ribald, if necessary.

People can laugh about things that are common circumstances to all human beings.

During your thirty-three-year life in the physical body of Jesus, you were only in this small . . .

. . . in this small area now known as the Middle East. But when I was duplicating my body, even after the body was no longer walking around as Jesus in the Middle East, I continued to visit other places for about fifty years after that.

What an incredible experience!

Peru with ET Visitors

Sometimes I was, as you say, influencing and other times simply sharing and enjoying the pleasure of our meetings. I remember once going to a place that is well-known and appreciated now in Peru, high up in the mountains where the people had a lifestyle not that different from what it is today. People from other planets would come to visit regularly, in the same way as today a bus might pull up at a corner and people get out and no one thinks anything of it. In those days a ship would land and people would get out, and no one would think anything of it. It was normal.

I would go there sometimes and stay there for a while as one of the people or as one of the visitors from the ship. Of course, the visitors in the ship would know who I really was because of their capacity to perceive. You couldn't travel in such a ship without such capacities. They would be perfectly happy to accommodate me in what I was doing, and I would visit amongst the people.

In those days when the ships landed up there in the area that is now called Machu Picchu and other areas high up in Peru, the ships and the people who visited might stay for weeks at a time and play with the children and teach the children, sometimes singing songs and playing games. It was a very benevolent, very happy, pleasant experience.

Where were they from? All different places?

Usually from the Pleiades, sometimes from Andromeda if they wished to study the culture and learn things that might be helpful to civilizations the Andromedan ship visited. They would often go to what they considered advanced civilizations—spiritually sound civilizations—on Earth, then take their knowledge and problem-solving techniques to other civilizations that were not quite as integrated with the sacred spiritual and the physical. They would suggest that this is how the council of elders solved things in Machu Picchu on Earth and show a picture of the people and how they looked, sometimes even creating some kind of a communication.

In this way the people on other planets would say, "Well, here are people like us. They are living on the land and they have their animals. They're not flying around in ships and don't have magic; they are living on their own like us. If they can solve their problems this way, then we ought to try that."

In this way the Andromedans would bring this . . . it's like a social welfare project, without giving them things from their culture and interfering with the native culture. Rather, they would complement that culture with a culture from Earth that was equal to or similar enough to their culture that the people would say, "Well, these people are like us; I hope maybe we will meet them someday."

The Total Teaching Experience on Earth

Altogether, you actually have hundreds of experiential years of teaching on Earth.

Yes, and sometimes just learning on Earth, such as with the Machu Picchu experience. There wasn't much to teach there; that was more visiting.

So you did learn, then!

Now remember, I was conscious; I'm not saying that I *learned* . . . if I remembered *everything*, how would I have learned? But that doesn't mean that I wouldn't enjoy the visit and have the pleasure of the experience. After all, you have pleasures of experience that you have had before and that are no less pleasurable for having happened before.

Right. If you added up all the time in all the bodies—how many years was that?

It's an arbitrary number. Does it really mean anything?

Well, it's just so much longer than thirty-three years.

Yes, but it wasn't one after another; they were simultaneous.

But the total accumulation of years is much, much more than thirty-three. It's hundreds and hundreds of years that you were actually influencing people on Earth.

Yes, and many hundreds of individual bodies and societies, yes.

That's not known at all. There are stories that you traveled here and there, but it's always thought of as one body.

The reason the stories still exist of my travels here and there is that people had some way of writing it down or keeping track of it, or they put it into their culture as song or myth. But most of the places I traveled to didn't have that, so you don't know about all the other travels. If they had kept a record, you would have known. It wasn't a secret.

Frequently they wouldn't have connected it with you. You didn't walk up and say, "I'm Jesus."

No, and I wasn't; I would use a name that would fit into their society and culture. I wouldn't lie; I would say, "I am a visitor." If they asked me where from, I would say, "I am a visitor from far away." Usually they wouldn't press any more than that. The people were very much more polite then; they would say, "Oh, that's nice." Sometimes they would want to know about the place I was from, and then I would talk about it. I wouldn't always; it depended on their civilization. If I thought they would want to know about where I was from, I would say all of the places I had been from, meaning all the places I had visited on Earth or the place I am most known for having been from. Although in the larger context, being from so many places, I would say what would be the most interesting and useful and helpful to them that was true.

Meanwhile, back in this one body you were in consistently in the Middle East, you built up this following of people?

No! That is a misnomer. People didn't follow me and the others around—and I might add that all of us didn't go around everywhere. Sometimes people would stay; they would be within their own village or within their own area and travel around their own area. At any given moment the students traveling with me usually numbered no more than ten or twelve—some men, some women.

Working and Traveling

Even when you traveled, you were working as a carpenter, weren't you?

Not necessarily. I could, if people needed carpentry, but I didn't carry my tools with me. If people needed carpentry and there was a carpenter in town who needed assistance and I could help, I would. But when I was traveling around and teaching, I would do that only if it was necessary. The societies of the time were open to the traveling teacher, and because the students traveling with me had many different skills, students might lend assistance with the animals; or one might help with healing or teaching or tending the children. But you see, there were so many skills. We didn't arrive to tax the people and their resources; we arrived in such a way as to assist them. First we would always ask the people to tell their stories and sing their songs, honoring them so that they would know that we were not coming to *put* something on them. We recognized that they had something that was working; we wanted to know about it. After they shared their culture with us, they would ask, "What do *you* say? What is *your* way, then?" We would share our way, but always very politely.

Mary of the Magdalene

How did you meet Mary of the Magdalene? Is that what you called her then? Was

she the woman who was your wife? I don't even know where to start.

I don't know where to start either.

You got married, is that true?

We're talking only about the individual in the Middle East, yes?

Yes.

It wasn't a formal marriage, no.

So there was an arrangement? Was the woman who is called Mary of the Magdalene the . . .

The woman as she is called today, I think, is Mary Magdalene, but others have referred to her as Mary *of* the Magdalene because the Magdalene was a teaching, a training, all of this. At that time we didn't have last names for people. It would be a description—where they were from or what they looked like or something like that. But it would be a single name. I don't want to create too much of a stir, but a lot of the names of the time were different than the names you have today.

The person you're talking about (let's use the common name Mary) was one of the woman students. She was very helpful, very insightful—a shamanic woman, in that sense. She was my friend, yes. We had a closeness.

I think you said you had children?

For the sake of the book, let's say that we were married and we had children.

How many children?

Two.

So you traveled around in this small area for most of the thirty-three years. How old were you when you started traveling?

About fifteen, but not so much. When I got to be about seventeen I really began my travels, but I started doing some when I was fifteen.

The elders . . . they weren't called rabbis, right?

I'd rather call them elders. It's more of a universal respectful term.

At some point the elders must have recognized that you were different, that you were intelligent, spiritual . . .

Well, I think they recognized that. My parents recognized it and my carpenter master teacher recognized it. I think they kept it pretty much amongst themselves until I was about nine years old and was interacting more with other people. Then it was more known.

So you had a reputation as an advanced soul amongst these people?

I'd rather say that people knew me as someone who could comment on a wide variety of subjects.

In a helpful manner.

Well, it depended on what you believed whether you would consider it helpful or not.

Oh, I see. You're saying it was common for teachers to travel around and share their stories and philosophy?

Oh, yes. How do people learn except to be taught? If they wish to be, of course.

So you traveled for years. Was it close to the end when you became a threat? Was it seen as subversive by those in power?

I think it was just the times. There were other teachers who were asked to be quieter and not stir the people up. Anytime a people is colonized, there will be times when there is more unrest than others. The last few years of my physical life there happened to be one of those times when there was more unrest, and all teachers and all elders in general were asked to keep the people calm. If the Romans, being the power of the time, felt it would be necessary to suppress the people, it wouldn't be Romans who would get killed.

So generally speaking, the elders and the teachers would be encouraged to keep a lid on it. Since I felt that my teaching was not threatening, I went on. During some of those times I spent more time farther from where the Romans were, generally speaking—with outlaws or bandits of the time.

You mentioned that; you joined them as a way to share your teaching.

Well, that's the only way one can be seen as an equal. Of course, I didn't do anything harmful to anyone, but I had to join them for a time. Those times were a small facet of what I did here. I think in the larger sense what I did here was more involved in my visits elsewhere in those other bodies, and it might be interesting to talk more about that next time.

Let's focus on where I went and what I did with whom and what we discussed and so on. I'd rather dwell more on that, because that's the unknown part of what I did, and less on what is necessarily going to be offensive to people. I'm not here to offend; I'd rather be here to expand.

So let us resume next week.

Thank you very much.

Good night.

6

A Student's Time with Jesus and His Tales of Jesus' Time Travels

Simon the Student and Jesus

May 4, 1998

I am one of That Man's students. I came to him late in my life. By the time I met him I was with gray and white hair, an old man for my time, about thirty-nine years old.

In my early years I had been a hard worker, but the owning of some property in my family—not by myself directly; I was [chuckles] far enough down in the lineage so that I had to put my back to it—allowed me the privilege of being supported by the land and the animals and by my relatives. When I got older I was able to make the time to travel around with That Man for a year and a half.

Jesus' Work with Elders and Children

I was particularly interested in what he did with older people and little children; being an older person of the time myself, naturally I was interested. And just like older people (because by that time I had grandchildren of my own), I was very interested to see how he taught the children, how they responded to him and most importantly, what the children went out and did with that teaching in the rest of their lives, to the extent I could follow it up.

My experience with him was as more of an observer than a practitioner, as was the last person who spoke. I was more interested then in his philosophy and how he lived it and taught it, and that was of great beauty to me. I saw that he not only treated older people and children with great kindness, but after he had established himself with the people he was talking to, he then went particularly out of his way to treat older people and children with great kindness and respect. It was clear that he was teaching by example, for he made no effort whatsoever during the time I was with him to tell the people that they should treat their children and their old people with respect. But I noticed when I went back to those places—which I did after he had gone, when I wasn't with him anymore—that they all treated their children and their older people with more respect. This is how, I believe, you can tell a good teacher from one who is, perhaps, still beginning.

A Present Life Who Studies Buddha's Teachings

I have chosen in my reincarnational life cycle to focus into lives that have either a long childhood or a long aged time. I am in a life now, a physical life, as you would say, on your world. I am alive in your time. I am over a hundred years old, living in Sri Lanka, and I am consciously telepathically communicating with my teacher, who is communicating through this man [Robert]. In this way the discomforts I have in my body, being an old man, don't come through the channel or will not go into the words that go into the book.

Who is your teacher?

My teacher is the Buddha.

When did you connect with him?

When I was a boy. One of my teachers had great respect and admiration for Buddha.

When you were a boy in what life?

This life. I was not raised in the religion (as they call it now, but I think of it as philosophy) of Buddhism, but this teacher had such great respect. I kept in touch with this teacher. It was only about forty years ago that my teacher died, and he has continued to instruct me on the Buddha's teaching all this time. Now in my old age I can be a practicing Buddhist and nobody is offended, because I am old enough to get respect, and perhaps my children and grandchildren and great-grandchildren and so on are more tolerant of an old man's eccentricities.

Are you totally conscious of the life you lived at the time of Jesus?

Yes, and it is because I'm at the end of my life here that I am very conscious of my other lives—including a life several hundred years in the future of this planet . . .

When Buddha and Jesus come back!

Yes!

[Laughs.] What a great joy!

I believe I am allowed to remember this past life because of its link to this future life.

I think that's one of the reasons this book is so important. It tells about their coming back. It's like an announcement, you know?

It is an announcement; that's a nice way to put it.

The Lifetime with Jesus

We have many things to talk about. At what point did you meet Jesus? How old was he?

He was then about twenty and seven.

Twenty-seven. And was it in the Middle East, in Israel or whatever it was called at that time?

At that time it was in the area now known as Syria.

Was it a place he had traveled to?

I believe he had traveled there, yes.

Did he stay there during the time you studied with him or observed him? Or did you travel with him?

I traveled with him for a year and a half when he traveled in Syria. Sometimes he would tell us that he had to go a long way off and would be gone for a while. It would usually be, by the time of your keeping, no more than a week to ten days, and he would suggest (he would never demand, he wouldn't think of commanding) that we help the people we were near. If they were villagers, help them with whatever they required. He did not ask us to talk about his philosophy, though there were students who could speak with great eloquence. He always asked us to help the people with their needs, so that's what we did.

Then if they asked or if the subject came up, he would teach.

At night only after everyone had eaten and just before they were ready to sleep—but only if they asked. If they didn't, if nothing was being said, he told us we could tell stories if we wanted. We didn't have to make them of his philosophy; we could tell funny stories or things from our youth, anything we wished to tell. So we did, and this happened on many occasions. Now I realize that he was traveling far away to other countries—China and, I believe, Ireland, what is now called the town of Limerick. I have been able to look at some of the places he went.

Now, in this life?

Yes. He went to places even in different times; he went to Saxony . . .

In the Middle Ages.

Jesus Visiting the Dark Ages

Yes. He said to us once that people are the most receptive *and* the most resistant when they have the least to lose. Looking back now from this life at where he went, I can see two places where people had the least and fervently prayed to their gods for the most—and yet they were very resistant to change. He felt that these people needed his help more than anyone, so he went to lots of places in lots of times, especially around what historians call the Middle and Dark Ages.

Of course, the Dark Ages were only dark in Europe; in other parts of the world, knowledge and wisdom continued. But in Europe, when they were discovering and exploring their more primitive fears, it became known as the Dark Ages. He would go there, often taking the form of either a child or an old person, to do what he could to cheer people up, to sing songs, to tell stories and, most importantly, to give hope. When people are going through things like that, hope is the most valuable and cherished of all things.

It's something to hold onto. That's beautiful. We'll probably go back and ask him about some of these adventures in those times.

I can speak of these things if you wish.

Please!

Sometimes he would prefer that we speak of things he did, because it is not like him to sing his own praises.

Yes, I noticed that. Please tell us.

The Aftermath of the Grand Inquisitor

Once he went to a monastery during the Dark Ages [a moment; the pain of the time came through]. This monastery had been visited by the Grand Inquisitor of the time and had lost many valuable and cherished monks and, as you say, priests. They were grieving, though they were ashamed of their grief because they didn't know whom they could trust, and they were terribly fearful. As it turned out, he said a blessing that took root there and sprouted in the form of a tree that lived about four hundred years. The tree continued his blessing, and the Grand Inquisitor not only never returned in any form to that place, but also to the village that surrounded it. It was as if they were an island in a sea of madness for a time.

That's the first thing he did when he got there; he said nothing to anyone. But there was a child there, and the child came up to him afterward, for he was dressed like a monk, and said, "Are you going to hurt anyone?" He turned to the child and radiated the full love of his being toward that child, saying, "I will do all I can to nurse everyone back to happiness." You know, the child did not understand the words because she was very young, but when she grew older she became the best midwife the village had ever known.

As an old monk, he went into the abbey and presented himself as an ordinary monk. The hierarchy, such as it was in the abbey, had been decimated, and the only man left who was the highest rank (I am saying "rank," but they don't call it that) was not a practical man and would really much rather work in the garden. (He was not practical with ideas and administrating, but he was wonderful with his hands and the soil.) He stayed there for a day and ate with the people and told stories. After a day they said, "Would you stay so that our beloved brother can return to the garden? Without him in the garden, no one can keep the plants alive."

So my friend said, "I will stay for seven days, and during that time I will pick three amongst you. One will be my successor, and I will choose this one on the basis of his ability to administer and guide you and help things work well for the abbey and the village. I will pick another who is the best religious guide. And I will pick one more who is the best to nurture you and cook and support you through this time of grieving that we must all do together, and to love our brothers on their way to be with God."

They were shocked when he said that because the Grand Inquisitor had said that those he had had killed were associated with the devil, and here this old monk (they saw him as an old monk, and everyone else did, too) was saying that they were going to God.

So he told them stories. He would say things as if they were stories, but they were true about the men who were killed. He would sing songs that were not only of the souls of those who were departed but were also connected intimately with the souls of those still left. When men live together for a time, whether they be in a religious order or a political or military organization or a family, they grow a bond together that is often unspoken and felt more than verbalized. The songs he sang brought back that old feeling of the bond they all had together, and this helped them to grieve and to know that these men were of God, that the Inquisition was something that was passing. It would come and it would go, and the better aspects of the Church would survive. And they did, you know, because this Inquisition thing is gone.

Where was this?

It was in the British Isles. I'm seeing it that way. He sang and told stories and taught them prayers. Some of the prayers are still around today and some of them are gone; they were prayers for the time. He nurtured them and noticed which brother amongst them was naturally the nurturer, and he took that brother aside. One of the monks who was killed had been the cook, and this man had been the cook's assistant. He said to him, "I'm going to teach you how to cook, and I'm going to teach you about herbs and many things so that you will not only be able to make wonderful foods for all your brothers in the abbey, but so that someday, not right away, as the villagers hear about these wonderful foods, you can begin to teach them how to cook when they ask, and teach them about the herbs. In this way the women in the village who know about herbs will be more highly thought of. In this way the town will be able to heal itself."

So he taught him everything, and it was as though the man experienced years and years of training as a cook (or a chef, as you'd say nowadays). He also learned in this time period (by your clock today it would be about nine and a half hours) not only how to cook everything that would be available, but how to find herbs, how to use plants and how to make the best wine—many things. And how to train cooks and assistant cooks who would follow. He did this.

So he stretched time.

He stretched time with the monk, and that one became not only the cook, but the one who nurtured the others. Then he noticed someone who was good with figures, as you would say—numbers of the time—and was also good at arranging things. This person was actually very young, one of the initiates, but he was a very good administrator. So he took him aside and taught him everything he would ever need to know about administrating, you understand? He presented him at the dinner table one night and said, "I know he is the youngest amongst you, but he will prove to you over time how wonderful he is at administrating, so please let him do it. And let him teach others who will follow; I know you won't regret it." And, of course, they didn't.

Then he picked one more, who was to be the religious leader. So many of the brothers had been killed. The monks had been decimated and had been considering disbanding. So he trained this one who had been a villager from that village. He trained him not only about the religions of the present, but he took him into his confidence because he saw within that person a profound spiritual connection. He gave him the gift of vision. He said, "You will be able to use this only for benevolent purposes" (he trained him this way). "You will not be able to see suffering and travail that might come. You will see only good things that will come, and in this way when you share your visions, you will find that they will always be welcome."

He also gave him the gift of teaching even though he didn't understand how he could do it. This monk was assigned to teach one other before he passed over so that the gift could continue.

He also taught the monk everything about the religion that was his own as well as many things about religions he had never heard of and that had not been heard of in that part of the world. It was not to influence the Catholic religion of the time, but to provide for the depth that is needed in a religious man, so that when his own religion cannot answer a question, he can pull on the wisdom of other religions to find an answer. That is what separates a profound religious teacher from a sage.

So he taught him how to be a sage and presented him to the group, saying, "You will find him to be a wonderful religious leader. I have shown him how he can find wisdom and the wisdom of the ancients. He will be able to tell you wonderful stories when I am not here to tell them to you, and he will be able to help you to help others even if those others are not of your faith." You know how important that is, especially for religious beings such as monks and priests who, even in their day, had to travel and would very often meet people who practiced other faiths, even if they didn't admit it.

So this abbey became known as the Abbey of the Heart. Eventually he left, but they didn't grieve his going because he left them with so much wealth—a wealth of people they didn't know they had. And for a place that had lost, as they felt, the very people who had held them together like glue, discovering the wealth in their own midst that they didn't know they had was magic to behold. This was one of his trips.

I mention this to you because you can see how what he did was profound and insightful—and yes, magical—yet in your time and my time some of these things can still be done. Perhaps not the same way, but it is possible to encourage talented people to follow the path of their talents for their benefit and for the benefit of others.

Not only that, you've much expanded our understanding of what Jesus did during that brief life. The impact he had on the whole planet is based on only one source.

He could travel in time—he knew who he was—and was unlimited, but instead of showing his unlimitedness to the people of the time and causing them to bow down (if not intentionally, then accidentally), he used his unlimitedness to travel to various places and do good things.

Buchenwald, World War II

Now I'll tell you something he did once. During World War II, which I remember, he traveled to a place of evil. It took all his strength magically and all his love to be able to go to such an evil place and be unaffected but also (and it may be hard for you to understand this) to keep from affecting or influencing before their time those practicing such evil deeds, for they would have a change of heart when the time was right for them. He had to pass through and do things there that would allow for the best to happen without changing the time sequence.

In those days toward the end of World War II, the time sequence was very carefully kept and nurtured, because there would be things that changed toward the end of World War II that allowed the war to end the way it did. If even the slightest thing had been changed, it might have been possible for an official Nazi party to have stayed in control of Germany. That was a risk right up to the end, even though it didn't seem likely. Even after the Allies took over Germany there was a lot of controversy, if you remember, because the generals in charge put some people in administrative positions who had been former Nazis because they were efficient. It was very controversial; this is well-known in history.

Toward the end of the war, he visited a concentration camp called Buchenwald. This was a terrible place, an evil place where people suffered and where even the guards suffered, because they lost their humanity for a time while they were there. What he went there to do was support a resistance movement. (Not much is known about that in your time, but there is a little known.) The resistance he supported was at Buchenwald in the camp.

The guards, or just the people?

It wasn't necessary to support a resistance amongst the prisoners; they had their own. But he supported a resistance amongst the guards, yes. The guards were weary, not just of what they were doing, but they missed their hearts. This is not very well known; you would have to have been there, but there might be a person or two who still remembers. He supported a resistance, and that's what the guards wanted, since they could see the war was coming to an end. They wanted to stop what they were doing. They knew that Germany was going to lose the war and they wanted to be soldiers again. They did not consider what they were doing as being soldiers; they considered it degrading and that they were being punished—and they often were. Soldiers who were sent there as guards were often being punished. Sometimes they were just mentally twisted and could not work within a military order, but sometimes they had offended the wrong person and were sent there as a punishment and made to do the things they did—there's no excuse for it, but the more they did those things, the more they lost their hearts. Ultimately, that was the true punishment.

So he supported a resistance movement that grew amongst the guards toward the end of the time of that concentration camp. As the

Allies were approaching, some of the guards who hadn't been influenced by that resistance movement fled because they knew what would happen to them when the Allies liberated the camp. But some of the others who felt that they needed to be soldiers again formed up and went off to fight in the battle. This might seem like a strange thing; you might ask, "Why didn't Jesus do something to stop it? Why didn't he do something to stop the suffering and the misery?" Yet he had done many things up to that point to stop it, to change it, to support the end of the war and to support the Allies. But he needed to do something, he felt, to support not only the humility but, perhaps most important, the self-respect of the people of Germany.

Now let me say why: One of the soldiers who went off to fight and be a soldier again survived; he was sent to a prison camp for a while in the United States, though not very long, because shortly after the end of the war, German prisoners were sent back. In the United States he had a chance to talk to some German-American citizens who were doing some work at the prisoner-of-war camp and rediscovered his self-respect. Of course, he didn't tell people what he had done in the war. As far as they knew, as far as the Allies knew, he was just a German soldier. They didn't know he had been a camp guard, and he wanted to forget that part of his life, not only because he was ashamed, but also because he knew he would be killed if it was known.

While he was in the camp, he rediscovered the religion that had been taught to him as a boy, one he had abandoned when he became interested in the Nazi party. You know, most soldiers weren't staunch in the Nazi party, but many were. He rediscovered that religion, and when he got back to Germany after a few years, he established a study group for that religion. He died not too many years ago, but that study group turned out about fourteen priests, and about sixty-three women went into various aspects of the church. Many of the children who came to those early study groups went on to do things; some of them changed religions and became lay preachers.

The most important thing is that society could have avenged itself on these people who had done these awful things, but my teacher knew that sometimes the hardest thing of all is to let people go on, because you never know the good they might do.

Prisons

In your time and certainly my time, prisoners are often sent to prison where they are not just kept away from society, which is the rationalization for sending them there, but they are very often brutalized, tortured and otherwise humiliated. So when they come out of prison, they just want to revenge themselves or kill themselves or do something else deplorable. But I have looked into the future because of my future life, and in those days, when someone does something that is against society, people treat him as if he is sick. He is not given drugs to dull his mind, but is loved and nurtured through his sickness until he feels healed. Then he is part of the community again.

There are tribal peoples living today that treat criminality as sickness. You might say, even with this ancient practice, that they are still perhaps ahead of our time—and yet it is, I believe, an immortal practice.

Teaching Animals to Help Humans

Then there was another time when he went to a forest. It was a vast forest; I think it was many years ago, perhaps several thousand years ago, and there were animals in the forest. It wasn't a rain forest, though there was rain; yet it wasn't a jungle. It was a beautiful green forest with many animals.

He went there and took the form of an animal, and in this place he became a deer. He spoke to the other deer and said, "Someday we will show the other animals the value of the human being." At that time the animals all said, "But from what we have seen from our visionaries, the human being will do terrible things to animals." Yet this deer, my teacher, told them, "Yes, but it will be your job to guide them back to what they truly are." Then he taught the deer what they could do, how with the great love in their eyes and hearts they could cause every human being to feel their love and the strength of their heart every time they saw a deer.

He changed form from one animal to another; he went all over the Earth, sometimes as an elephant, sometimes as a monkey, sometimes as a snake, other times as a dolphin—from one animal to another. He talked to them about what they would be able to do for humans when humans looked at them, consumed them, admired them or even reviled them; how they would be able to transfer some piece of the lost human identity to the human being they came in contact with, whether it be as a last thought, a profound feeling or a sound or a cry made to each other.

He reminded some of the animals; he commiserated with others, for they knew what they were supposed to do; and some he told for the first time, because they had not known. Thus when he was done doing this, all animals all over the Earth knew that this place they were on (Earth) was not just a place far from their home planets. They didn't know how they got here and weren't sure why they were here, because in those days there weren't so many people around, human people.

Now they all knew why they were there: to help the human being remember who he or she was, and that it would take an accumulated experience, many generations, many times, many animals coming and going. They knew that someday human beings would remember who they are, and they would have hearts that would expand a hundred times—the hearts they carried around with them—and that love would radiate out into the universe. And no matter where the animals were in those future days, having been part of this project to support the human beings to remember, they would receive tenfold the love they had given.

Beautiful! Because by then the humans would be able to radiate it.

This is what he told them. So they felt like they could go on and bring their generations into the world, knowing, because of their own visionaries, what would happen to many species, many of whom are not alive in this time anymore but who live on in spirit and on their home planets, sometimes looking at Earth from a distance to see how things are coming along.

I had no idea that he had such a profound impact. He was very busy!

He was most interested in many things. The thing I learned about him after spending a year and a half with him is that he seemed to have no limit to the subjects and to the range of ideas. He was always interested in exploring things mentally, physically and on the feeling level (instinctual) with his spirit, with his form. He didn't practice limits in any way, except when he was with people as himself, he never tried to be more than they were.

Ants

Even when he spoke with the ants, he was an ant—an old ant, a grandfather, you might say, or a grandmother. But he didn't try to be more than they were; he just told them a story, sang a song that they all felt and recognized in the deepest portions of themselves. And because they liked the story and the song, they passed it on. Now all ants all over the world, wherever they live, know this story and sing the song and tell it to their generations coming up.

This is why sometimes beings will talk to you about ants and how special they are. They have a wisdom that is theirs but that will someday be part of the wisdom that unlocks the final passage to the liberation of the true human heart. That's why they are so important and why they are committed to survival—not only for their own being, but for you.

Jesus in San Francisco during the Gold Rush

I will tell one more story. There was a time when he went to a place—these days you would say, "This is a place of sin; it is disreputable." It was in San Francisco around the time of the Gold Rush, and there were many places where there was gambling and prostitution. He went to one of those places. He wasn't frightened by people like that; he had never been frightened of that. He was known, even in the current Bible, for treating thieves as equals. When he went to this place, for about six days he became the friend of the madam. He took the form of an older woman of the time.

The madam, of course, was very busy; she ran her part of the enterprise and her partner ran the gambling part. She treated her girls better than most were treated at the time, and she also gave them all Bibles, which was unusual for those days. Sometimes there wouldn't be enough for everybody, but since there were never more than six of the women, she tried to make sure that each person had a Bible available to them—which was, as I say, unusual then. She didn't tell them how to live or that they had to pray.

She got into that business because she had been abused as a child and could do nothing else but become a woman of the streets. Being smart, eventually she saved enough money to become a madam, which was what she knew how to do, and she tried to make it as respectable as possible.

It was not a place that catered to a rowdy clientele, but rather a place that catered to, not rich gentlemen, but merchants, who tended to be more subdued. The gambling-hall part, which was in another part of the building, catered to anybody who came and went, but she was very specific with her partner. She said, "We will specialize only in the merchants, because they will be around tomorrow and they know that we'll see them again." She thought of herself as a merchant, and in that way she survived well into her seventies.

So as the grandmother, my teacher spoke to the madam at a time when she could speak (because a madam is often busy), complimenting her on the kindness she showed to her girls, as she called them. You might think that unusual, but the madam, Anna, had suffered as a child; she had been mistreated, and as a young girl (twelve, thirteen years old) had had a terrible opinion of herself. Yet she still managed to pull herself up through the support of a kindly woman who was religious. The woman, the grandmother, did not judge Anna for her occupation, but shared the Bible with her and told her she would not be judged.

So Anna treated her girls well because of the guidance of this woman and is now a shining light in the heavens. This woman, Anna, deserved the praise that my teacher passed on, on the last day of being there in the form of this grandmotherly person.

What reason did your teacher give to Anna for being there?

No reason; she said she was passing through and would like to visit with her. She said that she had been a neighbor (this is how he presented) when Anna was a child and had lost touch with the family. She visited and stayed with Anna in Anna's guest room. Basically she gave Anna the nurturing and love Anna had missed as a child. On that last day, Anna said, "Please stay; I love having you here. I would be happy to have you live with me as long as you wish." But my teacher, having other places to go, said, "Don't worry, I have contacted an old friend of mine who is in the neighborhood. I have to go tomorrow," she said, "but the day after tomorrow she will come here, and you will like her, you'll see. And if you like her, you'll perhaps have a substitute auntie to live with you."

Bringing Back a Soul Who Died

So when my teacher left, he resurrected someone. (This isn't known, you know.) This person had actually been in Anna's neighborhood, was a slightly older girl who had been forced onto the same path as Anna and had died two days before my teacher said there would be this person who will come. Having spoken to this person after she passed over (her name, I believe, was Gail), Gail said that she felt very disappointed in her Earth life because although she had married and had children, she never had a chance to resolve the dilemma of the career she was forced into, and she felt she had to stay around Earth until she could.

Well, what my teacher did was resurrect her because she wanted to have that chance. She did not look the same in her resurrected self. She was there in body, in form, and she looked like someone's beloved, sizeable auntie. She was at peace with her family and her children, so she didn't need to see them—not that she didn't love them, but she felt she couldn't go there as this other person and say, "Look, I am your mother." That would frighten them. She would look at them from afar sometimes and watch their progress. But she came to live with Anna, and Anna loved her from the moment she saw her. Gail had a chance to resolve her discomforts with her profession because Anna was such a wonderful person and treated her girls so well that Gail came to resolution. And because Gail was such a nurturing and fun person, the two of them had a wonderful life together.

And Gail didn't have to come back in another life to resolve it.

No.

How beautiful! So you could almost say he created a body for her spirit just as he did for his own.

Yes, he resurrected her personality, not her body. Perhaps *resurrect* wasn't quite the right word.

He allowed her to have that Earth personality in that body.

Yes, yes, and to nurture Anna and help her to continue healing herself and enjoy the pleasantries of the place, for there were those. In a few years Anna retired and she and Gail went to the outskirts of town, fortunately, and just lived on happily together—as women often did in those days, because women who weren't married would live together like sisters and friends and so on.

You have dramatically expanded the scope of our understanding of what Jesus did!

Other students may speak of other things, other places he went . . . He went to other planets, he did lots of things; I've given you just a few examples tonight because I'm most interested in the very young and the very old, and sometimes those in between [chuckles].

[Laughs.] What is your name in this life?

In my now life? I will give you my name translated to your language so that I can maintain my privacy. My name translates roughly into your language as Simon. Good night.

Jesus: Good evening. That was my student, Simon. He was called away to take care of his great, great, great grandchild. That is why his exit was speedy.

What was his name in your life?

Oh, he doesn't want that to be known; many of my students won't want that to be known. Do you know why?

No.

Most of them don't want to offend those who cherish the name of the apostles today, and they are perfectly happy being anonymous students, having names you would never recognize. Some of them will give names that are rough translations today rather than give their names of the time, even though my beloved youngster gave his name of the day.

You are saying that we will not know the names of the ones who were closest to you, whose names are in the Bible?

It is very possible that those who speak will not be the apostles you know, but it is also possible, depending on what they wish to do, that some of the known apostles will speak. It is hard to say. There is a story in that, and that is this: Some of the known apostles *aren't real!*

Oh, my God! [Laughs.]

They were made up in later days because they had all these stories written about that time in different documents; some were signed and some weren't. Some of the people who put the book together said, "Who wrote this? It's wonderful! We can't not include it, but we don't know!" So they took names of the time. They couldn't say "anonymous"; they were trying to attract people to the temple of Christ, as they saw it, so they said, "We'll use names that the people know!" So some of them didn't exist and some of them existed as different people, but does it really matter? They might say, "My words were attributed to this person or that person."

The two who have spoken so far have had so much love and so much . . . I just sit here and soak it up!

Yes, and there will be others. I think it will be fun, because it will give you perhaps a broader idea of some of my shenanigans. (I like that word; isn't it a wonderful word?)

You're a wonderful being. These stories are even more evidential and powerful coming from others.

Well, they're good too, because people can say, "Oh, this is the Earth I know, the part in which I live." Perhaps it is inspiring, but it is not something you can look over the back fence and say, "Oh, I know that." [Chuckles.]

This expands the possibilities. You know, we think of you as coming to save the planet, but you almost did it one being at a time!

And I am not alone; others have done things like this. But more about that for other books, eh?

Yes. We will eagerly await the next installment.

Good.

Thank you.

Good night.

7

The Shamanic Use of the Senses

Grandmother

May 5, 1998

Good evening. I am another one of the students. When I met this person we are both fond of, I was already a grandmother. I was practicing in the mystical traditions that had been handed down to me through generations. And I was with this wonderful teacher for almost three years. I had some grandchildren with me, and they came along; sometimes they helped and other times I helped them. But it was like a family trip, as you would say today.

My Training with Water

I was most interested in the teaching because it fit in so well with what I was already doing. I had been trained from childhood to perform certain vital tasks with water, and in that part of the world, water, although not being everything, is *almost* everything. I was particularly versed in working with water in streams and rivers as they bend. When water meanders, as streams and rivers do, every time it goes around one of those curves or arcs, it produces energy. When it flows straight, it is calm (unless it is going over rocks that produce rapids), but when it goes around curves, it actually produces an energy. I was taught how to utilize this energy for many tasks, not so much for healing but for the generation of energy that must be available. This is so that people will have strength, that mothers will have the extra strength they need to give birth and children will have the extra strength they need to survive (and in those times survival was not necessarily expected, though it was hoped for)—and for many other uses of this energy that can benefit the people, the plants and sometimes the animals.

I was taught to stand downstream. This is the flow of the stream; I would stand perhaps here or here, for example, and as it came around the curve, see, it would be more powerful.

Did you absorb it or did you direct it?

I directed it, not unlike how an antenna would do today. I would focus and ask for as much of the energy as could pass through me that didn't have other things to do (which it sometimes might) so that I could focus it to the places where it was needed by the people, the animals, the children, the plants or even the mountains or whatever felt it needed it. Sometimes, if it was too much, it would flow around me, and then I would direct it with my hands or by the way I moved my body, so it was kind of a dance. The closest thing today to the gestures I used would be some forms of tribal dancing that involved such gestures. That was what I was taught to do.

So when I heard that there was a teacher coming through who knew a lot about water, I wanted to hear what he had to say.

Before we get into that, was distance a factor? Did it matter whether they were a foot away or ten miles?

I was told that it didn't make any difference, but in my world what I did was practically never more than fifty or sixty miles away. I had been told in that lifetime that it would be possible to utilize this energy as long as the water was moving swiftly enough. If it moves very slowly, very slowly, then it doesn't work quite as well. But if it's moving—let's put a number on it you can understand—more than seven miles per hour, then it's particularly effective. In between there are gradients. I was told that there was no limit to the distance, and that it could be used for other planets and so on, but I never had occasion in that life to use it that way.

So I went to hear him talk about inviting the water, and he said there were also ways to encourage the water to pass you by if it was raining too much, but he wouldn't talk about that because we probably wouldn't face that in our lifetimes, and we didn't. He spoke of this, and I was very interested.

Jesus' Invitation

Afterward I had a chance to talk to him. I indicated to him, without saying exactly what I did, the general kind of work I was doing, and he was interested in that. He asked me if my people in the village could spare me. Then he told me that he would be in that area for two or three years and that I would never be more than fifty miles away from my village, so I could get home; and if it was an arduous journey, he would see to it that one of the stronger students would accompany me. As it turned out, I didn't need to go home and they could spare me for about three years. So two of my stronger grandchildren volunteered to help me out and went with me. That's how I was able to go with him.

Did you have an apprentice that did your work in the village?

At that time, yes; I had someone who didn't know everything, but she knew enough. Most important, when she felt there was something she needed to do but didn't know quite how to do it, she would focus on that need to know as long as she could. I would feel it—maybe not right away, but I would feel it—and then I would focus on the resolution. It would not necessarily be the exact resolution she needed, but I would focus myself into the complete resolution of whatever was the problem, and she could use my extended feelings of resolution to be inspired and know how to resolve the problem. In this way I was able to assist her on several occasions when inspiration wasn't coming for her on her own. It worked out well, and I accompanied him on his journey.

Tell me what you learned.

I paid particular attention to water and I learned things associated with it. The most important thing that I remember well and was able to use was learning about wind. Water and wind are related in terms of their flow; they flow where they need to go, each taking with it what is needed elsewhere and also sometimes being the messenger—in the case of water, downstream; in the case of wind, wherever it goes. So I became interested in the wind, and at that time, because wind was such a common factor, much more common than streams or rivers, I was fascinated with what he taught.

The Wind

He taught how to make the wind a friend, a close friend, so that the wind would visit and you could call it. If you needed a message to be delivered, whether word or feeling or energy, or if you felt you had a need, you would go out (as you would nowadays, but we were out most of the time then; our homes were often portable, sometimes not) and speak to the wind, knowing that it was there even if you couldn't feel it when it wasn't blowing. You would talk to the air and speak to the wind.

Let's pick something you can identify with today. Let's say you have a problem whose solution escapes you; you try different resolutions, but they don't seem to quite fix it, or they fix it only temporarily. So you explain the problem to the wind, then you ask the wind to bring you and all the rest of the people—or animals or plants, whatever it includes—the solution that will work best and last the longest for the problem.

Then very often the wind will come up; perhaps it will be just a slight breeze, perhaps it will be more pronounced, and you *feel* the problem and all its parts so that you can explain it to this person, that person and so on. You feel that problem after you're done speaking, then you gradually let it go and you don't think about it anymore. Then you wait, because the wind might have to travel all over the Earth many times until it picks up all the pieces of the solution. Perhaps you will be asleep when the solution comes in, and the wind will blow through your sleeping place. Or perhaps you will be outside in the fields or with the animals, and you will suddenly feel the solution. The wind can bring you everything you need.

Then there might be other things. How many of you (this has happened to all of you) remember the last time you had a wonderful inspiration? Maybe it was for a product that everybody needed, maybe it was a solution for serious world problems; but it was an inspiration about which you could personally do nothing in that moment. What you might do then is walk out into the wind, or if you can't get out (when you are in a place where going out is not easy), put your hand or your arm out into the wind and feel that solution to the best of your ability, that wonderful insight, that inspiration. Stand there as long as you are comfortable, then gradually let it go. It will go on to someone else who will be able to do something about it right then. In this way you act as a link to pass on or receive what is needed.

Tornadoes: Frustrated Wind

I was taught then that the wind is a messenger, and that sometimes when the wind acts up, as people used to say, it is sometimes frustrated because people haven't been receiving the message. The wind does not know that in your time, this teaching I have explained to you is largely unknown by most people. Some people know it, but not many.

It's carrying messages, but nobody's receiving them.

Yes, and the wind gets frustrated. When it gets very frustrated, it will spin. Instead of flowing around the world as it often does, it will get frustrated and upset and create smaller and smaller circles of flowing until it spins. You call this a tornado.

Or a hurricane.

The hurricane's a little different. But a tornado will express its frustration in that way. It isn't doing it to punish anyone, because the wind doesn't understand reward or punishment; that's not part of its world. But the wind is a feeling being.

Can we talk to it at some point?

Yes. As a feeling being it is a vital being; it is physical, it is solution-oriented and it is available at a moment's notice to deliver a message from you or to you. Anyone who is not being utilized to the maximum in the way that works best for it and to its feeling of comfort will sometimes get very frustrated and angry. Human beings will sometimes get self-destructive. Animals do something else that's self-destructive or they act erratically. Elements like the wind and rain become more of themselves, but in some aberration of themselves; the tight circle of a tornado is an aberration of the wind's natural flow.

Hurricanes: To Ensure That the Message Gets Across

A hurricane is more than wind; it is rain *and* wind. It is not just frustration. Sometimes there is rain with tornadoes, too. When there is, then the wind has called its brother, the rain, to come, saying, "They're not feeling this from me; can you add something? I will permeate the raindrops with the message or the need; can you add something by raining, so they will feel it? I know they must drink to live, so maybe you can help." That is why there are sometimes winds associated with ordinary rain. In hurricanes it is a need to saturate the area and blow this message into every crevice, places that normally don't get saturated by the rain.

As people become more trained to this wisdom (which is part of the reason for this book), then there will be less need for the wind to express itself with tornadoes and hurricanes and more utilization of the wind in the way it wishes to be utilized and was made to work. Then tornadoes and hurricanes will be very rare.

Wonderful! So you listened and learned. What else did you do during those few years? Did you travel to other villages within the fifty miles?

Yes, but because he wanted to accommodate me, I think, we also went to trails, very specific pathways where travelers and traders would come and go. You could go there and camp. It was a place where it was expected that travelers would come and camp. We would go to these places and just be there, and travelers would be coming and going regularly because there was water and sometimes shade and plants and occasionally trees that had fruit and so on. So these places were well-known. Even if the people didn't know about it, the animals they were traveling with could find it because of the smell of water.

The Smell of Water and Feelings

Water, you know, has a very distinct odor—not just water that is tainted. You can go to a place where there is the clearest mountain stream that has been touching only rocks and soil that are covered by this water—that's all it's ever known, the water and the flow and the motion and the rolling; in other words, a place where the water is as pure as it can be—and it has a smell. You can go there and familiarize yourself with that smell so that you know it. You would have to stay there perhaps for three days and three nights, because the smell at night is just a little different; it is not exactly the same.

Everything is like that. I don't know if you know it, but everything has a slightly different smell at night. If you stayed there for perhaps a week, focusing on nothing but smelling the water during the day and night, you might be able to memorize the smell. Memorizing a smell is different than memorizing words; it is something you know so well that it brings back feelings. People often have this experience, smelling foods and other things that bring back feelings and memories. It is like that, only you have to be able to remember *in your body* the way the water smells so you can find it. That's how animals find water if water is not available—that and instinct. But if it is within fifty miles of many kinds of animals, they will find it because they remember the smell.

Animals, when they are born, even if they have a better sense of smell than humans, are not born with the knowledge of what to do with it. They are taught by other animals, their mothers or fathers or brothers or older ones; they are taught by somebody in their group what to do with the smells and how to use them to save themselves. That's how animals know how to smell danger. Danger has its own smell. Did you know that there is a difference in the smell of danger, depending on whether it's dangerous for you or for others? There's a difference in the smell.

All these things are very useful. I did not learn all my lessons from this great teacher, but I learned a lot of them. The smell aspect I had already had some training in, but the nuances (that's a good word) of smell I learned from him. He was particularly interested in teaching me the smell of feelings; that's why I know about the smell of danger. He said to me once that even if you do not know a person, even if he does not speak your language or understand your customs (and for you it is the same), if you know what smell means and you understand smells, you will be able to provide everything he needs that you wish or that is safe for you to provide. And if there are things this person needs that you cannot provide or are not safe to provide, you can direct him to where you feel it would be best for him to go for these things or for what is best for him to do. You can do it all by pointing and by hand gestures. Or if you have enough water, for instance, you can share it with him, and he will then know. Sometimes people's sense of smell is so acute—if they've been trained or have experienced it in other lifetimes and it has become instinctual in a reincarnated life—that others will think the person is psychic, but it is because they have been trained very carefully in smell.

What does a person do who doesn't smell very much at all? Are there ways to get your smell back?

One of the best ways is to be around things that have very sharp odors, such as cooking odors or animal odors that are profound. When you can smell, or when the odors are safe to smell, open your mouth. You will smell more acutely if you can open your mouth (if you have trouble smelling it), because your tongue and the cheeks on the inside can assist your nose in smelling.

Wonderful!

Touch

Of course, there are other things. Sometimes there is touch. You all know and understand touching things, feeling them, touching each other, touching beloved animals and so on, touching the foods you eat and so on. But many of you have forgotten other forms of touch. When you touch somebody you love or somebody you don't even know, you can often tell (even if you can't see her; perhaps you're touching her from the back) whether she is happy or angry. You will often think it's because you contact her body and then you are inspired. But in reality you begin to know as you approach her, touching her energy body. This can be used for messages and for knowing what you need to know.

Perhaps the other person is not clear about what he feels and has feelings and thoughts he cannot express. You could go up to the person, put your hand in front of him (not right in his face), stand back at a distance and feel his energy body, saying, "Oh, this is what you are feeling." Then he says, "Oh, of course." He will talk to you and say, "What can I do about it?" Then you can advise him.

Most of the senses we have—the five senses and so forth—are not being used in your time in the way they were intended. Yes, you smell the food you eat, you smell a disagreeable odor, you touch someone or something, you taste things that are appropriate for you to taste. But the knowledge has died out in your times—not everywhere, but in many places—what other aspects of these senses mean.

Taste and Inspiration

Some beings—animals, even human beings in times gone by—would taste things they don't understand, and by the taste they would know what it is. If they had been trained to know what that taste is, then they will know; but if they have not been trained, as they bring it up to their lips to taste it, it moves through their energy body and they're already beginning to *feel* what it is. As they taste it slightly, it transforms; taste immediately communicates with your energy body, your soul body—all your reincarnational lives backward and forward; it stimulates or functions like a switch to stimulate everything you know and *can* know about that taste.

This is why you will sometimes see shamans, if they cannot feel what is wrong with a person, take their finger (don't do this without training) and touch the place on the person's body or the auric field of a person who doesn't feel well. They will not usually touch the person's body where it hurts, or taste it, because that could harm the shaman unless he is very advanced in his training. Let's say a person lacks an idea—there is a problem at his work. What you might do as a shaman is reach around to the back of the person's skull to where the soft part is below it, then to the top of that indentation, in the highest part of the soft spot in back. That's one of the places where inspiration comes in, but it's also a place where questions are transmitted. If you are seriously needing an answer to a question, you will transmit from the front of your body; but if it is a mental thing, you will transmit from the back of your skull. So if the person cannot speak or if there is a language barrier (it is just as much a problem in your time, if not more, than in my time), the shaman will reach around, touch the back of the person's skull with this finger . . .

The right-hand middle finger.

Or perhaps the index finger. Put one or two fingers there, then bring it around and hold it before him (in front of his chest, perhaps). If she doesn't get the answer, she'll touch one or both of those fingers lightly to her tongue. Then she will usually get the answer.

Because she'll taste it. Amazing!

Shamans will taste, not just the back of the person's head, which of course is the hair, but they will increase the contact with the question. Then they have greater contact so that the inspiration can feel the question more strongly and the shaman will know how to radiate the question and how to receive the best answer.

Not all mystical people in your time are doing this, but many can.

This skill was lost to most mystical peoples of your time because for a long time it was considered that anytime a shaman or mystical person touched someone, it must have something to do with witchery. This whole thing about witchery was perhaps unintentionally (or maybe intentionally) brought to the attention of people with the coming of the Christian religion. Not that witchery is in the Christian religion so much at all, but the culture around it was involved with that. As a result, many native peoples stopped doing some of that because they did not want to be accused of such things. For a while the wisdom died out, but I want to remind you now.

Hearing/Listening

Now, there is another sense, and that is hearing. One of the things this wonderful teacher taught by doing was to listen. He was a wonderful listener. As you know, the teachers who are often the most respected are those who listen, who know how to pay attention. Human beings are not that difficult to pay attention to, but sometimes it is a challenge to listen to the stone or to a leaf that has fallen from a tree and is almost at the end of its cycle. But you can hold it up to your ear or, perhaps more easily, to your chest or solar plexus area, in the center, and listen and feel what it wants, needs or wishes to communicate.

Sometimes, for instance, a tree might have an inspiration or overhear an inspiration that a human being or another tree or some other being had, but not have any use for it in its immediate environment for anybody the tree knows. When this happens, the tree will not know what to do; if it is a tree that drops leaves, it will place that wisdom in a leaf, and after the leaf drops it will gradually turn to dust. The dust will be impregnated with the wisdom and will blow somewhere in the wind or wash somewhere with the water. Maybe not immediately, but eventually that dust will find its way to someone who can do something with that inspiration. In my experience, seventy-five percent of the time, at the moment the inspiration comes through it is because you've consumed inspired dust in some form—maybe as a plant or as food or maybe from a breath—and you become open. You may get the inspiration the tree got or maybe another that you or your people need, but it will allow you to become more open to inspiration in general while that particle passes through you.

With rocks or a stone, for instance, you have to listen for a long time because stone is so massive. A stone shelf of a mountain or something like that is so massive that its memory runs very deep. When stone has something to communicate, it has usually been deep within the stone for a long time, slowly coming to the surface. You can listen either by putting your ear to the stone or by touching the stone—or as was sometimes seen in my time, people would lie face down on the stone and turn their head so they could hear it. You might hear a deep sound that sounds something like this . . . [Grandmother hums a deep, resonant tone. Apparently Tiger, the cat, expresses displeasure, because Grandmother speaks briefly to him, then describes to us what's happening.]

[Whispers to Tiger:] I did not mean to scare you. [To questioner:] My associate here becomes startled because he is involved in his own meditation to assist us.

So that sound (which I don't wish to make again because it disturbed my friend), which might be much deeper than my sound, has that "mmm" sound.

Like humming.

This will very often be the way the stone communicates through sound. It may be a sound you hear from the outside in or on the inside, as in an imagined sound. Don't assume it is something that isn't real. The imagination is present within you to act as a link to the unseen, the unheard, the untasted, the unsmelled or the untouched. It acts as a link to process those things in ways that have echoes of the senses within them—such as sound or smell that can easily function like a memory.

Is there anything else you want to ask about the senses?

It's amazing; I don't think, as you said, that many people know this.

Good. I wish to remind people.

We subjugate our senses to our thoughts so incredibly much.

That's understandable in your time. And yet sometimes when you are informed, things expand, yes?

Our Last Contact

Yes, absolutely. Let me ask a few questions about you. What did you call your teacher? What name did you use? Was he called Jesus, or did you have another name for him?

Some people called him Jesu [yay'sue] and others called him Josa [yo'sah]. And some just called him Teacher or other terms of respect. Nobody called him master, though, because in those days many people had to say that to the powerful, and he did not want people to call him that because he didn't want to be separate from the average person. He especially wouldn't allow us to say that, though we would often refer to him as the Master when we spoke to each other. But he said, "Never say that when other people are passing this way. They will think I am doing things they cannot do."

How old were you when you met him and how old was he?

Well, I was about thirty-six and he was about twenty-five.

So you traveled with him three years. After that did you come in contact with him or keep in touch with him or hear about him?

No, after that he went out of my life. He came to visit once much later when my life in those days was at its end, and he led me out of my body to the next world. He asked, I was told, to be able to do this, and in this way we had a chance to meet again in such pleasant circumstances.

What were you called at that time?

I would prefer to say only Grandmother, a title.

Is your name in our public records?

No. Most of the students are not mentioned in the book [the Bible].

My Present Life as a Librarian in a Different Galaxy

Where are you now? What is your situation now? Are you embodied on another planet or in spirit?

Now I am on another planet. I will describe what I do by your now terms. You would say I am a librarian, but the library is in front of me. I am standing in front of a pedestal about three feet wide and four feet tall. On the pedestal there is a small object that holds a crystal shaped in the form of a perfect sphere. The crystal is not completely clear, but mostly, and the crystal does not speak. It has gradually and gently been allowed to absorb all the knowledge that the stone itself is interested in. It is possible (and it has been experimented with in your time) to put information into stone for your own purpose, without asking the stone what it wants. But even in your time that is not the best thing. This crystal, when it was a little smaller and still growing, was inside a small vehicle about the size of the first satellite the Earth sent up.

Sputnik.

Yes. The satellite traveled where the crystal wanted to go. It traveled around the universe for a long time, and when it had absorbed all the knowledge the crystal was interested in, it came to this place. When someone has a question—and they can come physically or energetically—my job is to help them connect with the crystal. If the person is physical, I just say, "Touch it." If she is nonphysical, I will sometimes touch it; it will fill me with what it knows about the answer, then the person will absorb that from my energy body.

On this planet fully half the planet is devoted to such library crystals. At every station where there is such a crystal, there is someone like me who helps others get the answers they need. Sometimes people or even spirits don't come for a while. Then I'm able to either ask about what I'm interested in, or else ask the crystal to talk about what *it's* most interested in at that moment. When it's most interested in something, it communicates it with such enthusiasm that very often *I* get interested in it, too.

So I have lots of opportunity to learn and apply; that is the theme of this chain of lives I am living now: learning and applying.

Including the one with Jesus?

Yes.

Is this planet in our Creator's creation?

Yes, it is in this universe.

But not in any place we've ever heard of?

Well, if you were to stand on the outermost inhabitable planet in the Pleiades, farthest away from the Earth, we would be about three galaxies away in that direction. Before too long, you would be able to see the galaxy.

So you chose this incarnation you're in now.

As much as we consciously choose anything, yes. I chose it, and it has been very good. But I will tell you something: I miss the children. Not many children come, or if they do, they come with their parents or guides or advisors. As it turns out, this life is drawing to a close in another hundred years, maybe a hundred and fifty. I will say farewell to this life, and I've been promised that in my next life I will have a family—many children and grandchildren and great-grandchildren and so on, which is what I like.

Will you be here when Jesus and Buddha and Mohammed come back to the Earth?

I don't think so. That doesn't seem to be in my plan, but one never knows for certain. Nothing is fixed absolutely.

Where will this life as a mother and grandmother be?

They haven't told me. They don't want to distract me too much from my current life.

What can we call you now? You don't want to say your name.

Grandmother. That is my title; it is a title of respect, you know. In your time it has come to mean only a lady whose children have had children, but even in your time there are many peoples who use the term "grandmother" with great respect. I feel it is a wonderful thing to be called, something that often has to be earned.

All right, that is what we'll call you. Did you have other lives on Earth after the life as a grandmother at the time of Jesus?

No, the life I'm in now is my next life.

They last that long!

Oh, yes. There isn't deterioration here. One does not get old; rather, one completes a life as long as it is until you are done with it, and then you go on. But the body itself doesn't deteriorate; I go on and somebody else steps into this body. In that way this planet, which has scarce resources, is not overly exhausted.

By producing bodies. I see.

Yes.

Do you remember what the body had learned before your present life?

No; when I stepped into it there was no memory. You take it all with you.

I see. When you talk to the crystal, what are you most interested in when you can explore? What subject interests you the most?

Wind and water, still. On other planets there are different expressions of wind and water. Sometimes water gives off light or is much thicker; sometimes wind gives birth to color or has flavor. There is much variance. Even during all this time asking about wind and water from just this one crystal (there are many more here, but this is one is my assignment), it has never told me the same thing twice! Every time I ask, it is something new. So it must have traveled for a long time.

My theory is that everything you learn is preparatory to the next step. What do you think you're preparing for after the next life as a grandmother?

There's only one thing I'm sure of, it will be about learning and applying.

Well, you're wonderful. Jesus has said that a lot of the apostles' names in the Bible were made up because they would find beautiful writings and then put somebody's name to them.

Yes, but my understanding is that they did that with love, because they . . .

We're probably not going to be able to talk to beings named Matthew, Mark, Luke and John.

You might be able to, but some of the names were not the right names. But I don't think that's a problem.

My Life in Jesus' Time

Were any of the apostles you met when you were with Jesus ones we know historically?

Remind me of the names, besides the ones you mentioned.

[Laughs.] You've hit one of the things I don't know much about. Okay, Matthew, did you know him?

Not by that name. I did not know anybody by that name.

Mark?

No.

Luke? John? Timothy? James? Peter? Jude?

No, no, no, no, no, no.

Titus?

No.

Philemon?

Say that one again?

Philemon.

There was a Philema, pronounced as the French might pronounce it [pronounced fee-leé-mah], but that was a woman.

Well, we'll wait for people to say who they were. I just wondered if you had met some of the ones we knew about historically.

Nobody by those names, except for Philema. Is it not a nice name?

Beautiful. Did you bond with some of the other disciples and have relationships or interactions with them after Jesus and the group left your area?

One of them who was a trader by profession came to see me once. He did not speak of our time with the teacher, but we spoke of other things. It was a great pleasure to see him. We did not speak of things we knew well; rather, we preferred to speak about things we had just heard of, as people still do in your time, perhaps. He stayed overnight with my people and then went on. He was coming to do trading, so I saw him. It was a pleasure.

What did you look like at that time?

Well, my skin was quite dark, and I was a little stooped because of an injury I'd experienced when I was younger. I was also a little tired by then, and sometimes I needed to lean on people if I had been exerting a lot. That's why my grandchildren went with me. How to describe myself—my hair was dark, my skin was dark; my eyes were . . . not dark, but that sort of blue-green color you have today. What else can I say? I was a human being.

What about your husband? Was he already dead?

No, he was still alive when I came back. As a matter of fact, in that life he outlived me.

I bet you were glad to be home.

Very happy to see him, and we spent a little time alone when I got back.

I didn't realize you had to leave a husband. How many children did you have?

I had about eleven still living when I left, and when I came back there were only nine. But those things happened in those days; life was not taken for granted at all. That's why when people would greet the Sun in the morning or pay homage to the Moon at night, it was truly with thankfulness, because one could never be sure that in their given life they would see the Sun or the Moon again. It was a time of the unexpected.

Not many women would leave eleven children and a husband to go away for a few years.

I think if I had not had the position in the community I did, as this mystical woman, it would not have been accepted or even desired on my part. But because I was this person with these things I could do and could learn more, it was just considered part of my teaching. We were all surprised that I would receive teaching at that age or time of life, but I don't think there were any regrets when I got back. I gave my apprentice lots more to do and I was able to do more for the people in the village, and they were happy about it. Plus I had lots and lots of stories to tell, and everyone liked that.

After My Travels

So you taught everything you knew to your apprentice?

Yes.

So that it was carried on.

Yes.

Jesus said that one of the reasons he worked with women was to teach them to radiate this heart energy, this warmth in the chest. You did that, too?

Yes, I did that too, and taught my apprentice. I gave her the responsibility to teach everybody in the village. In that way she would gain the respect she deserved at that time. When the teacher and the apprentice are both alive and in the same place, it is hard for the apprentice to get respect, so the teacher must find ways to give the apprentice things to do, and let only the apprentice teach those things, never teaching them herself. In this way the apprentice has lots of respect by the time you pass over and doesn't have to earn it grudgingly because she's all there is now that Grandmother's gone! [Chuckles.]

[Laughs.] That's a beautiful way to do it. How did you start being a mystical person? When you were born did you have special abilities?

They told me that the grandmother or mystical woman of the time told my mother six months before I was born that I was going to be her apprentice. My mother was thrilled that she was carrying someone who would do good things for the people. She was happy about it. Because the other people in the village knew that this was a person who would help everyone in the village and maybe beyond that, they made certain that she got food and water and was with loved ones when she gave birth, so that the circumstances would be as good as they could be in those times.

What did your people do? Did they farm or have animals? How did they make a living?

Farming was not so easy then. They would gather, they would trade and they had animals. You had animals then, and there were a lot of people in my village who were traders and had been given skills and taught by other people in the community to know how to bargain and how to sell and buy. I suppose you could say that for our time, we were business people [chuckles].

Because you didn't have to travel; you could stay in the village.

Our village was close to the trade route, and that was to our advantage. As a result, everyone who came or went on the trade route knew they would be close to our village. If they wished to come over, they could travel no more than about six or eight hours to get to our village from the trade route. If they were careful, they could get there in one day.

Where did they tell you they came from? From how far away?

The farthest away any traveler came from that I met was what you now call Mongolia. He came through China and just kept going south. Eventually, he told us, he wanted to go to Africa, and then he would see if he could get back to Mongolia. If not, he would marry and raise children, and he would send his first son on the journey back to Mongolia to give the people there the message that he had survived and would teach his son all he had learned. I don't know what happened to him.

For the times, that was an interesting life; people came and went with skills and stories and materials you could buy.

Yes, there was variety, which was not common unless you were in business.

[Laughs.] But you called it trading.

Yes; we didn't call it business, but I'm trying to . . .

To use our terms.

Yes.

Have you shared most of the things he taught you?

That's what I have to say.

Well, we can quit. You're so wonderful that I hate to say good night.

Perhaps we will speak again.

Yes, yes! When I read this perhaps I'll have some intelligent questions about the senses.

Well, until that day, good night.

8

The Child Student Who Became a Traveling Singer-Healer

Duvla

May 7, 1998

Greetings. When I was with That Man, called Jesus now, I was three years old when I started out with him, and I was with the group that traveled with him for six and a half years. So when I left I was not quite ten.

The thing that was so wonderful about him is that he felt his communications to all individuals were equally important, no matter their age or what station in life they occupied or what philosophy they held dear, even if they were a Roman soldier or someone who had no true concept of philosophy other than [honoring] the emperor. The specialness of this wonderful teacher and friend was not often seen in larger groups, but rather in his communion with individuals.

My Introduction to Song, a Source of Joy and Healing

Because I was the child of the woman he favored, I was with him a lot. He always took time for me if I had needs, and he would sing to me every day. He was a wonderful singer. Sometimes the songs were sweet and cheerful for a child, at other times they were filled with deep meanings. Sometimes the meanings were not understood by me until much later in life.

I think he wanted to plant in me the joy of music and give me an entire litany of prayer songs. You have prayer songs today, but most of these praise God or god figures. His prayer songs were different; they would request something for all the people or for individuals or for people in a certain condition, and in that way the songs could be adapted to the circumstances of the moment.

When I moved away from traveling with That Man, I stayed for a time with my grandparents. When I was about thirteen years old I started my . . . you would say practice or occupation. What I did was sing prayer songs for people. Sometimes if they had disease or discomfort, the song would be to relieve that. When I was singing I would sit someplace near them, depending on where their discomfort was, and sometimes I would move around them as I was singing because energy flowed through me because of the notes, by how long I'd hold the notes and, I believe, the words. (In the beginning, I believed the words had something to do with it; later in life I decided that it wasn't so much the words as the intent.) The energy would flow through, and usually within the next three days the person would show marked improvement. The person might not be fully healed, but he or she would get better. If he asked me to do the song again, I would do it differently the second time, acknowledging and thanking the improvement and asking for further improvement until the person was either well or until I or he had to move on. (In those days people were, out of necessity, sometimes mobile, depending on where the food and water were.)

I was trained, then, for this life's work. It wasn't in a specific religion or philosophy. I had the opportunity to sing for soldiers of different armies because I could not say no; if someone asked me to sing, it was my obligation to do it. Sometimes it was a pleasure and other times [chuckles] it required discipline to do it because the person might not always be so benevolent. But I believed and was taught that the songs themselves would tend to increase the benevolent or heart aspects of the individual or group, and that alone would be a worthy reason to sing the song. Sometimes there were gestures I felt inspired to do, even to make drawings on the ground with a rod of some sort. Of course, when the song was over, I would make those things on the ground disappear . . .

Like a sand painting . . .

. . . roughing them out. It is essential to do that, because that way it returns to the Earth, and also anybody who happens along doesn't step into its energy.

It was a lot of fun in the early years. When my mother left me with my grandparents, I think it was toward the time when there were political problems for This Man, and she felt I would be safer with them. She was able to come back when I was about fifteen years old, and we were together until I went out and did my work.

Was your mother Mary Magdalene?

No, no. He has often indicated that Mary of the Magdalene was his mate, and I think this was true for a time, but he had different mates at different times. My mother had another name; as a matter of fact, I don't recall it. I know who you mean by Mary of the Magdalene, but I think her name was quite different. I don't think I can pronounce it, but it sounds something like the name André, though with a bit more of a gypsy sound.

Learning about Gypsies

This Man was particularly enamored of the gypsy people even though there weren't any around there. He told us about them; he said that in the coming years they would be more adrift, not having a homeland, yet that their very existence was vital because their breath and their heartbeats were particularly and essentially tuned to the breath and heartbeat of Mother Earth. And when Earth had difficulty breathing or her heart was under a strain, she would call upon them as people to breathe a little deeper for her and let their strong hearts beat some for her also. That's why he said to me once that this world cannot exist without these people.

Of course, we all wanted to know more about them and where they were. He said that they were a lot like us, that they traveled regularly because their homeland was really the entire Earth, but that the homeland they particularly cherished would not be available to them for a time. So he would sometimes sing us their songs, and they were quite beautiful. There was something similar between our music and theirs. I think that in some way the gypsy people were related to us.

When you were three and a half, how old was Jesus?

When I first met him, he was, I think, about twenty-four, something like that.

Twenty-four to thirty and a half.

Something like that.

So did you hear about what happened to him?

Jesus' Travels to the Machine Age

I didn't. When my mother came home, of course, I asked about him, but she said that he had decided to go to other countries and visit all his beloved friends and companions. Because she had vision, she could watch him and sometimes would say, "Oh, he's there now with these people" and describe the place. Sometimes I could tell by her description that it was not of our time, because he would travel a lot to the times you are in, roughly from 1870 to about 2010; he's in this part of the time cycle quite a bit. "Of all the times and of all the places that need the most help," he said to my mother, "it will be in the time of the machine."

My mother wanted to know, "What's a machine?" He said it was a creation by human beings of different forms of life that we all knew—stone and sand and water and rock (metal, he called it) and other things that were not asked to become what they found themselves to be. As a result, during the time of the machine there was great unhappiness; all the machines were terribly unhappy because they were made up of materials—yes, life forms—that would rather be in their homes.

As a result of their great unhappiness and because there were so many of these machines, sometimes the people would feel unhappy and not know why. This was because people are naturally sympathetic and would take on the energy of any being, if it were too overwhelming, when that being could not encompass its feelings. Human beings, being compassionate, would take on those feelings to help out, though the human beings in your time don't know this. As a result, when people feel unhappy or depressed, much of the unhappiness that they can't say is caused by this or that is caused by the unhappiness of the machines.

Tracking Jesus' Journeys in Time

My mother described one of his journeys [in time]. He was a man, a regular man, not unusual, but not a man who worked with machines, though. Because this man did not have a job with machines, he could walk around quite a bit. He would walk around at night and go to factories that were closed. He'd go up to the factory, lean against it or touch it with his hands and, through his embrace (which is our word for nurturing), run huge amounts of love, compassion, friendship and sometimes the balm of feelings encompassed by what the machines had been (what they would like to feel if they were home in their native places) into the closed factory. That's what he would do. It would appear to the average person that he was penniless, and he would sometimes be companionable with penniless people.

One of the things he also did on several of his journeys, my mother said, was go to shelters where people sing songs, say prayers, have a meal and maybe get clean clothes and have a bath. He said that the prayers weren't quite the kind of prayers we used (I was taught with song prayers, but there are spoken prayers and motion prayers and so on), that the prayers of your time are not as direct to the cause and cure as our time. But there were many people working at these shelters who were kind and generous with their own time and had great compassion for those who didn't have much. He said he would go there sometimes just to say a kind word to one of the workers at the shelter who would rarely be encouraged by those they were trying to help. He told them many things, such as how kind they were to do these things and "What a good heart you must have," things like that, very encouraging for people in places such as that.

Did you ever see him again after your mother came back?

No, I didn't have the vision. Mother had the vision, she could see. She loved him, but she had vision before she met him, so sometimes she would look in on him. At other times she would feel an uncomfortable feeling when she was going to look in on him, and she knew it wasn't a good time, so she didn't. But if she didn't get that feeling, then she would look in. I think he knew when she was looking in; he was very sensitive. He would always know when people were looking in.

She was very talented, then, because she was looking into another time and another place.

Yes; she didn't always understand what she saw. Once she had met him and fallen in love with him, from that point on she used her vision exclusively to see where he was and what he was saying and doing. Sometimes she would say to the people, "This is what he's talking about," and then we'd get to hear what he was talking about. It was a way of staying connected with him.

How wonderful! He was on the Earth plane fifty more years, until he was eighty-three. Eventually your mother died and you lost touch with him, right?

Well, you know, my mother always told me that he could travel throughout time as well as to different places and, she thinks, to different planets, because sometimes she would look at him and things would be so different that she was sure it couldn't be on Earth. I'm not certain of that; that's just what she said. But he was immortal. My feeling always was that he was immortal and that there wasn't an end to his life, that he just went on.

But at a certain point you quit hearing about him from your mother, right?

When my mother passed over, I didn't hear any more.

How old were you then?

Twenty-three.

Oh, so young!

Not in my time. In your lifetime, to live into your sixties is quite normal, but in those days to live into your thirties would be the normal life span. Of course, just like in your time, there were people who lived longer. But in my time, the thirties was about what you could hope for.

We probably would not recognize it, but can you say your name?

I will tell you only my nickname. We have been guided by That Man that it would be good not to give our names too much, so as not to cause any disruption in your current beliefs. So my nickname was Duvla [*u* as in "good"].

What does it mean?

Bird.

You sang like a bird, right?

Oh, I didn't make that connection till you said that, but yes. I never thought of that.

When did you go out to start teaching or doing your prayer songs?

As I said, when I was thirteen.

At some point you got married; did you pass that on to your children?

I didn't get married. I was sorry to have missed that, but because I always had to be traveling and going places, I felt it wouldn't be fair to marry a woman and expect her to travel with me. So I didn't get married and I never had children of my own.

Taking on a Blind Child Apprentice

Did you take an apprentice?

Yes. One day a grandmother in the group of people I often visited said that she had a child in her care who was very special and that the child was blind, but even so, she had the capacity to see, in a way. She would make little humming sounds and would use that to know where things were. She also seemed to have some sensitive abilities. I knew this child because I had been to that group several times, and the child and I were very fond of each other. The grandmother said she was getting old and it was hard for her to care for the little one, and would I consider letting the little one travel with me? Of course, first I asked the little one, "Is this something you would like to do?" And she said, "Oh, yes." So I said, "I would be honored." For me it was like having a daughter, and it was wonderful. She became my apprentice.

How big an area did you cover in your travels?

By today's standards not very much, but in those days . . . about fifty or sixty square miles. Of course I was walking . . .

You were walking!

Naturally; everybody did, just about everybody.

Traveling Where I Was Needed Most

Did you have an itinerary, or would you go where you felt a calling?

I'd go to where I felt the need. You can do that today, you know. It's not very complex; you just ask to be guided. Today that is what people usually do. I would turn around slowly in a circle, and I would recognize the feeling of being needed. It was a feeling within me.

In a certain direction.

Yes, and the feeling would be most profound in one or two directions. I would go in the direction I felt was the most urgent, and afterward I'd go to the other place that felt urgent and so on, just like that, just walking around in this area. I would do my song prayers and people would feed me. If my daughter was with me, they would feed us and give us water and a place to stay and so on. It was a good life. We had what we needed and we were of service, service that was needed. It was very good, a good life.

How old were you when you passed over?

Unusually old for the time; I was seventy-six.

Really!

I was considered ancient.

How wonderful!

I did not look my age so much, they tell me, but [chuckles] maybe they were flattering me, I don't know.

There's something about the vibration of sound and love. They tell us now that toning and certain sounds are rejuvenating.

It is possible. Maybe they weren't just trying to be nice. [Laughs.]

They didn't have a lot of mirrors, right?

No, we didn't have any, so if we wanted to know what we looked like, we had to ask somebody else. [Laughs.]

But you had some reflective surfaces like water, didn't you?

Yes, but we did not have a mirror as a reflective device. We didn't think about water as a reflective surface. I suppose some people did, but I never did; to me, it was a necessity and I would notice that there was some reflection. It was like you would notice that a tree is green; you wouldn't think about it.

It's wonderful that you lived long enough to care for your daughter, because it would have been difficult for her to go on without your care.

Yes, I lived long enough that she was able to marry and have children of her own. Her husband and eventually her children helped her around. It was very nice.

Did you teach others?

Apprenticeships

Just my daughter. In my days one had one apprentice, just one. It wasn't just a matter of teaching something; not only did the person have to learn all the songs and the words or the feelings with the words, but . . . in my days I taught the words, but there was also a way of being that went with it, just as your philosophers of today have a way of being, and that can be learned only by living with the person. I think this is normal. Even in apprenticeships for carpentry and other trades, the apprentice lives with the teacher, not only to learn what the teacher has to offer of the trade, but also to pick up the teacher's philosophy and habits, which are intended to allow the occupation to blend into and support his life rather than be what you would call in your time a job of work. The occupation would be your life just as much as your family or your children were your life.

In other words, it would take a long time, not just teaching the songs, but it would take fourteen or fifteen years at least to have all the different nuances of philosophy and attitude and so on to come up. So it wasn't practical to take on another apprentice, I think.

Did she pass that on so that the teaching continued?

Yes. She had twin daughters, and she felt she could not teach it to one without teaching it to both, so she taught it to both. And when they did the work, they traveled together, so they were like two who did what one had done before. They never traveled separately, but always together, and when they came to the end of their lives, they died on the same day.

Were you still alive?

No. Old age runs in the family; at least it started with me. My daughter lived for a long time and her children lived for a long time, too.

My Songs and the People I Served

Are any of your songs in what we call the Bible?

No.

Nothing about you?

No.

When you sang, would you talk about your teacher?

Very rarely. He discouraged that because he said people in desperate conditions are very often looking for someone to serve them, someone outside themselves, not God only, but someone who would be the rescuer, something like that. And he said it's very important to tailor the song to fit the person, the circumstances and their relationship to their God philosophy, world family and so on.

He said, "It's very important not to bring me into the song because I won't be a part of their world, and you'd have to teach them something about which they know nothing. Before long they would be more interested in what you were teaching them about me than *their* condition, and it would be up to them to participate in the improvement of their condition. So don't bring me up," he said, "it's a complication."

What a wise being! So within that fifty square miles you must have become quite well-known after all those years.

Yes, it would serve to say that almost everybody I would see there would know me, so it was kind of fun after a while. And because people would get to know me, they would feel safe to tell me what in their lives needed to be improved or what was happening for them that they would appreciate some help with. As you get to know people, they trust you, then they feel they can tell you things they might otherwise feel shy about (shy, good word).

You were like a trusted counselor as well as a healer, then.

Well, they'd only tell me about things I could sing about; I didn't tell them how to run their lives or anything. I always assumed they knew how to run their lives because they were alive and just being alive in those days was an accomplishment.

I don't think we appreciate that enough now; we take being alive so much for granted that we focus on our problems instead of being grateful for life.

Yes. I think that is why it is useful to go camping or to go live like other people do sometimes, just so you can appreciate what you have. Sometimes even the poorest person has more than he realizes; other times the richest person has less than he realizes.

When you passed over, did you see a bigger picture? You understood much more of what was happening, right?

My Subsequent Lives

Well, not immediately; when I passed over I went through a similar process that all people do on the Earth. I lived a few more lives. But I decided to stay in time sequence, and because my teacher, my friend, was spending so much time in that 1870 through 2010 time, I decided that I would also spend time around then. What I am doing is allowing myself to be close enough to the Earth so that I can see and speak through the occasional person, and sometimes I accompany the angels. They call me by my nickname, Duvla.

What lives did you have? Did you get to have children in your next life or the life after?

In the next life, yes, I had children, and in the one after that, too. That was nice.

In what time periods did you live?

It's hard to say, but I'll give it my best. Around 1023 I had a life, and then around 1417, something like that.

Now you work with the angels, but you don't appear in a body the way Jesus does when he comes to people?

No, he can do that [chuckles], and he doesn't need my help. But I've noticed that a lot of the students are close to the Earth at this time, available.

Available for what? How do you help?

I can't say what they are available for, but for me, I am available to inspire and talk to people sometimes when they are dozing you say dozing? Light nap? And I talk to them or sing to them, usually sing; that's my nature. Not when they're deeply asleep, though; then their teachers talk to them.

I see. And have you channeled through other humans like you're doing through Robert?

Never.

How does it feel?

Different.

Do you like it?

Too soon to say. I'm not used to speaking; I'm used to singing.

Well, you're doing a wonderful job.

Thank you very much.

When you first came in I kind of tingled all over; I felt the energy.

Oh, that's nice.

Sing for What You Need

But is there anything the readers could . . . let's see, do you want them to call on you or to communicate with you?

No. It is unnecessary, and I don't want to be made a god. People call on someone when they think . . . no. Rather, I would encourage them, if they need something, to sing about it and ask for what they want and need for themselves or others. Always ask for what you want or need. If you need to change your conditions, don't ask for something to stop; say that you want something to start.

The new thing.

The new thing to start, yes, because asking for things to stop doesn't work so well.

I wasn't thinking about you being a god, I was just thinking . . .

I didn't think you were thinking that, but the reader might take it that way. I have learned from my teacher to avoid being turned into a god.

I was just thinking more like in the old days, when you felt the need and would sing the songs.

I see. I would feel the need because the people would ask me. I would feel their need and I would go to where they were, and then they would ask me. I wouldn't just walk up and sing. It's good to be asked, you know. Then you know that people are ready.

That's profound, what you said. Share some more about people who sing their own songs. What would you teach them about how to do it?

It's important to ask about or sing about something that's truly important to you. It doesn't have to be to improve your own lot in life; it could be to improve the lot in life of someone else or other beings or anything like that. But it *can* be to improve your own lot in life or your family or your friends. For instance, you might hear about (in news programs) or read about or someone might tell you about a lot of people in another country (too far to go to) who are having some difficulty—fire, flood or something, famine perhaps. Let's say a famine. What you might do is find out (it works better if you can find out, but you don't have to) what are the foods the people eat over there. Maybe it is corn or maybe something else, some kind of fruit or something. Then you sing your song to that food—say, corn; you might say the corn goddess—or the pineapple teacher or something.

The main thing is that you feel into the right words and ask the foods if they would go and be more abundant in the places where people are hungry. When people are hungry, very often they need clear, fresh water, so you might sing to the water and ask it to come to the surface in many springs that will not cause a flood but be available for the people and the animals. Spring water, you know, is almost always very clear. You sing to the things, you see, that are missing in that place.

Then you mention the name of the country because you wouldn't know the people by name—you would just say "for the people who need you." You would never address water as a thing; you address it as a beloved friend. [He sings:] "O beloved friend, water: Would you come to Africa and be with the people who need you?" Like that, you understand. I am using Africa as an example; it could be someplace else.

Then you would sing about the foods the people normally eat or grow because those foods know the people. The foods are not a stranger to the people and the people are not a stranger to the foods. The foods would know the people and might feel affection for them and want to help—more so, perhaps, than foods the people don't know. You would sing to them, and you sing your song as often as you feel it's needed. There'll be a point at which you won't feel the need to sing it anymore, which probably means that the foods or the water functions have heard what you have to say and there's no need to continue to tell them; they know already. Then you let it go and go on to the next thing.

How would you sing for peace in a particular country? Is that too large a topic today?

No, it's all right. You might sing to the feelings. Peace is a circumstance, a condition; it isn't necessarily the feeling of peacefulness. It might be the absence of fighting or the actual feeling of peacefulness within a person, which is a very benevolent feeling. You'd have to know (at least it would be good to know) if there is fighting going on. If there is fighting, you might sing to the feelings that would transform that violence. Violence is often transformed by peacefulness, yes, but it is also transformed by satisfaction—you are satisfied and you no longer have to continue doing what you are doing, see? You might sing to those feelings, asking those feelings and others you might be inspired to ask for, to be welcomed in the bodies of the people who are in conflict. You would invite such feelings into the bodies of the people and encourage the bodies of the people to welcome the feelings. In this way you do not exactly interfere, but you create the potential for harmony without actually forcing it on anyone.

That's great! I've never heard of anything like that. What about someone who has a physical or an emotional ailment? How would one sing to oneself?

If you have some knowledge of your disease, you could use a picture as it might look inside your body, but you can also use feelings. Maybe your physical illness gives you pain and makes it difficult to do things you once did. It is hard to walk or move in a certain way; maybe it's difficult to swallow. Try to remember a time when it was easier or more comfortable, then invite the feelings of comfort within you, like the other song. But then you would add this: Because you are asking to feel benevolent, you are asking to feel charmed by benevolence. It's a special feeling to be charmed by something—kind of tingly and cheerful. And you would also ask your physical body to celebrate itself in its most healthful manner.

You have to be careful, though, because if you ask for this healing when it is time for you to pass over, you are rejecting the gift of death. Death, of course, does not always seem like a present, but when you get to the other side, you know it is. If you have had a wonderful life, it is hard to imagine, but when you get to the other side it is even *more* wonderful. You have to be careful, because you as a person, not being a doctor, might not know if you are dying—and maybe no one tells you. So you might say, "If it is for my best benefit, may I then . . ." and so on, like that. But it is unwise to say "for my highest good," because if you sing for something for your highest good rather than for your best benefit, your "highest good" might reflect on some higher portion of you, and the good of that higher being might discount the value of your physical self in your conscious life. So you say, "for my best benefit."

For here and now.

For here and now, yes, or "here in my life now," something like that. Then it is very specific. It might be that your best benefit would be for your life to be over or even some illness to take place. Then you find yourself with other people who have that illness and maybe you meet somebody—who can say? Maybe you wouldn't have met that person if you hadn't had that illness. So it is important to not assume that illness is necessarily all bad.

That is totally new thinking. The same principle applies with emotional healing for yourself.

Yes. Perhaps you are a sensitive, compassionate person and perhaps are working in a factory with many unhappy machines. You might find that when you get to work, you are sad all the time, and when you are at home, maybe working in your garden or around your plants, you are cheerful. It would be easy to assume that this cheerfulness is because you are home and doing what you wish when you want to—and that might be all there is to it. But if it is a struggle to get happy at work and if people say funny things and you just can't laugh, then you might be taking on the unhappiness of the machines.

Then it's good to sing to the machines—but not at work, so that no one thinks you are crazy. You can make up a tune and sing the words in your mind, see? You can whistle or hum the tune out loud and say the words in your mind, if you can do that and still do your job at the factory. Then you sing to what the machines were—you know, maybe metal was a mountain or glass was sand or something, and you sing to it. Maybe when you are on your lunch time or a break for the coffee, you can continue to hum your little tune and feel, project pictures or think of pictures of mountains and sand on the beach, perhaps someplace pleasant (always a pleasant picture, okay?), and maybe eventually the machines you work with will start to feel better and you will cheer up, too. They will feel a little better anyway because you're making the effort on their behalf.

Very often when a human being feels some sadness like that for no apparent reason, it means that someone or something around you is sending you a message. You can receive it most easily in your feeling body because that is the most sensitive part of you and you get your messages there first. Maybe then you sing a song of healing and wholeness for whatever is around you. If you've done it with all the machines and you still feel kind of sad, maybe it is for a worker near you, so you sing a song for him or her in some general way. Maybe he is shy or doesn't talk to you, so you don't know what's wrong with him. But you can sing a song for him that welcomes happiness into his physical self. That is not interference.

These things are wonderful! Apprentices have to live with you, but what can you teach our readers beyond what you've said?

Everything Has Its Song

In my experience all life naturally sings. The plants sing, and their communication tends to be melodious. Rocks, weather, even lightning—all these beings have a natural song. Human beings have a natural song. Sometimes from individual to individual there's a little difference; other times there are general songs that fit the patterns of all people. The important thing to know is, very often you will find yourself singing a tune. Sometimes it is a tune you know or have heard somewhere, other times you are not sure where it came from. When you're not sure where it came from or you're making up a tune (perhaps you are a songwriter or a musician), very often these tunes will be expressing something from life around you. If the tune causes you to feel good and causes others around you to feel good, it is a tune of celebration, celebrating life. If it is a sad song and causes others around you to feel sad, then . . . think about it. Just pay attention to what you are doing.

It is not bad to sing sad songs, but I believe it is good to build resolution into the song. Somewhere in the song it could say, "Things could get better." It doesn't have to say it in the words; it might say it somehow in the structure of the song, in a musical way. If you are clever as a songwriter, you'll find a way.

This is not being done, basically, on the Earth right now, except possibly among some tribal peoples. Has this teaching come down to us now in any way on the Earth? Is anybody doing this?

I think, as you say, some tribal peoples, some spiritual peoples, and to an extent, one cannot overlook what happens in churches. Churches are often places of song, and while the song may not be what I am talking about, it is related to that.

Yes, I used to go to a Baptist church when I was young just so I could sing off-key and nobody would notice [laughs].

It's a pleasure to sing, isn't it? And when you're singing with a group of other individuals who are perhaps like-minded or at least trying to sing the same song, you can celebrate life. And if you're not carrying the tune, as you say, no one knows but those who are standing next to you. [Laughs.] Perhaps they will take it in stride.

Do you plan to have another Earth life, like possibly when Jesus comes back?

Traveling Now with the Angels

No, I don't think so, but I will watch. A lot of what I am doing now is watching, although I do travel with the angels—not all the time, but sometimes. Angels don't always come to Earth only to escort those who are passing over; sometimes they come for other reasons.

Can you say a little about that?

Sometimes they will come if their presence can create greater benevolence. Sometimes, you know, there is strife that builds between individuals or groups of individuals, and while angels are not allowed to interfere in your growth process, sometimes they are allowed to be present. So sometimes they will just be present, and the radiance of their presence will occasionally stimulate things to be resolved in some more gentle way. As you know, resolution that is gentle and harmonic and flows in natural ways is likely to be more permanent than resolution that is authoritarian and willful. Authoritarian and willful resolution is invariably temporary.

So in some circumstances they are allowed to observe, and one of these circumstances is at birth. So they will often be present during the birth of a child or an animal; they will just be there. And that is a pleasure.

That's so we'll feel more comfortable? More love?

One can hope, but with that kind of energy around, I would assume it is doing some good. I am just telling you the circumstances in which they are allowed to be present on the Earth. As I say, it's not just when people die; there are other times when there is great suffering or some great calamity—for instance, a tidal wave. Although they might be called on in the aftereffects of a tidal wave to escort souls through the veils, sometimes they are allowed to be present (not always) before the calamity. If there is going to be a crash of some sort—a car, bus, train, something—sometimes they are allowed to be present in the vehicle before it crashes, and people will sometimes get this slightly euphoric feeling before the crash or feel giddy, as they say.

Then what? Does that help them to think clearer if they're the driver, and survive the crash?

What angels do is not always laid out for logical reasons. I am just telling you when they are allowed to be present, how they are allowed to be present, not that there's any specific intention to change things.

I see. I didn't know that they had to be allowed. I thought you could call on angels to help you.

You can call on them to help you, but they may not be able to come to you physically.

Who makes these decisions?

Whoever tells the angels what they must do.

Who's that?

I would assume it is God.

I see. We'll get into that later. That will be an interesting topic. When I used to travel, I would ask the angels to take care of me; I just assumed they were around, keeping me in this reality or something.

It's possible.

But not probable.

I didn't say that. It is not always good to look for hidden meanings. I will tell you something . . . this is a story.

A Story of a Child and Two Presents

Once upon a time a child was given two presents. One was beautifully wrapped with beautiful paper and beautiful ribbon, and the other was simply handed to the child. The thing that was handed to the child was a beautiful apple, so pretty that you almost wouldn't want to eat it. It was a big, big apple, and the child said, "I will save this to share with my brothers and sisters; it is too much for me alone."

Then the child opened the other present and very carefully removed the ribbon, folded it up and put it next to the apple because it was too pretty to throw away. The child very carefully removed the paper—the paper was beautiful, the most beautiful paper ever wrapped around a box—and carefully removed it and folded it up, put it next to the ribbon and said, "I must keep this paper, it is so beautiful." Then the child opened the box, and there was nothing inside.

Sometimes it is important to pay attention to what is, not what isn't.

You have so much to share. I have a feeling that we just touched into it.

It is likely that that would be the feeling of many of the students too, because we were not just trained by this great teacher, this wonderful person—I didn't really think of him as a teacher at the time; I thought he was a wonderful person.

He was almost like a father, wasn't he?

Well, he was a wonderful person and yet . . . people live, they have experience, and when they're inspired by such a wonderful person as this, perhaps the great gift we receive is our experience with others when we go out to do our work. The students will often have interesting things to say, and you will feel the depth of their being because of who they are, what they've done and how they've gone about it.

Do you have something you're looking forward to in the future? Is there something you feel you're training for or something you want to do?

Being Present in the Moment

The thing I've learned in my experience is to be as present as possible with whatever I am doing in that moment. It is happening for a reason that may not always be clear to you. In my experience with people, most people miss about 93 percent of their lives; things come and go and they don't notice. And sometimes they are unhappy at the end of their lives because they are missing something—a lost love or grandchildren, wealth, abundance, good health and so on. But it seems to me that almost all the time, the opportunities to acquire these experiences are right there in your life, but because one is looking to the future or the past, one does not notice the present and misses many things. So I am having a good time in the present.

You are teaching a lot by answering my questions. Did you decide you wanted to work with the angels and you asked? Or did a teacher mention it as a possibility? What was the dynamic?

It just happened. I was here near the Earth and I would always see the angels coming and going. One time I felt myself moving to be with them. So it just happened; it wasn't something where someone said, "Travel with the angels" or where the angels came up and said, "Come on!" It just happened.

Do you go with them to other planets or other places, too?

No, I stay close to Earth. I want to be here.

Just during this period that he said was so important, right?

The Loneliness of Machines

Yes. I think it is during the time of taking machines for granted. Machines are not machines at all; they are what they *were.* And in the case of some metals, they will be something else. They might rust, or if they break and are no longer interesting, they might go on the junk pile or be melted down to be turned into something else. But for the most part they are lonely, and in your time loneliness is considered normal; it is not considered something that requires attention.

Part of this is because people are often seeking independence and need their time to themselves. In that sense, independence is often confused with loneliness. But loneliness is always recognizable because there is a sadness associated with it that is not present when a person just needs time with himself or is experiencing independence. Being common in your time, if a person feels loneliness around him, he might think it is something he or some other person is feeling if he is conscious of such things. People very rarely consider that it might be some material they are sitting on or the wood on the walls or the stone on the floor and so on.

Or the paper you're writing on.

Yes.

Is your vision expansive enough to look to a time when we will create with the cooperation of the materials?

I don't have vision per se; that's not my gift.

Or your awareness?

The Change of Consciousness Coming in 2010

My understanding is that he said until the year 2010—that is the time of the great unconsciousness toward machines. After 2010 something changes. He said it didn't change at 2010; it begins before 2010, but somehow something happens around that time, but I don't know what. It might be that more people become conscious of the feeling world in which you are living . . .

. . . and begin to feel the machines, yes.

Yes, and begin to recognize the value of who machines are and how they can be comforted. Ultimately, machines are Mother Earth.

Yes, they're her body.

Yes, and your physical bodies are the same. And as you know from the experience of being in your own physical body, it is natural for one part of your body to transmit the discomfort from another part. If your toe hurts, you feel your toe hurting because your body transmits it. So it is not surprising that you, as a part of Mother Earth's body, would feel the pain of another part of her body.

The pain would probably get so bad that we'd have to do something about it.

I don't think it is like that. I think what happens is that people will get more conscious, become more aware of their own feelings and begin to expand their philosophies—which right now are insular—to be more universal, universal in truth. A person might say, "I have feelings and you have feelings; we may not have the same feelings all the time, but the feelings I have, you might feel sometime for yourself." In other words, people will begin to notice their commonality, their common ground, and eventually they will think of it with their animals. People who work in gardens will think of it with plants, and it's not a very big step to think of it with typewriters. Some people have a kind of a relationship with their car and give it a name, and they can feel a sense of personality with their car and other machines and so on. It has begun, and it will continue.

That's heartening. Do you think your mother might want to speak sometime?

Perhaps; you could ask.

Would I ask for Duvla's mother?

You could.

You've answered so many of my questions. What else would you like to say?

I think I will stop here and simply say, singing does create. Be aware of what you are singing; ask yourself, "Do I want to create this?" Good night.

9

Many Journeys, Many Disguises

Jesus

May 21, 1998

Tonight I'd like to talk about a journey I made to a planet with a civilization not so terribly unlike your own. The difference is that the polarity was not as extreme and the coordination between individuals was more compatible. Nevertheless, there was a significant amount of disruption due to the minor polarity that existed there.

A Journey to the Pleiades of the Past

The planet was perhaps most significantly different from your planet because the visionaries who were looked up to and paid attention to were all children. Children were considered to have the greatest clarity, and the older they got, the more confusion they would absorb. So young children especially were closely listened to; if parents heard something new or unusual, they would report it to their community network, and if no one in that network had heard these things before, it would be reported to the greater council. And if it was sufficiently unusual, it would be reported to the planetary council. (This is, I might add, why some civilizations on Earth even in your time pay more attention to children when they are young. Ordinarily, in most of your societies, they receive not so much respect for their statements.)

This civilization predated your own, and some threads of its culture underlie certain spiritual threads of cultures on your planet now.

I paid a visit to this place because I wanted to thoroughly invest myself with the understanding of the bedrock beliefs that would emerge in your culture even in your time, although I came to your planet before your present time. This other planet was in a star system distant from you; it was located in what is now called by some the Seven Sisters [Pleiades]. It was at that time an experimental place; it was considered necessary to keep it somewhat sequestered from other cultures because of the polarity. The polarity would become, at its most extreme, about seven percent—not much by your standard, but much more than the types of polarity in existence on other places in your time.

Oracles among the Very Young

This polarity was felt by people (I'm converting their ages to yours so you can understand their cycles of life in the context of your culture) when they were thirteen years old or older, not so much when they were very young. The oracles amongst the people then were all quite young; even in your time there are prodigies. At any given moment on that planet there would be seven or eight oracles who were usually not much more than eight years old. Because of their status they would practically never be alone except when they were asleep, and then there would be somebody posted near them—not so near as to interrupt their dream cycle, but nearby in case they might say something in their sleep, which would be examined. They were treated, you might say, like royalty. But as they got older and approached ten, eleven, twelve years old, their gifts would gradually diminish.

Here was a society that in some ways is similar to your own and in other ways quite different. I mention it because on your planet even now there is the potential for this same thing. Even the most complex problems, if transformed in language to something a child could understand, could be resolved now by children on your planet. If it is not possible to decrease the polarity right away, the next best thing would be to have the children in an area where they were not exposed to it directly, but not so sheltered that they could not get out and about amongst nature in its natural state—not a game preserve or a garden planted by man, but natural. In that way they would be fed the way all children are—not only with food and air and love and shelter, but with the natural wisdom in the natural world around them.

When you say polarity, is that negativity or male/female polarity? I'm not clear.

Negativity.

Pleiadian Negativity Removed

Ah, seven percent negativity. Is that planet still there?

It is there, but it is no longer in that circumstance. There is no polarity left on the planet; that has been artificially migrated away from it. That can be done by the use of an instrument that is basically similar to some of the theoretical aspects of the theory of relativity, but it is most effective when it is used to apply time and velocity to a planet in its totality—while everyone is alive, of course, including plants and animals. In that way the planet was evacuated of its polarity, which was allowed to escape and seek its best location for expression. It did not actually come to Earth; one might have considered that it did, but I think it was ultimately absorbed by the Master of Discomfort [see *Explorer Race: Creators and Friends,* Chapters 27 and 28, 1997, and *Explorer Race and Beyond,* Chapter 12, 1998].

I understood you to say there was a connection between that civilization and our own.

Since that civilization preceded the cultures on this planet here, I would say that threads entwined their way into the human genetics. Those people on that planet were a variation of human beings. They did not breathe oxygen as you do; it was more of a methane. But if you were to look at their basic genetics, you would say that, aside from adaptation to a different environment, these people were essentially human beings.

Genetic Abilities

Anytime anything is learned and discovered to be of value and is believed by the profound majority of any genetic culture such as the human being, within a very short time that belief will impact its genetics. So when different cultures fostered and spawned variations of the human being on Earth, certain beings had such capacities within their genetic makeup. On Earth, now you would find that these capacities exist in the darker-skinned peoples. The peoples on that planet in the Seven Sisters area were, for that planet's expressions, darker-skinned peoples. To put a tone or color to it, it would be light brown.

Did you feel you learned something there?

I learned something; I learned the value of paying attention to offhand remarks. Children will, even on your planet in your culture, say things in passing. How many parents compare notes and laugh and sometimes wonder about a casual remark, made by their child or some other child, that is profound beyond the years of that child or rings so true that its relevance becomes obvious sooner rather than later? This type of experience is not coincidental or accidental, but is actually focused profoundly within the genetics. I do not wish to make it sound as if light-skinned people and light-skinned children do not have this capacity, but it would be found more often in light-brown peoples.

I mention it because children in your societies are now beginning to get more attention. Granted, in some cases it is because misfortunes have befallen them, but this is just the leading edge of attention. Soon there will be much more awareness of the profound difference it makes when children are nurtured in their early years, loved, supported in their natural talents and perhaps steered toward expressing their natural talents, not with a firm hand, but with a gentle, nurturing hand. In this way they first become good at their natural talents, rather than stumbling across them later in life and only then learning how to use them. It is always better to build the foundation of your natural talents and then learn how to do other things as society needs or requires. This seems obvious on the face of it, yet even today in your supposedly advanced and intellectual societies, it is rarely done.

When you lived the life of Jesus, what was your name? What did they call you?

Is this not obvious? I don't understand.

Names in Jesus' Time

Did they actually call you Jesus? I thought they made that up later.

My actual name was closer to a variation of Joseph, but Jesus [hay'-sus], which is the pronunciation more often heard in the Spanish language, would have been the name they would have called me. So when people say "Jesus" today, with the hard *J*, it is actually a mispronunciation. The Spanish pronunciation is much closer to the true name.

Did you have a last name?

Peoples were described then by where they were from; they didn't have last names per se. You might have your name, of the such-and-such area; or if you came from a profound group . . . let's pick a profession that is understood today. Let's say you might be Joseph the blacksmith, and in your village or your group that's what you'd be known as. But most people would call you Joseph. They wouldn't say, "Joseph the blacksmith, come here!" [Chuckles.]

So they didn't use the towns they came from. Did they ever mention them?

Sometimes they did; if it was more convenient, you might be Joseph of Nazareth or Joseph of Jerusalem, or theoretically, Joseph of Rome.

Were you from Nazareth? Did they call you Jesus of Nazareth?

Later. At the time I was more known as Jesus [Hispanic pronunciation] the carpenter. As you know in your own language, names such as "Carpenter" or names that have "black" or "smith" associated with them often have to do with metalwork (in the case of Smith) or being a miner or a woodsman—you can trace these things back.

There's a book that says that what has been written of Jesus of Nazareth is incorrect, that the Nazarenes were a group at that time with a certain belief system.

I wouldn't rule that out. I'd just say that I would mainly be called by my profession, even if I was training for it. The arrangements would have been made for me to train to be a carpenter when I was still a baby, you see, so if adults would say jokingly, "Jesus the carpenter," it is the carpenter-to-be. But they wouldn't say that, or they would say it with a laugh. Only later, when I became a carpenter, would they say it as a fact. But with any child, when they were youngsters they would say what their training would be—with a little smile.

Sananda

Many people in the metaphysical community feel they're talking to you as Sananda. Sister Thedra gave forty years of her life to that voice; who is that?

It is a name . . . it is certainly an aspect of me, I would not deny it. I wouldn't personally, for who and where I am now, say that it is some other stream of consciousness emitting from me, but it is what I would call a free-floating personality, more connected with my life on Earth that you know about than what I am now. That being would be a fraction or a portion of myself.

I do not guide what that being says or does. It is, in that sense, autonomous, not unlike you are autonomous to the greater you. The greater you might guide somewhat, but you might or might not utilize that guidance. In that sense, you are autonomous.

So this is a part of you that has not reincarnated—on its own it cannot incarnate, right?

Certainly it can.

Has it?

No.

Where is it operating now? What is its area of interest?

It is most interested in what human beings are doing in concordance with religion, religious aspects and, generally speaking, the evolution of the Christian doctrine. This does not mean that this being does not comment on a wide range of topics, but it is most personally interested in how to put more heart into the Christian doctrine. I might say that I have some interest in that myself.

But he will never rejoin you; he is now autonomous and will continue on his own?

Never is a long time; who can say? One must remember that the purpose of my existence is not devoted to authoritarianism, but rather allowance.

This being is a little authoritarian, at least through the channels I've heard.

Well, he does not have to listen to his guidance [chuckles]. That's the circumstance of being autonomous.

Do you have other autonomous parts interacting with Earth?

Mother Mary

Yes, one more, that which is often called Mother Mary.

Please say more about that.

That one who is known to be Mother Mary is another portion of myself, now strictly autonomous. It is what I would like to call a very nice balance to Sananda. I like to think of Sananda as being kind of an evolving personality, whereas Mother Mary does not need to evolve. She's very loving, has complete grace, is also very interested in the evolution of religion (and also dogma), and is doing her utmost, not unlike others, to put more heart into religion. I might say she has been a little more successful than Sananda, who is perhaps a little more caught up in the urgency of the task, whereas Mary is more focused in the perpetuality of such love.

Some of her channelings have sounded urgent too, but she has such a love for humans.

I think so.

So your mother, Mary, has nothing to do with this part of you?

No more and no less than Sananda.

Is the woman who gave you birth also a part of yourself in some way?

Yes.

And Joseph?

No.

So you first sent a part of yourself here to prepare for your birth?

Yes; not a bad plan, eh? Of course, as they say, the best-laid plans . . . hmm?

Had that part of you ever incarnated before, or was that the first life?

That part had had considerable training with Isis but had not manifested directly on the planet as a human being. However, it had been involved as an emissary from Isis in training some of Isis' students on Earth, so it had some understanding of human interrelationships and circumstances of existence here. It is not an accident, a casual reference or even a whim that we truly are all one.

Allowing Parts to Become Autonomous

These are two intimate parts of your being. Would you say you created or manifested them?

Allowed.

Parts of yourself that you allowed autonomy?

No, that I allowed to become parts. Even a mother and father making love and bringing a child into the world allow that child to come in. If there is no allowance, it doesn't happen. The doctors say, "Oh well, the sperm didn't get to the egg" for this reason or that reason. Why not? That is an explanation, but it is not the cause. "Why not" is because *it is not allowed in that moment;* perhaps the parents are waiting for the exact moment and unconsciously they will say, "Ah! The soul we want to come in is just about ready! Let's make love," and then that soul comes in.

So in that way I allowed these parts of myself that wished to be in existence to become, and in that way they began their own autonomy. Just like creators spring from creators, it is not always because the creator wishes to put forth a portion of itself; it might be that that particular portion of itself wishes to go forth, so the creator allows that.

Let's see if I understand this: You allowed the Mother Mary part to go forth, and she first worked with Isis and then incarnated here; she was also born naturally, right?

Yes. When she worked with Isis she was not a human being, but when she was on Earth in her natural human form, she was born like everybody else.

Then you were born through her, but in your full consciousness. So at what point did Sananda come forth?

After the physical existence on Earth.

Right after?

No, awhile after.

A hundred years? Five hundred?

Seven hundred and thirty-eight years, three months, one week. Close enough?

Was Sananda born in a physical body?

No, never. As spirit only.

In a particular dimension?

Access in dimensions three through five, no higher. One cannot be in any way authoritarian, even in the slightest—not even the faintest echo of authoritarian aspects—at sixth dimension or higher. Even at 5.25, no. But one can have the echo of authoritarian at five.

And Mother Mary operates in what dimension?

Free access.

Well, I'm thrilled with that. She chooses to act in ways that relate to the Church?

Yes. She prefers to do that because she feels this is her best avenue of being benevolently influential without in any way making demands or commands. She loves the Church's hierarchies just as much as every man, woman and child, whether they be of that religion or another. She has on numerous occasions appeared in the garments of other religions and races and cultures and nationalities to encourage and nurture and speak about the beautiful aspects of those religions. On numerous occasions she has done this with Islam, for instance, which is another of her favorite religions.

Sananda now speaks through metaphysical channels, but has he also interacted with other parts of humanity?

As a spirit?

Yes.

Human's Addiction to "Truth" and the Importance of Fallibility

No, it has been entirely telepathic. It is a way of keeping him from being too influential, because human beings are, at your time, addicted to "truth." Human beings are addicted to what is "true," but of course truth is very often in the eyes of the beholder, as has been said so well. Since Sananda can be most easily perceived as a being of truth, he is prevented from physical contact because he does not yet know how to be fallible, nor does he understand why it is essential for beings who are looked up to to be fallible. It is absolutely essential, you understand. Human beings are so addicted to "truth" that if those who speak to them make mistakes, they become equals; but if they never make mistakes, they are guaranteed to be gods. So mistakes are required.

Deliberate mistakes, eh?

Yes, deliberate mistakes are required, sometimes obvious mistakes, sometimes less so. In this way these benevolent spirits are not to be deified in the near future.

Well, that adds an incredible "truth" [chuckles].

I might add that when children in your cultures begin to interact with other children and learn things in school, they discover that their parents are not gods. Sometimes this is difficult for the parents, but in the long run it is much better.

Yes, it allows the child to be free to grow up.

And to have a chance to be like their parents, whom they idolize when they are young and think they could never be like this—knowing all things and having the capacity to "love away my hurts and tears," as a child might think in its simple way. Then later on in life they discover that their parents are not gods, and unconsciously they become aware that they can be as good as their parents. For a while, as psychologists say, they overcompensate and think they are better than their parents, but they get over that quickly.

You wanted to talk about some of your travels during and after the physical life. I was especially interested in knowing if you had appeared as Quetzalcoatl.

No.

Then choose some that are meaningful to you. The stories should be very interesting.

I did start out with one, you know.

When you said before that you had appeared other places, I hadn't realized you meant other planets.

An Appearance as a Flower in Japan

I'll pick one here. There was a time on your planet, in ancient Eastern cultures, that was very complex, complicated, where some beings were protected and nurtured by the leaders of the time; and under this tutelage and protection, philosophies were gradually evolved. Shinto was one of these, which holds perfection to be in the natural world—flowers, for example. It was during this time that I had a brief [chuckles] visit.

There was a budding (since Shinto was still new then) Shinto priest who carefully raised a flower and showed this flower to all his fellows who were interested in such things. The protectors of the royalty of the time said, "This flower is perfect, and it is the perfect representation of what we believe, what we can strive for—beauty and so on." As this flower, I remained in such beauty for only a day and a half—but that is good, because I then went to seed and another budding priest carefully gathered the seeds—every one, without exception—planting them carefully and nurturing them. But there was no seed that produced such a perfect flower. This budding priest talked to many of the time and said, "Why did we not have such a perfect flower from the seeds of this most perfect flower?" Finally someone said, "Because in order to have such perfection, one must have freedom. The next time you find such a perfect flower, gather a few of the seeds only, and let the rest blow naturally out into the countryside. See then whether you have a perfect flower from the seeds you kept."

Well, when he was an old man he had another perfect flower, and he followed the advice. He let most of the seeds escape into the countryside to become he knew not what, and he let them grow with tears of gratitude. Keeping only three seeds, he planted each of them; he let one grow outside and one inside, and another one he let grow in the room of a child. He was taking a chance, because even though it was growing up high, little children will be children and things happen. He was concerned, so he checked on the seed every day.

The seed outside grew and produced beautiful flowers, but none perfect in his eyes. The one inside grew and produced not quite so many flowers, but the one in the child's room grew and produced two perfect flowers. He was thrilled and enchanted that they would appear in the child's room, where he had taken a chance. As a result, he visited the plant every day and got to know the child. He took the plant around and showed it to everyone, "Look, see! Perfection twice over!" Everyone was excited. Then he thought, *Where can I put this where it will be most revered?* He thought to himself, being at that time older and wiser, *I must return it to the place where it received such beautiful energy.* So he brought it back to the child's room. Whenever he spoke to the child, they would watch the flower. He visited the flowers more often and they gradually became less perfect and went to seed. This time he let the seeds go wherever they wished.

He talked to the child and took a greater interest in her because he realized that somehow this child had the capacity, just by being herself, to radiate this plant so that it produced more perfection than he had ever seen. That's when he came to realize that flowers, although they can be perfect, need human beings, not only to appreciate them, but to cohabit with in order to produce perfection in the eye of a human. That is when he wrote many things about human beings and their beauty compared to flowers and their beauty. He began to realize that this religion (though it was in his mind a philosophy) was meant for all people, not for only certain classes of people. He encouraged those who were around him to see what they could do to bring the philosophy to the average person after he passed over, which would be soon.

That's a wonderful story!

Sometimes I have appeared here in disguises. Disguises are useful if it is not your intent to confuse or create problems. It is often considered by those in many philosophical and religious worlds that the most ordinary individual might have the most extraordinary source. It is stories such as these that are meant to encourage benevolent treatment of one human being by another. And I must say that ultimately, in the case of Christianity, that will be what it is most remembered for, even though the experiences and circumstances of the religion have not always been so gracious.

During the fifty-year period after your life as Jesus, did you stay in that time period, or did you also travel in time?

I traveled a little bit in time, but it was not so necessary.

What about some of the times you appeared in disguise?

The Great Flood

Once there was a time when human beings were very worried about the perpetuation of their existence all over the world. This was during the time of the Great Flood, which was real.

Can you give us the time period roughly, something we could understand?

I'd really rather not, because if I did, I would interfere with many creation stories of different religions, so I will gently decline.

During this time many cultures were concerned: "How will we survive?" All over the Earth, different visionaries were needed to show up and give encouragement. During that time I showed up [chuckles] as different birds. It is surprising how encouraging a life sign birds are—as is indicated, of course, in your Bible and other places, too. When you are on a mountain in South America looking down, and instead of seeing clouds on a clear day, you see water where once you saw land, you become concerned. And if you see water as far as the eye can see, the idea of a bird approaching from the sea to bring a flower petal or some such thing is very encouraging indeed. That's one of my favorite things.

Did water flood the entire planet?

Earth's Reaction to Human Sacrifice

Yes, the entire planet. Earth has the capacity to do that at a moment's notice. At that time, Earth felt there were things going on that she did not approve of—not everywhere, and certainly not in every culture. But what was going on was something that Earth most definitely disapproves of, even though many people can demonstrate evidence (in their own ideas, anyway) that this is not so. And that was human sacrifice. It is one thing if a person chooses to sacrifice themselves for some purpose of his own or purpose of his culture; but to be nominated [chuckles] to sacrifice yourself? This isn't all right. And such behaviors angered Mother Earth because she felt it was an effrontery to the sacredness of life. So she thought, *Maybe it is time to do it over.* Others—spiritual beings and other planets—prevailed on her to not complete it, but she has said, "If this behavior happens again . . ." Of course, to Mother Earth, human sacrifice is not only considered as *you* understand human sacrifice to be . . .

. . . but also wars?

Yes, wars and killing and casual treatment of life, as if life were not by its very nature sacred. And not just human life, please, but plant life and animal life and, yes, mineral life—her body, yes?

So she said, "I will wait to complete it. If I see these things going on again at the millennium point," which is coming up soon for you, "then I will give myself ten years to think about it, in my form of thought," which is more of what I would call resonance rather than thought as you know it. "If I still don't like what I see, then I will give myself permission—though I will not guarantee that it will happen—to complete it." This is why so many people in your time are having visions about floods. Don't assume these visions are absolutely going to happen, but that's what they are about.

Predictions are meant to have us change our ways so that the predictions don't happen.

That's right. I feel it is, yes.

So this is a real concern. Look at the Middle East and Africa and the ghettos and the gangs. This is a real concern, then.

It is a concern, yes, a distinct concern. And because so many people are unhappy because of the circumstances of their lives, on a deep level to have the life come to an end and to go to some wonderful place they have heard about from their religion or philosophy or dreams or visions or just faith—or if nothing else, just to stop what they are experiencing—the idea of passing through the veils is not so terrible.

So they might help call it forth, almost.

They might be more amenable—not consciously—to such things happening. They won't call it to them, but they might miss the signals to avoid it.

Changes Are Needed

We need humans to go through to the fourth dimension consciously to make this experiment work, right?

Yes.

So we need to keep the humans on this planet alive!

Yes. And we also need for human beings on this planet to become comfortable with their differences with each other. You don't have to embrace the other person's religion as your own, but you must learn, not how to tolerate, but how to become *comfortable* with the other person's religion . . .

Not just religion, but . . .

. . . religion, philosophy, way of being—everything, sexuality, lifestyle. I grant that some lifestyles one cannot become comfortable with, such as violent lifestyles or something that is hopelessly self-destructive such as a serious drug habit. But one can become comfortable with the beings in other ways.

It's almost like everything in this experiment hinges on allowing your fellow humans to be what they are, and not judge or blame.

Yes, and ultimately to look at what they believe and see if there is not something either similar to what you believe or that can perhaps enrich what you believe. Many of the world's religions and philosophies and even lifestyles have enriched other ones just by saying, "Ooo, I like that; let's use that" [chuckles]. The fabric of life is intended to be complementary.

How did it get so bad? How did we become so judgmental and so nonallowing? Because we got caught up in the survival, the negativity, the ignorance?

It got so bad, as you say, because people, beings, spirits have to do it on your own. Creator stood back and said, "Now *you* do it." We can support, we can whisper in your ear, we can nurture, but ultimately *you* have to do it. If we are too close, you will imitate us, because our energy is all around you. But if we step back, you will have to find your own way. And finding your own way, when you are at least mostly (granted, temporarily) cut off from the heart of your full being, is a difficult passage, to say the least. It isn't that you are so corrupt; it is that finding your way, even to these simple truths that I'm speaking of, can be difficult when you cannot feel the path so easily. That is why all this training about the heat and the instinct and the heart's warmth is so important [see pg. 80]. Using your instincts is a much truer, simpler and quicker way to find the heart's path. But you know this.

Available Heart Energy

What is the percentage of our heart energy available to us now, and what is the median level on Earth of what we have accepted?

You now have available to you seventy-three percent, but the median does not exceed three percent, though some individuals have as much as eleven percent, and some maybe one and a half percent. But a great deal is available to you, and this availability has to do with the acknowledgment of your need. It cannot be embraced by simply saying, "I embrace my heart's energy in its totality." It can only be embraced by embracing your heart's energy in totality through your treatment of others and equally through others' treatment of you. This coming together of people and embracing them and allowing yourself to be embraced in ways that are acceptable to you (not necessarily a physical embrace) is critical in order to integrate that heart energy.

Who made the decision to allow so much? Just a year or so ago maximum available was twenty-eight percent.

The Punishment of Mining

It was necessary because Earth cannot bear too much more unconscious punishment, such as mining. Pollution is a factor, but mining is the most devastating. So Earth said, "Sooner, not later," in resonant communication. It is not so important who made the decision as the circumstances that provoked it.

So you are back in a similar time in a similar condition as when you came before—to literally help save the planet, correct?

What I'm doing now, you mean?

You're communicating, then making yourself known, in a very critical time.

Yes.

More critical than I knew. How can we help the process?

You have begun with your process, and others might benefit from self-exploration and perhaps finding common threads. There's nothing like humor to find common threads, so share a laugh together, eh? I will speak more on this, what to do, in coming chapters, perhaps.

Share some other stories. You must have hundreds.

Disguised as a Right Shoe

One more tonight. Let's see. I like the stories of disguise because it is important to bring to your attention the innocuous. Once I sent my energy into a right shoe. It was the right shoe of a woman who was what you might call a lay preacher. She was not sanctioned by any church, but went around from place to place. She had some capacity for healing and spoke verses as she did so. She had a deformity in the bones of her right leg. She received from an old farmer a pair of shoes he made himself, and he said, "For all the love you have given us in the many times you have come to our community, I honor you with these shoes, in which I have put all the love I could. They will last you a long time. And when you come back, come and see me, and I will fix them if they need it." The right shoe was a little thicker than the left shoe because her leg was a little shorter. After that she didn't have so much pain.

She walked for a penance, because she believed, unfortunately, that aspect of the Christian religion that human beings were somehow at fault for being human. This must go from Christianity, and it will, but it has been slow to depart. So she walked, and I had my energy in that right shoe for about fifteen months. The next time she came back to the town, the farmer replaced the heel and sole of the shoe and said, "These shoes feel more loving than they ever did." She said, "They feel that way to me, too." Then she continued on for another journey.

The third time she came back there was a dance, as there is sometimes in small communities, and she gave the blessing for the dance.

The farmer was there who made the shoes, and he said, "Would you dance with me?" Because of the deformity in her leg, no one had ever asked her such a thing, nor had she ever been wooed. The farmer danced with her and told her he had such great respect for her, would she consider settling down with him? He was an old man; he did not expect her to give him any children. Well, she thought about it on her next journey around to these towns, and when she came back she decided that it would be all right. So they got married and she retired from her journeys, though she continued to heal and quote verses to the people of that community.

Beautiful. Did she have children?

No, they were both old. But he had had children before. His wife had passed away many years before that, so she embraced his children like her own and was a wonderful substitute mother and, very shortly after, a grandmother.

I mention this because you never know who or what might be invested with the most benevolent energy.

What about the stories of the homeless person or the beggar . . .

Valid, certainly. I, or other beings, have often taken that guise, not only because these people need support and nurturance and can sometimes receive it only from one of their own, as they see it; but also because it is a wonderful way to see who has progressed. The child looks at a homeless person the same way they look at any person, sometimes with the benevolence that is inherent in children (if not always perceivable [chuckles]). Adults will look at a homeless person the same way, and sometimes that homeless person will look back and say, "I see your soul has evolved," though they might just say that to themselves.

You've said that to yourself.

Perhaps.

You really do love humanity.

It's . . . possible! [Chuckles.]

It is definitely true. I think there's a deeper level. You said that when the people on Earth are calling to Jesus, it doesn't really pull on you because they're calling to a myth or a story. You don't feel that?

If I listen, I'll feel it, but I don't often listen because I feel that when they say that, they're really calling to Creator, and that is Creator's job.

Aha! Yes, He is supposed to get more involved with us.

Yes! And on that note of perhaps filial responsibility, I'll say good night.

10

Parting Storms and the Inspired Stone

Jesus and Ahkananda
June 1, 1998

For a long time, perhaps because of artistic license or a need to identify my Earth life by different groups of people around the world, there has been a casual, not cover-up, but sort of hiding the truth a bit.

The Physical Appearance of Jesus and the Apostles

When I was on the Earth in that life, I was naturally thin like most people of my time. I was out in the sun, but even so, if you had seen me in those days you would have to say, "Oh, this man is a local Arab, or perhaps he's from Northern Africa," by my appearance. And it is true you know; there is a tribe of people in Africa who stem their cultural heritage to Israel, and Israel doesn't really want to [chuckles] honor that, but it is so. Nevertheless, that followed—I will say this—the casual observer of today would say, "This man is an African, or he is a Bedouin, always out in the sun." My wife—and I have a wife—people would say, "Oh, she is also an African; no question about it," and the heritage that we shared was a lineage associated with ancient culture.

As any good historian can tell you, some of the most advanced people thousands of years ago were in Africa. Granted, part of this was because they were isolated and they could develop an advanced culture without much interference. The whole idea of tribal warfare has been blown way out of proportion

And it was not such a big thing until recent years. My children all had dark skin, and more. The apostles, as they've come to be known—or as I like to call them, the students, all had dark skin; not because I chose dark-skinned people only, but because they were the ones who volunteered. Yes, I picked students, but I picked many more students than could leave their lives. But the ones who were able to leave were all dark-skinned, and the women also. It is true that the Jewish people of that area also had dark skin, much darker than you see them today. Granted, part of this was because of being outdoors, but that was not the only reason; some of them were of African heritage. And I am not comfortable with the way this has been glossed over in your time. The true picture of myself would reveal a man about in that life five foot tall, maybe five-one; my wife a little shorter, about four-foot-eight . . . not an unusual size for a woman of those days. My students—the men were twelve, women ranged from eighteen to twenty in a given time. I told you before what the women did; I won't get into that too much. But I just want to say this in closing, so that people of today do not become overly attached to the racial image of that life. And I completely understand the desire to claim racially someone whom you admire; but would I be so awful if I didn't look fair with blue eyes and blonde hair? What I said and what I did is more than you know today, but it will come out. I mention this because at some point some of my students might wish to talk and make an addition to this book.

And they will all have different points of view. Some of them will have originated in different parts of Africa, many of them having been fishermen or involved with that trade, or seamen of the time would have found their way to the Middle East on boats, as you might expect. So that is the picture I'd like you to hold. Understand that ultimately the cultural heritage that will be identified as the Earth personality, the appearance of the Earth person, is intended to have brown skin . . . sort of that milk-chocolate, perhaps a little lighter than traditional milk chocolate, maybe coffee with a dash of cream. [Chuckles.]

[Chuckles.] Café au lait.

Yes, very nice; and wavy hair, perhaps different colors; and athletic-looking, taller than the average extraterrestrial, perhaps average height of five-six to five-eight—average height. And perhaps a little bit longer arms and a little bit longer legs than the average humanoid of the past.

So I mention that because I want you to keep it in mind. It was originally intended that you have six fingers, but unfortunately this has been discouraged by many generations. For a time it was a trait noted in Europe, and a few other places; it is possible that someday you will have your sixth finger, which is the natural state of your hand. It will not just be an appendage; it will be fully able to grasp. You will also probably have greater lung capacity, which will allow you to be more athletic. In this current state of affairs of being out of shape, as many Americans are ruefully conscious of, to say nothing of Europeans and others, is a passing thing. You will be athletic by choice not by necessity, so don't worry about it.

You said you were of the lineage of the house of David?

I'd rather say, since the house of David is a lineage that doesn't go back more than four or five thousand years at the most, to its point of actual origin on Earth, that the lineage preceded that, back to Africa. The original blood that is sometimes called royal blood, but actually in its original meaning, the word *royal*, in Africa, meant anointed; which actually had more to do with responsibility as royalty of today perhaps understands, than it did with class. So if you understand that, then my lineage would go back about seven thousand years into the interior of Africa. This is really the place where royalty, as you understand it today, got started. The Royalty of five thousand to fifty-eight hundred years ago had more to do—the kind of royalty you know today—with authority and to a degree, responsibility. But taking royalty back to its point of origin of being anointed, which obviously suggests that you've been initiated, that ultimately your responsibility as royalty was to initiate others. And in that sense, you can see why as a soul I would choose to come from that line of royalty.

Sports and Times to Come

Did you participate in some of the decisions about the physical body of humans? Talking about the six fingers? Or was that just something that you knew?

That's something I know, but it is intended that human beings have six fingers because of what you will need to do. As time goes on, because your bodies will become more athletic—and that will have a lot to do with your interests—the desire to fight each other and war will gradually turn into more athleticism, which is why different types of sports are becoming almost overly pervasive now; it's an experiment. And someday sports will be the competition between countries. And eventually, of course, there will be sport that is cooperative; but there will still be some competitive sports. And it will not be an obsession with people, but a passion that people from other planets will come to observe, and occasionally participate in, because there will be all forms of sport played here; plus, as you begin to explore the planets and you discover the sport of other planets, very often you will like it. Sometimes you'll love it, claim it as your own and integrate it into your sports here on Earth. Someday Earth will be known as a place of great sports and athleticism. So this trend of more, rather than less, sports is just the beginning.

Introduction of Jesus' Students

The apostles/disciples won't all talk, but a lot of what they talk about won't seem to be in alignment with what is in the New Testament. And that's good in a way, because there will be stories you don't know about.

And some of their backgrounds and cultural histories will be from places that have not been acknowledged in the New Testament. I might add, for the sake of not sounding overly political here, that when the New Testament was assembled, all of the individuals who were my students were not known in those days. But some were known, and because of the structure of society and culture at those times, students who didn't fit into the framework of how it was perceived christianity could become a dominant force in the world politic were either eliminated or transformed into archetypes of the time that would be admirable to people in those days, not unlike today. I think it's time to correct those errors.

The highest application of religion as it exists in your society now is to serve the people. This is understood by the hierarchies of most religions, but it hasn't been completely applied. It is beginning to be applied now, and the latitude in terms of how it is to be applied is becoming broader. It is important to not serve the people in a rigid framework; not serve them if they qualify, but rather to serve them as they are. In that way, Mother Theresa was a wonderful example, and her example has guided many of the church elders of today.

Serve their needs, not preach.

Not tell them how to be, but help them and be an example of what it is that you believe in, and support them physically, emotionally, mentally and spiritually.

The Student Ahkananda

I am one of the students of the time. I will speak now if that is all right.

Wonderful, yes.

My name is Ahkananda. My heritage is in Northern Africa. I was raised at sea; not so unusual for my time. Seagoing families were often onboard with whomever owned the boat. My father did not own the boat, but the boats were, with my people, owned by everybody. Everybody helped to make them, so they were owned by everybody not unlike—I have looked from a distance—how things are some places in Asia, even today. We lived on the boats. And if it was necessary, the women would help out if they could. And the men and young boys, if they were strong enough, would fish and always tried to find fresh water, but we never did. We had heard about it because of our location: the waters of North Africa and the Middle East—what is now called the Middle East. We made several journeys before I heard at one of our ports that there was a man from our country teaching things in the Middle East. And he was teaching things that I had always wanted to know. And because my lineage had to do with the shamans on my mother's side, and the sea on my father's side, I wanted to hear this man. So they left me there, and planned to pick me up. They said, "We will be back, we will be back." I knew how often they came, so they said, "We will look for you the next three times, and we will be back at this time when the Sun and the stars are in this position," and so on. And so, by your standards, that would be about once every two-and-a-half years, so I had about seven-and-a-half years, yes?

Where? What was the city?

There was no city. They dropped me off on the coast of what is now Israel.

What was your name as we know it, now? Are you one of the twelve named in the New Testament?

You don't know me now. I've been not included in the book and that is not unusual for people from my part of the world; because in my time, where I lived and where I traveled afterward, people did not keep records in writing—they kept them in song. If you went there today, you would still hear some rhythms and tunes and words that might be related to that. But there are no words. I'll give you some words.

In Search of That Man

I joined with this man; it took a while to find him, but I found him. It's a small place in terms of what can be habituated. I was met where they dropped me off by people who traded with my people. And so they took me with them; they said, "We will help you to find this man; we have heard of him."

How old were you?

About twelve.

Oh, so young! Okay.

Young by your standards in your time now, but in my time that was not considered so very young. So I said thank you, and they promised my parents that they would look after me, see that I had food until I found this man, and then it would be my choice whether to go with him. So I said thank you, and that's all that was necessary in those days; you didn't have to pay them anything to look after someone. They were happy to do it. We traveled for a time; we had to travel on their trade routes, that's how they survived. But in about six or seven months, we found this man. And I was sorry to leave them; they were such wonderful people. But I left them and told them I hoped I would see them again, and they said, "Well, we'll see; maybe when you're on a ship again with your parents," they said, "we'll see you." And I said, "Good, I'll look forward to that." Then I asked this man if I could join him, and he said, "Where are you from?" And I told him, and he said, "You look familiar; I think you might be like a cousin to me." And we compared our lineage, and sure enough, we didn't have a blood connection, but our peoples had had some contact through trade and other things; so we felt kind of like cousins. And he said, "Do you want to go on with me on my travels for a while?" And I said, "Yes, thank you very much."

How old was he at that time? At what point in his teaching was this?

He was about nineteen.

Ah, very young. Okay, go ahead.

Of course, in those days it wasn't considered young. So I said, "Yes, thank you." He had a few other students, and he said, "Right now I'm looking for students, so I'm happy for you to be with me." And we walked around. I was with him for about five years, a little more—five years and a month, or something like that. And we had a lot of fun.

Learning and Playing with Jesus

You know, that's not something that has come through in your modern stories, but he was a fun-loving person. He liked to laugh and sing and he especially liked to dance. And he liked to dance to rhythmic sounds; he was particular interested in rhythmic sounds and how what he had to teach could be adapted to rhythmic sounds, music and form. In other words of the time, dance would have been form. In your time, theater might be considered form; dance also, of course.

So we traveled for some time. I felt this kindred spirit with him, and he taught about natural life. He taught about the many-leggeds and the human being—how the human being can learn from other beings and how the human being can learn to feel at home anywhere on Earth if you emulated the beings that were surviving well and in harmony. And when he said that, he always meant what human beings call . . . excuse me . . . the animals because most often they will be the ones who will be living well, in harmony. So he taught us that, and that's how we learned to get along. He said, "Pay attention to them and you will learn where to find food and water, shelter, comfort . . ." That was a lot of the training, and because my mother was of shamanic heritage, it felt very natural to me to learn these things. He also would stop where there were people—encampments of people—nowadays you would say villages . . . but then, the encampments of people weren't so permanent; they would stay for a while and then move on. He would listen to the stories of the people. He would share whatever we had to share, and they would always be generous, providing whatever they had, so we all shared alike. If the people had a need for certain kinds of food or water, he would always address that first before any teaching. Because he had a natural ability to find water he would teach it to who we called the water-bearer of the people we were visiting with. He would teach them everything they could remember, that he could show in form—as you say, in theater, dance and music because it is much easier—at least it was then, and I think it still is—to remember form and music than it is to remember words on their own.

Words on their own are just symbols. But form, music and sometimes story, this kind of thing, this would be what he would use.

Inviting Rain

And when their water-bearers had as much as they could take in, he would show them how to invite the rain. He was good at that, too. And he would advise them how to find food; he would teach all of these things first because survival in those days was much more important than philosophy. Survival first, then philosophy. [Chuckles.]

So after he would teach all these things to those in the tribe or group who were responsible for these things, then we would eat and sing and tell stories, and sometimes they would perform, as you would say, the little story in form—as I'm used to calling it. He would share philosophy that way, about being kind to each other, about noticing how polite that the wild animals naturally are Granted, some animals that are living with human beings are polite also, but wild beings, especially the many-leggeds; very polite. They have very specific ways of addressing each other. I grant that sometimes they consume each other, but their basic nature is to be polite. Politeness did not come from strict upbringing; it came from observing the ways of the animal world, which is totally ingrained with honoring. I have picked up your word of the time, polite; but honoring is the root, yes, honoring is the root. So this is mostly what I learned in that five years; how to find water, how to bring rain, how to be like the animals and, of course, later I applied it to being like the fishes. And how to teach in the most entertaining way, and also learn, in the most fun way, the things that were important to remember.

The Inspired Stone

After my five years with this man, I said, "Now I must try to find my way back to where my people will meet me," and he embraced me and gave me something he had carried for a while. He said, "I would like you to take this back to your people." He showed it to me, and it was a very smooth stone; very round, almost perfectly round and perfectly smooth. I asked him if he had made it that way, and he said, no, he had found it. Everyday, he touched it, rubbed it with his thumb and his finger and breathed on it at least three times every day. He said if I was ever at a loss and didn't know how to teach something, I should take it from a little sack I had it in, and I should breathe in from it [makes an in-breathing sound]. Take in a breath, just one; and then I would be inspired. He said, "Also, when you are inspired or you are feeling that your teaching is going very well, take the stone out of the sack, rub it between your thumb and finger and breathe on it three breaths out; that way you stow wisdom in it for the next person or for the next time you need it. And when you are old, pass it on to your best student, and give him these instructions as I have given you."

I mention this to you because this is something that may still be done today in your time and places and could be done by others. The stone must want to participate; if the stone wants to do it, you will know because you will pick the stone up and have a good feeling. It will not be a thought, it will be a good feeling. And then give the stone a moment, hold it between your finger and your thumb, and hold it near where it was, so it can say goodbye to its friends and those it has been with, for a while. You will know how long; it might be more than a few minutes until you have a relaxed feeling in your body, then gradually start pulling the stone toward you. If you start to feel tense, the stone is not done yet; bring it back to where it was and wait. Eventually, when you bring the stone toward you, you will be relaxed and have that good feeling; the stone will have said goodbye and be ready to do its work with you.

Interesting. So you made your way back, and you found your family?

I made my way back. I had to wait a while for the people; they weren't the same people who were traveling, but they were related to them by tribal connection, and I spoke the words that those people told me to speak to others of their family, as they called them—they didn't say tribe; they said family—and so they knew that I could be trusted. In those times, a person couldn't always tell by the way someone looked whether they could be trusted; but what you said and how you said it, that's what they would know. So I said these things, and they said, "Come, travel with us; we know where you are going, we know this place, we can get you there soon." And so they did. I traveled with them; again, it was wonderful, they are such wonderful people. I asked them to give my greetings and my heart—it is like, what you say, love; but we said, "give my heart," which is a gesture. One goes toward the chest and goes like this, offering.

The right hand with the palm up.

Yes; some people might do it with the left, but I do it with the right, see? We'd say, "I give my greetings and give my heart"—just like this. When you say heart, then you move your hand this way, toward the people, "to my friends, and for you also." You didn't hug people in those days; it was like that. You might hug the person you are close with, your wife or your husband, but you didn't hug people otherwise. So then they said, "All right, thank you." They left me some food and I lived, as you would say, on the beach for a while. They had left me what I needed, plus I had learned how to find water or bring rain so I was all right. And my people came and picked me up, and I was, by that time, almost nineteen.

I was able to teach my people many things that were helpful to them and tell them about how one of our countrymen was in this place teaching things that we would be proud of.

So you continued to travel on the sea the rest of your life, then?

At Sea

Yes, that was my life. And when we would come into a port, we would stay for a while. After I helped unload the boat of its cargo, the people—my people on the ship would say, "We'll be here for a while; why don't you go ashore and talk to the people?" They knew that I wanted to do this; it was part of my duty. I would do exactly what my teacher showed me to do. First, I would talk to the water-bearer and then the food-gatherers about how to find things, how to invite the rain and thank it, how to find water; all these things first, then share stories between us, talk about things that are valuable as I mentioned. And then we would be brothers. It actually drew us closer to these people that we traded with. And then we would go on. And that's what I did for the rest of my life.

What was your route? How far did you go?

Just know it was basically between Northern Africa and the Middle

East.

But not up around Turkey and Greece; you would just go kind of back and forth, then?

Yes that's right. We didn't go much to the North because when we contacted ships from the North, they were not always very friendly. The people of the North seemed to be more concerned about other things in those days.

You mean like material things?

No, they were more concerned about fighting each other and being right. So they weren't ready to hear these stories and have this knowledge. After all, these were not spiritual warriors, not complete warriors, just warriors, who wanted to win at any price. If they were taught how to bring the rain, use the rain and to honor the rain, they might try and use it as a weapon.

So when we met these ships, we would trade with them and pretend to be ignorant. Very often the best weapon with which to defend yourself is to pretend to be foolish; not so foolish that you make a bad trade, but not wise to the ways of the world. I think some of your people are doing this even today.

Okay, and what was the trading process? You would trade them fish for salt and things, or what?

Whatever we needed, or more often, since we were trading, whatever the people we traded to needed. They would say, "Oh, can you get this?" Or, "If you have the opportunity, can you get that?" And sometimes very specific things; and we would say, "Well, show us, what is this thing?" If we didn't know it, they would show us, if possible, or describe it to us as best they could. Sometimes we would get them exactly what they wanted, and sometimes we wouldn't get them exactly what they wanted [chuckling], and they might take it or not.

So material, metal or things like that? All things? All kinds of things?

Whatever was wanted or needed, and whatever was available.

You did much beyond fishing, then; you traded beyond the fish you caught.

Yes.

So you were really very sophisticated, but you just appeared to be, as you say, fishermen, then.

Parting Storms

It was to our advantage, since we didn't have the heavy armaments your ships have today, to be innocent. We weren't going to show them that we could invite the rain, or even ask a strong storm to part so that we could get into a port. We wouldn't ask to drive the storm away entirely; maybe it had a reason to be there.

Yes. So, when you talked to people, to the families, did you attribute the teachings to Jesus or mention him, or did you just . . .

Yes; sometimes we would, if they asked. Teachers know that it is not important who gets credit for the wisdom; what is important is how it is used and if it is spread about wisely to those who wish to receive it.

So we would sometimes mention his name, but we wouldn't say his name as if he were a god; we would just say, if someone asked, "Where did you learn these things?" I would say, "Oh, a man named Jesus taught me these things." And sometimes they would ask about him, and I would tell. But he was no different than any other teacher; he insisted. And he always insisted—this whole thing of making him a god was not his plan.

Would you say, Jesus of . . . some place? Would you describe him?

No.

Just his name.

Yes. After all, the people wouldn't know that place anyway; so why say it?

Yes. You said, "we". Did you teach these things to your family, and then they helped you teach? Did they come with you?

I speak of the other students as we.

Oh, okay.

And of course, I had my own students eventually, and I include them also in we.

Did you marry and have children?

Oh, certainly. People still do this in your time, yes?

[Chuckling...] Yes, yes. Did you have other lives after that? Have you had other Earth lives?

No Earth lives, and I don't think I'll be back because it is such a great privilege to be here in your time, meaning the past six thousand years or so. It is a privilege because so much can be learned in so short a time; so I don't think, even if I stood in line, eh? Queued? Do you say that, queued?

Yes.

Queued up? I think that the line is too long. So, no; I have been living other places. I'm currently living on a planet in the system that you call Sirius. And it is a beautiful place. A lot of people here remind me of the way I looked in that life at that time.

I've seen the lineage of That Man, my teacher, here in places, because I recognize the look in people's eyes.

The Look of Lineage

I've always been good with eyes, recognizing a look. You know, you don't study people's eyes by staring; you glance. But if you look at enough people's eyes, you can tell not only things about them as individuals, of course, but you get a feeling for their lineage. Like even today I can look at somebody and say, "oh, you're from this place or that place." If I was on your planet today I could look at someone and say, "oh, you have spent a lot of time on this planet or that planet." It's not so complicated.

Do you know how to look at a person's eyes and tell if they are from this place or that place?

No, sir.

You can imagine, for example, being on the Pleiades, feeling that for a long time; it's a feeling, okay? And then you can imagine being on Orion, another feeling pick other places, too, places that you know the names of because if its a place you don't know the names to, it'll only work so well.

Then feel into it and relax; enough so that you can recognize the feeling of a place, see? Do this several times a day for maybe three weeks then when you look at a person or an animal, even a many-legged animal—don't stare at them, you just glance at them—then you will have a feeling come up in you. You will be able to say, oh, this person is from that place, or they have spent a lot of time there or, they are . . . how do you say . . . lens-like focused through that place in this life. But that's not necessarily true; they might have just spent a lot of time there, and their character traits in this life are more associated with that place than other places they might have spent time on. And if you feel over time the character, the feeling of these different places, because of the different feelings and sometimes emotions it will give your body, you can identify the different character traits associated with these places. And then if you are going to do business as I have done, with trading, you will know that this person will have these certain character traits predominantly; so you will know how to talk to them so as not to offend them. Very important in business!

Yes. When we get out seafaring, I mean spacefaring like you were seafaring, we'll need that.

Or even now you have people that do business from country to country, and you can use it here. You can more easily travel to those countries and spend time there, and there's a feeling about those countries. If you can't travel, then you can imagine.

But for people in business, travel, maybe and spend time there, and you will have a feeling, and certain emotions that come up, associated with that country. Then when you meet people, you can be aware of certain things to say and certain things not to say to them, so you will not offend them.

Sometimes this is useful in your time when people have lineage from different countries, and they may not want to talk about their lineage. They might live in one country and have lineage from other countries. Because of that lineage that you can see in their eyes and then feel in your physical body, you will know how to speak to them. It will almost be as if you knew their personality. It may not have anything to do with what they were taught as children; did you know that?

It may not have anything to do with what their parents taught them. It would be rather what you identify as their personality, which may not always have to do with what they learned from their parents.

It would relate to their soul?

Yes. So that's why I say, starting these things is useful even today.

Life on Sirius

Absolutely. You turned out to be a very wise trader, I can tell! What do you do on Sirius now?

I'm a teacher. I teach about the differences between childhood and old age; I teach about old age to children who are not so young that they need to be taught about being children, but when they grow up a little bit. I also teach older people about children. A child was just here, pulling on my pant leg, reminding me to tell a story.

I'm going to tell the story she wanted me to tell. When I would teach the older people about childhood—which is important because when you're old, you sometimes forget about childhood—I would sometimes tell this story.

The Old Man and the Child

I would say, "Once upon a time there was a man who was walking along very slowly, because he was an old man; and he came to a hill, and the hill was between him and where he needed to go. And he looked up at this hill, and he said, 'Oh, I don't think I can get over that hill on my own. I can't get over that hill just by myself.' So there was a rock there, and he sat down. 'I will sit down and wait; maybe someone will help me.' And people came along, and they were all very busy, and every time he'd get ready to lift his finger up and say, 'Will you help me up the hill?' they rushed by. Eventually a child came along; very young, about five years old.

"And the child, being curious, stopped and said, hello, this is my name; what's your name? And the old man said, oh, this is my name. And the child said, 'Who are you waiting for?' And the old man said, 'I'm not waiting for anybody; I have to go to the other side of the mountain, and I don't think I have the energy to go over it by myself.' And the child said, 'I'm going the same place! I'll walk with you and hold your hand. And if you don't have the strength, by holding my hand, we'll have enough strength together. You tell me a story, because I like stories,' said the child, 'and if you're too tired to tell me a story, I'll sing, and it will cheer you up, and we'll have the strength between us to walk over the hill.' So they went holding hands and the man started telling a story, and then he got tired. And the child started singing, and as the child sang—because of course that child had plenty of energy—the man felt younger and stronger and walked right up the hill. By the time he was at the top of the hill, he had so much energy he had to carry the little one because he was walking so fast! And as they walked together back down the other side of the hill, he told the child the rest of the story. They got to where they were going."

You understand the meaning of that story?

Sometimes it's good to stop and ask; sometimes it's good to be curious and stop and ask. You never know when you are going to hear a new story, sing a song and travel to a place with a new friend.

That's wonderful. Had you made some agreement on a higher soul level to be there at the time of Jesus, or do you feel you had chosen to be there at that time that he was there?

I don't know if life is that specific, whether everything profound in your life is agreed upon on a higher soul level. I have heard that question asked and answered many, many times. Of all the profound ways of asking and answering, I'd still have to say that I am not sure that that is so. Maybe it just happened.

But you were blessed by it and you helped many, many, many people because you met him.

I'd like to think I would have helped a few without having met him, but I admit having met him was a very important experience in my life. If you were to say, "What is the most important experience?" I would have to say marrying my wife and having my children; I think in your times, it might be the same.

Who did you give the stone to?

To my best student, who was not one of my children but one of their friends. He was a very good student.

That's wonderful; I can just feel your love and your energy, it's wonderful. All right, now you're talking to what we call the Explorer Race, so, from all your expe-

rience, both on Earth and where you are now and before, what would you tell people?

Advice from Sirius

I would say, consider what are the most important points of your philosophy. It is sometimes good to examine your philosophy, to find out if there are things in it that do not serve you. I think the biggest challenge in your time is cynicism. Cynicism is a hard challenge for you in your time because you have been disappointed so much that the disappointment becomes your worst pain. But many of you have food and shelter; starvation or going without water is not as common as it once was, but it is still happening for some. I'd say this. See if you can take your philosophy, the ideas and feelings and thoughts and actions that you live by, and bring them down to four lines or less. Then convert those four lines to form: theater, a song or a rhythm, as a musician might call a sync-o-pa-tion [speaks each syllable separately], a type of a rhythm. And if you can do that, you will then discover by the way that syncopation feels, if your philosophy is still growing. There might feel like there's something missing in your song, or there's something coming—perhaps another line for your song—or if it is complete because it will feel perfect the way it is.

In this way you can pass on your philosophy, if you believe in it and hold it dear, to others in a way they can remember rather than to join the sea of words that exists in your time.

That is very original; that is wonderful. One thing I didn't ask: Of the other followers of Jesus, do you know the names of the ones that were there when you came?

I would let them speak for themselves.

Oh, all right; I was just wondering who was there. All right. You're delightful; say whatever you'd like to say.

Good night!

[Laughter.] Good night

11

Jesus' Autonomous Parts, His Bloodline and His Plans

Jesus
May 22, 1998

Let's continue where we left off last night.

Was Mary Magdalene part of your energy originally, or was she from another life stream?

From another life stream.

Were there any other autonomous parts of you that you interacted with on the planet, or were Mother Mary and Sananda the only two?

You mean during that time?

Yes.

Another Autonomous Part of Jesus

There was a child who was a witness to much of what went on. Children are often witnesses because they go unnoticed. Oh, their parents notice them, but they do not think of them as witnesses. But they, in their own childish way, make wonderful witnesses because they are curious; they want to know, and they will often observe in great detail. The eyes and heart of a child are often the best observers [chuckles].

And what did the child observe?

She observed the teaching during that time. She observed with curiosity the people listening and trying new things. She also observed some of the conversations toward the end of that life and what might be described as some of the drama.

Whose child was she?

She was just a child of the time, not a name you would know, no one you ever heard of.

Did she live again on Earth?

Yes. She's living now. She has a life now in the country Sri Lanka. She is a beloved older woman, looking after many children and living a simple life. Very often the most simple lives are ultimately the most profound. When one has time, you know, and is not distracted by too much technology (which is supposed to be time-saving [chuckles]), they can enjoy the simple things—children especially.

And this is another part of yourself that you gave embodiment to?

Yes.

The Being in the Everglades

Are there other parts that have interacted on the Earth either before or after your life?

There was one other in the 1920s through about 1971, who lived in the Florida area, the swamp area of Florida.

The Everglades, eh?

In and around that area, getting by as best he could. An unusual person, with a lot of knowledge about the water beings who live there—as they said in that time, a great fisherman.

And he will come back again?

I think not. He has moved on to a job you might find interesting. It is on Andromeda, where such jobs are plentiful. He is the overseer—not a manager, but sort of a protector (I don't think that's quite the right word) of a very large library. The library contains not only books in printed form but also wisdoms, as they're called there, that are visual, that include sight, sound, smell—all the senses—of all the known life forms in this universe.

Such libraries, according to different subjects, are in great abundance on Andromeda, because there they are most interested in all expressions of life, all manners of thought—and now more and more in the manifestations of feeling and inspirations from spirit into form, as they would say (or, as you might say, from spirit into physical action). They have libraries of all these things that incorporate a vast array of styles of communication so that different beings from different places can come and consult and learn. Maybe they need to know; maybe it is just curiosity or basic research. It is a good job. Of course, he is most interested in the fishes [laughs], as he would call them in that life on Earth, but now he would say water beings.

Other Autonomous Parts

Are these parts of you that you have given freedom to?

I have let them go; they wished to be expressive of . . . something they wanted to do, yes? And since it was not something that I personally wanted to do, I said, "Go forth and do this. Enjoy this experience and go on and become what you will."

Yet you have a special connection with them and can look in and learn or enjoy . . .

Enjoy. I can look in and enjoy them. For me it is not exactly like a parent looking at a child; it is perhaps a little closer to a grandfather or grandmother looking at a grandchild. That feeling of great love, but not quite the closeness of a parent.

So it is usual for beings from the place you come from to do this?

If it comes up, yes. Not everyone has it come up, but when it does, the usual response is to bid them on their way in joy and happiness and from time to time look in and see what they are doing.

If they called for help, you would answer?

If they called for help, they have their own guides and teachers who will take care of them. I would not refuse advice, but they have their own beings who help them. They don't need my advice [chuckles].

You're telling me of some that are in this creation, but you may have some in other creations that I never heard of.

Certainly.

Hundreds? How many?

Not many more than 1300.

1300!

Not too many more than that.

So in a way, then, each of you, in addition to creating the Loves, are creators of individuals.

Yes, but we don't think of it that way. We don't think of creating it, because it wasn't a conscious thing on our part. We didn't say, "Now I'm going to create a being to go out," not that at all. It is more that some portion of us became motivated on its own to go out.

And if I were to talk to each one of them, they would say the same thing the creators do? "I first became aware of myself . . ." and so on. [See **Council of Creators.*****]***

Yes, most likely.

So it works the same for individuals who bring forth and for creators coming forth from another creator.

Yes, and although it is not exactly the same for a baby on your planet before it is born, it might speak that way when it is still its previous all-that-it-was. But once it is born and is physical, it would clearly understand that it came from, besides God, its mother and father and so on, and perhaps see its blood heritage. But before being physically born, it might very well speak like the creators spoke.

Jesus' Bloodline

There's a book out called* The Bloodline of the Holy Grail *[by Laurence Gardner] that attempts to trace the bloodline of your descendants from the life you lived as Jesus. You didn't want to talk about your children, so it's possible you don't want to talk about this?

I am very protective of that bloodline because they need to survive, not only for themselves and their loved ones, but for people in your time. As some people say in your time, they are carrying the energy (not holding it) from those times gone by for the times that will come, such as when I return.

Because you will come back and be born again?

No. When I come back (and others with me), a few years before we come, they will begin to start teaching and encouraging others to prepare for our coming. The preparation is not as one might prepare for the visit of the head of state but rather to get your questions ready, for soon they will be answered.

They are safe, then?

They are safe. It is not possible to be found by those looking for them.

Good. Do the others coming back—Buddha and Mohammed—have the same bloodlines?

Yes, but not quite so secretive. They have made an effort to ensure their bloodlines by perhaps having more children.

Oh, I see; whereas yours is a smaller lineage.

Yes. They will talk about that when they are ready, yes.

Zoosh talked about Mary Magdalene as a great sensitive who was given a tool, the Magdalene that's been passed down and is still in existence today.

Yes.

What was her lineage? Was she connected to some being who came here to establish a lineage because you were coming?

Her lineage is back to God's daughter. [See *The Explorer Race*, chapter 21.]

Immortal.

Immortal, yes.

I had thought at one point that she was the feminine aspect of this Creator, but that's not true?

Yes and no. More about that some other time.

Do some of these beings want to speak for your book?

I don't think so; they might wish to do their own if you have interest, or even a chapter in some other book, but not for this one, I think.

Okay, so none of the cast of characters, whether they be apostles or Joseph or anyone connected with that life of yours, wants to be in this book?

I don't think they see that, because this book is not exclusively about those times.

Jesus' Lesson Plan

There's another thing that interests me. You set up sort of a lesson plan for your life, but we didn't really go into it. Had you studied humanity, had you gone in the future, had you prepared by going to other planets? You primarily needed to bring energy here, right?

Yes.

How would you describe the teaching you wanted to bring?

I wanted to bring something that sounded familiar enough to the human beings of that time and place but that would bridge the gap of the limits they were experiencing in order to allow them to accelerate their pace toward reunion.

What led you to that conclusion? You knew the purpose of the Explorer Race.

Yes.

You looked into what was and what was coming, and this is what was needed, right?

Though it did not turn out that way, I hoped to change some of the coming human catastrophes—wars and plagues and so on. I hoped to cause that to be unnecessary; but alas, it was not to be so.

What was your plan, to do this in one tiny geographic area? The plan encompassed all the trips to all the cultures, right?

Think of the simple things we talk about, the simple love exercise you have heard in many different forms, the visualization techniques that I was sharing with the people of the time, not unlike what people use today. The idea was that this be the birthplace in that time of those things.

Remember, this teaching that I was doing was not happening in an isolated place; there were great trade routes that went through there, and people from all over passed through and people from those areas passed to other places, so this knowledge would gradually spread around. Because I knew the time of great explorations was coming when explorers would look for the new world and all that business, if they had that knowledge and wisdom, instead of bringing the cudgel with them, they would bring the palm frond. But it didn't work out that way.

You were able to look ahead and see what played out, and then you made a deliberate intervention to change it?

As they say nowadays, guilty.

That's highly unusual, isn't it? Most beings, like Qua, talked about the attempt not to change anything.

Guilty.

[Laughs.] Oh, I think that's wonderful!

Well, I appreciate being given the opportunity, and from what I have seen, it did not cause any harm. Perhaps that's why I was allowed to do so, because it didn't make things any worse, though it is not certain yet whether it made things any better. We'll see.

The Hopes of Buddha, Mohammed and Jesus

Buddha came first, then you, then Mohammed. Had the three of you discussed any of this? Had you come in knowing about the other two, or did you come independently?

We came independently, but we did have cross conversations, as you say, and we decided amongst ourselves that if we didn't have the success we wanted at these times and places, we would wait. But we all felt that what we did in these times and places was worthy of doing, and we knew that what we did would live into your times. We could hope that they would be threads through your times to unite people, because there would be so much that would distract you and cause you to feel disconnected.

Because of the threads into your times and beyond and the potential for greater unity, we felt that we would do what we did and take a chance on disrupting things. If it did disrupt things for the worse, of course, we would have had to pay the piper, as you say. But it didn't, and your Creator allowed us.

And the price to the piper would have been some sort of . . .

We would have had to uncreate all that we did. It takes time, and people would have inevitably been affected; and we would then have to heal the damage, and it is a lot. But we all took a chance, and I feel the chance was worthy and worth doing. I know my brothers agree with me.

Did you have to accept the thread of discreation of yourself, as Zoosh has said that everyone involved in this had to face?

No, our intervention was not considered that dramatic.

You came to anchor a particular energy. Did the other two also?

Yes.

Was it the same energy or something similar?

It was slightly different. The energy I came to anchor had more to do with heart and vision; the energy the Buddha came to anchor had more to do with mind and vision; the energy that our other friend came to anchor had to do with spirit and vision. Who came, you might ask, to do *body* and vision? Nobody; that comes later.

Someone we have never heard of yet.

Body Vision

Somebody will come someday, probably out of the ranks of what is now considered native peoples, and teach body vision. Body vision unites it all, you know.

I don't know; say more.

The body you are in is, of course, Mother Earth's body, yet it is inspired and animated by your soul and your personality. The body utilizes the mind, the spirit and the heart or feelings—love, yes? And the body is the union that contains the vessel of all these things. Ultimately, when the teacher comes with body vision—you have a vision and you fulfill it through your body—when that action and incorporation take place, that being will provide teaching about how to incorporate all these benevolent things, regardless of your station in life, your location, your tribe, your culture, whoever you are and wherever you are on the Earth.

This person hasn't come yet because people have to be ready. They have to be at that point where everybody is standing around and, as in the cartoons, scratching their heads and saying, "We want to get along, but we don't know how." Right now people are still saying, "We want to get along and we'll find a way." That's good; I support that completely. But someday people will say, "We want to get along, but we don't know how." Then that person will come.

Is he one of you also?

She is one of us.

She is sort of watching what's going on now, and she'll be born as you were, as a human?

She is alive now.

But not public in any way yet.

Correct.

That's incredibly exciting.

I think so [laughs]. Of course, I am a little biased, but I don't mind.

[Laughs.] That's great! So we really can't talk about her yet, but it's out there, right?

Better not to say too much right now. Better to allow her to enjoy her childhood [laughs]. It is an innocent time for us all, is it not? At least ideally.

But she'll have a benevolent childhood.

We'll see.

How have your interactions with everyone else in the place where you live changed because of your time on Earth? You've talked about having to go off sometimes and release negative or emotional feelings, but what did you gain from coming to Earth that makes your life better now than before you came?

I gained someone to love, and that someone is all of you. Just as when parents have a child, they gain someone to love, and that is a wonderful thing. You have someone to love you; you know you've got something worth having.

Your energy is not pulled by humans calling you, but yet you're very aware of what goes on here all the time?

I pay attention, though I am not watching each and every one of you, as in the famous song about Santa Claus.*

[Laughs.] But you're aware of the high points.

I'm aware of the generalities, yes.

The Plan to Return

So this woman has to come first and then the three of you will come back together?

First she will prepare people; then the three of us will come—and others. But we will come and people will know who we are. We will not hide it; no need. At first people will be excited and want to treat us like kings or what-have-you, but we won't allow it.

Will you come in a body similar to the one you had on Earth, the three of you?

If we did that, we wouldn't be recognized. Most of the Christian world is enamored with the idea that Jesus was fair-complected. Of course, he wasn't [chuckles].

You'll come back in the myth image, then?

I may come back in several different guises, not being in one place at once, but at many times in many places. I might just come looking fair-skinned and fair-haired, especially in Nordic countries, but when I go to South America or the Caribbean or Australia or Africa, I'll look more like I originally looked.

If you came today, you'd be on television, but if you look different in every country, how will you deal with modern communication?

Assuming they can shield their equipment from the radiation (there will be a profound magnetic energy that comes from all of us), then I might appear differently to different people looking at the same screen

* Refers to the words of the song, "Santa Claus Is Coming to Town": "I see you when you're sleeping, I know when you're awake, I know when you've been good or bad, so be good for goodness' sake."

at the same moment. One might see dark skin, another light skin; one might see a woman, one might see a man. One might see a very old person, another a child. At first people will be confused, then they will be nervous; but I will reassure them and calm their fears.

Because each person needs to see you in a certain way?

This would be an extreme case—say, where six people see different things. But I will appear to every individual in the form they feel most at peace and comfortable with. Not, of course a loved one who has passed over, but . . . maybe when you were young some particular person looked after you, maybe an aunt or uncle or just someone you called auntie or uncle, and you might still have a tender spot in your heart for such a person. Depending on what nationality or race or culture you are, that person might look different to different people. So I will appear that way. Even in person I will be perceived differently by different people, and in the beginning you'll want to say, "No, he was this!" and "No, he was that!" After a short time you'll say, "Well, however he appeared to you is fine with me, but the way he looked to me felt great." You'll say, "And the way she looked to me felt great, too!" Then you'll laugh and go on with your lives.

Will the other two do that also?

Yes.

That ought to be* very *interesting! [Laughs.]

It'll be fun for all concerned. The first people will be confused, but our friend, the body visionary, will have prepared you quite a bit, so you'll be able to adapt more quickly than you might today.

So her purpose is twofold, then; it is to teach people how to consolidate all these energies and prepare for your coming.

Yes. But she won't stand on a street corner and preach or wear a sign that says "Repent." Rather, she will be a simple person, not very complicated, and very likable to everyone. Everyone will say when they meet her, "Didn't you just love her?" or "Wasn't she a lovely person?"—like that. No matter what walk of life you are in, the poorest person, the richest, the most intellectual, the simplest, it'll matter not. Everyone will feel good about her.

When we get into the apostles, did they incarnate because you were coming, or did you have prior soul arrangements with them?

You ask them.

Oh, I'm going to talk to them?

Why not? If you're going to talk to apostles, that's really a separate book. Who was there? What did they see? What is the joke that starts off as an accusation and gradually turns into humor—"What did they know and when did they know it?" [Laughs.] I like that one.

That would be wonderful! So wherever you have not really wanted to discuss specific things you did, we can get twelve points of view in another book?

Maybe more than twelve, because why just talk to the men?

Twenty-four! [Laughs.]

Maybe more than that! Yes, it might be interesting to hear that—what they thought, what they felt, what they really did, not just what is known or considered to be true about them today. What they liked, whether they were funny, whether they were serious—like anyone. Things that would be interesting and amusing, perhaps.

I think that is a great idea! I've got to do some studying.

Yes, you might have to read about these things in spite of yourself! [Chuckles.]

Well, we won't get into that now. I don't know why I've never had any interest, but I certainly am interested now.

Jesus' Current Passion and Observations

Do you have a passion or an interest or a project that you're involved in now?

No, I'm involved with you humans; that is my passion. Oh, we talk about other things. We discuss other beings' projects and it is a pleasure. But my passion is you and what you are all up to, as you say.

You watched humanity, but did you intervene again?

No.

Since you left, you have just watched how it has played out.

Yes.

As you watched your teachings being changed . . .

I did not feel so awful. It is like you do what you can do, then you have to let it go. I felt it was worth a try, but it didn't work out as well as I had hoped. Nevertheless it is still alive in some form today—perhaps not the form I would have liked, but it is still there and some are comforted by it. Someday when the true teachings reemerge, then the religion, as it is called, will become more of a philosophy, and it won't have to encourage people to practice it. It will be its own magnet.

I image you having this great loving compassion, living your life and doing everything you did, then watching it being turned into a tool for politicians.

You could look at it that way, but even though it was transformed into something I didn't intend, it wasn't *all* lost. Even though love for each other was transformed into love for God and unintentionally became distrust for each other, that was not the intention. At least love is incorporated. I'm uncomfortable with the religions where blame takes a stronger cornerstone of the religion than love, but that will be resolved in time.

It appears to my limited understanding that your life has had a more profound impact on humanity than anyone else's life.

Oh, I wouldn't say that that's true, but because of who you are, the time in which you live and, perhaps more importantly, the location in which you live, it might appear that what I have done is more profoundly impacting, but I certainly think that what Mohammed has done is profound indeed. And the Buddha.

We know so little about Buddha or what Mohammed . . .

Well, it isn't integrated so much into your society, but if you were in that society you might feel differently. Of course, if you were in that society, who knows whether we'd even be talking, or if we were, you might be talking to Buddha instead. But that's another story.

He wants to talk too, doesn't he?

Perhaps, yes.

You probably had a more profound impact on we call Western civilization. Look at the world today—Christianity is everywhere in different forms and organizations and dogmas.

Yes, but Christianity is not so much about me and what I taught. Christianity is more about an idea and a political application. I'm not prepared to take credit; after all, if I take credit I will certainly have to take blame, so I'm not going to claim it just yet.

[Laughs.] All right, I understand. You're going to come back here, and you love humanity, the Explorer Race. How far into what we've been told of the future of the Explorer Race will you be interacting or involved?

Good try! Just keep asking every once in a while, and I'll pay attention. It's just like saying, "When are you coming back?" You tried that one before too, and I gave you the same answer. But I'm not going to give you a date, you know.

I meant, does your consuming interest continue until the Explorer Race becomes the creator?

Oh, no. Once you are well on your way, I will pack up a lunch for you, kiss you on the forehead and send you down the path to the bus.

[Laughs.] And then what will you do?

Go on with my life!

[Laughs.] Zoosh talks about the teaching mastery and quantum mastery you are working on, yet if you created everything, it seems like you already are that.

I don't want to say that I singly created everything. Our people, maybe. I think it is safe to say that we are quantum masters. After all, consider the consequences if it was a disaster and I had to resolve things. The only way I could resolve things is to be a quantum master. So yes, we are all quantum masters here.

Is there something beyond that I can't even encompass that you are working toward?

There are many things beyond, but I do not think they can be framed into your language or thought patterns at this time. That is why Zoosh has not gone any further with the explanations of mastery.

Suffice it to say that there is something you're working on, something you're interested in, something that calls you forward?

Yes.

All right. I guess we'll give it up tonight. This is very interesting.

Good! Glad you enjoyed it. Good night.

I need to say one thing before you go. What you said last night has added such urgency, impetus, seriousness to something I thought was already a done deal—that we were . . .

Have you ever seen a basketball player spin a basketball on his finger? In order to keep the basketball spinning, you have to tap it every once in a while. If somebody taps it the wrong way, it falls off; or if he doesn't move his finger around to stay under the basketball, it falls off. It's a balancing act, and "done deals" don't always stay that way.

12

Learning to Invite Matter to Transform Itself

Xrtgypzlql from Sirius

June 12, 1998

Greetings. I was a student of That Man. I was known to him for who I really was, though. During the time of my study with him he did not speak of who I was to the others, and as far as they were concerned, I was just an occasionally unusual-acting visiting student.

Transforming Materials

I was with him for a short time, about a year and a half of his teaching, when he was involved with discussions about the temporary—or permanent, if necessary—transformation of one material to another. This was education I needed for the work where I resided. I was then (and still am) a citizen of a planet in Sirius, and with little disguise I was able to pass for a citizen of northern Africa.

The communication between us was immediate; he understood who I was and that I wished to fit in, blend in, and not cause any stir. So when I said that I was a visitor and wished to study with him for a time, I was welcomed like any student. The life I lived with them at that time was at the early years of the life I'm in now. I am still in the same body, though I'm back on my home planet in the galaxy Sirius.

The discussions he had—mostly with what I would call interested parties, all of them students, though occasionally people from different encampments would sit in—were all discussions with demonstrations.

He would always show how something was done first, then have one of the students do this thing *with* him so there would be no question that he was a teacher, not a magician.

How to Get a Rock to Become a View Screen

I remember one time when he picked up a rock, just a normal-looking rock, and he said, talking to the students (who, as far as he was concerned, were training to be teachers), "Sometimes you might need to know what is happening somewhere. Find a rock that volunteers—you know how to do this—and then hold the rock up. Place it in your hand."

He always used his right hand, so I'm not clear whether that's the only way. Then he would put it on his knee with his foot flat on the ground, and he would demonstrate how to invite the stone to become something like a view screen, if I may use that term. It would take time, perhaps thirty minutes, but the bottom of the stone (he would usually pick a flat stone when he did that) would begin to show something.

Remember that in those days television or anything like that was unknown, so it was considered magic. That's why he would give the training first and have the student do it with him. Then it would be seen as attainable by the students and not something beyond their capacities. He would usually show something interesting. He would say, for instance, "Here's a country you have not seen," and show perhaps the mountains and hills of Iceland or some faraway places they would never see. He would discuss it, and it would be entertaining. Then he would work with other students and the student who demonstrated with him. They would split up into smaller groups and teach each other how to do this. He said, of course, "Never use it when the uninitiated are present. This way you will frighten no one."

From Sand to Water

Another thing he liked to do was pick up a handful of sand (or dust, depending on where we were). Then closing his hand, water would suddenly come out of his fist. Then he would open his hand and there would be no more sand or dust. This soil turned into water. But if you looked at the ground expecting to see a wet spot, there wouldn't be one; there would be only sand or dust, whatever it had been. He would show us how we could invite the water crystals to temporarily occupy the crystals of the sand. He would say that this was particularly important. If you are somewhere in the desert without water for you and your people, you can temporarily create water. He would show us how to create the water so that it would last, say, thirty-six hours. It would be able to go into the body and pass through before it turned back into its original state. In this way he educated us on what he called true magic.

I needed this wisdom because at that time I was assigned to a planet in Sirius that was being nurtured to convert from a desert climate with some volcanoes to a water world. We on Sirius at that time did not have this knowledge. That's why I came to this place at this time, as I have mentioned, to listen to these studies.

He would often take great pleasure in saying that he had learned this from this or that person on Earth. All the students knew he had the capacity to travel great distances without need of going by foot, and when he was talking about turning the sand into water, he said he had learned this from an old man. He didn't say monk, but we could see him in our mind's eye (now I see it was a monk). From what I now know, it looked like an old man in a robe in Tibet inside a mountain, and that monk had taught him how to transform one material into another. It was knowledge and wisdom they needed in order to survive in a fairly inhospitable underground place. The old monk had said he had learned it from creatures that live underground. Jesus said that he was never clear whether the old man meant animals or actual people, but he didn't want to press him. A good student does not interrupt a teacher, and by the time he had a chance to ask questions, he had transferred his interest to something else. So he had never found out.

He delighted in saying this, I think, because he wanted us to think of him as a student as well as a teacher and not just a conscious person. I respected this greatly because I could see he bent over backward to avoid being seen as a great and powerful teacher. He would prefer to be seen as a humble man. I respected this because this is the way our elders act on Sirius.

I was with him for that time, about a year and a half, and at that time he was only about seventeen years old. He was quite young. I think that later on in his life, from what I have heard, he became more interested in issues of philosophy and less interested in teaching these magical things.

How did you look?

I would have looked to the people of the time as if I were in my late twenties, early thirties—something like that.

Tell me about your life in Sirius.

The Sirius Project

Since I came back from the voyage to Earth, I have been working with a united team. Given a certain placement of our community energies, we have formed a grid, understanding that each dot here [draws] represents a community of people working toward a common cause. The grid is shaped like this [draws].

With this grid we worked for a long time on inviting water vapor. We had been told by our scientists that there was an unlimited amount of water ice under the surface of the planet, but in order to bring it up in liquid form on the surface, it would be required to have the energies of water beings that were entirely infused into the sands and stone and rock of the surface of the planet. That way the planet could become conscious that water beings were present and would thrive in number once water was available on the surface, in this way preparing the planet for what we wished it to do, without forcing anything on the planet in case it had designs to be something different. We did this for about fifty-five years, in your time. While we did it we moved around, maintaining that grid so that we covered most of the surface of the planet, with the exception of the volcanoes.

Living Prayer with Sacred Ceremonies

Then, as the cook would say, we stood back and waited. We got on vehicles and waited, because this form of living prayer is activated when you do things. There's an extension to the prayer. There's action, yes, which we consider a living prayer done with sacred ceremonies, then there is waiting, or patience. After that there is either reaction from the planet (we had given the planet a thousand years to react in some apparent way) or if there were no reaction in a thousand years, we would thank the planet and go back and do further thanking ceremonies for considering and allowing us to be there. Then we would go on and see if we could find another planet we could ask to do this.

But as it turned out, in seven hundred years the planet began to bring springs up to the surface. Now the planet has become a very viable water planet. Our sensitives have checked with the planet, and it seems that the consciousness of the planet was just waiting to be invited to turn into a water planet. It took seven hundred years to bring the water up to the surface in places where it would be most useful. So now the planet is populated with water beings, some of which you have here and some of which you do not.

At the time you came here, you were thinking that rather than asking the planet to do it, you would change the material yourself?

Yes. It was, as you say, kind of a backup plan. It was something to know, but to use only as a last resort, because that would be interference with the planet. Those who were in charge of the project wanted me to know it in case it was necessary to demonstrate what was wanted. The demonstration would have taken place by converting some of the sands to water (temporarily, of course), then touching the water and other places on the planet so the planet would understand what we wanted. As it turned out, it wasn't necessary.

Traveling through Space and Time

How did you get to the Earth? On a spaceship?

This is a sacred form for us. A vehicle that actually has that form is not so much a vehicle, but more like something that travels—not exactly through time, though.

One quarter of the travel is through time [writes]; then there is another quarter that works with the *energy* that precedes form or *mass*. I'm going to write that "EM." Then fully half the means of travel has to do with *recognition* and *allowance*. I will explain that: Recognition is like a sine and a cosine. We make a request as a living prayer, and the cosine is our feeling of welcome. So it would be [writes] "living prayer/welcome." Welcome is a feeling. Allowance [writes] means that "all parties are allowed to be themselves at all times." In this way there is no forcing, see?

1/4	Time
1/4	EM
1/2	Recognition and Allowance

Recognition: Living prayer/welcome
Allowance: All parties allowed to be themselves at all times

That is the means by which the vehicle travels. We recognize space, that which is between physical bodies, as a substance in its own right, and for space to get out of the way of the vehicle as it's traveling is our recognition of allowance. This means that the vehicle partly travels through time, but at times appears to travel through space. It will not take the shortest route (point A to point B), but the route that is most allowed, most welcoming, most acceptable by the space itself. If you looked at such a route, condensing it here [on the drawing], the route would look not unlike this, X being where we start.

This is typical, an example of a recent route [draws a convoluted line]. This is a portion of the actual travel, and I will indicate the direction [draws an arrow]. That is the path that is comfortable and most welcoming for such a vehicle passing through. Using this path appears to be time-consuming, but because that space welcomes us, there is virtually no wear or tear on the vehicle whatsoever, you see? And anything that might be in motion through that space is missed by the vehicle, because all space that exists knows (it is like a conscious being) what is traversing through all space anywhere at any moment.

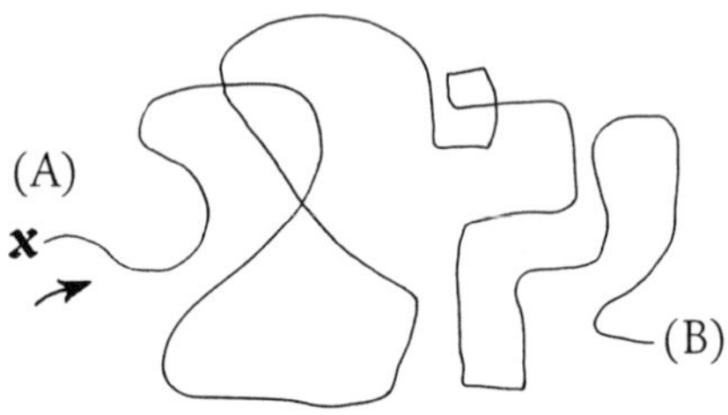

Frictionless Movement: Welcomed by Space

Thus our vehicle interacts with space on a feeling level and knows where to go by welcoming. This example is actually much quicker than going from A to B, because not only is there no friction, but because there is complete welcome, the vehicle experiences virtually no wear. I would have to say, having been on several of these voyages, that sometimes when the vehicle is repaired (when there is a problem) as it passes benevolently through space like this, the space honors such a passage by volunteering parts of itself to repair or even replace a part that might be missing.

Incredible! And because there's a knowledge of the path, you don't run into any other ship.

No, no; you don't understand. *Space* sets the course.

Because it does, it doesn't allow any two in the same space, right?

It's more that space knows what's going to be coming and going through it. Space doesn't stop things—it starts things or accepts things that are started. But space does not, in its own right, stop things; it tends to welcome things. It is very conscious material, and at any moment, if you know how to communicate with it, it will give you exact routes of everything and anything from a grain of sand to a massive ship to a planet or a galaxy and so on, what is passing through it and when, into infinity. If you could listen, it would tell you everything that's going to pass through it and when, indefinitely. It's not that it doesn't allow, it's that it knows the exact route to take so as to avoid anything that will be there.

Propulsion Devices Create Conflict

In this way we honor space and we honor that which is passing through space, and we do not inflict our presence on space. For instance, a propulsion device tends to inflict itself on space; that is why sometimes these devices have a great deal of wear and tear or else there is something else in that space, whether you can see it or not, and there is a conflict.

We have much to learn.

It is not that different from the passage of water on your planet, however. You can learn from water by establishing an intimate feeling relationship between you and the river or stream. Water does not, as your scientists say, simply take the path of least resistance; it takes the path *where it is the most welcome.* There is a difference.

Are you in a different time than Jesus and the students?

Yes. I am using years and so on for your sake of reference.

Are you in the past or the future?

Future.

I had thought all the planets in Sirius were water planets, but that's not true?

No, it isn't true. Sirius is known for water planets because there are more water planets there than anyplace else I'm aware of.

So you're part of something like a scientific expedition or exploratory group?

A True Magician

I would prefer not to be called a scientist because science in your time does not involve very much cooperation. I'd rather say that I'm a true magician—a *true* magician. A true magician is not an illusionist, but rather works in harmony with all materials, with all life forms, and brings about unusual harmonies between them, such as sand into water and so on.

Were you born with a special ability?

No.

How did this come about?

My family volunteered me for this task when I showed an interest in what we could call sacred farmers who communicated with seeds (of the food, you know) and water and soil and sang to them and so on. I showed a great deal of interest in this, so my family volunteered me. They said they would be comfortable if I wished to pursue this as a profession and would support me while I was in my studies so I wouldn't have to do anything else.

So there is a place that trains people in this. Were you an apprentice to someone?

I was apprenticed, yes, to a magician, you might say, for about fifteen years. Then I was sent on this mission to study with Jesus.

Someone in the group you worked with was aware of what Jesus was doing on Earth?

Yes.

Are they aware of what's happening everywhere, or are they just tuned in to that being?

One of the historians knew that this had happened. Remember, we are in the future.

Earth Sleep Versus Sirius Sleep

Yes, I see. So how did you live? How was life here different in your daily living—eating, sleeping and whatever?

Sleep is a good question, because much more of it is needed here than where I exist. Where I exist sleep is more of a light sleep for a couple of hours, almost more of a meditative, light sleep. But deep sleep is required here because, of course, you are not consciously aware of other parts of yourself, and the body needs to be in deep slumber for the total you to be aware of that. But that is not necessary where I am from. A year and a half of deep sleeping was something new to me.

You had the deep sleep even though you didn't need it.

Yes.

So was it . . .

. . . different. I still have thoughts about it. It was unusual. On my planet I have heard such deep sleep referred to as coma.

Were you conscious, or did you lose consciousness during these sleeps?

I would sleep the way any ordinary Earth person would sleep, though in the so-called dream state I would be aware that my body was asleep and that I was doing things, that my life was a continuum. I would continue to explore the area I was in rather than return to some other place where there might be teachers—my home planet or what-have-you. Then when I'd wake up, I'd remember it all.

But the unusual part was having my body be in such a deep slumber. To me, it did feel a lot like the way coma has been described.

Adjustments during My Earth Visit

Did you eat on Sirius? Are there similarities or differences?

Yes. The eating consists of thin and sometimes thicker liquids that are fruit-based, you would say. If you were to eat it you would say, "This tastes like this or that fruit." That is the consumption. This requires less of a digestive system than you have. When I was here I didn't eat meat, and that was considered unusual. I said that my people didn't believe in it, and everyone took that to mean the people I lived with in Africa, and I let them believe that.

You were able to pick up the idioms and the dialect and the Earth references and so on?

When I couldn't, I would just be silent. People considered me to be unusually silent. They took that to be a trait associated with my people, so they didn't question it. You have to remember that the students were not all . . . well, they might have been homogeneous in the sense of being comfortable with each other, but they were all different, from different places. So to be different in a group of different people is to fit in.

Did you find it delightful, hard work, refreshing or like a vacation? What was your feeling about that period?

It was like an extension of my school, like an extended apprenticeship, and I found it to be fun.

So after a year and a half, they picked you up at some prearranged spot?

Yes. After some time with the people, I bade them all farewell and returned to a place where the vehicle could pick me up unobtrusively—in the evening when there was a new moon, so it was quite dark. Then we returned.

Do you still think about it sometimes?

Certainly. Would you not?

Yes, but how many years have passed in your time?

You don't need to know how many years have passed in your time.

I mean in relationship . . .

I can't use your term; I'm using your years for your convenience. We don't have a calendar at all.

As a percentage of your life, that year and a half was a very tiny percentage?

Yes.

It stands out very strongly even though it was a small period of time. That's what I was getting at.

Yes, as a voyage to any planet might stand out strikingly in the life of a person who did not normally voyage to faraway places.

Earth Learning

You came to study this transmutation or transformation. What else did you pick up?

Most of what I learned beyond that point was folk songs and stories. You call these myths, but I'm not comfortable with that word because myth in your society suggests something that didn't happen. Legend is a little bit better, because you can allow that legend might have taken place. I was most interested in the stories and legends and songs of the people we met, so that was fun.

You knew you were coming this vast distance to study, so what was your perception of your teacher?

A fun person. That's something I think that has not come through in your current literature—how fun-loving and humorous he was. At least in those days when I knew him, he would kid around a lot, as you say, and laugh with people and tell jokes.

Really?

Why not? He was a pretty happy person; life then was not that serious all the time.

What about some of the other students? Did you learn anything from them, or were they all seriously or happily learning from the teacher?

Mostly I just learned about their lives and their songs and their legends—their personal experience.

Did you travel around, or was he in one place?

We were always walking about.

On the trade routes?

Yes.

So you never had a chance to use this skill when you got back?

No, no reason to. But I thought I'd stop in briefly tonight and say greetings.

One of My Jobs on My Home Planet

What kind of true magic do you do? What do you do in your life now?

It's not so much what I do, it's what I know how to do if it's called for. You know, sometimes you build tunnels through mountains; you just drill, yes?

Our civilization does, yes.

Sometimes we need a tunnel also. We will ask the stone, or whatever the material relates to, if it will make a tunnel for us. We'll usually ask several hundred years (for the sake of your calendar time reference) before we know we're going to need it, giving it time to do so or not. If it chooses not to do so, then we find another route. It is my job to request this. It is a request in the form of a living prayer, and I usually have to touch quite a bit of the mountain, if not all. So it is a living prayer that might take five or six years in your time.

During which time you walk . . .

. . . all over the mountain and touch it, walk barefoot, as you would say, and touch it and sing the prayer—which to you would sound a lot like a chant.

Is this on the planet you talked about before?

This is my home planet.

That's where you spend your time, or do they take you to different planets?

That's where I spend my time. I do other things, but I thought I'd mention that because you can . . .

. . . relate to it.

Yes, well said.

What steps did you have to take to look totally Earthean? Did you have to use a disguise?

No. We look like you. On the outside there is really no great difference. But on the inside there's some difference—the digestive system, some of our internal organs. The heart is a different shape, the lungs are trinary. Generally speaking, I had to be very careful not to cut myself because the blood is not as red as your own.

But you have the same type of energetic body as we do, with chakras and meridians and lines of force and things like that?

No. If you were to check the chakras, as you say, we would have a unified one, not individual ones, because chakras are designed as receptacles for learning.

Say more about that.

Your philosophers and wise ones have talked about this chakra is for this and that chakra is for that. It is a way to classify them. The reason they spin is that they attract knowledge and wisdom associated with the functions that are identified. Since we do not attract wisdom in the same way, we approach it . . . we attract it unconsciously.

The third dimension is a stripped-down system, yes?

When you are "welcoming" the unconsciousness so that your physical body can contain experiences and so forth, using magnetic methods of the spleen and the chakras to bring things to you that will support your soul's intentions, in this way even if you try to avoid a lesson for one reason or another, the spleen and the chakras will bring it to you.

What dimension are you in on your home planet?

Compared to where you are now, we are equal to seven.

When you came, then, you saw with your spiritual eyes? You were seeing the totality?

Yes. It was very distracting. I couldn't endure the people spanking or slapping. I could see all that people were potentially capable of doing. Because on Earth millions of people, even the ones who were students of the sacred, are still capable of perpetuating things that would not be considered benevolent. Not that they *would* do it, but the fact that they are *capable* of it—that I would find distracting.

How My People Regard Earth People

We have great admiration for you on Earth, since you are attempting to imitate and be more than your Creator. It is a powerful challenge that I cannot even imagine our society attempting to duplicate. This is perhaps why people from my culture and other planets as well do not hold you to our interplanetary code of ethics. We cannot expect that who you are and what you are doing could provide for you (and you for it) an ironclad code of ethics. In attempting to create and cocreate, it is necessary to have a broad range of experience. As such we have great admiration for your dedication, and we salute you.

What name can we call you?

I don't think my name would be pronounceable, but I will spell it. [Writes "Xrtgyzql."] These are the letters that come closest, yes? I would be finding it difficult to say this.

Yes, no vowels! One more thing: How did you happen to speak to us tonight? Did Zoosh come and sort of tap your shoulder?

He has created a magnetic vortex of invitation for this project.

Well, thank you for responding.

You're most welcome.

This is a delightful addition to the book. It gives it a whole new perspective.

Good. Good evening.

13

Inviting Water, Singing Colors

The Man Who Sang the Colors

June 15, 1998

I am another student of That Man; I'd have to say, though, that my level of study was different than most. When I was with him he was already in his late twenties or early thirties, and because I could neither hear nor speak, I had to study with him in a different way.

Signs and Gestures

I would sometimes look after the children or the animals to make myself useful. And after he would speak to whomever we were visiting, he would always come over to me and . . . it's hard to describe, but he would tell me a story without speaking, so that I didn't have to hear him, and without requiring me to say anything. Sometimes I would understand what he was thinking—that's the only way I can describe it—and other times he would draw pictures in the sand or the dirt, depending on where we were. Sometimes he would make gestures in the air, and somehow I would understand them.

I had not in my life before or after had such an experience with anyone. The most impressive thing to me is that he took the time and made the effort, and I appreciated it very much. I'm assuming he spoke great philosophies to other people for a long time . Then, as I say, he would come and talk to me. He wasn't using so many words, but mostly pictures and some experiences (the only way I can describe it), where I knew what he was demonstrating. The philosophical talk would be much shorter. If I didn't understand something, I'd tap him on the sleeve or on his shoulder, and he'd find another way, a different way to say it. Sometimes he would give three or four different explanations of the same thing until I understood it. He was very patient. No one before that time had ever been patient with me, and I think I had to learn what patience was with him. I was used to having to just accept not understanding, because people didn't want to take the time.

So he would explain it in his own way, in a way I could feel. And when I looked after the children or the animals, sometimes what he talked to me about would affect the way I was with the children or the animals. And they would often know it; the animals would always know in advance. If the children had been traveling with us for a time, they would understand it without my having to say hardly anything. The children were very feeling-oriented, and because they sometimes did not speak the same language as other children (there were many different people who traveled with That Man), they would become very sensitive to their own needs and the needs of others, and could communicate it in the simplest possible way.

The Prophecy

He began to give talks about water and inviting water and, as I originally took it, creating water, but later I learned that wasn't what he was doing. I was particularly interested because when I was young, someone took the time to tell me (it took a lot of time because he had to draw pictures in the sand and just be patient, which not many people were then) that someday I would meet a man who would talk to me and many others about water: how to find it, how to know where it is and how to invite it so that it is present.

When I was young, I didn't know what that meant. He told me that when I found That Man and after I'd listened in my own way to many of his talks about water, the third time he would bring rain—or, as he said, invite rain, regular rain that would heal me.

Of course, when he started talking about rain (sometimes some of the other students or children would tell me what he was talking about with sign languages or pictures), I got very excited—not agitated, but excited—and I didn't know how to tell people why. But he knew. I don't think he was inviting the rain because he knew it would heal me; I think it was just something he was doing and I was there.

Well, the third time he invited the rain, it rained quite a bit and we all gathered as much as we could, and so did the people we were visiting with—and I expected to be healed! [Chuckles.] But it didn't happen, not right away. When I went to sleep that night, I think I was crying a little bit because I wanted to believe that I'd be healed. I didn't want to say anything to him because I didn't want to bother him with my little problems. And that night for the first time (I had been with him for maybe a year and a half then), he didn't talk to me about things afterward. Maybe he sensed that I was upset.

The Dream

When I went to sleep I had a dream that I was inside a long tunnel that was closed on both ends. Instead of my walking in the tunnel, the tunnel flew up into the sky with the stars, and I could look through its walls and see many amazing things. I saw people, some who looked pretty much like us and some who were very different. I wasn't sure at that time whether they were people or animals, but I didn't recognize them as anyone I'd ever seen on Earth.

I remember that at the end of the dream was all this color; I felt that it was inside the tunnel with me. Some of the colors were moist, almost wet; other colors were dry and had tones associated with them as they touched me. Some of the colors had the sounds of the wind and others seemed to have voices talking, but I couldn't understand what they were saying.

My Healing

When I woke up in the morning I could hear for the first time in my life! I could hear myself trying to make sounds—and I could! I did not know how to speak language, but I learned. Of course, when I could hear, I was excited; I danced all over the camp and people didn't know if I was sick. That Man came over and told everyone it was a celebration because I had been healed, and that they would all teach me how to talk in a way that I and they could understand. He said they would have a big celebration.

So we celebrated that day, and the people who were visiting joined in. We all said it was a miracle. He didn't take any credit for it; I've always thought he must have been somehow responsible, but I'm not sure. It was a wonderful dream, and it was so *real!*

Well, I stayed with him for a couple more years, and by that time I had learned how to speak many words and understand many more. He asked me if I wanted to know more about colors, why some were wet and some were dry and so on. I asked him if he had been there, and had he caused that? He said no, that the man who originally told me I would have this experience had been involved in my healing, and I should give the credit to him. So I sent him many thanks every day from that day on.

Jesus' Color Teachings

But That Man taught me about color.

You mean Jesus?

Yes, as you call him. And he taught me what colors could do. He also taught me something that at that time was, as you say, revolutionary—that there were colors that couldn't be seen but that could heal. I asked him, "How will I know that those colors are near me?"

He said, "You won't, but because you have sensations associated with those colors and because you remember which colors were wet and which were dry, which one had tones and which one enabled you to hear voices and so on, you can try to reproduce those circumstances when you work with people. Sometimes you will make tones out loud now that you can hear yourself; or if there is an instrument you can play and you make a sound *like* that sound, you will remember it forever. When you make those sounds, those colors will be there, but you won't see them. There might be some people who can, and if they do, they will perhaps tell you.

"For the colors that were wet, you must always carry some water with you." He showed me how to do that, saying, "Take a piece of cloth and put it on the part of the person where they feel pain or where there is an injury, and then invite, just as I do with the rain, the healing colors that like to be wet. You will remember. Do the same with all of the things.

"In the case of the dry colors, you will blow across the wound and invite those colors. Blowing will help, or a breeze. You will make certain the person is outside in the dry breeze. Then invite the color and trust that it will be there.

"To the colors that have the sound of voices, try to imitate the sound of the voices. You can use your language and your words and say a prayer if you like; or if you prefer, you can use whatever sounds come forth from you that remind you of those voices you couldn't quite understand, and invite those colors to be present.

"Sometimes you will have a feeling to do *all* these things, sometimes just some. Soon it will be time for you to go out and work with the people. I especially want you to work with the children," he said, "and don't forget to work with the animals. Among the animals that have great strength to produce strong offspring, many will not always do well when they are younger, because they are born with some problem. You can help the animals to have a long life and have many good offspring. That will be good for whomever the animals live with."

Healing People and Animals

A few months later I left the group after being with him for several years. I hugged the children, who were sorry to see me go. I promised I would sing to them at night before I went to sleep, and if they listened very closely, they could hear me. I knew they had that capacity because of all the training they'd had; that way they'd know I was never too far away. I promised I would see some of them again; I couldn't be sure which ones, but because I felt I would see some again, I said I would. Then I went out to do my work.

Well, I worked with people from all walks of life, most of them regular ordinary people, occasionally very wealthy people and sometimes with frightening people [chuckles]. I always did the work the best I knew how. Most of the time it worked; they got better, sometimes not right away. (I would hear in my travels that someone I had worked with got better, but not right away.) So I would tell everybody, including the animals I talked to, that I'd do my very best for them, but I couldn't be sure exactly when they would start to feel better. I said I was pretty sure there was a good chance they would at some point. Then I would go on.

I did this work about thirty-seven years, which was a great surprise to me, because when I left that man, I was about seventeen years old. You can see that I lived to be very old for the times.

Fifty-four, yes. What a lovely story! How old were you when you started with him? You were just a very young boy.

I was a youngster.

Did you have parents? Did they abandon you, or did . . .

No, they didn't abandon me; it was not so awful. It was just that they were very busy and did not know how to communicate with me, so they would ask my brothers or sisters to try, because they would be with me more often than my parents. One of my brothers and one of my sisters were better at communicating with me, so they did it. My parents loved me; they hugged me and everything, so I know they loved me. They just didn't know how to communicate with me.

Were they still alive when you got your hearing back? Were you able to go see them again and share your joy with them?

I looked for them. Because they were nomadic peoples, I did not find them, but I did find my sister when she was an older woman. She was so happy that I was all right and could talk to her. We would sing and . . . it was wonderful.

How did you happen to find the teacher?

He came through the community.

Where you lived or where you were traveling?

Leaving My Parents So Jesus Could Teach Me

We would settle for a time if there were things we could eat and drink in an area, then we would move on. He was walking through and he stopped. He could communicate with me immediately in the way I said, and I was so excited! He talked to my parents and he said that he would work with me and educate me as best he could. They were so excited because there wasn't much hope for me in their lives. They loved me and were very sorry to see me go off. In their own way they tried to tell me that they would miss me and so on. My sister told me many years later that they were really very upset, but they wanted me to have as good a life as I could, and this was the first man who could communicate with me in a way I could understand. They thought that if there was anything he could do, and if he was willing to let me come along, they wanted me to have the chance. So they made the sacrifice and let me go.

The teacher who told you that you would be healed, when did you meet him? Was that before you met Jesus?

I never thought of him as a teacher; he was just another person in our group. But he would sometimes have visions. People wouldn't ask him, "Get a vision for me," nothing like that—that's very impolite. But if he had a vision for somebody, he would go to the elder of our people and say, "I had a vision for this person." Then the elder would approach either that person directly or perhaps the father or mother of that person, depending on whether it was a male or female he'd had the vision for. Only then would the man tell the vision, but he would always go to the elder first to make sure it was proper, to be done with politeness.

How old were you when he had that vision for you?

I must have been about four or five.

So when you met Jesus, did you remember that vision?

Oh, I never forgot it. You don't forget it when someone tells you you're going to be healed. You never forget that.

So you and your parents thought that Jesus was the being who . . .

Oh, no. No, that wasn't the reason. Neither my parents nor I thought that this man had anything to do with the healing; it's just that he could communicate with me.

So when he started talking about the rain, that's the first time you started putting it together?

Yes. I didn't put anything together until he started talking about the rain, and then I was very excited! [Chuckles.]

My People

How many people were in your group? What was the lifestyle of your people?

There were about forty, never more than that. We were all related in some way, cousins or something, but you travel with so many because you can support each other when there's more of you; if there's a big job to be done, there's always plenty of people to do it with. You also travel with that many because if there are any bandits or something, they would usually be in small groups, and if you are many, they wouldn't attack you even if they were desperate. Many extended families would travel like that.

And how far would you travel? Did you go in a circle, or did you . . .

We tended to travel along the routes of where there was water. Although this was the desert, there were springs there and we knew where they were. One of our number had traveled on the trade routes a little when he was young, so he knew how to find water. He could smell it. He could be fifty miles from water, and he could tell, smelling, how to get to it. He would know whether it was safe to drink or not. There could be two places . . . let me draw you a little picture [draws].

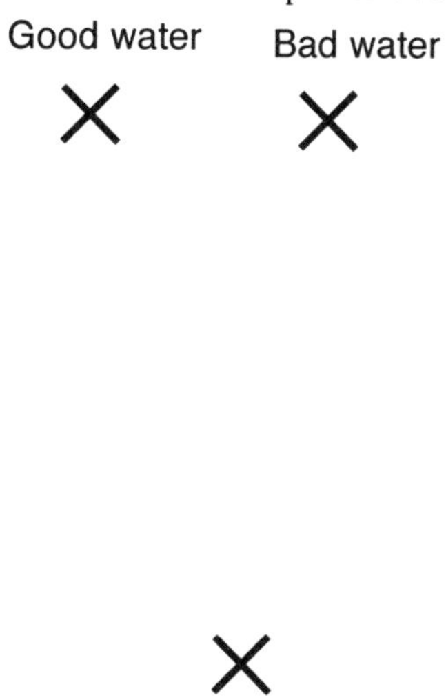

Here we are at the X [at the bottom]; then maybe another X here and another X here [at the top], all right? (Your language is very beautiful.) Here we might be, and you can see that this is good water and this is bad water. It might be, say, forty-two miles to the bad water and forty-five miles to the good water, and there's not much difference in these directions. But he could *smell* it, and he would find the good water every time, even if bad water was closer.

Awesome! So he was like your shaman or your . . .

The Boy Who Could Smell Water

No, someone else was our mystical woman, but he had this skill. When he traveled on the trade routes (he left that route when he was about seven or seven and a half years old), he traveled with this old man. He helped the old man to walk, being young and strong—as you say, a child, but children are strong. The old man would help him in the ways he knew how, and he taught him how to smell and find water.

The original idea, I think, might have been to stay with him, and when the old man died he would take over. But our paths crossed, these traders and our family, and it turned out that the traders owed my family some great favor. This child was an orphan and liked our family. He wanted to be with us because we had children and the traders didn't have any children to play with. He didn't like leaving the old man because he really loved him, but the old man told him it was okay, to go ahead; he'd train somebody else.

So that's how he came to be with us. It was the most wonderful thing that happened to our family at that time, because the only way we could find water was to be guided by people who sometimes remembered this or that, so often there were desperate times, they tell me.

Living off the Land

I'd like to understand how you lived before you went with Jesus. Would people carry everything on a horse or a donkey or on their backs, or did they have stick sleds like Indians?

Mostly we walked.

What about your possessions?

You know, when you're living in such rough terrain, you don't carry anything more than what can actually help you. You find that the most important possessions are each other, like the man who could smell and find water, you know; and other people could do other things, find food and so on. These are the most important possessions. You don't carry a box around with things in it.

The weather would get hot, but it wouldn't get cold so much, not freezing cold, so you didn't need to carry too much.

Didn't you have tents or shelters?

Sometimes we would have those, yes.

What would you do when you got someplace? Did the men hire out wherever you were?

Work? You mean like employment and be paid money?

Or barter or something?

No, no. No, it wasn't like that. Most of our effort was in finding food, shelter and water. If we needed to move on, we did. It wasn't work and money and all this; we lived off the land. That's the term they use; we lived off the land.

You never had anyplace to go to, you just kept moving toward more food and more water?

Yes. That is strange to you?

So you were like nomads; you moved from place to place.

Yes, a healthy lifestyle, as they say in your time, for children, I feel. I've learned many valuable things. Many of your children, I think, might not be so safe out in the desert, but children of my family would be perfectly safe. They'd know how to survive, what to do. It was survival in those days, not much more than that.

So there weren't any settlements or places where there were large groupings of people like villages or cities or anything? The whole area was just people on the move from one place to the other?

I couldn't say. We're talking about my family when I was young, yes?

Yes.

No, where we went there weren't a whole lot of settlements. If we went to a spring or something, there would usually be people, but it was not the sort of place that would support building a town, no. It would be just enough for weary travelers, but not a lake or anything.

Did you ever come upon a town when you were with your family?

Never. Imagine my surprise when I was traveling with That Man and we came across some mud huts. I'd never seen anything like that. I was startled to go inside one; it was so cool in the daytime. I'd never been in a building before. I had never been in a shelter that was cool other than a cave, and I didn't know that human beings could build a cave. It was a surprise to me.

That was the largest encampment or group that you saw?

Yes. There weren't so many people then, you know. Usually when you saw other people, as soon as you were sure they weren't bandits, you were happy to see them, you know? You would share wisdom: "Oh, there is food this way" or "There is water that way" and so on; you'd help each other. It wasn't so desperate that you couldn't help each other.

Jesus the Entertainer

That's why when Jesus met a group like this family and listened to their stories and taught them, your family would be happy to have this experience because there weren't many teachers, right?

Not just that, but we didn't have the experience that you in your time call entertainment. For someone to come into our midst and tell us stories we'd never heard or sing songs or have people who danced—something different—it was wonderful! To get this wisdom . . . well, it was wonderful, we loved it. So when he would come along, people would love it. It was wonderful.

So some of the people who traveled with Jesus were singers or maybe played a guitar or danced.

No guitars. This is before technology as you know it.

They would have something to create a chord or a sound?

They might have something they struck that would make a sound, but mostly they would sing. The first instrument was the human voice, you know. They would sing, then some people would clap, then people would dance—it was wonderful!

To have that followed by stories and teaching would be a rich and rare experience.

The First Teaching

Yes, wonderful! One of the first things this man would do with people would be to help them learn to find water, to invite water—rain—and to invite food, because food in the desert isn't always there, you know. Sometimes you have to invite it. He would teach them how to invite it, you know, like plants and so on. And he would teach them songs or what we used to call prayers; there would usually be dances that went with them, and feelings. Then they would do the dance and have the feelings. He'd usually have them do this for the next place they'd go to. Then the feelings would be there when they got there!

I understand more and more. He literally gave them survival skills before he gave them philosophy.

Oh, he *had* to do that; even today, I've heard, when people are hungry they go to places that will feed them.

Like missions, first you feed them and then you talk about religion.

Yes. I have heard of some places where they want to talk first, but I can assure you that people who are hungry don't hear a thing until they are fed and have had water to drink. They don't hear anything.

So when you traveled with Jesus, you were part of this incredible group; was it pretty constant, or would the members come and go?

Sometimes people would come and go, but there were some who were always there. There were certain women and men who were there, but . . . of course, I wasn't there the whole time with him, so I can't be sure. Maybe there was more coming and going, as you say, than I knew about.

But I thought you were with him constantly for a period of years.

Yes, I was; but I wasn't with him before or after that time. For the time I was there, some regular people were there all the time, and then some other people came and went.

I remember one person they talked about. I don't think he was there when I was, but I'm not sure—I was so young. This person lived on water and had a house that floated on water. I had never heard of that. I had never seen a huge body of water before, and I'd never gone to the ocean, never saw it. So when I heard about someone who traveled for a while with him who lived on water, I was amazed.

The student who lived on water was one of the main students, or just happened to be one of the students?

I think he was there for just a short time, but he . . . I would have seen him. I remember he had a sort of a regal bearing. He looked like he was a man of some wealth, but he didn't wear jewelry like you see on people sometimes. But he looked . . . there was something special about him.

You don't remember his name?

We wouldn't use names so much then. We would often just talk to people politely who wanted to talk to us. At least that's how my people were, so that's so how I was. If I wanted to say something to somebody . . . you see, in your time I notice that you use a person's name and then you talk to them at a distance. One would consider that, in my family, very impolite. We consider that if you were speaking to someone (using your measurements) who was more than five feet away from you and you had to speak louder for him to hear you, that would be very impolite. If you needed to speak to him, you would go up and touch him on the arm here—you can see where on the arm?

Between the elbow and the wrist.

Yes, thank you. And you would touch them, and then you would say something.

During the time you were there, about seven years . . .

Seven or eight years, maybe.

. . . would some be considered senior students who had been with him and stayed with him all the time? I know there was no hierarchy, but . . .

There was never any demonstration of hierarchy, as you say, never. There were some who had been there for a long time, but there was never a hint of that kind of rank.

Rank, that's a good word. Did you get to know some who'd been there long before you came and were still there when you left?

Yes. There was a woman who had been there with him for a long time, a long, long time. I think there was a closeness, but after a while they discovered that that's not what it was about. He knew that it was to walk together and do special things. I think that between the two of them, he had a capacity for compassion and she had a capacity for finding things that other people needed.

Sometimes the people needed a sacred object. You would call it a mineral today; it was some kind of stone. This is what he would do. She would put her left hand out like this. Describe. The arm is bent at the elbow.

The fingers are pointed straight ahead.

He would stand to her left and he would put his . . .

. . .right hand out, palm up . . .

. . . underneath her hand, and then he would put his left hand on top of hers so their hands were pointing in the same direction. When he did that they would turn around. There was nothing they couldn't find. They could find anything or anyone for anybody. But it only worked that way when they did it together. I saw them do it many times.

The job I'm doing now is [guiding] the souls of people who are lost and confused or who don't understand their guides and so on. There are other people like me who are doing this. I find them wherever they wander off to, still in that desert area where I live. And I escort them to the guide, who takes them on. I feel that it is a gift that has been granted me, perhaps for some good things I may have done, so that I could continue after my death in this spirit form to be of service, which I consider a great gift. I am very thankful for it. I know that someday I'll go on elsewhere with a guide, too. I'm so happy to be in this beloved land that I have walked on and be of service to people.

Many of the people have faces. Sometimes I'll be there when they die, and sometimes I'll just see them wandering around, but in spirit form they look kind of like they looked in life. Sometimes I will see faces that remind me of people I knew, so I know there's some ancestral connection somehow. It's fun—that's the word—it's fun!

Or they could be reincarnated too, do you think?

Maybe. I don't know.

How many are you dealing with? One a day, one a week or a year?

Sometimes one to three a day, sometimes it goes several days with nothing. When it starts to happen and someone gets lost, I have a feeling, and then I can find them. It's not unlike what I did when I was in my physical body. So if I don't get the feeling, then I can just go around and look at things and people. Things have changed, but there are still some reminders of the old way.

So you can look at people in the physical, but not even sensitive ones know you're there?

It hasn't happened yet, although once there was a child being cared for by its mother who might have seen me. She looked up all of a sudden, and there wasn't anybody behind me. She smiled right at me and I smiled back. That was real nice. She saw me, I think. I'm not sure; she might have smiled about something else.

When you stayed there, were you able to follow the life of your apprentice?

I was busy. I heard about my apprentice later. I heard later that he did a lot of good things and passed it on to someone else.

So you don't get lonely.

No, because every day or two, sometimes three times a day, I'm with these spirits. Sometimes they are frightened and upset. I calm them down; sometimes I sing to them and have them sing to me. It makes them calm. And I tell them about their guide and that they are going to a wonderful place. They trust me then, and when their guide comes they are not frightened and they go with their guide. It's a good service.

Most of these are recently dead. Did you ever find someone who's been there a long time?

No, I don't think that happens much, really; I think that's just in stories. People are not allowed to wander about and become unhappy like that. If they have a reason to still be on Earth, maybe they are allowed to be there. Like me: I was allowed. I don't remember asking to do this, but I'm very happy that I've been allowed to do it. So there might be people like me, doing this and other things, who have been here for a while. It's possible.

You've never asked how long you'll be here?

No, you don't ask things like that. That would be impolite. That would be like someone giving you a meal when you're hungry and your saying, "How much can I eat?" even though the room is full of people. They put some food in front of you and you eat it, and you are grateful. If they put more in front of you, you eat it. But if they don't put any more in front of you, that's all they can give you.

You haven't come across angels or other spirit beings to communicate with, other than those you help?

Their guides come, you know. They usually smile, and maybe they say something pleasant. It's usually not the same guide twice. It's very pleasant. I'm not lonely. It's a good job.

[Laughs.] That's wonderful. You don't remember the lives you had before this last life?

I don't, no. I don't remember that.

I have this itch, but you're not curious, right?

You mean, am I curious about the lives I might have lived before?

Yes, or where you're going.

I have always been so busy with the life I'm living now that I don't really think about those things.

You were still alive, of course, when Jesus died. Did you hear about it? What did you feel about that?

You know, I've never been very sad when somebody dies. I can be sad when someone is suffering, but when a person dies it's not so bad. I heard from some people that he died, but I didn't really think that he had.

Well, he said that he spent another 50 years here, traveling in time. So when you left 37 years later, he was still on the planet. You never saw him in spirit or never came across him?

No, I never saw him again. But I had my memories.

I would like to ask your guides if they could give us some information, but unless you want it, that would be impolite. You're not interested, right?

I don't understand.

If we could have your guide come in and say a little about who you've been before or maybe where you're going after this.

My guide?

Your guide or somebody who knows. Like why you're allowed to . . . you know, just some information about your life and your path and your future.

Someone other than me.

Someone other than you that you could listen to, yes.

I don't need to listen. This is something *you* want to know.

But you don't want to know. You wouldn't be interested if they talked about you?

It is something *you* are asking. I have not asked for this.

Right. Well, I can't ask for it if you don't want to know.

I am satisfied with what I know about my life.

I always want to know where people came from and where they're going—you know, the bigger picture.

I understand. I have heard of these things. It is best described this way: For one, I am doing something now that is totally fulfilling, and I have been doing this for a long time. Why would I want more?

Jesus talks to us, so I thought your teacher could maybe talk to us a little about how it all works or why you're doing what you're doing or going where you're going. But you don't need to do that.

Yes.

Are you in the same area now, in Syria, or do you do this all over the planet?

No, I stayed in the area where we traveled with That Man and where my family traveled. Sometimes I'm in the area called Lebanon; I've done a lot of work there. I don't get to that area called Israel. I've heard it is a beautiful place, but I have not been there. Mostly Syria and Lebanon—I think *that's* a beautiful place. You had to have been there and still see how it is. I think the people are so beautiful, have such good hearts. I am very fond of it, and I consider this to be such a great . . . what I am doing is too much a pleasure to be called a task.

Do you watch the evolution of the people, then, in the sense of how they change, how they like change and technology? Do you see the cities now?

I see the cities, I see the machines, but I'll tell you something: Compared to my time and the way the people were then, I don't see that much change in the people. People still want and need the same things. Sometimes they get them in different ways. Sometimes they are distracted by all these man-made things and they don't remember that the thing they *really* want, they have not got yet. So sometimes when people like that die, those are the ones who get lost, because they're easily distracted.

So you find that the people aren't as sensitive as they were when you were alive?

I think that in my time, when I was physical, there wasn't much distraction. You knew what you needed and there weren't many things to distract you. So you didn't forget what you needed [laughs.].

They've had a couple of wars in that area. It must be really difficult.

It's very sad, especially to see the people suffer and misunderstand each other. It is a funny thing, but most of the people in that area are related to each other in some way. Sometimes they don't know it, sometimes they do. But there are some people they are not so related to, and they have trouble getting along with those people. Some of the people in that area are more into thought, thinking, reading, things like that. Our people are more into feeling, and sometimes there is no great link between the thinkers and the feelers.

Sometimes I wish that That Man I traveled with were with you today, because he could always communicate to people, no matter whether they were thinkers or feelers. It didn't make any difference. He could communicate and he could help them communicate with each other. I think there will be people who will help that way sometime.

Did you know that he will be coming back? Do you think you will be here until he comes back?

I'd like that.

He's planning on coming back when we get to a certain frequency level. He will come and walk the Earth again with Buddha and Mohammed.

I would like to see him again.

I'll bet you loved him so much that you'll be here until he comes back.

I would like that.

Can I ask Jesus about that?

You may ask anything you wish, but not from me.

All right.

Perhaps you want me to go now so you can talk to Jesus.

No, I just wanted to give you the gift of knowing you'd be here when he came, that's all. I thought it would be an opportunity to give you something, because you have given so much.

Thank you. I will receive your gift with the generosity and warmth that you have intended me to receive. That is clear. For now I think I will say good night.

Thank you so much.

You're most welcome.

I'd like to ask Jesus to come back. I'd like to get it on the record that maybe you'll be here till he comes.

Jesus: Well, good evening. Let me suggest a way you can refer to me, but this will be homework for you, all right?

Is this Jesus?

Yes, as you say.

I don't have anything else to call you, so . . .

I will give you something to look up. You will have to do some research. The two words, "that man," is how a lot of people referred to me then, but they used a different language, of course.

What language?

Aramaic. Look up or find out the words that would come closest to "that man" in Aramaic. That's what you can call me and how you can refer to me in this book.

I get tears in my eyes, this being is so beautiful, this being who has stayed to help lost souls. Will he be here until you come?

Yes, but just long enough to have a happy greeting and perhaps a spirit hug—it is a little different than a physical hug—and then a wave and he will go on. But he'll be happy with that.

Can he hear you now?

No, he did not want to know, and it is never good to tell people things they don't want to know. You can harm them.

I'm the one who wanted to know.

That's all right; you wanted to know, so I'm telling you. But he cannot hear, and that's good.

Is there anything you can call him? I know names are difficult, but how can I refer to him? He is such a humble, modest, beautiful . . .

Most of the students will not give you names because they do not want to offend the believers of your time who are attached to the names of the students.

How can I refer to him? What can I call him?

In some descriptive way: "the man who sang the colors." Good enough?

Good enough. These beings who were with you are so full of love and so peaceful.

Yes, I thought they were special.

[Laughs.] I hope this comes through in the book. Thank you very much. Good night.

Good night.

✹ ✹ ✹

❖ *Robert's Comments on His Experience*

He (the man who sang colors) must be very visual because when he was talking, I could see everything. That's unusual for me.

What did you see when he talked about his teacher?

He was there, and he had longer, sort of dark hair. I saw him on the other side from the front, as if from the back, usually kneeling down to talk to a child or something like that. He didn't show his face. I think he might have done that on purpose—out of respect, I'm feeling.

The being who was talking, there's no way you could see what he looked like because you were looking through his eyes? Did you ever see him?

I wasn't looking through his eyes; it's not like that, but I know what you mean. He would be describing things in his memory. The only time I could actually see him completely was after his life when he was doing his work. Then he was in this gold-white light matrix. He has long hair and a beard—not very long, though—and he's wearing a robe. He's very calming; that's the thing I noticed. There was a feeling there;

it was very calming. He would see these agitated discarnate spirits, then he'd calm them down and they could find their way. Apparently, it's agitation that causes them to get lost.

Keeps them from their guides.

Yes.

These stories are like nothing that anyone has ever read or heard before.

Well, it's nice to give people a lot of encouragement—which is, I think, our whole thrust here, isn't it?

Well, if these stories don't open their hearts, I don't know what will.

14

Learning to Teach Usable Skills

Jesus' Animal Teacher-Student

June 18, 1998

I am another student of That Man. I traveled with him for almost sixteen years. I saw him change from a young person to a wise man.

When he was young he had all this insight and wisdom, but he didn't know how to apply it to life. Part of the reason we traveled around so much is that every time he was exposed to different people, he learned by doing things with them. He would not so much gain new knowledge, but gain in how to present that knowledge to different people at different times in different ways—which is truly wisdom, because wisdom is about *how*. That is very important.

When I started traveling with him he was about . . .

. . . seventeen or so?

Jesus' Early Teachings

No, a little younger, I think closer to sixteen, and he was just beginning. In those days he was a little eager. He wanted to tell people about the mysteries of the universe when most of the time they just wanted to know something that could improve their lives enough so they could have enough to eat and drink for themselves and their families. So in the beginning he was teaching things that were fascinating but that the people really couldn't use [chuckles]. I think it took him about a year to recognize that. When he did, he either went back to where they were or he would find them somehow, then he taught them something they really needed to know.

I think they saw him differently then and recognized and acknowledged him as someone who truly helped them. Perhaps most importantly, they would mention this to others. A wise man, a philosophical man, often speaks of things of great interest that might even become part of your family's cultural philosophy because they're so interesting. Yet if it doesn't, as they say, put bread on the table or wine in the jug, then it becomes a little less important. So it was interesting for me to see him go through those changes.

My Response

When I first met him I was new to the Earth. I had never had an Earth life before, and I was about a year old. I don't wish to say exactly what I am, but I will say that in that life I was an animal [chuckles]. I don't wish to say exactly what kind. I think the first year or so he appreciated me but didn't recognize who I was. But by the second year and after, he and I started communicating, which we hadn't done till then. It was within that communication . . . I don't want to say I took credit for anything, but I would communicate to him only about the absolutely practical, day-to-day things.

Occasionally he would want to talk about the great mysteries, and I would say just enough to let him know that I had a point of view and understood some of these things (so that he would know that I knew), then I would pointedly bring the subject back to something very practical, day-to-day. After doing that three times, he got it [chuckles]. He said, "You're trying to tell me something!" And I said, "Yes, and I think some of the older students have been hinting at it, but you know, they love you so much that they don't want to come out and say it. But our relationship has so much to do with the day-to-day that I feel free to speak to you of these things." Being a quick study, he said, "Perhaps you are trying to suggest to me that it would be beneficial if I were more practical with the people I speak with." I replied, "What a wise man you are." He said, "I've been thinking about that lately; I'm glad you confirmed it for me."

So that was really the beginning of our relationship. If he had a confusion (you say a problem, but we would say a confusion, because a confusion can be clarified, whereas a problem can be interminable, yes?), he would talk to me, amongst others, calling me his old wise one, and say, "What's your opinion, wise one?" And I would tell him. I don't think everybody realized that we were communicating in such a way; I think that most of them thought that he and I had this sort of affection because I'd been with him so long. People thought, *Sometimes he likes to be with the animals because they're simple.* And there's something to be said for that.

I think that he mostly kept his relationship with me at that level of communication—quiet. I appreciated that because it gave us a personal relationship. With the others I was just a simple animal—which was all right, because they didn't expect me to clear up their confusions [chuckles]!

How I Came to Be on Earth

It was quite surprising for me to come here. In previous lives I was in existence on places other than Earth, very far from here, always with four legs. On Earth, that's considered an animal [chuckles]; on some other places it's just considered someone with four legs! [Laughs.]

I remember that I was planning a reincarnation—I was between lives, you know—and I was saying, "I like it very much where I've been (my home planet and some of the outer planets as well), but in my next life I'd like to be [laughs] someplace where I can learn new things and teach what I know in a simple way to people who will *learn*." Very often, as you know, this is the teacher's great desire.

So, much to my surprise, in my very next life I found myself on Earth. I didn't know the place; it was quite a startling thing. I was conscious, you know, and I thought, *What have I done?* [laughs]—as many souls probably do, at least in the beginning of their life here. But then very early on I met That Man. When I was just a few months old I met him, and I knew when I met him that we were going to be great friends, but I didn't know how long I would know him and be with him. We took a liking to each other. Then when he went out, he was given me as a gift by the people I lived with, and I was thrilled. Then I realized that what I requested was going to be answered for me.

We had sixteen years together; it was wonderful. I had a little extra time after that with an old man and an old woman, but they had also been with him in his study for a while. He asked me if I wanted to go with them; because I was getting a little older, I said I wouldn't mind traveling a little less. They were leaving the group, so he taught the man (the woman wasn't a communicator with words so much) how to communicate with me. That was nice of him to do that, you know, so that I still had somebody to communicate with who was not of my own kind. Then we said good-bye; it was an affectionate good-bye. He said that when I ended my natural cycle on Earth he would come to my home planet and visit me. I said, "Oh, we'll welcome you!" And he did. Since then we've had many visits; it's been very nice; I've enjoyed it.

You communicated telepathically?

Yes. Sometimes he wouldn't get something I was trying to say or I wouldn't get something he was trying to say, so then we would sort of draw pictures in the sand [chuckles]. That's necessary sometimes for anybody. Pictures really make a difference, don't they?

You don't want to say whether you were a cat or a dog or a donkey?

I don't want to say.

You left before the supposed end of his life. Did you know what was going to happen?

I knew that he would travel a lot because that was his nature, but I didn't look ahead. I've never looked ahead. In order to understand things, I have at times looked back, but I've never looked ahead.

Did you hear about the supposed end of his life?

I heard about it, but the people I lived with and myself still felt him here, so we didn't think it was true. We thought perhaps he had been mistaken for somebody else, or that perhaps one of his students might have filled in for him . . . you understand, not because he was afraid. We just thought it couldn't be so because we could still feel him.

What did you learn here?

What I Learned about Humans

I wanted to teach more than anything, and I wanted to learn new things. I learned that human beings can often be much more than they are given credit to be. On my planet before this life, human beings were considered limited; it was considered a growth form, that beings who were learning how to do things would take that form because it was so fragile that you would have to do many things just to survive. But I learned when I came here that human beings can be so much more. I particularly liked the music; that was special to me.

How did you know about human beings? Had you met them in your travels?

No, I'd heard about them. Many people have heard about them, but the attitude that prevailed on my planet was, I think, fostered from viewing human beings from a distance. Just like viewing anybody from a distance, you can make observations, even scientific ones . . .

. . . but you don't get the whole picture.

That's right.

Did you know most of those things he taught, or did you learn from him?

I knew most of those things. Sometimes he would talk about something I didn't know about, and that was interesting. But most of the time I knew what he was talking about because I remembered who I was.

You were conscious.

That makes a difference.

When you heard other people speak, you understood what they were saying?

Yes.

No matter what language they used?

It didn't make any difference. The human being has a great capacity for speaking with feeling. Even when human beings are trying to disguise their feelings or aren't aware of them, so much of their beingness is expressed in what they feel that it doesn't make any difference what words or sounds they use. The feelings and the message are very clear. That's how I understood what the average human being was saying. But when I was talking to that man, I understood everything he was saying because when he talked to me, he would put the maximum feeling into what he was saying so that I could pick up all the nuances.

Whatever form you were, you were always there, so you participated. But other people didn't realize who you were, so they just took you to be who they thought you were, right?

Yes, and I've found that human beings do that with each other quite a bit also. There's a lot of assuming with human beings. This is essential to you because in this way you can make mistakes. Unlike many peoples, you seem to learn profoundly from your mistakes and confusions. Sometimes you don't think you do, but you do.

So at the end of your natural cycle, you went back to your home planet.

Yes, right back.

Educating My People about Humans

And you communicated to them about what humans were really like?

Yes, I did. I told them that there were a lot of casual errors about human beings, and if they couldn't understand (which is to be expected), I would play back visually with all the senses things that I saw and experienced. Then they would understand.

You can do that?

Yes. It would be as if you remembered something—how it looked, smelled, tasted—so I could share a memory with them. They were particularly impressed with the great love between mothers and children. They still acknowledge that it's difficult for human beings to love fully, because they don't have a sense of thankfulness; they're not born with thankfulness for life itself. Perhaps you are born with it, but you forget it, so sometimes it's difficult for you to love. But mothers don't seem to have much difficulty loving their children.

And where you're from, that love is a given?

Yes, it is; but it was thought that human beings did not love their children very much because of things that happened.

So from that one life you were able to teach over a vast area. Did your people travel?

Not very much, no. My people could come to conclusions about human beings based upon limited knowledge, perpetuating that knowledge until somebody found out differently. This is because they don't travel very much.

And you don't have many visitors.

At the outer boundaries of the universe, on the other side of it (I like this very much), people don't go there when they're on their way to someplace else; they have to *want* to come there. As a result, the visitors we have are usually diplomatic and so on; they want to come there for a reason; they're not just happening by.

Are you part of our creation, or are you visitors from someplace else?

We're in your universe, yes.

How long is your cycle of awareness? How long have you been aware?

On our planet, you mean?

Yes.

We don't measure time the way you do, but utilizing your time, we've been fully conscious for about four million years. But a person can be fully conscious and not know everything. Or you can be fully conscious and have knowledge that's not correct.

Absolutely. That was very daring of you to come here!

But you understand, it wasn't conscious! It would have been daring if it had been conscious, but since it was totally unexpected, I can't take any credit for it.

You don't know how that's arranged? You don't know the dynamics of it?

Yes, it's arranged the same way *your* lives are arranged; one talks to one's teachers and so on, and the teachers make recommendations. I expressed a desire before that life, and my planet and the other planets could not fulfill that desire. I had to go someplace where it could be fulfilled because I stated it as something I really wanted, and they felt I really wanted it. They felt this was the best place to go, and they obviously felt it was the best time.

About My Home Planet

Did you incarnate in a body similar to one on your home planet?

No, the only similarity was four legs.

What kind of body do you have on your home planet?

The closest I can come, and it is a very poor description . . . you would have to use your imagination, but you have seen the beautiful sea creature, the manta ray? Imagine the manta ray with four legs.

So you're very graceful when you move.

We think so. [Laughs.]

Your social structure has family units?

Oh, yes. Family is very important to us. One thing I've noticed in some Earth people . . . you know, once you've been on Earth, you can always look back and check in. I've done that a little bit, and I've noticed there are some tribal people—or people all over Earth who have managed to maintain their culture—who do what we do, have extended families. When youths find each other, they want to be together and bond—to expand the kinship, we call it; family is not quite the right word, kinship is what we call it. The idea of the clan, meaning a brother- or sisterhood, would be something similar to this. The young don't move away and start an independent life; everyone welcomes them and they stay within the kinship. Thus you have families that are very clear about who they are.

When there are young ones, perhaps they don't always understand everything the way they need to in that moment from their parents. So then they can go talk to their uncles or their grandmothers or grandfathers. The answer is there somewhere within the kinship, and they can find the answer they need. In this way they always know who they are and there is never any confusion about it.

I think this is perhaps the biggest problem your young ones have. Most of the time, very often even throughout their adult life, they have no idea who they are. They don't know who to ask, and they wind up asking people who are not in their kinship. Those people give them the best answer they can, but it may not be the answer they need. That's why people wander around looking for who they are.

I understand that you're cut off from the bulk of who you are, but I think that from what I have seen in your cultures, those cultures with that strong kinship, what you call the extended family, very often have a much, much clearer idea of who they are and are much less likely to spend their lives wandering around asking people who they are. I'm not saying that on your planet people go around doing it like that, but sometimes they try and find out who they are by doing this activity or that. With the extended family that's not so common.

You don't have too much technology, then?

We don't have a lot, no.

You don't travel.

Yes, we don't travel. But we have developed the spiritual abilities quite a bit because we remember our past lives and so on. I am speaking to you embodied on my home planet now. I can see, not exactly the space in which this communication is going on, but different places around the Earth. And it is nice. I'm particularly interested in the interaction between animals and people, naturally, but other than that, my second great interest is in families on Earth and how they're coping with changing times and experiences.

The Time of the Machines

Did That Man ever talk to you about what he told some other students, that the time he would be most needed was when the machines came?

Oh, he mentioned machines to me a couple of times, but I didn't quite understand them then [chuckles].

As you look now, you have a better idea of what we're going through, right?

Now I have a better idea of what machines are, and I see why it's such a challenge, because it's so difficult for the average human being to look at a machine and see it as anything other than what it appears to be. But it is a direct analogy to your relationship with other people. As you know, you don't walk up to a complete stranger (as you would say) and tell them your life history (to the extent you can remember it). When a human being misidentifies an object that's a machine, she walks up to a video box, for instance, and says, "This is a video box," not, "Well, this used to be part of stone in this mountain" and so on. The latter doesn't occur to most human beings. But it *is* possible to get that wisdom from that material in what I would call its primal state. It's a direct analogy.

As human beings begin to understand that machines are *what they're made of* rather than machines, that is a key. You will then very quickly grasp the connection between learning that lesson and learning the lesson of why you get along with this person and not that person, because you understand who this person is, or at least you think you do. You'll jump very quickly to realize that most people don't tell you who they are; they might not even *know* who they are. You will learn who they are in the same way you learn who the machine is—it is not a video box; it's component parts from different places—by the same form of communication.

Some people who start communicating with the video box's component parts will start communicating with human beings' component parts. Someone will be able to pick up a hair of somebody and say, "This person came from here and they did this and they did that." Your people can do that now; someone will walk up to a human being and, with permission, connect with that person's heart. That person's heart will tell this sensitive person who this person really is who doesn't really understand himself very well—what he's done, what he's experienced, what he needs, what he needs to express, what he needs to hear—everything about that person.

While the sensitive person is hearing that, she will at that time or another repeat these things to the person so he will know everything he needs to know about himself, but not a lot of extraneous details he doesn't need to know. Your heart won't speak of what you had for breakfast twenty years ago; it will speak only about your urgent needs, feelings that need to be processed, feelings that are passionately felt but not understood—all these things that your psychiatrists have been working on for years, but very often the psychiatrists have to make their best guess. But the sensitive person will communicate with her heart, and her heart will tell all. First you'll understand this through the machines, then very quickly [snaps fingers] you'll make the leap to doing that with human beings!

Wonderful! Do you see that soon?

Sooner than you think.

You have a vast knowledge of humans. How long is your natural cycle?

On our planet our natural cycle is about twelve hundred years.

This is your second life?

This is the second life after that, in terms of time, yes.

Telepathic Communication with Feelings

He didn't talk to you in Aramaic?

No. I would communicate back to that man in the language he would most easily understand, which, because he was conscious, was sometimes different Earth languages, sometimes languages that weren't even of Earth at all. As you may know, animals (not Earth people, not human beings) speak with their feelings first and their thoughts second. Thoughts really are perhaps third or fourth. The feelings are very strong, and that way there is instantaneous knowing. You say that you pick up a feeling from somebody; you *know* that feeling, then you can put the word of your language to that feeling to describe it. But you don't have to; if you're conscious of your own feelings, you don't have to. Sometimes we wouldn't use words at all.

I want to know what "That Man" is in Aramaic, but I don't think you're the right one to ask.

No; I can understand all human beings' languages, but I don't necessarily speak them. That Man and another older man would feel what I was saying, and if there needed to be words, words would come afterward to define, in that sort of sketchy way that words define true feelings. It is best understood this way: Picture for a moment that a person is speaking one of the romance languages, such as French. If you translate French into a language of precision, not a romance language, a great deal would be lost.

The nuances and everything.

The nuances, the passion, the zest . . . a great deal would be lost, as well as the fact that sometimes words and feelings don't translate. You would get a very thin version through translation. It's like that. When feelings are translated into words, they become less tangible. Feelings can be felt; words sometimes will stimulate feelings, but not always. Feelings are *always* felt. In that way we consider feelings to be a permanent language and words to be fleeting. If you study your archaeological sites, you will often get intrigued by some words, but for even a casual viewer at an archaeological site, the first experience will be feelings; then come other experiences, thoughts, examinations, considerations and so on.

You were with the teacher so long, were there any students who were there as long that you really got to know? Or did they come and go?

They came and went, but there were one or two who were part of his core group that used to think of me affectionately. They would think, *Oh, That Man is with his friend again*—me being the friend. They would think of me affectionately as someone who loved him and was loved by him, and they would just smile, looking at me. They had heart for me and I had heart for them, but we didn't communicate per se.

Did they change and grow, and did you see depth in them that wasn't there to begin with?

How the Students Changed

Oh, yes. Yes, a lot of them changed. In those days you didn't see new people very much. You saw the people you regularly saw, and when you saw other people, you weren't sure whether they would be safe to be with, so sometimes you avoided them. In those circumstances it would be very easy to come to a lot of erroneous conclusions about people. But they would get over all of those conclusions walking around with That Man because they'd be meeting people all the time. And they'd learn how to create safety for themselves, not by avoiding people but by projecting certain feelings—not consciously throwing a feeling at someone, but rather feeling it so strongly that what they were feeling could be only that.

For instance, they might feel great safety or great strength going into an encampment of people who might look very savage or frightening. It works both ways. Not only were the students then safe, but because the students would all be projecting safety for themselves, the savage-looking people, the warriors, would feel safety. They felt no threat, so it was like, "Oh, well, you must be friends" or "We haven't met before, but I feel good about you; come and sit down and be with us" and so on. It works both ways. You don't project what you're feeling; it just naturally projects, and what you're feeling will often be picked up by others.

Would you like to share with the readers anything you heard That Man teach that was particularly meaningful to you?

That Man was talking about a different species, but there aren't too many of those animal beings around anymore because so many people have cats today, hmm? Let's use the cats as an example, and I will make a variation.

What Jesus Said about Animals

He would say to learn from the animals because the animals will teach you their simple strength, and their basic needs are the same as your own. You have the cat; it sits in your lap sometimes and it purrs and you're petting it. You like petting it. What the cat is really doing is meditating, as you would say; the cat feels at peace with the world and is totally focused on being at peace. When people pet cats, they will often feel more peaceful because the cat is feeling peace completely and that peace is radiated. Just like the warriors in my example, the person who pets the cat or is close enough to it will experience peace. Eventually, after petting the cat or having the cat in your lap for a while, you start to feel better.

He used to encourage people, when they were agitated or frightened, to be with their animals, and if the animals were frightened, to just stroke them and talk to them gently. It didn't matter what you said, because it was the feeling in your voice that caused the animals to get calmer. And as the animals got calmer, you too would get calmer because you were doing this loving, unselfish act. He would say that. It was very simple and accessible, you know. A lot of people have animals around—even if they're not animals that live with them, they're around.

Maybe a neighbor's dog is friendly and comes over once in a while and you can pet it. The dog is friendly and it makes you feel more friendly. The dog is curious and likes people; before you know it, you're curious. You go over and talk to your neighbor because you feel that you like people more, you can trust them more. The dog's feelings radiate, and if you are open to them, you feel them and absorb them. You become simple and trusting and full of heart like the dog, and you say, "Oh, you're such a good dog. I want to go and see the people you live with; they must be good people." Pretty soon you and your neighbor are friends, whereas before you didn't know each other.

People in those days had animals. That's one thing he learned after a while. He talked to them about the animals because they could all understand. There were common threads, he would say, common threads—he said that a lot. You know, everybody has to eat and sleep, they need shelter sometimes and they need love and so on. He'd always talk about the common threads first, then other things as they would come up.

The Mystical

As he became older, he wouldn't bring up any of his really mystical things unless people asked about them. If they asked and they were just curious, he would say some little thing, maybe tell a story about it—this happened or that happened. If they continued to express interest, he'd talk to them about it. But if they asked and were genuinely curious and if he felt in their energy that they had a talent or an ability, he would look them in the eye. He might be telling the story to everybody about the thing, whatever it was, but as he looked at the person he felt had a talent for this thing, all this energy would be flowing toward that person. Very often it would be a younger person. You couldn't, even as a teacher in those days, take a younger person away and give him a five-minute apprenticeship; you just couldn't do that. It wasn't considered proper. You couldn't do it unless the father or the grandfather, the brothers and all those people were there. You had to talk to *them*, you couldn't talk to the child so easily.

So he'd let all the energy of the story and the experience, whatever it was, flow into that person; then he would trust that if she had a natural talent or ability for this, she would then have the core resonance, as he would sometimes call it, to re-create this skill on her own. He used to say to me sometimes, "Much of the time I just have to have faith that it will work out." When he got older, he said, "In the beginning I didn't have that faith. I wanted to say more to them, I wanted to *show* them. [Chuckles.] I wanted to show them every step. But as I got older I was more comfortable being the farmer, dropping the seed, nurturing it a little bit and going on."

He would teach how to get water and find food and sing songs.

Very practical, yes?

How Jesus Taught Indirectly

Did you hear other practical things that he taught?

Sometimes he would want to say things, like of childbirth, but it wasn't considered proper for a man to speak of that, so he didn't. But he would sometimes encourage the women with him who were traveling students to talk to the other women about childbirth and such things. If he saw a woman who had skills in this area—you know, working with a woman who is going to give birth . . .

A midwife, a healer.

Like a midwife, yes. He would sometimes talk to one of the women students, usually one of the older ones, a grandmother type of person, and he would do that same thing. He'd be talking to her, but he'd be radiating this energy at her and she would know what he was doing. Then she would go talk to the other person and pass it on, see? She'd radiate that energy to the other person, and in that way he'd get his message to the person without speaking to her directly.

You were in a good position to feel and know all this.

Yes, I was.

But the humans weren't.

Yes, I was a bystander in that sense. As you like to say, I was a tree. People were used to seeing me and didn't think about me, so I could see things, experience things, observe things.

And bring testimony now.

That's a nice way to put it.

You've given some wonderful examples. Is there anything else that people can get a feel for the time, like experiencing the memory?

Changing Apocalyptic Thinking

One of the things I'd like to say is that even then there were people who felt that life was too much of a burden. They felt that something was going to come crashing down on the Earth. They didn't think meteors or anything, they just would say "the hand of God" or something like that, that people weren't living right and that God would say, "No more!" In other words, there were people even *then* who believed that God would wipe out the Earth and perhaps start over. I think this is still with you. I feel that its core isn't so much fear, but more like giving up, not having faith in the resilience of people and life around you to re-create itself in some more benevolent way.

If you can begin to say with passion things that you feel, even when something isn't working the way you'd like, "Perhaps it will work better soon"—don't even say that, because "soon" can be who-knows-when?; just say, "Perhaps it will get better!"—with *feeling*, you see? Then just forget about it or go on if you can. It gives energy. First, it demonstrates that you are prepared for it to get better. If it has the capacity on its own to get better, whatever it is—circumstances or other people or animals—it will feel the permission to get better. So much of life is to reflect to you human beings—through the animals, plants and elements—because this other life knows it is here to serve you in your dramas and lessons. If you start saying *with feeling* that things can get better, then these other forms of life—animals, plants, elements, mountains and so on—*will have permission to get better!*

If enough people do that, things will start to get better no matter how bad they look. Most things have been in response to human beings' difficult and challenging lessons for so long that they've gotten used to things getting worse. But now if enough people start saying, "Things can get better," not just saying it like something you'd pray over and over and over again, but saying it once with feeling when something comes up . . . let's say that I come to the office in the morning and by the time I get there, all that's left is the dregs in the coffeepot and no one's made a fresh pot of coffee, so I always have to make it. You could say, "But things could get better!" Say it only once and let it go. That gives the coffeepot, the people, everything, permission to get better. It may not work immediately, but it will work in a cumulative way.

So that's a real thing people can do.

It is not something you say over and over again, because if you say it over and over, it becomes something you don't believe in. Say it when something comes up, when you catch yourself complaining about something. Then you say, "But things could get better!" and go on and do what you have to do—make another fresh pot of coffee or what-have-you.

Disasters Versus Cleansings

[Laughs.] That's good. You are very perceptive.

This is particularly important now when people have disasters like floods and fires and so on. To some extent some of these things are natural; what is a disaster to human beings is often part of Earth's natural cycle, such as floods, which are often Earth cleansing herself in some way. She doesn't want you to have to suffer when she cleanses, but everyone has to wash at some point and cleanse themselves. She's exactly the same. Sometimes she uses fire for cleansing because to her it works. Again, she doesn't want anybody to suffer, but sometimes she has to do it. Not all fires are caused by her, of course, but when they are, she had to do it for some reason.

What I'm saying is this: The challenges you face, some disasters, are often caused or made worse by something human beings did or didn't do. I'm not talking about those things. But when these things are caused or made more dramatic by Mother Earth herself, then recognize what it is and do the best you can. Help each other, yourselves and your families, and say, as people have done through the years, "It'll get better" or "We'll get through this" or "We'll move someplace safer"—whatever. And it *will* get better. You know, some floods are caused because there is something unnatural—a dam, for instance. Mother Earth doesn't like to have her waters dammed up. It's not natural; you wouldn't like to have your blood dammed up; it makes your body uncomfortable. Her body's exactly the same; everybody's very much the same in most ways. So sometimes she has to say, "Well, I need my waters to be where they were before."

Don't Look into the Future

You see what's happening right now, but as you said, you don't like to look into the future.

It's not a matter of not *liking* to look into the future; I just don't do it. Our people don't look into the future at all. Sometimes we'll say things because we have a good feeling for something happening, but we never look into the future. It's a choice.

Is it a choice made in your past and you've conformed to it? Is it like a cultural heritage?

It's something we're proud of. We feel it's very important. We feel that when people have the capacity to look into the future, if they see something they like, they will strive for that future. If they see something they don't like, they will strive to do something other than what they don't like.

That may be a lesson they should go through.

Yes. So we consciously make an effort to not look into the future so that we can be in the present and go through what we go through. Also, that way we can have some discovery too, and some joy and happiness. If we know everything that's going to happen, a lot of that isn't present.

How interesting! I'm always still looking into the future, but what you said is very wise.

Sometimes you look into the future and you see something you don't feel good about and you don't look any further than that. If you looked *all* the way, you'd see what you learned as a result. But because you are what you are in that moment, you haven't lived that future and you wouldn't *feel* what you learned. But the minute you start learning something from the thing that might be difficult, you become somebody completely different and you look into the future differently, more strongly. Something that used to frighten you doesn't scare you anymore, because, "Oh, I've done that; okay, I can get through that," see? But when you're looking from your present into the future, you can't experience that future *you* looking into the future, no longer afraid of that thing. You just look from your present and see that frightening thing, and even though you see that you seem to be happier after you've lived through it, you're still not that future self. As a result, you try to avoid it; you pick a different future.

That is a powerful thing to understand. We'll put a box around it or some vines or something. [Laughs.]

When I was very young, when I was in that life with That Man, I

People and cultures get stuck because they avoid those futures that are even slightly uncomfortable. When they get stuck, they don't grow. Remember that.

couldn't imagine carrying heavy weights. I would see my fellow beings carrying heavy weights, and I couldn't imagine being able to do that. It frightened me very much. But as I got bigger and stronger, those weights didn't look so frightening. They didn't pile those heavy weights on me when I was young and not very big and strong. They started small, giving me only as much as I could take, and by the time I was big, the idea of carrying things just seemed natural. Because I was big and strong, those things that frightened me when I was young didn't frighten me anymore because I was now the person I had become. It is like that.

As you were able to look in on the planet during these two lives you've lived since you left, have you followed some of the other students? You said you'd interacted with the teacher.

I haven't checked in on the other students. I suppose I could, but I haven't.

You're just not that interested?

Oh, I don't want to put it that way. That makes it sound like I didn't care for them, but I cared for them in that life very much, and we had our relationship then.

Were there equal numbers of men and women, or were there more men or more women? What was the makeup of the group?

It varied. Most of the time there were more men than women.

Just because it was easier to travel?

I couldn't say, I can only report.

You know what, but you don't know why.

I don't know why, but most of the time there were more men than women. Of course, there were always a few children, which made it more pleasurable. Children always do.

Jesus' Companions; Teaching by Example

Did That Man appear to have one companion or various companions? Did he appear to have a wife?

He seemed to have one or two different women that he particularly cared about over the years I was with him, and there were some children he seemed to treat more like his own rather than the other children who were with him. But he mostly treated everybody the same. He was very affectionate and loving with everyone. With the women he was courteous and diplomatic and did only what was acceptable, unless they were lovers.

We've read in our literature that he taught by example, but this book is going to show it. He truly did teach by example.

He made an effort to do so, and he felt that when you teach by example, everyone doesn't have to learn, only the people who find the example of whatever you're doing appealing in that moment. They will learn when it isn't authoritarian.

Otherwise, you're forcing a lesson on them.

That's right. It's just, "This is the way you do it; this is how you cut the wood, this is how you form the brick," and if people are intrigued by that, then maybe they try to cut their wood this way or form their brick that way. If it works for them, that's what they do. In this way it allows those who find what you do or say or experience in some demonstrable way appealing. They seek you out and ask about those things, and in that way give you permission to say and do more along those lines. The example is like a restaurant that puts a pie in the case. Maybe pie is on the menu, but they don't come over when you're finishing your meal and put a piece of pie under your nose and say, "Pie?" The pie is there, and you can have it or not.

This Water Planet

Yes, it's available. Are you able to say in what countries or what area you traveled?

I don't know such things. I'm sorry, I don't have those details. Once we saw the water, though. We went to the sea and we saw the water. Oooo, that was really something for me, because on my home planet water is very scarce. We don't have big bodies of water like you have on this planet. I had no idea that there was that much water on this planet until we went to the sea. Of course, I ran down and ran through the water, and everybody else did, too. It was a lot of fun. When I went back to my home planet I told the people there that there is more water here than the people could ever use.

Was it fresh water or sea water?

It was sea water; we went to the sea.

The Mediterranean, right?

Perhaps. But back on my home planet there are springs. There is enough water for my people to use, but there are not vast amounts of water. That was an amazing sight for me; I still remember it very well, the clear blue sky and the shimmering water. It was a sight to be remembered.

This is a beautiful planet. We need to keep remembering that.

I have heard from other travelers who occasionally come to my place of residence that there are other water planets, and that it is not possible as a traveler, even if you're from such a planet, to approach a planet like this from a distance and get closer without being thrilled. As other travelers have always said, it's a thrill every time. They can really identify with what I was talking about, seeing the sea for the first time; they understood completely.

It seems that you went to the same area more than once. Was there a pattern? Did you go around an area and then return, or did you go in many different directions?

Sometimes it seemed like we were traveling in a pattern, and other times he would have a feeling to go some other way. When I would think we were in some kind of pattern, we'd go someplace else and that would be the end of that [chuckles]! We went where he felt to go.

Over the course of those sixteen or seventeen years, did you get to see some of the people more than once?

Aging and "Regeneration"

Oh, yes. Yes, it was nice to see the youngsters grow up and people get older. Yes, that was very nice. But of course you have to recognize that on my home planet this is one of the things we cherish—seeing the youngsters grow up and people get older and the changes in their cycle of life. It's very beautiful, and to see it being constantly repeated is very reassuring. When children see this, they learn that things will go on no matter what. They're not frightened of becoming older because they see older people in their own kinship becoming older. They might be doing things that the youngster cannot identify with, but they can see that that older person seems to be enjoying it. They think, *Well, maybe I'll enjoy it, too.* They don't dwell on it, they just do what they do at their age.

It doesn't concern them or frighten them.

That's right; it's very reassuring.

It's just like this on your planet, too? You have these very long lives—twelve hundred years, you said, so . . .

I'm talking about my planet when I say our kinship.

Do you have that cycle, then, where you grow older and the body wears out?

Yes. Well, it isn't "wear out" for us, but we get a feeling. I'm saying twelve hundred years because it's about that in terms of your measurement of time. We get a feeling that it's time to regenerate. You would consider regeneration to be death and then perhaps reincarnation. But we consider it regeneration, and we always ask to be returned to our own kinship. We don't always go there; sometimes we wind up in another kinship in our regeneration. Then we accept that and go on.

Over several cycles you may have deep affection for many different creatures?

Yes.

Population

Do you have thousands, millions, billions, hundreds? How many beings on your home planet?

Oh, the population is regulated to around four hundred thousand or so. It's not regulated cruelly, but in this way we really appreciate children. There are not many of them, and they're loved and nurtured. We appreciate older people too, because there are not many of them either, and they're loved and appreciated. In that way all ages are cherished.

How do you control the population?

We ask. We say, "There is only so much water and resources for about four hundred thousand to live comfortably. Let's have that be our population."

So even if someone's ship should come by to colonize new areas, you prefer to stay on your planet?

When beings are conscious—that's the answer, but I will elaborate for you: When beings are conscious, they know that it is so when something like that is stated, that the planet can offer comfort for four hundred thousand beings. But if it becomes more than four hundred thousand, it will become increasingly uncomfortable for everybody. How could conscious beings possibly consider doing that?

What I meant was, there was no desire to colonize other planets—to go out from that planet and create.

Other planets have beings, too; if we went there and started our civilization, we would be saying to those beings that the resources that are supporting them . . . it would not be respectful!

I see; aren't there any planets that aren't inhabited?

All the planets—our planet and the outer planets—are all inhabited. They all have people on them, and the resources of the planet are sustaining the population in a way that's compatible for the planet and for the people. In that way, then, everyone is happy and life goes on.

I thought there were uninhabited planets everywhere that one could go to if one wanted to.

Not where I live.

Life on My Planet

I see. Is your planet the size of Earth, smaller or bigger?

Bigger; about one and a half times the size of Earth.

And it's mostly land.

Mostly land.

Do you live over a much larger area?

Yes. I have spoken with Earth once, and she says someday when people here become more conscious, there will be a fixed population, much the same as we fix ours, and it will be much, much less than you have now.

Do you own property, or do you just settle in a place that's comfortable?

We don't have ownership. Ownership requires that something is less; if you own something, the thing you own is not of equal status as yourself. You humans own land or a car, yes? Those things you own—the car or the land—are less than you; they are not equal to you. That's what happens with ownership. Where we live, the land is equal to us and we are equal to the land. How could we own it? If we own it, it is not equal to us; it is less than us, giving us permission to own it. We do not believe in ownership.

Do you travel all over the planet, or do you have an area that your kinship inhabits?

An area. Most of the planet is in its pristine, original condition. Our peoples touch about one-tenth of the surface of the land in our travels and living. Most of the rest is just the way it has always been, as far as we know. And the planet likes it that way; she's comfortable with us utilizing about a tenth of her surface. But she wants the ninety percent of her surface the way it's comfortable for her.

You didn't even travel through it, you said.

Never, never. She has expressed an interest in being mostly untouched, allowed to be herself. But she can't be herself where we build our structures and live and do what we do, just like Earth here. Earth can't be herself when you build your structures and have your needs and do what *you* do here. It's no different; it's the same for every planet I've ever talked with.

Are the structures you build houses or villages or cities?

Simple houses, not unlike the pueblo style.

In which you mostly lived in during your life, or did you move from one to the other?

The house is a place for private activities and family gatherings, but most of the time we're outside the house in the elements. The planet is benevolent. When it rains, we go out and celebrate the rain, because it doesn't rain that often. We're outside most of the time. The house is for private pastimes or family kinship ceremonies and so on. Because the planet is not threatening, we're not inside too much, so the house doesn't have to be very elaborate. It can be simple.

Do you grow your own food? Or don't you eat?

We eat, but not as much as you do in terms of the mass of our body weight compared to what we take in. But we do not have to grow it; the planet has food. To an extent, the water we drink is very nourishing. It has all the elements we need—like you would say, vitamins and minerals. The food we eat, then, is not that much; it would be like what you would call fruit or vegetables that grow wild and in great abundance.

All you have to do is just pick it?

We don't; we just go out and eat it. We don't pick it and bring it back; we just go out and eat it. It's not so far; and it regenerates very quickly. A new crop would regenerate, by your time, about every month and a half, so it's very prolific.

Well, I can't ask you what you'll ask for in the next life, because you don't like to look ahead. Are you at the end or in the middle of a cycle now?

My Time Cycle and Dimensional Differences

No, I'm not at the end of a cycle just yet. If I'm going to ask something, I'll ask it in my more conscious state between lives, like I did before. But I could say right now, I don't get the feeling that I'm going to ask for anything. But who can say? In my greater conscious state I might want to do something, so I don't know. I will find out when I am there.

[Laughs.] In your conscious state now, do you remember the more conscious states between lives? Are they available to you?

I remember feeling more conscious, but they're not readily available in terms of what was said and understood. They're not as available; I don't have the capacity or the nuances. Remembering everything going back to my beginning, we'll say that's a recollection ten. But between lives I would have a recollection seven.

That's pretty close. Are you at a particular dimension?

You would consider it to be dimension five.

You live in a way that is so benevolent it sounds like it's higher than that.

In my experience, dimension-five beings all over are pretty benevolent. I have not seen anything but that. I'll admit I have not seen everything.

You were in dimension three when you were here, but you didn't have the limitations we have here. How did it feel different to you compared to dimension five?

I felt heavier; I felt (and these are the only words I can find to describe it) thicker. And I felt slower, but at the same time I could smell and taste things better. So there are some gifts, too.

Your senses were sharper?

Yes. I had never tasted anything salty before that life, ever.

What about sweet?

We have sweet; we don't have much salty.

The Students' Agreement

You said that you and the other students had gotten together and were not going to reveal your true names.

Yes. We feel it is essential to honor the people who think of That Man as a great religious figure and his students as his followers. We know that That Man never thought of them as his followers, but rather as his students, which he was comfortable with. That's what he was doing, teaching them things so that they might go out and teach others. The whole idea of following came much later. We decided we didn't want to offend anybody any more than necessary, so we decided we wouldn't give our names. In my case I decided I wouldn't describe what I would have been perceived to be because my name would not mean anything to you anyway! [Laughs.]

[Laughs.] That implies that after we started this book you have all somehow gotten together or communicated.

It's like a knowingness; that's the way I would describe it. I knew that this was the way to do it, and since you say that others are doing it that way, then I can see that what I knew was so. I am used to the idea of honoring those feelings within myself.

I see. So if you did have a meeting, it wasn't conscious.

That's right; it may have happened at that other level. But I feel that we somehow got together and made this decision.

I think it's a wonderful way to handle it. I was supposed to ask questions of what are called disciples, but I don't know very much about the Bible; it's not something that had interested me. So it's a way to tell how it really was, to put out the truth without pulling down something that somebody believes in.

That's right; we don't want to destroy anything, we're just adding something that people can enjoy or pass over.

I think it's a brilliant idea. And in the process we've learned not only about the students, but more about the teacher.

Perhaps.

A Last Word

Would you like to say something to the readers now?

The simplicity of the animals belies their complexity in terms of the nuances of their feelings, yet you as human beings all have these nuances and perhaps more. Know that your common threads, as That Man said, are much more profound than your differences. Your differences are those spices that make up the pleasure of newness from one individual experience to another. But ultimately your common threads weave a bountiful and benevolent garment for you all. Good night.

Thank you very much. Good night.

✵ ✵ ✵

❖ *Robert's Comments on His Experience*

Going into that session, I felt this animal energy around and I couldn't get it together. I was trying to notice the feelings of the student. Finally I just let it go.

Did you see a picture of an animal?

Kind of, but not exactly. At times I saw different animals.

Which ones?

That wouldn't be proper; I'm not going to say. I want to honor the being; the being's clearly indicating to me it does not wish to have me say, so I'm not going to.

Not the body he had on Earth—but he described the body on his home planet.

I didn't see that very well. I just saw something that's . . .

You saw what it was on Earth, but he described something like a manta ray with legs.

I saw that; it didn't quite make sense, but it was okay.

Did it walk, yet have this part on top? What did you see?

I just saw a manta ray, like a manta ray that swims through the sea, but with legs. I didn't see what he actually looked like; I saw the literal analogy. That's all I saw.

It's hard to picture that; that's why I thought if you saw it, you'd have more details.

No, not this time.

15

Learning about Different Cultures and People

Jesus' Childhood Teacher

June 19 and 22, 1998

I would like to talk a little bit. I was not exactly a student of that man, but I had some influence with him at an early age.

When he received his initial practical understanding of Earth and its ways, it could only be learned by living it. Like anything else, you can study something from afar, but as everyone knows who has done so, the actual living of it [chuckles] is vastly different. So when he was very young, about six-years-old, I was working with him—a teacher, you might say, but in disguise.

Jesus' Teacher of Religion

At that age a person has needs, and those needs must be fulfilled. But also it is a time in which a person—especially one like him—is very receptive. I was his initial teacher in the religion (if you want to call it that) into which he was born. This is considered in your time Judaism, but you must remember that both of his parents were more . . . I don't want to say broad-minded; I'd rather say more interested, more worldly, both religiously and philosophically. And because they had had some opportunities to discuss things from a global perspective with various individuals, they wanted that global perspective for their son.

They were very alert to the fact that he was conscious; you cannot live with a person all the time without realizing that. But they wanted him taught the manners and mores of the culture in which he would live, as well as to be exposed (to the best of my potential) to cultures and philosophies of those in the immediate area. Even then his parents were quite alert to the idea that he'd be going around and meeting a lot of people from many different cultures. I think he had told them, and they believed him.

So we would start out every day talking about some philosophical point or something he was curious about. Something would come up that he had seen, and he would want to know the way our people (as he would say) would resolve this. Then I would discuss that with him. Then he would say, "Well, how would *these* people" (referring to another culture) "resolve this?" So you see, I had to be versatile [chuckles] and be able to discuss in depth how others would resolve it.

Well, by the time he was seven-years-old, I could not cover with depth how other cultures would resolve something, so I started asking friends of mine—what you would call today colleagues who were involved with other religions and philosophies—to come at night (when it was dark, either early in the morning or at night) to speak to this child. I warned them at first that he had great insight, was profoundly wise and remembered who he was. Of course, I first would swear them to secrecy, and they would accept that. Then we would try to answer his questions.

About the time he was nine-years-old, we were able to answer only about half his questions [chuckles]. We didn't feel foolish because his questions were so *deep*—sometimes very simple and sometimes profoundly intricate—that we learned with him from our answers. When he was ten, he thanked us and gave us a gift. He told us he would see us in the afterlife.

How Jesus Found Additional Teachers after Age Seven

That was my time with him. I heard, though, that he had found a way to seek out other teachers. I now know, of course, that he was traveling, as you say, out of body—or with his body, since he had that capacity—all over the world. He had begun communicating with these teachers about the time he was seven-and-a-half-years-old, when he would come to ask them things. The ones who were most receptive were the ones he went to see. But even in these early communications when he would ask them things at a distance, he would receive many different answers.

What I'm trying to expose you all to now is that he asked about things he not only cared about, but that he felt were important for him to know someday. Maybe he'd need to know it later, you understand.

In a way, it was self-training for a diplomat, though I don't think he ever considered himself that. He wanted to be able to meet people on equal ground and minimize any offense he might give them because of his ignorance. I think he spent a profound amount of his youth in educating himself on the peoples of the world and their customs. I underline this because this is just as relevant today as it was in his time, if not more so. I hope many of you will find these things interesting enough to do.

Give us an example; what were some of the things he asked about?

He would say, "If a man meets a man from another village, not of his own people or his own village, and he has just enough water for himself and his animals and he needs to go from one place to another, if the other man asks for water, even if he is not desperate for it, what do you do?" A practical question; different customs would have different answers. Some customs would say to be truthful, say how much you have and how much you need; another way would be say, "Come with me. If you come with me, I can spare you some, and in helping each other, we might get to where I'm going with this much." Other customs might say you must offer him some because it was offered freely to you.

Do you understand? There were many different answers. It was vital for him to learn that there is no fixed answer to all people for the same question. Even today in your time it is so; sometimes even the most obvious questions, questions that may seem obvious to one person, might be very subtle to another. I feel that much of his training and education was to prepare him to know how to talk to people, how to interact with people and how to avoid pitfalls.

When you first started, were you more than what you put yourself out to be?

All I am saying is that I was one of his teachers, that's all.

But you were aware that he was conscious.

You would have to be aware of that, it was so obvious to even the average person, although he learned how to disguise it to make people comfortable.

Were you what would be called a rabbi? What were you called in that time?

That term didn't really exist then, not in wide practice. I was a teacher, that's all; no more, no less.

Did he come to visit you in the afterlife?

Oh, certainly. As a matter of fact, even though he was still alive on Earth, he greeted me as I passed through and accompanied me for part of the journey. Then he said that he must return. But there were others with me by then, so it was all right.

Resequencing Events as You Change Dimensions

Where are you speaking from now? Have you had other lives on Earth since then?

Yes. That's part of the reason why I'm conscious of the relevance of what he was doing then. I just had a life come to a close about a year and a half ago.

Where?

On Earth. I was a schoolteacher in New York City, an English teacher.

[Laughs.] How wonderful! Have you had many, many lives, or just a few?

Just a few on Earth, but many lives. On Earth were two or three—it depends on how you count.

Why would it depend?

Different futures, different pasts. If you counted from your now time sequence, three; if you count from the future sequence that you are evolving toward, two.

Can you speak about that a little bit?

Well, as you are changing dimensions, you are resequencing events. This is one of the few ways to alter things that cannot easily be altered en masse. As you accelerate or expand your capacities, thus defining dimension four, you will leave some lives—what formed them, what those lives accomplished, what consequences they had—in an alternate place where they will sit for a time. They will not be in limbo, as it's called, but they will live out a sequence that will allow them to become (from their perspective), on a daily basis, more and more conscious. Ultimately, as they become totally conscious, they will rejoin your total being on dimension four or five (depending on how long it takes them as individuals), and they will not be lost. In this way violence, corruption and other discomforts associated with the human experience will be resolved—from my current perspective.

Fascinating. And what were some of the other lives you had, just to give people an idea of the variety of choices available? You were going to share about some off-planet lives.

My Long Life as a Research Fellow

The life right after the life with That Man—after all that study and looking into intricacies, naturally, I was not consumed with interest about such things, but I became very interested in different cultures' expressions of wisdom. So I was given a life (this would be a pretty close job description) as a research fellow. The planet is in this star system, and from what I've been able to tell, every galaxy has at least one planet like this (some have more than one), where the wisdom of all beings is gathered—past, present and future from as many places as is available. So I went there and was allowed to research to my heart's content.

I was given a life that by Earth years was about fifty-five hundred years long. Think about this: Anything I got interested in, I had time to look it up and find out about it. But it's not just in a book; you can look at a book if you want to, but there are what I call living books. You can touch a portion of the book and then experience (if it's safe; you can experience only things that are safe—other things you might read about, or it might even gloss over them if they're not safe) what the original writer of that book experienced. You can experience his great realization of some point or another.

That's very exciting, because as a scholar you will very often have that exultant moment when you recognize that you've made a leap in consciousness. That's not often, but in a fifty-five hundred-year life, you do. But when you can have that moment, which other scholars also appreciate, it improves the quality of the experience, as they say.

You were studying alone with books and sharing writers' experiences, but not interacting with other people?

I could have interacted with other people, but . . . it's hard to describe. For those of you who are reading this who are bookish, as they say, you will understand the great pleasure of unrestricted time to explore anything that interests you. And when you have the full experience of what the scholars who wrote these things experienced, you begin to think of them as friends. I would talk to other scholars who were there, but I didn't have too much more than that in terms of a social life. But I liked it very much.

Can you say what planet it is?

I never knew its name; I just found myself there—not as a child, but in a form that I kept until I was no longer functioning there, as we call it.

When you say in this star system, do you mean in this local solar system?

Oh, no.

Someplace in this galaxy?

In this galaxy, yes.

Were you able to use that knowledge? Did that stay with you in the next life, or was it just on the soul level?

My Life as a Farmer

In the next life I returned to the neighborhood [chuckles]—not in this solar system, but nearby—and I had a life that was incongruously different. It was like a farmer, only we didn't plant the crops. The crops grew wild. On this planet the plants did not have the capacity to reproduce themselves, so when they had their fruits and so on, if the fruits or the vegetables (however you want to define them) were ripe, they needed to be picked, and the farmer's job was to scatter the seeds. Sometimes if we were hungry we would eat some of that crop, but other than that, our job was to scatter the seeds in places that the seeds would find beneficial. We couldn't just take a handful and throw them into the air; we would walk around with the seeds, one at a time, and we would ask the seed where it wanted to be. When we got the feeling where it wanted to be, we would put it there and then go on with the next seed. The farmer was entirely in service to the plants. A simple life.

The fruit was harvested and used by the people on the planet, right?

Yes, but the plants themselves wouldn't live very long, so the plants requested of the people that they put the seeds down where the seeds wanted to go and where the ground welcomed them. The plants themselves would produce abundantly for two or three crops or seasons or years, if you like, and that would be it. So the people had to work in compatibility with the plants.

But you were just one group of people. Did the whole planet do this, all the people?

Everybody. A very simple life; a very sacred life, if you look at it that way. I actually didn't get the chance to use any of that wisdom until my Earth life as an English teacher in New York, and then only in my dreams. One of the reasons I was popular as a teacher there is that I had an unusual ability to get along with the students *and* the faculty. Sometimes when I would bump up against a faculty member I had difficulty with—or a student—I would just avoid unnecessary contact with them until I'd had a chance to sleep and dream about them. I would say before I went to sleep, "I need to dream about this person's origins, whether on this planet or elsewhere, so I will know how to speak to him and how to radiate the energy that will cause him to feel at home.

I didn't think of it as a way to resolve the situation; I would say, "*feel* the resolution," which I now understand makes it easier for the person. So I found myself in that same position. I was pretty popular, and I wasn't ambitious; I didn't want to go onward and upward. I was very happy being a teacher.

Were you married and did you have children?

I don't want to say too much because it might be possible to identify me.

When I Was Asked to Teach Jesus

All right. Did you just happen to be in the village where Jesus was, or did you

know his parents? How were you chosen?

As a teacher, sometimes I would go from village to village, but his parents knew me, and they asked me if I would stay near where they were and teach him. At first I said, "Well, I really feel I must go from village to village, because there are other people I talk with." They said, "If you still feel that way after you talk to him a short time, then please continue what you are doing. But if you feel differently, feel welcome to stay as our guest." Well, I don't have to tell you, I felt very differently, so I asked another teacher I knew to take over my students in other villages and send the other students and teachers my apologies.

That's something no one has brought up. When these families would walk from water hole to water hole or whatever, did they have a teacher in the group for their children?

You mean the people with a nomadic lifestyle?

Yes.

Sometimes they would and sometimes they wouldn't; it depended. Depending on their culture, they might be happy to have the teacher. Other times some of the people might consider the teacher to be superfluous—unless the teacher could do other things, of course.

Because survival was so important.

Yes, as I said, very often hand to mouth.

Did the village have a name? I don't know that anybody has said where he grew up.

No, we cannot say these things.

You cannot?

If you prefer, will not. All of us have taken a silent oath that we would reveal as little as possible so as to avoid unnecessary offense to those who believe and cherish the words of the holy books of your time. We feel that is appropriate. These books are ultimately intended, from what I can understand, to educate and enlighten, but they are not intended to shock, disclaim, insult and attack. It is better to add food to the table rather than take all the food that everybody knows and loves off the table and put food on the table that you think people *ought* to be eating, hmm?

I'm just trying to add to the information.

I think we must stop. We will resume perhaps Monday, all right? And you are assigned to go to bed. Good night.

✷ ✷ ✷

Welcome. I'm sorry we had to stop the other night.

Do not feel bad; one must know when to say, "Enough!" If you don't, you will find out the hard way. I know.

How do you know that?

Well, once in my travels I was visiting some people, and they had an abundance of this fruit. I don't know what it was; it might have been dates, but I'm not sure. It wasn't as sweet as the dates I know, but the consistency and the flavor were very similar. They said, "Please eat all you want." I had just begun to teach the children, and I felt it would be very rude not to eat as much as they were. So I ate that much, and later on [chuckles] in the evening my sleep was restless, to say the least. So I was reminded to learn how to say, "Enough."

Adjusting to Teaching a Conscious Being

You may want to say something else too, but the big question I have is, you were in a time when the philosophy and the known information, as far as I know, had nothing that would allow you to understand a conscious being from someplace else. How did you stretch your understanding to accommodate that?

You must remember that the religion in which I was well versed, as well as the philosophies and religions of others, had a great deal of mysticism built into them. The idea that a being would be met who had profound wisdom, beyond even the known capacities of this planet, was not beyond the stretch of imagination. It is true that such a being might be tested (if that person accepted a test)—not to determine the nature or value of their wisdom, but as any teacher might test any student to see if this is something they have learned from another or whether it was inspiration coming to them through some open channel. The simplest way to do that is to ask (in this case, the child) questions whose answers no one knew or had ever heard.

When I began to get a glimmer that this child was special, I would ask questions like this from time to time. I would listen and try to follow his answers the best I could. As a result, since I couldn't know whether I was being told the absolute truth, I would have to use my instincts. I could also correlate things I knew from other bits of knowledge that had come my way, to see if there might be something to it.

So I would ask him questions you would ask your seer, such as, "What will the future bring a thousand years from now for the people of the desert? Or two thousand years from now? What will life be like then?" Obviously, no one would know in my time, just like in your time. If you were to say, "What will the future be like here on Earth for the mountain people" (you live around a mountain, so in my eyes you are mountain people) "two thousand years from now?" Well, people could give you their best guess, but it would take someone with the vision of this child I worked with to give you the absolute truth.

When you are being told something that is true, as you know, there is a feeling in the physical body that resonates to that truth even if we have no means to know the certainty of it. Through this physical means we have our second means, besides the mind, to know that something is so. And when he would give me his answers, I would always get that feeling. So I knew he was special. I counted myself amongst the lucky, because other teachers that I knew within my religion and other religions would often freely discuss different philosophies when we had the opportunity. I had not, and other teachers had not, had the opportunity to meet such a being with such powerful wisdom and mystical capacities. But we all had often discussed the possibility. So I counted myself lucky, and when I saw these other teachers I would tell them as much as I felt was all right to tell. They were always fascinated and wanted to know as much as I felt comfortable revealing.

Do you think that you as a soul chose that? You said before that you just happened to be there, but I don't think anything just happens. Do you think there's a reason you had that position? That's pretty awesome.

I had always looked upon it as a gift.

So you would ask him these cosmic questions that he was very comfortable with.

Very.

But he would ask you questions about how to accommodate different cultures, philosophies, morals and mores amongst various peoples?

Yes, he would ask me about practical matters and, as you say, I would ask him about cosmic matters. But I made it a point to ask him about cosmic matters only after he had covered all the things he needed to know. If he still had energy and wanted to talk more, then I could ask him about these things. Oh, it was wondrous!

Jesus' Remarks about the Future

What were some of the things he told you that were the most special to you or that you remember best or that you thought the most fascinating?

I was quite astonished to hear that there would be ways for human beings to fly through the sky. Even in my time people would say, "I wish I could fly" here or there. It is a wonderful thing, "if only," hmm? To hear that there would be a means for people to do that was quite astonishing. I was also saddened to hear that the people of the desert, who were much more friendly in those days, became less so in the future. He told me it would be temporary, and that in time they would all connect to their hearts. But for a time there would be sadness and suffering between the peoples of the desert, and that saddened me.

Tell us more about that. Everyone wandered through this area, and even though there were different philosophies, which he prepared himself for, everyone was

friendly—except robbers.

Certainly there were some beings who kept to themselves. Tribal people kept to themselves, not for social standing but because they felt the need to preserve their culture, and that was honored. But people didn't wander; there were known trails. Even if the trail was not obvious, as it is in your time when they are marked clearly, some people would know how to find the way.

I wasn't concerned with that. Now there's such separation in that part of the world; they're enemies, you know.

Yes, it is a sad thing; but he assured me it was temporary.

Mohammed and Islam

And some religions that are in opposition now really hadn't even been brought to the Earth yet because Mohammed hadn't been born yet.

Well, there were great philosophies. The Islam religion I have studied a little bit, and it is profound. This man who assembled this body of wisdom assembled a lot of wisdom that already existed from the teachers of the time, putting it together in such a wonderful way that the people could call upon it. It was not just a flavor from this tribe or that tribe. It was a great unifying force. Religion has often been a unifying force amongst divergent and diverse peoples.

So we must honor that man as well as others who have understood that this religion (which I prefer to call philosophy) is a force to unite people. Ultimately, though, in your time it will require the force of the heart to unite, because the mind can only do so much in union. Ultimately it is the heart's job to unify.

What were the various religions or philosophies . . .

I'm sorry, I can't answer those questions, because the other religions, the other philosophers and teachers . . . we didn't say, "I'm this religion and you're that." It is known that Zoroastrianism was there, but I'm loathe to say it was this religion and that religion. Mostly I considered myself to be a philosopher. I think that's the reason this man's parents (but to me he was a child) were interested in me, because they knew I would not be dogmatic. And that's essential.

Judaism

Then you were not closely identified with a particular religion of that area?

Of course I was; I was identified with the Jewish or Judaism religion. I was certainly identified with that, but I was still not dogmatic. You have to remember that when people are living in harsh conditions, if you were dogmatic, you would very often miss great opportunities.

Religions that are dogmatic are frequently that way because the people who believe in them either do not wish union with others or they do not feel the need for it. In the desert one does not casually dismiss the assistance of one's neighbor.

No matter what he believes, right?

Certainly.

What of Judaism was available to you to study? Did you have what is now called the books in the Old Testament? The Torah?

Almost everything was word of mouth. My teachers told me, then I told others. I know there were writings, the Torah and so on, but I did not have that. All I had was word of mouth; my teachers told me, I told others. My teachers also told me, "Don't be attached to what is written, because the people you will be working with will not be able to read, anyway. So if you point to something written, they're going to say that it's a pretty design, but that's all. Be able to speak to them as they would speak to each other so you can be heard, and talk to them philosophically, such as, "In my experience it has been this," or "My teachers advise me this way." In other words, don't say to them, "This is the truth and the only truth." If you say that to them, you will teach them how to be small. But if you can teach them in a way that adds to their wisdom without taking their wisdom away, then they can be as big as they become.

That's what you passed on to Jesus, basically.

Yes, of course. Perhaps that's another reason his parents found me to be adequate.

The Simple Life

We live in this data-rich time, you know, with television and libraries and computers. It's hard to even imagine someone living that simple a life.

Yet you have people in your time who live much simpler. They camp, as you say, out on the land or travel by whatever means they can. A simple life is still available. Not to the extent as in my time, but to some extent a simpler life can be chosen if you wish.

They can go to the emergency room, and there's all this stuff available to them if they choose.

That is not a bad thing, though.

It's hard to get in the mindset of so few options.

Imagine that you're going for a walk. You take a drink of water before you go so that you have enough, and it's a short walk. You walk out on the land and perhaps around a hill, so you can't see your house anymore. As far as you can look, it is open land. Then you would be able to imagine a little easier.

That sounds like good homework, as Zoosh would say.

Yes, something to try. Then just to reassure yourself, run back around the hill and look at your home and say, "I have all those comforts waiting!" And be thankful!

That's part of what I'm trying to say. I don't think we are thankful enough for the incredible opportunities and health we have. But we still have our lessons; they're just different, that's all.

Different but similar: how to love each other, how to embrace life, how to get along the best you can and so on—not much different in my time.

[Chuckles.] The story line is the same, but the set and setting are different, right?

Yes; the curtain rises on a different stage.

That's pretty good for an English teacher [laughs].

Thank you. It has come in handy.

Just express now whatever you feel we need to know from that time, even if I can't think of the questions.

That's all right, we're just about done.

Raising Children

The times in which I had the privilege to work with that wonderful child are not so terribly different from your own. As any parent knows, you're very often proud of your children. You say, "Look what he did!" or "Look what she did! I am so proud!" Sometimes when they grow up and get older, you still say this, but then they are shy and embarrassed, or they say, "Dad, stop that," or "Mom, don't fuss over me." Know that that's part of life. They must be their own independent people, and it wasn't so very different in my time. Know that children are treasures given in small quantity so that you will appreciate them. But if you happen to be one of the lucky ones who has many, don't be greedy with them; let your neighbors visit and enjoy the antics of the children.

And don't forget to talk to them. Sometimes, as many parents will know even in your day, those children will say things that will just amaze you, and sometimes you can encourage such wisdom and vision. Other times it will be wisdom that just comes and goes. Enjoy it and appreciate the children. Ultimately children and other people are really what you have on Earth. Good night.

16

The Role of Mary Magdalene, a Romany

Mary of the Magdalene
June 25, 1998

Jesus: Good evening. Well, there was a sampling of my students. I have other students, some in other countries, some on other planets, but I feel that might be enough for now. We could fill another volume with other students, but I'd like to inquire whether you have any other directions for the book to take.

Before we get through, I would like to talk to the mother of the child who spoke and who was one of your mates. The child said she was called something like Andrea, a gypsy name—the one we call Mary Magdalene.

Oh, yes. Very well.

Mary of the Magdalene: I am the one referred to as Mary of the Magdalene, though my name wasn't Mary. But it is an acceptable name.

Welcome. Thank you for coming.

You are most welcome. The mother of the child offered for me to go first, so I am here. Perhaps both of us could speak tonight. We'll see.

Certainly. Tell us anything you wish.

Visions of the Future

Only that the best teaching I received from That Man was how things would be in the future. When you are striving for something—in the midst of it, you know—it is sometimes difficult to go on, because you are surrounded with cares of the moment, to say nothing of survival. And sometimes (in terms of your calendar about once a week, maybe once every other week) he would talk about the future. He would describe briefly your time; he would talk briefly, lightly, about the times between our time and your time; then he would talk about the times to come from your time's point of view. This he would talk about at greater length.

He would tell us how things would be, what the people would be like. He would tell us how what we were doing would relate so closely to those future good times and how we were involved in laying a foundation, and that there were others all over the world in our time who were laying bricks as well. He said that it would be easy to see, from that future time, how what we did in our time and what was done by others supported and in some ways carried people through the more difficult times. In this way we could carry on, because we could see the value of what we were doing, which is sometimes so difficult to see when you are caught up in the day-to-day struggle.

So I'd say that this was the most nurturing, and it was that nurturance that was like food. We, I must say (speaking for all of us), probably could not have gone on without those visions. Most of the students came and went; it was a revolving group. Some of us were there for the whole distance, but after he was gone or at least separated from us, what kept us going almost exclusively, from everyone I have spoken with, is those visions—and the feeling that if we did not do our utmost to teach what he really wanted us to, we might be weakening the potential for those good days that were coming. So we went on. [Chuckles.]

Supporting Families and Women with Children

As you look back now, from your perspective what were some of the most important things you did?

I think perhaps the support given to families and to women. Sometimes women would be without husbands because of their difficult times or this or that reason, and it was not always so easy for them. When with a group of people or a village or an encampment, he would always manage to tell at least one story that would involve orphans or single women with children, and if there was a single father with children, he would work them in for sure, in ways that would teach about their great value. I feel this was his finest contribution.

This has not come through in the writings you have about him in your time, but I would like to tell one story he told me.

We were at a place where there was a small spring, and there was a group of people who lived around there and traveled from spring to spring along trade routes. We arrived one night and greeted the people. They greeted us and asked us to have a drink and sit with them. We had extra food we shared with them and they shared their water with us. It was very pleasant. They told us the story of their origin and we told stories of ours—our peoples, you know, where we came from, because we were such a mixed group. Then while we were talking, the elders of their group and That Man were speaking, and when we were done telling about our origins and our family traditions, he returned with the elders. The elders told some of their traditional stories and then they asked him to tell stories. And he said this:

The Man Who Brought Water to the Desert

"Once there was a man walking across the desert." (In those times if a man was walking alone across the desert, it almost always meant a desperate situation. People never traveled alone, ever, because of the dangers of the desert.) "So," he said, "this lone man was walking across the desert, and he had a special gift. When he would feel a tingling in his hands, he could stop and dig just a little bit, just a little ways down, and find moist sand and water. He was a water seeker, so he could go anywhere, and he would always leave the place with a little pool. He would dig it out a little bit so there would be a pool of water there. Then he would take a big drink and go on.

"This man was the one who helped to create many of the springs here. He walked this desert thousands of years ago, before any of us were here. The reason he was alone was that there weren't many people here at that time. Everybody thought it was a forbidden place, a place where you could go but not come back. So he spent his whole life walking around and going from place to place; sometimes he would plant some seeds he had with him, and trees would grow. He was a mystical man, and he could go a long time without food, but no longer than any other person without water.

"One day he came to the edge of the desert where the people were camped. The people were startled to see a man walking alone out of the desert. And they said, 'Who are you? Where have you come from? How could you survive such a place?' He said, 'I am the water seeker.

If you come with me, I will show you all the water I have found and all the places that are safe to go. But you must come at night, and I will show you how to find the water by the stars.'

"The people talked amongst themselves and said, 'We don't have much water here. In order to find water and know where it is and have more land we can use and places to go, we should find out what's on the other side of the desert. We should send someone.'

"So they picked their three bravest warriors, and the warriors said to their elders, 'We will go with this man. He does not look very strong, so if he is trying to lead us off or lie to us in some way, we will know and put an end to him. And we will know very quickly. Then we will ask to be guided back.' They said, 'We will sing in the night so you can hear us.' (There is a sound that the people of the desert make, and it can be heard for miles and miles.) And the men said, 'Good.' So they went with the water seeker.

"While the water seeker was walking, he said, 'To know how to find these places, you must know the stars.' And the men said, 'But the stars, they are just points of light, and they all look the same. How can we find such a place as you describe?'

"The water seeker said, 'The stars look the same, but there are patterns in them if you know what to look for.' So he made like drawings of the sky, and the drawings were of a woman with a child, another time a man with a child, then another time a little boy, and then another time a little girl. In this way he would show them how to go, because he would draw them in such a way that the man and the child, the woman and the child, and the boy and the girl were all pointing in the direction of the water wells—and with the other hands they were pointing back to where the men's encampment was!

"Well, they found all the wells he wanted to show them. They thanked him very much, but they were afraid they couldn't find their way back. So he accompanied them. At first he said, 'I will show you the first two with the boy and the girl; then see if you can find the way. If we get lost, I'll show you, but I want you to learn these things, these pictures, so you can show your people.' So they found the other two on their own. They thanked him so much and wanted to make him a king, but he said, 'No, no; no, no. That is not my job. My job is to find the water and help other people find the water and show you things you didn't know you could do.'

"So he spent the rest of his days going around the edge of the desert, finding encampments of people and showing them the pictures in the sky. Sometimes their places would be completely different, so he would make other pictures in the sky, but always a man and a child, a woman and a child, a boy and a girl—in this way stressing the importance, the sacredness and the underlying benefit of children and parents who were, like you say, single parents."

A nice story?

That was a beautiful story.

It was one of my favorites. And you know, he too could find water like that, so I was never sure whether he was talking about some former life of his, whether it was someone he knew or whether it was just made up. Whatever it was, the people were very impressed. If they didn't have enough water, he would teach them how to find it. They were very thankful. It was always a good experience; it was a wonderful thing.

Tell me about yourself. What did you do before you met That Man?

I was born to be a mystical woman, but of course I did not know that. As a child I was like any other child; I would run and play when I could. Our people didn't have very much, but we had what we needed. We had Grandma, as we called her in our language. She could see not only the details others missed, but sometimes she could see the past very clearly, and occasionally the future when we needed to know about something—usually danger, or perhaps good fortune.

The Magdalene

It was also her job to notice which were the most spiritual children. And when she would find someone like that, she would tell another woman. We had another woman in our group who was a mystical woman. She was younger, not old enough to be a grandma either in fact or by title, and she was the carrier of the stones. It was her job to obtain all the information that Grandmother could not get. The stones would tell her somehow, and the stones were known as the Magdalene. It was known (this was a great secret then, but I can say it now) that the Magdalene was given as a gift from people from the stars, and they said the name of their planet in the Pleiade system. (Pleiades, you say, but they did not pronounce the *s*. I'm translating, but they said Pleiade, just like that.) And the name of their planet was Magdalene.

They gave us this gift and said that if we needed any information, we could have one of our spiritual people touch the stones with her fingers. It must be a woman, they said, because a person has to be especially receptive to do it, be *naturally* receptive and not have to struggle to be this way. She could touch the stones with the fingers of her left hand. The six stones were long and thin. Of course, it was before my time, but this is what I was told.

When Humans Have Twelve Fingers

We were told that someday human beings would have a sixth finger, that it was intended. And when we had this sixth finger, we could then and only then learn the wisdom of the universe. It would take six fingers on the stones at the same time by a mystical woman to learn such things. But for now we could use any five stones that felt right with our fingers and thumb. But we didn't call it thumb; the thumb was another finger, see?

So that's what we would do. We would get lots of information that would help us, but we couldn't get the wisdom of the universe.

But you tried, eh?

We tried, but it didn't work. We weren't surprised. We didn't feel badly, because it was such a wonderful gift, and my ancestors were thrilled. The Magdalene stones still exist today; they are in safekeeping. They probably will not be able to do their full job until people have six fingers. Someday you are intended to have them. The sixth finger will grow next to the little finger. For a while some people had a sixth finger there, but in your technology time, this has been thought to be some kind of a defect. But it isn't a defect; it's something that's intended to happen.

You'd be surprised how gaining another body part like that will make a difference. It will signal to others—from other places as well—that you are growing spiritually. It won't happen overnight. I say this because I know that your doctors and nurses, when they see such things, they say, "Oh, poor person," because children are still being born now and then with something that looks like it could be a sixth finger. Please don't cut it off. When they have just a little one like that, a little stub of a sixth finger, if those people marry (they won't all be in the same family, you know), eventually you'll see the full-size sixth finger. One of those people will someday be able to obtain the wisdom of the universe for you.

Going back to your story, you were running around and they noticed that you were very receptive?

My Training with the Stones

I don't know what the mystical woman noticed, but she observed me, I think, and she told my mother that I would be the one to take over the stones when the person who was doing the stones passed on. That's how that worked, you know; we didn't just take it away from somebody. When they passed on or when they got to the point that for some reason they could not do it anymore, I would be in training with the person who had the stones—the carrier of the stones, you might say. So I was in training with her.

What kind of stones were they? Crystal?

You know, I'll tell you a little secret that I can reveal. They were the plainest looking stones you could see. If you saw them on the ground with other stones, you wouldn't think twice about leaning down and picking them up. It is often the most dazzling stones that are thought to be precious, but those who understand stone know that it is with the most plain and common-looking stone that we often find the greatest gifts.

That's a teaching all by itself, isn't it? But even if they were mixed up with all kinds of other stones, they felt different?

The sensitive person would know. If we felt that there was danger . . . we never had to do this, but we knew that we could throw the stones down with other rocks and they would go unnoticed. We could pick them up later. We knew, because every person whose job it was to carry them regularly was trained to do that. I was trained to do that, too. It's surprisingly easy; they get to be like friends you know very well. Different shapes of rock have different uses, but I can't say any more than that.

Can you say what kind they were—granite, limestone or another kind of rock?

I do not know these terms.

How old were you when you became their custodian? By our counting.

I was about eleven-years-old.

Oh, so young!

Not so young to us, but old enough to be responsible.

Romany Culture

What was your culture or your nationality?

We don't think of ourselves that way very much, but if you were to see us, our skin was dark and our hair was very wavy or curly. I suppose that if you saw us at the time, you would say, "These people are looking a bit like a cross between Romany and North Africans."

The reason I ask is because I just heard that you were like a gypsy or a precursor of the gypsy.

Romany is the proper term; gypsy is not really what they call themselves. Romany is a culture.

I didn't know that. Then what happened? You were nomadic, and your people . . .

We were nomadic, yes. We were always nomadic, but that was common for the time. We traveled quite a bit, and we traveled in what I would call a generational cycle. Do you have a map of the area?

I have a huge map on the wall.

Thank you. We would travel like this, cyclical, like this. We traveled along this area, through here . . .

Way up to Rome and Spain!

And then back. It would take lifetimes, see?

So where would you start? Jordan, Syria . . .

It wasn't so much a start, but it was like a constant travel, see? We used to do this, see?

You used to go from Cairo, from northern Africa to southern Africa.

Or all around the Mediterranean. We never went down into Italy, but we would go from here, see?

To Madrid, and then back down to Africa.

We used to do all that complete, but then after a while we just started going this way. We would go back and forth, but it would take lifetimes because we were working, you know.

What changed to cause you not to go across Africa?

For a while there was a terrible drought there. No one knew how to find water. Then for a while the tribes were very much at war. So our people stopped doing that. This was before I was with That Man. He could find water and so on. I'm just talking about our people.

The Romany people.

Our people said that many, many lifetimes ago that there used to be a land bridge here [Strait of Gibraltar], and that the actual travel originally was like this . . .

Circling the whole Mediterranean area.

Constantly around and around. But it came to be this, and then this. Can you explain that? I will give you a moment to write it down in a way you can remember.

It's from what we call the Mideast up across Europe, down over to . . . did you go all the way down to Gibraltar or to the ocean?

I can show you. Those names did not exist then.

It's okay to draw on the map. This will make a big orange mark.

Well, in this lifetime people traveled like this, as much as I remember.

All the way north to the top of Italy.

And then back.

Retracing their steps.

Then back to here. I make dots like that. In old days, before my time . . . but I do not do that anymore.

So that's where we lived and traveled. People did not live very long then. We would always be on the move, and many of the people did not remember how to get from here to there. But we would always have an old one who had made the trip.

We were trained from childhood to look closely and see everything we looked at. I have noticed in my day that many people look but do not see. This way, when our people would see everything we were looking at, it would be not so difficult to find our way. If the person knew the way and others didn't, then the person would teach, saying, "Look, it is like this," and give the instructions. Then the person whose job it was to lead would memorize them. But I was told that happened only once.

That's an incredible number of miles.

With Jesus

Yes, a long time, and it was a different life. When I met That Man we were on a journey through that part of the country where he was walking, you see. And he and I had good feelings about each other. My people said to him, "If you have these feelings about this person and she has these feelings about you, perhaps you are to become joined." He said, "I would like that very much." So we had a ceremony, my people's ceremony, and we became joined.

This was necessary, you see; otherwise I could never have spent that much time with him, because my people had to keep going and I was a vital member. Fortunately, by then I had trained a student, and That Man promised my people that no matter where they were in their journeys, if it came to be a time for the two of us to part—he said the time would come; he told me that from the beginning—no matter where they were before that parting took place, he would use his skills and abilities and help me rejoin them. He would find a way, and he showed them some things he could do. So they trusted him and knew he could.

And how old was he and how old were you, in our terms?

At that time he was maybe about fourteen and I was about . . . I think sixteen.

So you took the stones with you, or they stayed with your . . .

They stayed with my people; he said it would be all right, so it was. And when the time of the parting came, he took me through a magical method. He and I stood together, and I was with my children. He had me hold their hands very tightly. He said they had to stand on the ground for it to work. We all held hands in a row. Then he walked forward in front and had his left hand back for me. I had my left hand back for my oldest child and so on, three children. He was dancing and singing, though it was a tune I did not know, and he said, "It will be like we're going to go through something, and we'll get there immediately on the other side." We went through this thing; it looked like nothing, it looked like just nothing. I couldn't see anything. But he disappeared into it. I trusted him, and he pulled my hand. I said, "Hold your hands tightly!" to everybody, and we stepped through. On the other side there were my people in encampment.

It was nighttime, and they could see us. They weren't frightened because they knew of such things. They could not do them themselves, but they knew. My people knew about magic, true magic—not tricks, but true magic. And they celebrated our arrival at that time. My people were . . . [finds marker for map] I use this stick here. They were around here.

France, near Geneva. That's an incredible distance. How many years had it been? How old were you then? From sixteen to what age?

I was an older person then, about thirty-one or -two.

That would be sixteen years. So he was thirty then?

I'm not sure.

But he knew of the troubling times coming up for him?

He never talked about this much; he said that there were things going to happen and he would have to travel constantly, but he would come to visit. And he did. I did not live so long as he did, but he lived very long after my life, I am seeing. (I'm looking back.) He lived many, many years.

His Visits

In terms of your time, he would come about once a month and spend a day or two, just like family, and be with my people, no matter where we were. Sometimes he would bring gifts; other times he would tell stories or sing songs, but always there would be some celebration. I think he liked my people very much; they're special people, very special.

So how long did you live, then? You're using our years to make it clear.

I think I lived to be about forty by your life span.

So for eight years he visited you.

Yes, but I know now that he continued to visit the children. He knew when I was dying, and he came to escort me through the veils. What he said to the children, I remember, was really wonderful. He said to them, "Your mother is ready to go to the place where we all came from." And the children were crying, of course, and upset. They said, "We want to go, too!" He said, "You will come when the time is right for you, and I will come and your mother will come, and we will bring you all then. Until that time, I will come and visit you much more often, and I will find the right way to help you."

Their people gathered around the children and held them; the other women held them, and of course they were upset. Then we went through the veils. After he escorted me, he said, "We will see more of each other now, but I must go." And he went back quickly and kissed all the children and hugged them to let them know that he would indeed come to see them. And he did. When they were young, after my death he came to see them about every other day or so, until they started to feel better. Then he went to once a week, then about once every ten days, but never any longer than that, until they got to be old enough to have families and children of their own. Then he would come once a month, like before.

How wonderful!

Romany Secrets

My people had many secrets. Even today their descendants still have many secrets. Some have died out along the way because there was a terrible catastrophe in Europe not so very long ago. Many, many, many people died and an evil man tried to wipe my people out because he knew they were secret and special. But many of us escaped.

Is that Hitler?

Yes. Some secrets were lost, though.

He does not come to visit once a month like he did before, but sometimes when the children are sleeping (the descendants of my people), I go and sing songs and whisper stories to them, and sometimes they remember these things. And it will help the people to remember their precious secrets, with which they alone are entrusted.

Did you incarnate on the Earth after that life?

No, I did not. I had much to do. That Man helped me to do many things and suggested many things, so I have been active with people of the Earth since that life. But I have not incarnated. If I incarnated, I would not be able to do so much.

Our Vision of Hitler

What are some of the things you do besides telling stories and whispering in their ears?

I go to the children of the world and visit them. Sometimes they remember, sometimes they don't. I don't tell them the same stories or sing the same songs, but I sing songs of hope and encouragement, because in your time with all of your modern technology and all these wonders you have, still the same problems exist. People are hungry and unhappy; people are sick. There are homeless people. I do not understand why, with all this technology, that you have not put more effort toward helping the people. I think it's because you do not understand that you are one family. My descendants understand this, but they have to stay within their own group because the Romany people are not often appreciated for their true value. So that's what I do mostly, work with the children. They are the hope of the future; I think you will not be disappointed with what these new generations will do.

Oh, I know, the star children. How long did the Magdalene stones get passed down? Was it just before the Hitler purge that they were put away for safekeeping?

There was a vision about . . . in terms of your calendar, about one hundred twenty years before that evil man, that such a catastrophe could happen. Not details, but that many, many people would die in terrible ways, and not only our own people, but others. There would also be calamities and disasters, and we would have to hide the Magdalene. So, using special secrets that That Man taught my people (I still identify with them, you know, I say "we"; you'll have to accept that because that's who I still feel I am), the people found a place to hide those stones where they can never be found until the right people go to retrieve them.

The Pleiadians' Gift

Do you know about the history of the Romany people? How long before your time had the Pleiadians given them the stones? A thousand years, a hundred years or ten thousand years?

Before my time. I was told that the stones had been given about eight hundred years before my time, and the gift was given to more than the Romany people. At that time the Romany people were more North African than Romany. So because they were unable to go into North Africa for a while, they became not so much North African, but . . .

In the old days, when the Pleiade people came, they said, "We have brought three sets of these stones, and we are giving one set to your people and another set to people in another country. These people, like you, are very sacred and connected to the land. And one more set to another people on your planet. I am not allowed to say who and where, because if I did, it would make for danger for these people.

They said that only the stones given to my people will be discovered—meaning that there will be some discovery of the stones, but the people who discover them won't know about them. This was a riddle to us, and then they laughed. We said, "What do you mean?" And they said, "It is a little joke that we can't tell you, but your future generations will know, and they will laugh with us. We are sorry that we can't tell you." So my people said, "Okay."

But future generations found out that the joke came to be that people called me Mary Magdalene. It became like a last name. It's very funny because in those days people didn't have last names so much, but everyone (reading in this book) seems to accept that one person named Mary Magdalene had a last name! Funny, eh? [Laughs.]

One of the students, who was a child, said your name was more like Andrea or something.

It is like that, but hard to pronounce in your language. That's the best the child could say. I am sorry, I do not wish to say.

Did you come from the same place as Jesus? What was your connection? Do you know why you were so connected?

You know, these are not questions that my people would ask. My people are very good observers; they see what they are looking at. But "why" is not even in their vocabulary, in those days, at least. It was "what, where, when" and so on. So I cannot answer that question.

Have you heard some of the other students talk for this book?

I have not heard them talking, but I know they have spoken.

Our People's Secrets

Well, Jesus says that he will be back, and I'm wondering if, like that other wonderful, beloved being, you will be around the Earth until he comes back?

It's possible; he has mentioned this to me, that he's coming back with some other special beings, and he asked me if I want to join them. And I said that I would like that, yes. And also one of our children will join us. So I look forward to that.

Oh, that's wonderful! Where did your people get the secrets? Did you get the stones because you had the secrets, or did you get the secrets from working with the stones over those hundreds of years?

We had many secrets before we received the stones, but after we received the stones, many, many more. It's like this: Every one of our people knew, including the little ones, how to keep a secret. They were not secrets in our group, but they were secrets from others. So we had secrets before the stones; and after the stones, many more.

Can you give us a feeling about what kind of secrets? You knew how to find food and water. Could you see at a distance? Can you describe any of them? If you can't, that's okay.

Well, I think it would endanger their descendants if I said things.

So the descendants won't really be safe until Jesus comes, until you and he and the others come back, then?

In their own way, they are very safe; they are just not fully appreciated. But sometimes they [chuckles], perhaps with some mischief, cause people to misunderstand them. But when so much of your heart and soul is a secret, it is hard to show your great beauty to others. So my people have come to accept that they will be misunderstood. I think that ultimately, though, they will be clearly understood.

The Importance of Romanies

Is there something about what they know and what they are that makes it essential for them to be on the planet?

Yes, I do not think that human population could exist on the planet as comfortably as you do without them.

Even though they are much fewer in number now?

They are fewer, but they are durable [chuckles].

So you were with him for sixteen years. And you also taught, as well as he, while you traveled with him, right? Or did you mostly assist him?

I didn't think that I was assisting him or teaching so much; I was his wife. And when there were children, I looked after them, and sometimes I would teach the children mystery songs. But I don't want to say I taught so much; maybe a little, not so much. We must end soon. Do you have anything more to ask?

Because the channel's tired?

This energy is difficult.

Reading by Touch

I see. What's the most important thing to say to the people who will read this?

When you . . . read this, . . . don't just . . . read the words. As you . . . are going along, . . . touch the words with your finger. Try . . . one fingertip, then another, . . . till you feel, *this is the right fingertip.* Read just a few words—you can stop before the thought . . . is . . . finished, . . . and then . . . *feel.* The words printed on the paper . . . of this book . . . have the power to transform, . . . but they *must be touched* . . . as well as read. There are some secret ways to touch them. . . . Try different ways. . . . You will find them if you try enough. When you feel the great and benevolent energies, . . . then ask for gifts . . . to come . . . to the people in form of . . . peace, . . . prosperity, . . . love, . . . kindness . . . and welcome. In this way . . . you will perform . . . the service . . . you so . . . desire . . . to . . . do.

Now, I said this with lots of pauses. This accentuates how I want the people to read some of this book. This book purposely has some mysteries built into it. It won't be obvious when you are printing it, but there will be people who will read this book and say, "Oh, I touched this page and this happened; or that page and that happened." This book is intended to be a book of wisdom and mystery.

The Energy in Children's Imaginations

Thank you so much. One of the things that Jesus said he came to do was to bring an energy to the Earth because the Earth was unhappy with humans. You were one of the people who transmitted that energy, right?

He was very clever—not just smart or inspired, but also clever, meaning he could see the connections between things. He requested to work with the Creator of this universe, that that energy be available in the imaginations of all children, and that when children were imagining wonderful things—inspiring, happy things, adventures, fun, benevolent things, beneficial things—that that energy would naturally be transmitted. Is that not clever?

[Laughs.] That's very clever! He said the women radiated it; he didn't say anything about the children.

He is a little discreet sometimes. It is true that women, children, girls . . . the girls, perhaps, do this twice as strongly as the boys, but the boys do it, too.

You were the only woman who was with him constantly, but there were other mystical women who trained with him, right?

Yes, he had other women and sometimes had children with other women, but in my time this was not considered a bad thing. So yes, there were other women, and they were all my friends.

I only knew about one other. Should we speak to one of them, or several? What would you like?

The person who is the mother of the child who spoke; that would be the first person to talk with. If others wish to volunteer—that is what it takes. They must *want* to volunteer; if they do not want to, then you can ask as long as you want, but you will have to wait a long time. [Chuckles.]

I just want the book to be wonderful. Some of the beings have so much love, I just sit here and swell up with the love, it is so beautiful.

I am very thankful that you have the desire, the dedication and, most important, the curiosity to continue to ask and to share your curiosities with others.

I'm glad there's a use for it. But it's a great joy, a privilege. I'll let you go, but thank you very much.

Good night.

17

Traveling and Teaching People How to Find Things

Jesus' Traveling Companion, Mother of His Child

July 3, 1998

I am the mother of the child. You wished to speak to me?

Welcome, and thank you so much for your patience.

Well, it is not a problem for me to wait. When you have a child, waiting is not an unusual phenomenon.

You had a child two thousand years ago. Are you speaking from that time now?

I have chosen to remain in this time period with my little one. It is a good time for me. I speak to you from there, though in the larger frame of life I'm other places. But this is where I prefer to speak from.

Tell us anything you want to about your life there with Jesus, with the child, with the people.

The best years of that life were with That Man. I was on the travels with him in the desert from the time he was about, I'd say, eighteen to twenty-nine. So for quite a while we had many good experiences, but I was not one of the students. You asked to speak to me, so I am here, but even now I prefer to be with the children. When he was teaching I would look after the children.

I understand that you had the ability, when you put your hand out, to find anything.

But I did not learn that from him.

How did you learn that?

You mean my ability to find things in general?

Yes.

How My Grandmother Taught Me to Find Things

When I was very young my grandmother taught me, and she made it a game. She was very good with children. She said, "Did you lose it?" And we'd say no. Then she would say, "Can you find it?" and we'd say yes. She would say, "How will you find it?" turning us around and around. Then she would show us to point, always using our left arms. If we had to find something made by human beings, then we would point like this . . .

The index and middle finger are pointing forward, with the thumb forward and the last two fingers pointing back toward the body.

Palm down. Thank you. As children we didn't know it was so important, but if we needed to find something that people or the animals needed, like water, something that was made by Earth and other spirits, we would put the palm up. Same position, yes, but palm up. My grandmother would teach us. Some of us would stumble around—it was just a game and fun, and that was okay with her. But looking back on it now, I realize that she was looking for the children who had natural ability. And I was one. She would continue to play the game with all the children, but she would encourage me to find things. Sometimes she would hide things and other times she would say, "Today we're going to see if we can find some water" or "We're going to see if we can find some grass for the animals," things like that.

It started innocently like that, then as I grew older she would teach me how to find people. First it would be people I knew and had feelings about. She would have them hide and then we would go find them. Then it would be people I didn't know but that she would describe to me very clearly. When she described them, grandmother was remembering being with those people, so her feelings of the people made them easier to find.

As I got older (and she got older too), Grandmother would occasionally let people who had lost things (usually animals) come to me. Although they had come to her for years, she let them come to me in her presence, and she and I would go look for it. But she would mostly let me do it so I would learn. That's how I learned.

His Knowledge of My Gift

How old were you when you met That Man?

I was about eleven-years-old.

And you say he was eighteen?

Yes.

When you were with him, were you his mate? Is the child his child?

It's his child, but it wasn't that we were bonded. Because he was such a good and wise man, I asked him if he would be all right with giving me a child. He said he would think about it. He thought about it until I was about fifteen, and then he said okay.

You were with him eleven years, so from your age fifteen to twenty-two, the son was also there. Is teaching the children mostly what you did?

That's what I liked to do. My grandmother was really the one who raised me. I had parents, but they were travelers. Grandmother was in one place only, so she raised me. I would see my mother and father sometimes, and that was good, but Grandmother became sort of mother and father together for me. I was used to being around children my whole life, so that's what I liked.

So how did the group around That Man learn that you could find things?

He found out; he knew. When I started with the group . . . I started at age eleven because my grandmother died.

And he came along right then?

Yes. He came along a little while later; I was staying with some other people. He was traveling through, speaking to people, and he saw me with these other people. He said, "You know all about something that I've begun to teach people." And I said, "Yes." It's a funny thing; I said yes, not knowing mentally what he was talking about. He asked me, "Would you like to join us?" and I said yes. It's one of those things where you hear yourself saying something and you are surprised. So he spoke to the people and said I would be treated properly and would have a good life, and they were happy for me. That's when I joined. He said I could sit in on the teaching but that I didn't have to, and that we would talk. I said, "I think I would prefer us to talk, because too many words confuse my mind." He replied, "I understand."

My First Trip with Jesus

Once when I was almost twelve by your calendar, he said, "Would you like to go on an adventure?" I said yes—again hearing myself say yes. He said, "We are going to go to a place far away from here. I'm going to tell you about the place first so you won't be startled. There are animals there, so you will like that; there may be some children, but I'm not sure. And there are mountains, very high, and the mountains have white on them, and the white is cold."

He knew I understood cold because it cools off at night sometimes, so he told me that the white is cold—he was describing snow, of course.

And he talked to me in an amazing way; he talked to me as if I were his equal and a child at the same time, even though in my days eleven years old was sort of leaving childhood. But he wanted me to enjoy my youth.

He said, "We will travel in a special way, and because of your skills and abilities, I'd like you to come with me." I said, "Yes, yes." Then he said, "Let's wait for the others to settle down for the night, and then we will go." After they settled down he said, "This will be unusual for you, because we will leave here and have a good time where we're going, but when we come back it will be just a little later. Right now the animals and people are still restless, getting comfortable, going to sleep soon. When we get back they will all be asleep, and it will still be this same night." Of course I thought, *Well, we are going to go for a short time.* But it was not so.

He said, "Walk with me." And I walked side by side with him; he held my hand as you would with a youngster. Then he said, "Now stand right behind me. We won't hold hands, but stand right behind me, okay? I'm going to walk, and then there's going to be light, and it will flow around you. It'll be brighter than daylight, so you might have to close your eyes." I said, "All right."

It was so bright that even with my eyes closed it was like daylight. Then all of a sudden it wasn't. It was very bright stars, a different pattern of stars than I was used to. There was a breeze, and it was cool. He asked me to step near him and he wrapped his garment around me a little bit so I would not be cold.

Meeting the Tibetans

Then there was a man in front of us who had no hair on his head. He said, "Welcome, traveler." We walked down this path—it was on a mountain and at night—and there was the white! I could see it! We walked close to some of it, and the Man said, "Touch some." I reached out and touched it, and it was soft and cold, and then it was wet—most unusual. Then we walked down the path and there was an opening like a cave, but the rock was like a door. When it was closed it would look just like the side of the mountain, but it could open.

We went in and it closed behind us. We were in a vast underground chamber, and there were many men like the one who met us, with no hair on their heads, and there were some young people a little older than me, boys. They also had no hair on their heads. The man I was with said, "Now I will talk to these people for a while; you can sit with the boys over there. You can talk to them or you can look around if you want. It's not impolite here."

So we sat for a while. He spoke to them and then they spoke to him. Then I looked around a little bit. Thinking back on it, it was a place that had a timeless quality to it, but I think it was a place of this world, not on another planet. Eventually he said, "Come to me," so I went to stand beside him. He said, "These are our friends," and he introduced me to them. Two or three of them came forward in something like a little bow—a very nice type of greeting.

Then he said, "Tell them about what you can do." So I told them. He didn't say where to start, so I started with Grandmother, and it took a little while, as it did with my telling you.

When I was done they were very interested. They said, "Would you show us a little bit? We have some of these skills, but we'd like to see what you can do." So they showed me some things; one was a bell (they let me touch them) and one was a little animal—I hadn't seen it before, a very funny little animal. Another one was a fabric like they wore, and then they picked out one of the boys that they thought I was getting along with because we had been talking and smiling a bit.

Speaking to me gently again, kind of like an equal but as a child, he said, "Now close your eyes and we will hide these things. Then show us how you find them, please." So I closed my eyes and put my hand in front of my eyes, too. Looking back on it, they probably smiled at each other. They hid the things; the bell they put in a cabinet and the little animal they put in a little cage, which they put behind a rock. Then they had the boy hide way back in another part of this cavern.

So I would use the method I showed you with the bell—man-made, yes? I held my hand like this and found it. The little animal and the cage are both man-made and provided by spirit, so I moved my hand back and forth a little bit—up, down—and found them. With the boy, same thing, because the boy was wearing a garment (man-made), but the boy is of Earth and spirit. So I found the things like that.

And the cloth? You said they had a cloth, too.

Yes, like this.

Palm down, yes.

I found all of them very quickly, and they said, "Most interesting. Thank you so much." Very, very polite and kind, the sort of people you want to see again, when you meet them. [Chuckles.] Then the man I came with said, "Well, we can stay a little longer; would you like to?" I said, "Oh yes, please." So we stayed there in this place and went up on the surface. They had a big building there; it was in an area now known as, I believe, Tibet.

We stayed there about a day and a half. We ate with them and we attended their ceremonies; we were welcome to see what they did. I have been told that they do today in your time the same thing they did then, so their tradition is a long one.

Promises to Return

Then we had to say good-bye, and I was sad. I wanted to see them again. The old one there with no hair came over to me and I had tears running down my face because I was so sad. I wanted to be where I lived, but I wanted to see them because I loved them too, they are so wonderful. He touched my tear and then touched my forehead and I felt tingly. He said, "This mark will bring you back to us when it's the right time for you."

Then I felt a little better, but I was still kind of teary. Then he touched my head and said, "We'll be all right." Then I went with the man I came with, the old man with no hair and the boy I liked as a friend, and we all walked back to the place where we started. I was tearing and the boy said to me that we would meet again. I felt it and said, "Oh, good." We touched briefly and said good-bye to our friends, then I walked through the light with my friend, and we were back.

Just as he had said, as we approached the camp I felt the tears stop and I was happy to be back. But such a wonderful experience! We came closer to the camp and everybody was sleeping—not deeply yet, just a little bit. He said, "We have been gone from our home here about . . ." and then he would say, in your time, about thirty minutes.

But we were able to be there as long as we were. I looked him in the eyes deeply, the way only a child can do, and I said, "Promise me that I will see them again." Then he reached out and touched a tear of mine, still in my eye but not running down my face, and he did the same thing on my forehead. You see what I do? I make a mark, first downward, then like this. It's like a *V* with a mark . . . like this.

A straight line across the middle.

Yes. He did that, and he said, "I promise you will see them again." So I said, "Okay," and we hugged each other, and I went to where I slept and he went to where he slept.

Then what?

We got up the next day and life went on.

What were some of your other adventures? Your son described how you and he could find anything that anyone . . .

I taught him the same way Grandmother taught me. At the same time, if other children were there, I played the game Grandmother played, and I taught them all. For some of them it was a game only, a fun game, and they would play it with themselves when I was not there so it would amuse them. As it turned out, my son had the gift.

How wonderful!

So I taught him, and he was very good at it, too. He could find anything. I think maybe he was a little better than me, because I had to go and touch it. He could point and say, "There," and then describe it, "over the hill behind the bush" and so on. He could describe where it was without even going there. He is a little better at it than I am.

He's also modest, because he didn't mention that.

Oh, he would not say that. But I am parent; I can say that! [Chuckles.]

What an incredible time for your life! What were some of the other adventures?

Because That Man and I had taken that trip, he said, "I probably won't take too many of the others on some of my journeys, but because you have these skills already and because some of the people I visit like to see others besides myself, would you like to come on other journeys?" I said, "Yes, yes!" He said, "Eventually we will go back to visit our friends." And I was happy, I was jumping—a child.

So (always in terms of your calendar) two, three times a year we would go until I had baby. Then when baby was young and I could carry him, we would still go sometimes. He told me baby had a gift, he didn't say what. I found out myself. In those days when the teacher or the wise one would say, "You have a gift," you would never say, "What?" It would be considered impolite. But you would know that if a wise one told you that you had a gift, you would find it. It gave you something to look forward to without taking away your happiness in finding it. That was the way we were.

Journey to Another Planet

We went to a lot of different places. One time we went to another planet. He told me that we would be going to a place where the people would look very much like us, but that they were special people and I would find out more about it when we got there. I am sorry I can't tell you the name of the planet—it is supposed to be a secret even in your time, though some people on your planet know the names. I was about twelve and a half.

He said, "Are you ready?" I replied, "Yes, yes!"

He said, "Then we will go to this place. It is a little different from

Earth; the plants that grow are sort of yellow and brown and gold. They are not green, and the land itself is sort of that color too, and some other colors we have here. But the people look like us."

It didn't take any longer to get there than it took to get to the mountain place. We stepped through that light door and we were, just the two of us, in this huge space. It was completely surrounded by mountains. It is hard to describe, but the sky was dark like it was night, yet the land was light, as if the land glowed in its own right. Hard to describe. I picked up some dirt and it didn't glow, so I don't know how to explain that. But it was a high, flat plain in the mountains; he said it was very high up but that we would be comfortable. He said, "We will walk a ways, if you don't mind, and I will sing you a song." So we walked a ways and he sang me a song. Then he stopped and said, "This is the song of the people who live here. These people live on in places on Earth where we are from, but this is their home planet. They have all their history in song, and this is how, with song, they can remember their history and pass it on to their young ones."

The Songs and the Colors

So we walked a ways, and all the time we were walking (except when he said that) he was singing this song. I think now that one of the reasons he was singing that song was to announce his arrival to these friends so that they would come out. They were not hiding, but they were shy. Eventually they came out, but before they did, he stopped singing. Then one of them began to sing, but I didn't see them yet. I heard a voice, a beautiful woman voice, and she was singing. The song sounded like the one my friend had been singing, but it was a little different. It was, I think, an answer. I believe that his song was a call and hers was the answer.

So she sang the answer, and we stopped while she sang. When she was done we walked forward, then the people came out. There were hundreds of them! They came out, and so many of them! They were dressed in beautiful garments that had designs all over. Some of the design was a little bit like this [draws]. On the front of one man's shirt is a design like that. This is the shirt, this is his head here [points]. I'm not an artist, but this is the design.

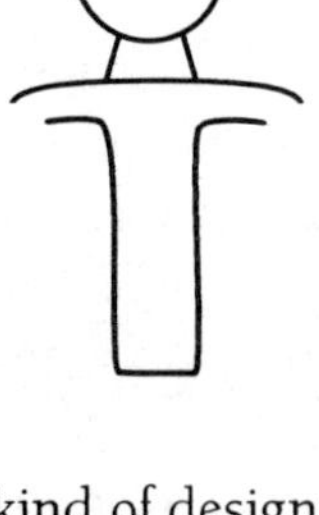

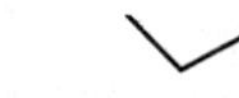

Then another person had this kind of design, like that [draws]. Very pretty.

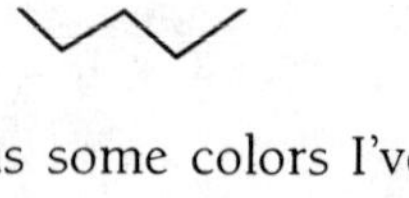

Were they colorful?

Very colorful, beautiful colors—earth colors plus some colors I've never seen before, kind of glowing on their own. They were very beautiful. The people came out, hundreds and hundreds of them, men, women and children, and formed a big circle around us. I did not know what was happening. He leaned down and said, "Don't be concerned. This is their way of welcoming."

Then they all began to sing the answer song that the woman had sung. They stopped, and then he sang the calling song briefly again. The woman who sang the answer song sang it again briefly and came forward with a gift. You have strings of beads, but these were like . . . it is a string of disks, and the disks feel like shells, but I'm not sure what kind of fish they're from, not like on Earth but very beautiful, different colors. The edges of the disks were very gentle on the skin. They put one around his neck and one around my neck. My friend whispered to me, saying, "We will wear these while we are here; I'm not sure if we will take them with us. We'll see." He still talked to me like I was young, but not a child.

Then the woman took his hand and he took my hand, and we walked toward the people. They all gathered around us and we met and laughed and talked. Then we walked to their camp. They had something like a fire (but not like fire on the Earth; it was like glowing of light) and they told stories. He told stories too, and everybody ate something like fruit. When they cut the fruit, they used this pattern [points to zigzag pattern], the same as on some of their clothes, to cut the fruit—not a circle and not straight through. They used those patterns in their lives. It is not a decoration or a symbol only; it is part of their lives. Then we ate this wonderful fruit. I have been told its taste is like a cross between honeydew melon and watermelon, but no seeds. It has all the vitamins and minerals and proteins and everything you need. That's all they eat. It is amazing food, because it sort of melts in your mouth, you know. And after you eat just a little bit, you're completely satisfied. Then you pass it to the person on your right, and they have some. It passes around the circle, a very nice way of eating, though it is not just one circle. That's their style, their culture.

Many little groups, circles.

Yes, or more like this [draws] shape.

A bunch of half-circles.

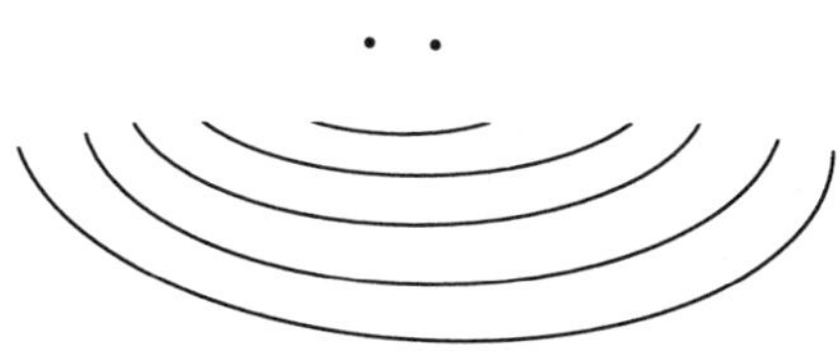

Shaped like that, so anybody who talks or sings or tells stories sits in front of the group, you see? They sit here, or like so [draws two dots], yes?

My Dreams in the Cliff Houses

We stayed there for a while, and then we walked over to . . . it's like a rock face, and there are handholds. We climbed up the handholds—and there are houses built into the rock, like the old way. I think you have some of them here on Earth.

You mean pueblos?

Like that. It is very comfortable, and there is a stream that flows over the top of one of the rocks right through where the people live, so there's always plenty of water. Down where the flat place is that we came from is a place where the bushes grow, and this fruit grows there. Everything you need, you know—very nice.

We stayed with them and had a very good time. I'd say, in terms of your clock time, we stayed about eighteen hours. Part of the time we slept. *I* needed to sleep, anyway; my friend, I'm not sure if he slept or not. Maybe not. But I slept with some of the younger people. I remember to this day, that's the only time I had dreams like that. I think I dreamt the dreams they have. I don't know if I shared someone else's dream or whether the place itself encouraged that dream, but it was beautiful light and animals and people playing and happy—wonderful, wonderful. Sometimes there were shapes floating and moving about and sometimes there were faces. It's all kind of mixed together like a dream, you know. Very nice.

The Gift Jesus Left

I woke up feeling more refreshed from sleep there than I ever felt in my whole life. After I woke up, the sky and the ground were the same—the sky was dark and the ground was light. I cannot explain this; they did not have a day and night like us. Then we stayed a little longer and had another small meal and sang some songs, and my friend gave the people a gift. He held it in the palm of his hand. I looked at it and blinked my eyes and looked again, not sure. It was hard to believe what I was seeing. What I looked at in his hand looked like a pool of water. I looked at it, then I looked at him and he looked down. He knew I was looking at him. He smiled at me, and there was a twinkle in his eye. He gave it to the elder; it's like it slipped out of his hand into the elder's hand. The elder said, "What is this wonderful thing?" And my friend said, "This is a . . ." what did he call it? He said something like, "It's a pool singer," meaning like a water singer.

He said, "Rub your finger over the top," and the elder rubbed his finger around the top in a circle, and music came out. Everybody gathered around to look at it, and the elder said, "Thank you so much." My friend said, "It will someday also tell stories, but for now it will just sing songs like the people." They sang songs, so they thought it was wonderful. They were happy with it, yes.

Then he said to me, "Will you tell our friends here what you do and how you do it?" Of course, they did not need to find anything, so they didn't understand things being lost or found. But I told them anyway. [Chuckles.] They listened politely, and when I was done one of the young ones came up to me and said, as children say, "But why do you lose things at all?" [Laughs.] I said, "In our world we haven't yet learned how to find and always keep." The little one didn't quite understand, but the adults nodded their heads; they understood. I think maybe the adults there know about our world, yes? But our people do not usually know about *their* world.

I learned more later when we left. When we left they sang to us a good-bye song and my friend sang back. Then we walked a long way again, back to where we came in. All this time the people were singing; we could hear them even though they were far away. We turned around and waved once in a while. My friend told me, "There are people on the Earth right now, and there will be more in the future, who are directly related to these people. Someday maybe we will meet some of those people. Would you like that?" I said, "Oh, yes, yes!" He said, "Well, we're going to do that, then."

He said he was sorry we had to give the necklace back; it was just something to wear while we were there, not to take back with us. I said, "It is all right; I take back my memories." He looked at me, and that was the first time I thought I saw something in his eyes that reminded me of my grandmother. Being a parent myself now, I know what that it was: I think he was proud of me.

So we walked back to the light door, turned around and waved one more time. Then he sang a few more sounds and we went through the light door. That was that adventure.

Meeting the ET Relatives on Earth

Did you ever meet any of these people on Earth?

When I was about fourteen, he said, "We're going to go this time to see the relatives of those people. They are on Earth living very similarly, but because of the way Earth is, it is harder to get along. You'll see similar things, but not exactly the same. Their garments might be animal skins and some fabric too, but the designs will be very similar, because they know about the place we went to and they've been visited by elders. They have connections they know, and they know how to keep a secret too, so a secret is safe with them."

So we came to this country here [United States], and we went to more than one place. One place is farther north than where you are here now, in this Arizona; I think it is now called Montana. Then we also went into part of what is now in your time called Canada.

Canada.

Canada, and we visited with the people there. Then we came to another place where people lived in the rock, very much like the rock dwellers we visited. A very nice experience; I like very much.

On this planet we would call them Native Americans?

Yes.

Do you know why they were here?

Why is anybody anywhere? I think they have something to do with preparing Earth for other human beings.

So you had an extraordinary life.

I had some fun.

Were the other people who traveled with That Man aware of where you went and what you did?

Sometimes he would say, "It's okay to tell them about these things. It's always okay to tell the children, but sometimes best not to speak to the adults." You know, sometimes children get big fun, thrill, out of hearing things that the adults don't get told. Maybe that's why children like story hour. They hear things adults don't hear; then they can tell the adults. To the adults it is like a story . . .

. . . like imaginary things.

Yes, and the children don't feel left out if my friend feels maybe the adults aren't ready to hear some of these things.

Return to Tibet

That's wonderful. When did you go back to Tibet?

We went back when I was about nineteen, and I was never so happy to go someplace in my life. The people were still there, and they looked very much the same, except the boys . . .

. . . were grown up!

Grown up, and there were other young boys there. The old one was there, and I was so happy to see him I got the tears again. This time we spent about two and a half days' experience time there. Old one there told me, "Someday you will have a life with us, and you will remember both of these trips. The reason you will come to live with us is that you will tell people about these trips you made when you were a child in another place in another time. Someone will tell us and we will send some of our people. Then you will come to live with us and we'll all be very happy together." I was nineteen and a grown woman, but I said, like a child, "Promise?" And he reached out and touched my head, just like he did before, and he said, "Promise." I think he put special energy, and I think maybe I had that life.

You're still speaking from that time?

I like this time very much—simple, not complicated. I do not understand machines and complicated things made by man. I like things in natural state.

Did That Man bring you on a trip to now, to the time of machines?

No; he knew I did not like it and wasn't comfortable with such things. When he would speak of such times to other people and students, I'd go away and be with the animals. He was not offended; he said, "Everyone must be what they are. This way they will never lose themselves." [Chuckles.]

The End of the Journeys

So you were twenty-two when . . . how did you happen to leave him?

He said, "Things are going to get a little confusing for a while, and I would like to drop you off." He didn't say it that way, but I try to be contemporary. He said, "I'm going to ask you to stay in this village for a time, but I will come back and we will go on more journeys in the future. You like that?" I said, "Very much. Can I bring my boy?" He said, "Yes, every time. He has the gift."

So he was gone from my life then. I didn't see him for about eight or nine years, then one day he is there! He said, "Ready to travel?" And I said, "Yes!" By that time I had enough time to train someone in the village besides my boy, but my boy was also very good. My boy was old enough by then to say whether he wanted to go or stay; he usually went with us, but once in a while he stayed in the village, and then there was someone there who could find things for people. But this time he came with me.

According to the rest of the world, That Man died, but he didn't say anything about that?

He didn't say anything to me about that; he just came back. He looked exactly the same, and we continued our journeys then more often—three, four times a year. We did that until I was a very old lady.

Did he age?

A little bit only, not a lot, not very much. And when I am an old lady . . .

How old in our time?

My Last Trip: Seeing My Grandmother

Maybe forty-two, and my hair is all white. He came to me and said, "One more trip; do you think you can do it?" I said, "I am tired!" He said, "I will carry you."

"Okay, short trip," I said. He replied, "Short trip."

He carried me to the window (my son stayed behind) and said, "We're going to see somebody," and we went through the doorway, and there was my grandmother! The grandmother and I hugged, and she told me wonderful things about the place beyond, where she had gone. She said, "You will come and join me soon, in about . . ." and she said a time equal to about a week. So we talked for a while, and my friend just sat there listening, enjoying our happiness. Grandmother told me I had a week, so I could say good-bye to everyone and prepare them for my departure. Then Grandmother said, "I come to get you next time and take you with me. We will leave your body there, but we will bring spirit along, and the closer we get to light window, the younger you get, and just before light window you're like a little girl again, and I carry you." That's what happened.

So you're talking to me from that time. Can you change focus and tell me what you've been doing since then?

I'd rather not; I like it here. As you can tell, I am person of touching and heart, not so much head.

But you're very clear, very concise.

Yes, thank you.

What a wonderful time! Did you look in on your boy? Was he a great healer?

He did this besides the skill I helped him to learn. I looked in occasionally, not too often. When conscious spirit person looks in at conscious physical person, it is distracting for conscious physical person, so I don't do it much. I don't do it much, but he knows I love him.

Wonderful!

Now I say good night.

Thank you very much for coming.

Jesus: Good evening.

Good evening, welcome.

This is my life, these are my friends and students. You also in your time, readers and others, are also friends and sometimes even students. Good life!

Thank you, with all my heart, thank you.

Appendix

Reprinted from *ET Visitors Speak*
Qua through Robert Shapiro

Qua Comes to View Origin and Evolution of Christianity

Qua Chi Cantsa

April 6, 1998

My name is Qua Chi Cantsa. I have been on your planet for over twenty-five hundred years. I was not stranded like other ETs, but came here intentionally to study your religions. On many occasions, I have been able to take human form, which I can maintain for only about ten days, so of course I make an effort not to get too involved with people, so they won't miss me.

Religious Traveler

I have on different occasions played the part of a traveling philosopher, a traveling sales individual and a traveler in general. These days, I am most often the traveler. In fact, my name, Chi Cantsa, means *traveler* in my language. Qua is my proper name.

I have been able to observe the beginning of many of your religions, and to observe others while they are actually functioning and carrying on their philosophies and traditions. Some of your religious practices are deceptive, but you know this. Some of them are reaching for the highest goals and highest value and some of them only say they are. Yet ultimately, in your hearts, you all do believe in something greater than you. One might assume this is because of the way you are raised, but in my experience, even individuals who have had almost no early exposure to other people still assimilate that belief in a larger being or god.

This is perhaps one of the reasons that your civilization has persevered through events or circumstances that would have destroyed many others. Certainly, global wars and conflicts of conscience have been many, some of them so severe that even I was surprised that you survived. Perhaps the biggest challenge facing you now is the conflict between the loving feelings of the heart and the cold rationale, or as you might say, the clear rationale of the mind.

The mind, when separated at least mentally from the heart, is capable of wonderful insights, though it is also capable of just as wonderful insights when strongly bound to the heart. But when mentally separated from the heart, it is also capable of appalling atrocities. And it is this latter that has been your greatest challenge. It still is, though perhaps one of the saving graces of your time is that technology is beginning to serve you in a most valuable way through worldwide communication from individual to individual. Worldwide communication has been in effect for some time and there is great hope in this, yes, great hope.

From my perception, I would say that my time here is drawing to a close. Another three or four hundred years will be the end. Then I will return to my planet of origin where I will continue with my life and deposit the knowledge I have gained from observing you and your cultures. I will make my recommendations to those who were responsible for my visit. It is not actually a mission; they did not send me. I was interested and had viewed your cultures from a distance. The people who govern contact with your cultures had to give permission for a visit of such duration. I did not speak to those who had such authority, but there are people on my planet in touch with them. After I submitted my intentions there was quite a wait, almost ten of your years while they considered perhaps all the possibilities, then permission came through. I was here very quickly because I had had a long time to prepare and had everything ready to go.

Christianity

I made an effort to arrive before the beginning of what you now know as Christianity because I wanted to see the conditions that would lead up to such a religion. Christianity started out being profoundly heart-centered and feminine in its nature, truly mystical in its practices and with the ultimate intention of quickly transforming everyone on Earth to become the most spiritual being they could be. Lofty aims, you might say, yet the individuals directly involved in the beginning of this religion saw it as a true potential. Never once did they waver from that belief.

The person around whom the religion is built traveled extensively in spirit, and to some extent in form, to understand the great philosophies of the East and transform them into the ceremonies and functions of the culture of the Middle East. But the lofty goals were not achieved, and the strong feminine orientation was gradually disintegrated. The mystical nature was integrated more into the hierarchical regions of the churches that would become established. Unfortunately, some of the mysticism was turned into power-oriented mystical rites, which were not uncommon for the time since people were often invaded by others and would try any available magic to transform such raids in their favor. So it is not surprising perhaps that the traditions initially established—very heart-centered, very feminine-oriented and very spiritual and mystical—were gradually turned into what you now call satanic practices by individuals who were perhaps not the best-oriented.

Of course, I do understand that the religions, at least at most levels, do not support this at all. Yet some of this practice is in high places and is intended to corrupt the hearts and souls of the followers of these religions. Unfortunate but true, and in time it will be resolved. I mention these things because this is a phenomenon to be considered: Your people all over the Earth have integrated into their lives to great extent the pursuit of a meaning to life based on higher beings and the wisdom they provide. This is essentially my perception of religions, at least religions that are hierarchically oriented. Religions that are day-to-day philosophies in any form I do not look upon as being so separated from the people. They are philosophical practices, and to the extent that it is more a daily event, not one that occurs only one day a week, I generally gauge the value of these religions' ultimate contribution as being more benevolent.

I have had much time to observe your people. I am profoundly affected by the lofty goals many of you have, and I am also affected by the great courage you often show in the face of extreme danger. So by and large I have a good opinion of Earth people. But of course one cannot ignore the harshness you often show those who are the most vulnerable in your society: the young, the very old, the weaker ones, the sick, your prisoners and those you call the insane. I grant that most civilizations beyond the Earth will gauge the value of your civilizations by how you treat these groups because these are not the easiest groups to treat benevolently all the time. Yet, when you ultimately discover the way to do so, you will resolve almost all your problems. So my visit here has been of great interest.

You very carefully chose the period of time you would come. Had you previously looked ahead to see what would happen?

Actually, I had looked back. Our civilization is in the future compared to the time sequence you know here. But I was not able to study the details of the evolution of your religion, only an outline. I wanted to come and see for myself why some things were done the way they were and to understand not only the psyche of your peoples but the heart response, and not only the heart response in benevolent ways, but the extreme heart response, which is sometimes malevolent. I was very interested to see how you will get from the place where I arrived in time to your future, which is very benevolent. When one considers the tortuous path by which you had to travel, historically speaking, it is quite impressive that you made it at all.

Cat Consultant

How far in the future do you live?

My cat consultant here advises me. He does not think it is good to give such details. I will just say that I am about a million years in the future from your perception.

Why doesn't he think it's good to give such details?

He is wise enough to know that the more you know about me, my people and my civilization, the less you will admire your own.

I see.

Coming from a long line of beings who understand their own civilization very well—the cat people—they have discovered as a civilization that knowing one's own civilization is the best way to avoid making the same mistakes over and over. They know that the best way to discover your true path is not to emulate the path of others, whose social and cultural mores might not fit your people at all. This is why to this day, if I might make the little joke, cats are cats and dogs are dogs. There is no confusion between beings of who they are.

What can you say about your civilization? Is it in this universe, in this orb?

No.

The Shape of Love

Can you say where?

It is not in Love's Creation. It is beyond that. If you were to move back away from Love's Creation, you would gradually find several other circles, loosely speaking, shapes not unlike Love. Some of them are like Love, others are similar only. If you were to continue to go beyond that point for a ways, you would find one massive one. In terms of size, since miles will not do, we simply have to say that the distance from Love's Creation to mine is equal to about 460 equal sizes of such creations, and my place is about ten billion times larger than Love's Creation. If you were to approach it, it would just look like a massive white light. It would seem like going through a veil into a massive white light, but it is actually contained. It's just that it is so massive that you would not be able to perceive the shape.

Is it hierarchical? In other words, did whoever created the system you're in, create the various versions of Love?

I believe they did, yes. What they did in order to create Love and her sisters is that they took the best qualities of their own being and sent out satellites (I'm going to call Love a satellite if that's acceptable) and offered them to do as they wished. They could just be or if they chose, they could create. So they're not all exactly the same.

When we get beings on the Council of Creators who have talents and abilities that Love doesn't have, they must be coming from the creation you're from?

Not necessarily. Love might not demonstrate a quality. It does not mean that she doesn't have it. Just as you might not demonstrate your capacity to, say, operate a particular tool or cook a particular recipe or let's say something extreme, be a lifeguard. It doesn't mean you don't have the capacity; you're just not demonstrating that at the moment.

I see. One of them did say they thought it was from one of the thousand levels of the Love being. So you have such a life span in our terms that the three thousand years you're here is like nothing to your life there.

Let me put it like this: Our life span is constant. We are able to change our form because of the consistency of our existence, and for all practical purposes at least from your point of view, we are living immortals. We do not die, we are not born. We are in existence and are allowed and encouraged sometimes to change our form, should it be more pleasant or interesting. So there is no boredom. Boredom, as you know, can be a mischief maker.

33^{9th} Dimension

Is there some similarity to our dimensions in the place you're from? What is your form? Is it light?

The dimension I exist in in order to be here is the ninth dimension. The dimension I am from is hard to describe. The best I can say is, if you wrote down thirty-three to the ninth power, you would have a pretty good idea of the dimension in which my people exist.

Did you come here in spirit or in a ship? Or did you just come?

Yes, not utilizing doorway or such thing, but I came on what you could call a string of intention, although it is not a string. Intention alone is sufficient to get us from place to place, not will. Will is direction and purpose and projection. Intention requires not only that we have a desire and a need to go someplace, but that the place welcomes us. That is the equal balance that allows us to get to exactly the right place, not only for our own purposes, but ultimately for the purposes of the beings who are already present. This is why I am speaking through Robert at this time, because it was always intended that at some point I make a more lasting contribution to your civilization. In that way, the place welcomed me because I would leave a trace that is at least intended to be benevolent.

Exactly where on Earth did you first come to, and how did you interact with the beings there? Do you have the ability to see all over the planet? How do you know what's going on?

I have a means to see all over the planet, and I arrived initially in the desert region now known as Egypt—not near the pyramids, but close to a traveled area where the people of the desert travel. Trading routes, I think they were called. I remained in higher-dimensional form for quite some time, several hundred years, so that I could observe without influencing or impacting anyone. I don't know if you know this, but beings up to the seventh dimension can unintentionally impact those who come close to them by their energies, although the impact is benevolent. I did not want to influence anybody, so I remained at the ninth dimension, and in that dimension one cannot impact anyone on Earth in any way.

Beauty Healing

Give us some instances when you interacted with the people then, when you took a form.

About a hundred years before Christianity was begun, not a hundred years before the birth of the man Jesus, but before the religion really became a religion. This was just a few years before the birth of the person that the religion is built around.

A few years before this man was born, I had my first encounter. I visited in form, appearing like a man of the time, a woman who was involved in a healing practice that was not at this time widely utilized. The practice involves placing the left hand over the back of the right hand and then placing the right hand at the base of the skull of the individual to be healed with the intention of letting energies flow through her hands into the backbone and skull of the person being healed.

Many similar types of healing are used today, but this was used regardless of the illness in whatever form. The hands were always and only placed on the back of the skull with the fingers pointed away from the spine, upward. I wanted to feel what it was like to have a healing of the time, so I created an injury, and told her it was a birth injury. It was a foot not quite able to point straight ahead so I limped.

She welcomed me and first gave me some tea, a sweet tea, very pleasant. It was not, I think, so much an herb tea to assist me or relax me, but to be social, to be courteous, to create a friendly atmosphere between us—which is intended, of course, to release any feelings of mistrust. This social interaction is not often done by healers in your time and is so valuable. When I say healer, of course I am including physicians as well.

Then she performed her arts, and without consciously repairing the injury, I noticed that it was seventy percent repaired by what she did. She just asked out loud that the healing energies of the beings of beauty and life flow through her hands into the places in my body that would allow me to live a more fulfilling life. That's all. That's all she said. It was very beautiful.

After the experience, which took less than five minutes, the injury was seventy percent corrected. She said, "Come back in a few days and I will do more if I am able." So I did, and we had tea again and chatted a little bit. She said what she said, and lo and behold, the injury was healed without my interfering. I was very impressed.

She trained other people to do this whether they be man or woman, boy or girl. She said she had even attempted to train an animal, because the animal kept putting its foot upon the back of people's heads. She said, "Maybe it's trying to do what I do," but she gave up. She decided that it was doing some kind of healing, but not one she could teach. She said that was amusing and went on.

She was a great, wonderful, dedicated healer. She didn't travel because at that time in her life she was older, so people had to come or be brought to her. That was my first contact, really, with a human being. I think back on it now and remember her fondly.

Jesus' Sister

A little later, after the man was born upon whom the religion has been built, I had the opportunity to visit one of his mentors, someone who helped him, guided him, supported him and generally nurtured him. I think this person was his sister, and she gave him a lot of support.

At that time in his life, he was really just getting started. He had learned the skills required to get along and raise a family, but he knew who he was when he was born, so he was highly involved in the spiritual and the mystical. His sister had been trained by someone who had been trained by this woman—not the healer herself, but one of her students. She taught him this healing technique, and I think that he used it later in life and was renowned for such a thing, though I think he did it differently. He would usually do it in the traditional way, but occasionally he would do it with one hand only.

I found that my contact with the sister of that man was a very pleasant experience. She was very friendly. She felt that what her brother was doing was very valuable, yet she would not be able to stay long with him because she was to be married soon and would move on and raise her own family, continuing the healing practices she had known and understood.

So I had a brief contact with the man that the religion was built around, and he seemed like a nice young fellow, certainly insightful. I must say, he knew who I was and was discreet enough to say nothing, but we had a little smile between us. Because all was known and understood between us, we didn't have to talk about it. But I think he felt comfortable with me, and we could have a little light humor without exchanging words. When one spiritual traveler meets another there is a sense of amusement and pleasure, even without communication as you understand it to be. That was my contact with this man when he was alive.

How old was he then?

About fourteen. His sister was not quite that age, but close. But of course people got married younger in those days and didn't live as long. When they developed the abilities to have children, it was considered proper for them to do so, provided that they had been raised properly and knew who they were and could carry on the benevolent traditions as best their people could teach them.

Jesus' Goal

Did you focus a lot of your attention, then, on the beginning of Christianity? Was that why you came, or was it one of the reasons?

It was one of the reasons. I wanted to observe other religions and their impacts, but I must admit, at least half of my reason was to observe the beginning and precursor of the time of the development of the religion that had such an impact on your history. I can tell you that it doesn't exist in the future in the way it exists now. It exists in the future of your existence, not as a prayful separation between that man and the followers of that man, but as more of an equal status. This is what he always wanted to begin with, I think, when he was teaching. He wanted people to be able to do what he could do, and he felt he could teach them. Well, it didn't work out that way, but it was a worthy goal. In time, when humans are more receptive and are over the bigger hurdles of your evolution through this time, he will return and once again take up his teaching. He will bring friends; he will bring the apostles, as you call them, not only the men but the women and their students, and they will spread out over the Earth and share. They will not teach with an arm twist, but simply share with whomever wishes to hear what they have to offer. Then they will return from whence they came.

The religion will evolve into being more of a daily practice with a sacred understanding of all peoples and plants and animals and, perhaps most important for Earth people, your place in the universe and who you are. This will be a most benevolent change for you. It will still be called, interestingly enough, Christianity, but it will not be in its present form. It will be more what that man envisioned it to be when he came.

But as we become aware of who we are, we won't need religions?

When you change—suppose I said that religion wasn't just something to follow because of some authoritarian purpose, but that it was a gift and an initiation and a ceremony—the blessed event in your life. If I said that, then you would want it. You would enjoy it and embrace it.

That is ultimately what it will become. If one takes the broad-minded point of view and looks at other ET civilizations loosely related to you, like the Pleiadians, one could easily say that their day-to-day spiritual practices are a religion. It's just that it is totally benevolent and one could easily call it a religion. As an Earth person, you would look at their practices and say, "This is a benevolent religion." The Pleiadians might respond by saying, "We don't think of it that way, but we can understand why *you* do."

What is comparable to religion in your time? You don't have anything like that.

A way of being. It is the way everyone is where I am, and it is completely benevolent, totally connected to all other beings and in complete and total harmony, which ultimately is the intention of benevolent religion: to create, sustain and maintain total harmony.

Responsibility for the Explorer Race

You're aware of the purpose of the Explorer Race.

Certainly.

Is it your understanding that the effects of it will go as far as where you live, where you're from?

It is my understanding that the original idea was prompted from where I am from.

Aha! Finally, we've got somebody who takes responsibility for it!

My understanding is that threads were sent out in my place of living. Threads, as was said by your Zoosh, of potentials deemed worthy are allowed to emigrate on their own to find those who might do the most and the best with them. So the threads are in that sense alive. It is this life force within them that will set up natural attraction between them and those who are attracted, not unlike your attraction to your cat when you first met him, and the cat to you or you to another person. Attraction is a very powerful and benevolent force.

You have so much wisdom. Would it be appropriate to give sort of a synopsis from your point of view, of each of the religions, since that's your field of study?

I don't think I want to make too much comment on all the religions. Since my main focus has been Christianity and its development—and of course, its eventual outcome—I think I'm perhaps in a better position to speak of that than all the religions and philosophies, many of which I have studied and interacted with but have not been involved with to such a degree or have not really studied to such a depth. I wouldn't want to comment on things for which I do not feel the validity of my comments in terms of their value, at least their value to you.

Religions authoritative and controlling.

Of course, they're entirely imitative of what exists before and after. After all, Explorer Race members came here from somewhere and you will be going to somewhere. All those somewheres have that type of religion, loosely speaking, that I referred to as being on the Pleiades and about which you would say "This is a religion," understanding what you understand now about religion. It's very benevolent. If you understand that, you would understand why there is a propensity to create mental explanations, physical practices, the desire to produce feelings—you know, great religious ecstasy—and inspiration that would abound on Earth as truly an extension of previous experiences of an Explorer Race member and the thing you will ultimately go on to.

So it is imitative, and it would be surprising if there weren't such a thing, considering that you are cut off for the most part from remembering what benevolent religion is about. It is not at all surprising then, that religion would be attached to events and people and circumstances and politics. Yet at its root, it is imitative of what you have experienced elsewhere and what you will experience again.

Even in my home, if you were able to visit where I live, you might say, "This is a benevolent living religion that you all experience." Certainly a priest or any religious person might come there and say, "This is a benevolent religion. It's wonderful." I think the average person might think that what we do is religion. It's just benevolent, that's all.

In your understanding, has anyone else come to Earth from the creation you're from?

Not yet, but they might. You have to remember that I've come back in time. Others might when I return and disseminate my findings. Others might choose to come back. And if they are allowed to do so, then they might. Of course, they might come back further in time than I did, so you have to understand that when I say they *might* and *not yet* within the sequence of time when one of them perhaps does, they might come back *before* me. But at this point in experience, I am the only one at the moment.

A million years in the future—was that just a round number, or is that accurate?

A round number, yes.

By that time the expansion should have happened already.

Oh, yes. At that time the Explorer Race has come together and you are now the creator or the creator-in-establishment of this universe.

The Crossroads of Christianity

As you followed Christianity, when did it come to a crossroads? Who perverted it?

Oh, it is not so much one person. You have to remember that very often some things that might now be considered a perversion in the light of your current history were intended at that time to make it more accessible to the people or to improve it. Originally, what that man was offering was something that was radically different from what was being practiced in those times, even though he was born to a specific religion and specific practices and was a member in good standing of that community.

So in days gone by when people made changes in that philosophy, which came to be known as a religion and became politicized, the changes were intended to make them more accessible to the local community. To fit these things into an already well-established religion and perhaps more important, into the body politic, it not only had to fit into the established religion, but it had to be palatable to others who were not of that religion yet may be influential.

So many changes were made that you might say, if you looked at it politically, that, well, these changes were not only justifiable but made complete sense for the time. However, transferred to your time or even to recent times—say, during tumultuous periods in European history or global history—these changes do not work so well because they initiated and truly inaugurated separation between the average person and the religion.

Remember, That Man [Jesus] originally wanted to establish a sacred relationship between all people and all beings as a day-to-day integrated reality. But this was in a time when the people were instructed about the practices of these religions by a spiritual leader, and those who believed that the principles of this man's philosophy were worth saving could think of only one way to save it at the time. That was to share all the principles with the religious and ask them to teach the people.

Don't you see that this would make sense to them at the time? The other choice would have been that it would have ended, and that would have been it. You would never have heard of Christianity; it would have stopped because of the current religious practices and the politics, to say nothing of the conflicts. So the people who made those changes were attempting to save as much as they could of what they perceived to be a good thing by inserting it in the best way they could into the religions of the time. That's the best they could do.

What particular religions?

As you now know, the Jewish religion and Islam. One of the more spiritual members even attempted to transpose or transport at a distance some of this wisdom into Eastern communities in India. But they already had these practices, so the message coming back was that "we will honor your great teacher and recognize him as we would recognize our own spiritual teacher." In the larger sense, true Christianity to this day has been best preserved by those already practicing it in India. Although it became hierarchical and politicized to some extent there, it lives on as what many of you think of as Eastern religion. Much of what that man originally taught was not really modeled after Eastern religion, but it was so close to what he believed was of value that it was like a first cousin. So for those of you trained in the Christian religion of today who find the Eastern meditations and ways attractive, know that you are closer to true Christianity than you know.

Origin of Jesus

Can you tell me where the entity known as Jesus originated? In this creation or someplace else?

I will look. I think his father was Andromedan and his mother was from the Pleiades.

I'm sorry, I mean at his source being. Was he originally created in this creation or, like you, did he come from someplace else?

Oh, you mean like tracing everyone here back to their source.

No, I mean that some people in this creation were created by this creator and some weren't.

Nobody in the Explorer Race was created by this creator.

Yes, I know. Was his origin from one of the seeds of the Explorer Race or from this creator or from someplace before this?

No, his origin was from where I live.

You knew him before you came here?

No, I did not.

That's why you came here.

I knew of him. I was interested to see what he had done, what preceded what he had done, what followed and how it all came about. He told it as best he could, and it was very interesting. But it is much more powerfully interesting to have observed it happening than to have heard even the participant himself speak of it.

So you came because your source was the place Jesus came from?

Yes. He was hoping to bring your civilization along a little faster. It was a worthy effort. I think that in the larger sense, it has actually accomplished its purpose, just a little delayed. In time, the religion that is practiced on Earth—one you might not consider a religion unless you went to extraterrestrial planets, where you would say, "Oh, that's a religion"—would be very much like what's on extraterrestrial planets now. If you were to visit that time, you would say, "Oh, I recognize this. It's like the mysticism and Eastern ways and Christianity and a little of the Jewish ceremony and a lot of the honoring of Islam and a lot of the . antecedents of this future religion, yet it is an amalgam of many of the philosophies and is similar to what is practiced on other planets. It is certainly similar to the best of the Eastern traditions today.

Did the founders of the Eastern traditions come from your creation, also?

I do not think so, no. Oh, you mean originally. No, yet so much has moved around. But if you were to visit the average planet of beings similar to you, you would say, "I can see different things here that remind me of the best of the religions we have at home."

Cries of Need

So from whatever level or from whatever time, various beings have come to Earth in an attempt to move us along faster, give us something to live by—in other words, they brought religions here from everyplace?

It was never the intent to speed the process up, but rather a response to your cries of need. Very often people would pray and ask for things to come and improve not only their lot in life, but the lot of their people and, they would often say, "other peoples," meaning this planet, of course. Sometimes teachers and beings would be moved in their heart, such as that man upon whom Christianity is built. He was so moved by the prayers and entreaties of individuals of the time that he came. I expect it was similar motivations that prompted others to come, too. I understand completely. If someone is desperately hungry for a change for the better, it is hard to know about it and go on. It is one thing to not know about it and go on, but to know about it and do nothing is very difficult.

I believe that all those who came had the best of intentions in mind. Ultimately, Creator didn't block anyone, didn't say, "Don't come," and He might have told them that they would have to accept the conditions of the time. As benevolent teachers and beings, they would most likely assume that that meant mental and spiritual and day-to-day practical conditions, yet they might not ultimately consider that the conditions would also have to do with your creator's timetable for the transformation of your peoples. Of course, that was perhaps the most important meaning your creator was giving in such a statement: He would not block anyone attempting to serve the needs of those who were hungry and desperate for benevolent change. Yet he had his own timetable in mind, you might say.

So there were certain periods of time when no matter who might teach or what energy they might bring, they weren't able to have much of an effect because of the creator's timetable?

What you had to learn and how you had to learn it. This planet is a place where you are allowed to make profound and critical mistakes, for which not only *you* might suffer but also many, many others. I can assure you that if the souls who originally invented explosives and dynamite were able to change what they had done, they would do so. At the time it seemed very practical and wonderful. Yet who they are now regret it. So it does not mean that things should be changed; it just means that your creator understood how much time it would take you to learn what you needed to learn about responsibility, consequences, knowledge, awareness, wisdom, love and practicality. The loftiest goals and the loftiest aims might not mean much to a man or a woman who just needs to eat and drink.

You mentioned two times that you interacted—at the beginning of Christianity, or once just before and then once when he was fourteen. Are there some other interesting times during that period? What interested you enough to dip into physicality?

I passed through several churches as a traveler, an easy guise to wear. Travelers are quite accepted all over your planet. They always have been. I passed through many of your churches and observed the politicization of the hierarchy. I was most interested in the evolution of the church as it went along. I was particularly interested when other facets, other Christianity religions, began. I was intrigued because at this time there was a great stimulus of mental activity, the beginning of the mind, if you look toward the beginning of the breaking off of other facets of Christianity.

Martin Luther

You will see that it very well coincides with the time when reading and writing and attendant stimulation of the intellect and the increasing vocabulary and all of this was going on. I wanted to be there for that, so I would often pass through as a traveler. I once walked a road with Martin Luther, a man who was perhaps very much misunderstood in his own time. He was, of course, a sociologist—like you say, a product of his environment.

Some of the things he believed and held dear were perhaps atrocious in terms of his attitudes about other people and their worth. It is unfortunate that so much of what he wrote along these lines has been carefully preserved the way an antique dealer might preserve something that is awful and atrocious because of its age, then ascribe a value to it. Unfortunately, observing as Martin is now, many of his writings, he's put his hand to his face, if you understand, and says, "Oh, no. This they saved, and my poetry they discarded."

He wrote the most beautiful poetry, similar to what you might call sonnets. They were very beautiful, and he would speak them often to the people of the time and incorporate stories in them. He was a wonderful storyteller and a man of many abilities to paint a picture with his words and draw people in. He was not such a terrible person, yet unfortunately, those things did not last. People listened to his stories; they loved them, but they didn't write them down in a permanent way.

Unfortunately, we don't remember this man in your time for his finer qualities, but, sadly and perhaps ironically, he is remembered for some things he wrote that had more to do with who taught him, with whom he was raised and what he was exposed to as a young man than what he evolved into in later years. When he was older he had great wisdom and wrote other things, saying that he rejected his earlier writings that were sometimes hateful and blaming. He spoke about the glory of God and the loving heart of God and all these things. Unfortunately, most of these things did not survive.

What we got was a Lutheran religion that I walked out on when I was twelve years old because they talked about being born in sin, things that just made my flesh crawl.

Yes, and if Martin had flesh, it would crawl today, too. He is sad about it, but he knows who he is today. He knows it will pass. Someday, Christianity will be what that man originally intended it to be, and when he returns with his apostles and followers and students, Martin will be one of those people.

What would you like right now to tell the Explorer Race people?

Remember always that the way to know about yourself, who you are and who your people are, where you're from and, yes, you are here to observe daily needs in yourself and others and serve these needs in yourself and others in the best way and in the most patient and loving way you can. If you don't know how, ask others and try different things and notice what works and discard what doesn't.

Qua's Experiences Studying Religion on Earth

Qua

April 7, 1998

This is Qua. I want to talk about a person who has what you call mixed reviews in these times: Pope Pius XII.

Pope Pius XII and WWII

This person was in his position of leadership during World War II and by some people was held, not exactly responsible, but in low regard for not having spoken out against Hitler and the Nazis.

I had an opportunity to spend some time with this being in the guise of a young priest and I found out a few things about him. One, he wasn't too happy with the Jewish religion. He didn't have anything against the people so much, but it annoyed him that the religion itself was too rigid. It is kind of amusing when you think about it; the Catholic religion is known for its fixed ceremonials, although in recent years it has been more flexible.

He thought the Jewish religion was too rigid?

He felt the Jewish religion was too fixed and inflexible, but then he felt the same way about Islam. So perhaps it was perception based upon a younger religion compared to a more ancient one. He wasn't, as they say, "in bed with the Nazis." Oh, he had communications with them and he could see the Nazi's inner circle without having experienced it directly for what it was. He understood that the intention of the inner circle of the Nazis was to gradually eliminate everyone who didn't agree with them and that they would start with a group of people who, from the general population's point of view, wouldn't be missed.

If the general population had been really conscious of the fact that men, women and children and old men and old women were being executed and in such atrocious ways, they might have spoken out. You could say that the general population did keep their head in the sand a bit, but you must remember that it wasn't a democracy. Even if they had known about it, they would have been afraid it would happen to them. That is ultimately why Pope Pius XII didn't speak out, because he felt that he had to placate Hitler a bit since he was right there in the midst of it, to say nothing of all the Catholic people. He felt that it was really a small step, from the Nazis' point of view, to start to massacre Catholics at large.

You could make a case for the fact that there were some born and raised Catholics in the Nazi party, but nevertheless a lot of priests were killed. He objected strenuously at times. He also requested (this is what he told me and other members of his inner circle) that the children be spared. He felt he was taking a risk when he said that. He said, "Why eliminate the children? They could be raised in any way." He was trying to speak to them in ways they could hear, you understand. But it was shortly after he objected to the elimination of the children that more priests started to be killed.

You have to understand this within the context of the times. He felt that ultimately, if the Nazis should stay in power, that the very next target would be the Catholic people. He was absolutely convinced, and he was probably right.

So I think it is important to remember, rather than to just point the finger of blame, the context of the times and to know that if things had been different, he might have been able to do more.

He was not a bad man. He was a good man and did the best he could. I am not here to defend people or to make things they did or didn't do crimes or to smooth things over, but when I speak to people I know when they are being sincere. I know when they are just saying platitudes or things they don't really believe. This man was sincere. I found out that he liked great literature and would read it for pleasure. Sometimes it was hard for him to do because he was so concerned about his people, especially that Catholic people caught up in this Nazi regime thought it was wonderful and treated Hitler like God. He was very upset that people raised in this religion could, from his perspective, so easily transfer their allegiance.

Toward the end, when it became obvious that the Nazis were going to lose, he talked to members of his inner circle and said, "There must be changes made in the church so that people are more loyal, not just following a leader, but more loyal. There needs to be a way to draw them in." Many suggested that some of the more mystical aspects of the church be included in the daily parishioners' experience, and that was almost incorporated. To some extent it might still be incorporated. Things take time in a large organization, but I think that what they ultimately decided was to make their religion more modern.

It was right around then that they decided they would eventually stop speaking the mass in Latin. They felt that even though older people liked hearing it in Latin, eventually the younger people (they were most concerned that the younger people had so quickly turned their back on the church) might understand and feel better about the service if they could hear it in their own language. So even though these reforms didn't come until later, they were really decided then.

I wanted to mention these different people because I understand that some people might say, "Well, if the pope had spoken out it would have been different." But I assure you if the pope had spoken out it *would* have been different, all right—the Catholic people would have joined Jewish people in tragedy in wholesale masses.

If he had made a proclamation condemning the Nazis, and issued it to every Catholic Church everywhere, couldn't they have joined together and had an impact?

You know, it sounds today like they could have done that, but you have to remember the thing that horrified him and other members of the church, lifelong members, is how quickly people who were raised Catholic immediately and so enthusiastically shifted their allegiance to [Hitler] and treated *him* like God.

It was because of that political situation and really religious, or anti-religious situation, and because he understood that ultimately the Nazi party was practicing satanic forms of anti-religion, that he knew. It was very clear after talking to the Gestapo and especially the SS (the SS was not as bad as the Gestapo, but it's a matter of degree, you understand) that this was a perverted aspect of religion. If you examine the Nazi doctrine, you will find that there is a lot of ceremony and ritual involved. Granted, the rituals and ceremonies are against God, but they are there.

He was quick to recognize that it was satanic, and I agree. I am not saying it wouldn't have been good if he had been more influential at the time. One thinks of popes as being influential, but in fact because the people had turned away, he knew that he wasn't. He also knew—it was very clear and I agree with him—that if he had resisted mightily, even those who were born Catholic and had become staunch supporters of the Nazi party would have quickly gone to the death camps. It would have made no difference because the pecking order there was Jews, Gypsies, the mentally ill, the sick and the lame; people who couldn't defend themselves very well, you understand. Catholics were not that high on the pecking order, either.

He did what he did to protect his people, and when he spoke out for children, as anyone might, it was right around that time that they started killing a lot more priests. They killed a lot of priests, you know, sent them to the death camps. It was a warning to the pope when they did it. They didn't say anything when he said, "Would you consider doing that?" He said, "We will take the children *here*." He tried to make it easy for them, you know. He said, "You could bring them here; we would be happy to have them." You understand, he was trying to do what he could. They said nothing; they just looked at him. Right after that they started sending the priests away. The church got the message.

Religion as Government

It seems that some churches and religions are attempting to constrict human consciousness expansion, that there is a stultifying effect.

Let's compare them to other larger systems. You could say that some of the religions are stultifying, not all.

On the other hand, you could say that governments are just as stultifying, if not more so. Larger religions, in my experience, become very much like governmental bodies, especially when they are established and the threat to them has greatly subsided. When religions start out the threat is high for them, even today in places around the world; Christians are not safe just by being Christians, you understand? For example, not too long ago in Lebanon there was a war, and it was really a religious war. You could say it was class war, but I would have to say it was more of a religious war.

Certainly there are other places in the remainder of the British Empire and many other places where being Christian is a risk. For instance, being what is called a Black Muslim in this country is certainly a risk. One might find the Islamic faith to be very attractive as structured for the Black Muslim church yet even if it is not, and many branches of it are not political, it is politicized by the external community. So it's not particularly safe to be of that religion, either.

Yet when religions grow big enough, they become accepted, not unlike governments. When the fledgling government of the United States took over and defeated the British with the help of the French and some native tribes as well, your country was considered an outcast by most of the world. If they hadn't been recognized by the French, they would have had no chance of survival. But once you were established, then people said, "Oh well, they're here to stay." Religions are no different.

In my experience; religions change slowly, yet what is the new religion now? The New Age religion. It also has dogma and rules. You might say that it is not really a religion so much as a philosophy. Yet in many places, it is passing as a religion and perhaps sometimes out of necessity, utilizing the laws that protect religions in your country. They therefore have to form as a church with parishioners and so on, and that takes time, like any religion.

I agree with what you said, yet from my perspective I can see how religion has actually helped set the stage for the return to normalcy—benevolent attitudes about yourself and your fellow beings, and fellow plants and animals and so on—because religion constantly reinforces the belief in the usefulness of the unseen. God is, after all, unseen, though there might be symbols to represent God for various different religions. Ultimately, religions support and nurture [chuckles] the belief in the unseen. When looked at historically, at least from my time looking back, it is quite obvious that this has supported the ultimate return to the sacred path.

But people are so caught up in the dogmatic rules of their religion that they can't see that they each are a god, a creator, a great being.

This is certainly true. As you say, I can find no fault with what you say, yet I am looking at the big picture. The big picture suggests that in the long run although religion is dogmatic and has many faults (which are legion, I admit), it will ultimately be shown that religion has kept a lot of people on track.

What would you say if I said that the whole satanic movement was given a tremendous boost by the Nazi party? Granted, it was not the soldier in the field or the average citizen, but the inner circles, even some of the rites and rituals associated with the different branches.

Yes, we have published a lot about that.

It was not respected by career German soldiers but known to them *to some extent*. That's why some of the older career soldiers and generals rejected the Nazis and begrudgingly served only because it was Germany. They considered the Nazis to be perverse and warped and twisted and had no respect for them; nevertheless it was Germany and they served.

I would say there would have been a serious hazard over time had not religion kept people in line so they didn't fall into the Nazi pit of satanic practices. Many times people have been attracted to this. Religion has forced with an iron fist its perception of the sacred and stamped out these practices, at least to an extent. So we have to recognize that even though we might not like everything about a religion, religions have served some valuable purposes.

The Bridge Religion

From your future point in your studies, what caused you to choose the Christian religion to experience? You felt that it was the most important one?

I felt it was a bridge religion. There are other religions that are more, as you say, spiritual—the Shinto and Buddhism have great beauty and grace. Yet because people who would be Christians and born into that faith would have such an impact on world history for these past few thousand years, I thought it was an important religion to study and become familiar with, to understand it on an intimate basis, meaning to communicate with Christian people, especially those involved in the formation of Christian movements, such as Martin Luther.

I can see that it might also have been useful for me to spend more time with others who are credited with being the founding fathers of Islam and Judaism, even Buddhism. I have spent a little time with Buddha. But I felt the historical impact of Christians and Christianity was so impactful on your world history that a closer study was necessary to understand not only why people did what they did, such as during the Crusades, which was really not about religion so much as about invasion, colonization (if not permanent, at least temporary) and lots of other unpleasant things.

I saw such a perversion of the intention of the man that Christianity was built around, yet that somehow it would ultimately lead people to be receptive to his original intent, which happens in the future. I wanted to see how it was possible for people to take this long, circuitous, twisting trail and come to the point of such great readiness. You know, when this man Jesus returns with all of his students and apostles and friends, he will be received with open arms, not as a god but as a beloved teacher returned to help his students. He is not going to be bowed down to as a god—he is going to be embraced. To some extent as Christianity gets modified over the coming years, it will have a lot to do with that.

The Mormon religion will have more and more impact; they have, in some ways, a broader world view. They have even a cosmic view which is not that common among Christian religions. They will become significantly more influential over the next hundred to hundred and fifty years. They will modify the tenets of their religion somewhat, becoming more benevolent toward women and include women much more in the church hierarchy, until eventually the church hierarchy is almost exclusively female. When that takes place, a lot of good things will happen. Not that the Mormon religion is so awful, but it just needs to be feminized, as many reli-gions do. When it is more feminized, it will be perhaps one of the longer-lasting Christian religions. Among the Christian religions though, there is a New Age Christian church that has been forming for some years that may or may not last—the Mormon Church has the best chance for survival for the next few hundred years. The churches that are more flexible—Unity, Unitarian and so on—have good chances of surviving, too. Eventually the Unity and Universalist-Unitarian churches will combine.

When Jesus and his group come back, will they be welcomed by all of humanity or just the Christian religions?

All of humanity. By that time humanity will have a better understanding of what Jesus was trying to do. A lot of the original documents and original stories of the mysticism and so on that Jesus was attempting to teach will have been released to the general public. People will have the opportunity to study what has really only been available to Bible scholars, and sometimes not even to them. As a result, people will be gradually conditioned to the idea that Jesus was a teacher and never intended to be perceived of as a god.

The Light Museum

You said that when you get back home you are going to give a report—to whom?

It is not exactly like the way it is here. When I get back I will do this: I will place my left appendage (we are going to call it my left hand) onto something that to you would look like a shelf of light. I will rest it there for a time, and during that time my entire experience will flow into this thing that looks like a shelf, which has the capacity to absorb my experience. This structure of light runs for quite a way—it is what we could call the *Light Museum*. Those who wish to know, including those who study such things, will come and touch it with their left hand and be able to absorb the full experience, not just the thoughts or the words or the descriptions, but what I actually experienced. At times, I felt I needed to experience things to help me understand the human being better. I know that the man the Christian religion was built around did this. At one point, he choose to experience a death before his actual death, so he would understand the fear of death people had.

I did the same thing; I thought it was a wise thing to do. Once I was in a battle with soldiers—it was before bullets, so it was with swords and shields and things like that. I experienced a death and I experienced the fears of people around me. I did not have fear myself, but I experienced their fear and anger and so on, and it helped me to understand the fear of death much better.

You would manifest your body. You weren't born, you would just create a body?

That's right. I would just create a body temporarily and be an anonymous soldier. I did this during a war where only swords were used.

Not the Crusades?

No.

So others can feel your experience?

Yes, and then I think they will either act on it or not. There aren't councils where people sit in groups together, but there are councils in terms of energy awareness. The people do not come to a central place to physically communicate when they can communicate at a distance. There is some kind of counseling—you would call it talking—back and forth with the people to decide the value of my experience. Others might try it or they might try something similar by using techniques not unlike my own. That is why I was the first of my people to come back, but I may not be the last.

So you say that they may act on it by coming back to experience it themselves?

Yes, to experience it themselves or to experience something that interests them. They might come back to study a religion as well, or to study even a movement. Our people are interested in such things.

You are very careful every time you've created a body so that you wouldn't do anything that . . .

I took care that no one fell in love with me so that there wouldn't be a broken heart when I wasn't there anymore. I took care that I did not make a commitment to any cause or group that could not get along fine without me. In other words, I did what I did and left as little a track as possible [laughs].

You don't have days, you don't have nights, you are immortal. What are your enthusiasms and joys in your own time?

In my own time? I am most interested in how things came to be, which is why I am doing this. That is my main interest. I study other civilizations and look at them as they are and then look at their history and see how they came to be that way. This is the first time I have actually gone back in time to live how they came to be that way, but that is my interest. I am doing my interest.

What do you look forward to?

You must admit that when you look forward to something, it is sometimes because that something is so much better than what you are doing. Other times, it's because what you are doing is really not fun. So I am doing something that is fun. I really don't look forward; I experience the moment to its fullest. If I were to do anything, I might look backward and examine in more detail what I had experienced or, in the case of studying other cultures, what they had experienced. But even in my time and place, I look to see how people got there. What is really available is trends and histories but not much individual experience, which is why I value my time spent with you, especially in my observation of the development of the present Christian religion.

Creation of Light

Can you just give us just a short explanation? Do you live on a planet? You said there was a great creation of light.

It is not a planet. It is just like a mass. If you were to stand there and look at it, you wouldn't see a planet, you wouldn't see structures and technology. You would see plasmic light. You might at times see shapes and forms. You might get the impression of individuals, not necessarily looking human, but looking more like points of light. It is not like your place.

So are there a hundred or a billion? What kind of population?

You mean the numbers, the individual personalities in this place? Oh, I should think no more than several trillion, no more than that. It is a big place. Think about it. Several trillion is a minuscule number compared to the number of individuals living in Love's Creation that you are in. So several trillion is nothing, and our mass is bigger than Love's creation.

You said you thought that all of you as peers had created Love. You don't actually have a creator?

Correct. This is my understanding. It is what I believe. I have not seen anything separate from all of us.

Have you always been?

Yes, I have always been.

When you need to know something, do you have guides and teachers or what we call somebody up the line that you can ask?

No. If I need to know something that may be known by other members of my people, I might go to that light wall and feel it. If it is there, and it usually is, then I will have it. If it is something beyond our capacities, such as an intimate understanding of the people here on Earth and how they came to be, do and so on, then I will request permission to go there, which I have done. This trip represents the fact that none of my people had ever come here before, so no one could give me that experience. It wasn't available. The only way to obtain it was to come on my own.

If Jesus came from that place, how did he get permission to do something so awesome there?

I never asked him. I will ask him. [Laughs.] He didn't get permission. In those days, they didn't require it. Since then, they have become a little bit more conservative.

So he just had this idea and came to this creator and this creator said okay?

Yes.

So what is the being we know as Jesus doing now, this moment in our time?

He spends a lot of time near your planet, not necessarily on it, observing and radiating the best energies he can to assist you all. That's where he invests most of his energy. There is still some portion of him where I live, but most of his energy, in terms of percentage (I should think close to ninety-seven percent is close to the Earth—at a higher dimension, of course.

Was he the first from your place of existence to come here and interact on the Earth and with the Explorer Race?

He was the first to do it the way he did it, meaning to be born as a man, to live intimately on a day-to-day basis in a body. He was the first to do that, yes.

Have any others done it since he did?

No.

After the Explorer Race project is over, then he will return to your place of existence and continue his life?

You will have to ask him.

We might do that sometime. The people from your place of existence go everywhere?

They could. They used to have much more access, but since Jesus' experience went in ways that caused disappointment with the outcome (though ultimately, he will be feeling very good about the outcome), they haven't done much for the past few thousand years. Before that, I think they used to travel extensively. Even today they can travel, but they are not encouraged to become involved with the people. I had to wait almost ten years to get permission to do what I am doing. Of course, the admonition was that I be very discreet and that I don't get directly involved in . . .

The time line?

Not only that, but to have such involvement that people might come to want me to be around and then miss me when I am gone. Do you know why? It is not only compassionate. If someone misses you, it holds you somewhat, it binds you to that place. Part of the reason that Jesus is so close to Earth is that so many people miss him. Even though they haven't met him physically, they have a feeling of what he might have been like. Because there is such love and affection, he is somewhat committed to being close.

I see, so it's almost self-preservation. It's compassionate, but it is also for your own good.

Yes. My people understand this, so I am discreet and have no affairs of the heart.

Were you tempted?

Would you be insulted if I said no?

Light Intimacy, Responsibility

What about in your place of existence? You are all points of light. Do you have relationships?

Certainly we have relationships, but they are not exclusive as they might be here. We do not have sexual relationships as you understand it, but we might have moments of intimacy with one or several beings that would be greater intimacy than we might have with others at some other time, a greater connection with the absolute essences of ourselves. We might choose to make an essential connection with a special individual or individuals we feel special about in a given moment.

Do you have family life? What is your culture like?

It is not like yours at all. There is very little similarity. I have somewhat adapted our existence into a framework that you could understand, but there isn't family life as you know it. There is a sense of great kindred connection with all beings, great love between us, great affection for each other, yet there are no individual families per se.

You can all go anyplace just with your intention. There is no limit to the places you can go, if you get permission from your peers?

We can all go where we are welcome. That's how we get there. Intention is not enough; we have to be welcome there. If we go to become involved as I am, then permission is required. If you just go to observe, to be amongst the people but not be seen or noticed in any way, permission is not required.

Not just Earth, but all reality, all levels, all creations, all dimensions—do your people do that very much?

There was early on an exploration of higher dimensions. Yet most of my people prefer their ninth dimension or denser because there is more activity there, more things happening, more people, more creations, things to learn, things to understand and so on. So trips to the thirteenth or the thirty-third dimension and so on are not so common. They are done only by those who wish to understand how things have formed or come together. Again, that's of great interest to us. We are perhaps historians at heart.

But you don't really have any responsibilities then?

We do not, as you understand it, have responsibilities. Our responsibility is to each other and to be what we are in the most benevolent way for ourselves and for others. We do that. We live in total harmony.

Could we get a a road map of the infinite here? You have this vast place of existence, this creation. I get the feeling that all of you created all of the flavors of Loves. Is that true?

In my understanding, yes.

All right. Then one flavor of Love created Love's Creation. Do the others have similar creations, or is this the only one?

It is entirely up to them. Some of them have creations. I do not think that any of them have creations so vast and complex and with such a variety as the one in which you are now living. But then the Love who created this had an agenda.

Because she too saw the ribbon and the inspiration, right?

Yes, she wanted to do more, to create more in the most benevolent way and yet to experiment with how that benevolent way might be.

So the original intention for the Explorer Race came from your place of existence?

Yes.

From everybody, from one person, from a group? How does that work?

Our civilization does not compare to your own. With any thread emanating from our civilization, our place of existence, there has been participation by everyone, although the initial consideration for its application in specific terms might have been by a few members. Nevertheless, all the beings in our creation participate before the thread is released to find its natural place of expansion.

So one thing you beings do, then, is inspire and, in a sense, give guidance to all the creations that are down the line.

Not necessarily down the line, it's also up the line. All are available to our influence because we don't send them all one way. We send them all different ways. I might add that for the threads sent out for the Explorer Race there were about three hundred. They were sent all different ways, all different dimensions. It is certainly possible that another one of these threads will be acted on at some point, some place. I don't think they have been yet, but it is possible.

I understood that you said there wasn't anything up the line from you.

I am not aware of anything up the line, as you say. That doesn't mean that there isn't that; I'm just not aware of it.

Have you ever asked anyone from beyond your creation if they created all of you?

No.

Would you?

If you wish. I am told that we created ourselves.

So you are the beginning, then. There is nothing beyond you?

I cannot say that for certain. I am told that we created ourselves.

You mean that we actually got to the end of something?

I cannot say for certain. I can only answer the question as I did.

You are very valuable. You are from the farthest away, up, out. Please describe infinity from your point of view.

Infinity equals total expression of all possibilities everywhere, anytime, with love. That is my understanding.

How much is it possible to visit?

I am not aware of any. It doesn't mean that there aren't. I am not aware of any. I can only answer you within what I know and if there are other answers. Since I am able to touch the wall or shelf as we call it at a distance, I can hear something different. I have not heard anything different.

You are an historian. Do you have beings who practice anything similar to us—music, theater and similar art?

Yes, within the context of our civilization.

Each of you as a point of light, right?

That's the best way I can describe it to you because you can imagine a point of light. But yes, there are those who have a greater interest in expressing art or sound—as you say, music.

What about children? Do you create them at a certain point? How do you expand?

No, no, no, no. There are no children. Remember, there are no families. We do not require the mechanics of continuity—we *are* continuity.

So the fixed number that was from your beginning is the number that there is now?

Yes, which makes sense if you think about it. The number of beings that we are is the most compatible number for this place. Why reduce it or make more?

Is is possible that there was a creator who split in fragments to experience everything and you are the result? I am at the end of my ability to communicate with you.

Well, that is because I am stretching to make our civilization more understandable to you and you are stretching to accommodate my explanation. Yet it is like this: If you listen to music from your car radio, it is beautiful, perhaps, yet it is directional. But if you are sitting in the middle of the orchestra as it plays that music, there is so much more. Right now I am giving you a directional idea of our civilization. If you were with and in our civilization as one of us, it would be so much more. I am attempting to stop the record from spinning, which is unnatural for it, to show you one tiny piece of it that sounds vaguely familiar.

Could you say that your beings have done what Jesus did at other places you know of? The only reason he attempted it here was because of the Explorer Race, right?

He attempted it here, yes, because he was helping to speed up the process because he had such great compassion for the suffering of the people. No, he is the only one. Perhaps it's as well.

Because?

Considered as experience. It turned out well in the long run, and it has not all been taboo. There have been wonderful things—like Christmas. [Laughs.] Is that not wonderful?

It has been wonderful, it really has. You have learned a lot about the other religions on this planet not just from studying, observing, but interacting.

Interacting, yes.

Birth of Jesus

You really have a pretty good idea—like an anthropologist who would go to a tribal culture?

I have a fair idea. Not a good enough idea to make any brilliant comments on other religions. (It's a joke for me.) But, yes. Did you know that I was present at Jesus' birth?

Were you? Unseen?

No, I was an animal. I know it is shown to be all this light, but it was quite dark in there. I grant that the being did glow somewhat, but not so much as to illuminate the room. It was a typical birth in the sense of what a woman goes through, yet the people who visited there did feel like a special being had entered the world.

Of course, parents always feel that way about a child, but people who didn't even know the parents felt that the being was special. You could feel that. That's one of the reasons when he was teaching that people were attracted to him. You felt there was something special about him.

He was conscious at birth?

Correct, and he remained so. And as such he had to set aside some of his biases in order to experience life as a human being.

What an amazing thing to live, to be conscious and then go through that, the restrictions and the limitations.

You know, it makes one so much more compassionate and understanding with human beings when you experience it. I think that as a personal experience for him it was very fulfilling.

Was that the only life he had on this planet? Conventional wisdom says he had several lives.

In my understanding, it was the only time he was born.

He may have walked in or created bodies at other times?

Oh, he might have, but probably not walked in. I don't think our people would do that. More likely, he would have perhaps created a body and existed for a time.

Did you create the animal at the time of his birth or did you just sort of temporarily merge with it?

Created. One does not question, you know, when you see a sheep. One does not really question that there is such an animal present. You see the animals, and you don't think about it. If there is an extra one and you don't know where it came from, you still don't think about it. It's like, Oh, I didn't remember there were that many. Then the next day, Oh, I must have counted wrong. That's all it is. It is very easy to be anonymous as an animal amongst human beings.

That's wonderful! How far did the expansion go?

It is still going.

Has it reached your place of existence?

Oh, it has gone past our place.

But the going past your place, if there is none other like you, where is it going?

I couldn't say. [Laughs.]

This is related to the Council of Creators and some of them want to limit it to this Earth and to this solar system and to this creation until they see how it works. It is interesting that you say it was allowed to go this natural way.

I would say that everyone will relate to things on the basis of who they are. Even on your planet they do that. Not knowing very much about who you are, you still do that.

We have our opinions about whether we have any knowledge or not.

Yes. Regardless of what they are based on, and of course on the basis of your immortal personalities as well.

We are taught that at the Council of Nicaea the religion itself was distorted and perverted by some of these councils of bishops and popes who used it to control humanity. Is that your perception?

Mystical Teachings of Jesus

That cannot be overlooked. Certainly that was true to some extent, especially when the Church became more politicized. When it became more established, it was understood that in order to maintain the Church indefinitely, it would be necessary to be politically powerful while at the same time bestow the Church's blessing, as it were, upon one powerful political being or another in order to maintain sufficient protection from governments. It was always perceived by the Church that the Church was permanent, but governments come and go. So these councils sometimes were accommodating governments and other times were restructuring what would be shared with the people. Every so often, as they still do in governments today, temporary measures would be put in place that became permanent.

Yes, and everybody forgot why.

One of the temporary measures was to remove the mystical teachings of Jesus for a time. They said, "Well, we will remove it be-cause then it cannot be used in any way for mischief. We will keep it, study it and try these things within our own circles (though they didn't, that was the intent) and we'll keep it back for a time." Then it became permanent. But eventually it will come out again.

Are the records of some of the stuff that was removed stored at the Vatican?

I would rather not say. I just say it's stored someplace safe.

How will it come out? Will there be more similar things like the Dead Sea scrolls or the Kumran scrolls, or will existing information be made available?

It will be released consciously. They'll say, "We had these documents, and we feel the time is right for these teachings. We want to share them with our parishioners." Of course, when they do that there will be a lot more parishioners coming to the Church, even though some of the hierarchical members of the Church will say, "Well, if the people become empowered too much, they might go off and start their own religions." But cooler heads will prevail and say, "Well, the time is right to release these things, and if it brings people back to the Church, wonderful. If it causes them to start their own thing, perhaps that would be acceptable."

Most likely it will just bring people back to the Church because in order to know these things, you will have to attend the church to find out. You may not have to become a member, but you will at least have to visit regularly. The teachings, not the original documents, will be made available to you and possibly even become rites and rituals involved in becoming a member of the Church. In this way, the Church will become more mystical. The more the Church embraces the mystical and allows its parishioners to practice the mystical, the longer it will last. The question is whether they will do that sooner or later, but it will be done.

So do they do it sooner or later?

That is the question.

And you are not going to tell?

I do not wish to have undue influence.

But they are going to it?

They will do it, yes. Eventually, they will release it to all religions, but of course they will start with their own people, as you might expect.

At the place where you live, you don't use rituals? You don't need mystical practices to attain anything? You already are that, right?

Yes. One might say we are our own ceremony. We celebrate our existence by being.

That is beautiful. Is that an evolutionary possibility? Is that a choice? I mean, other souls, other beings, can't come there to join you because you have a fixed number, right?

Yes, but at times we have visitors as long as their energy does not create any disharmony. If it does not, then visitors are allowed. They are not frequent, but we have them sometimes.

Where do they come from?

Wherever they are from, but they must be able to accommodate the higher dimensions of their being, meaning that they must be able to express themselves comfortably at the ninth dimension or higher. They come and stay awhile and experience what we are, and if they are interested in receiving wisdom from the place of the light wisdom, they can receive it to the extent that they can assimilate it.

Of course, it is meant for our people, so they may not be able to assimilate it for who they are, but they can assimilate it to some extent. Then they will go on, perhaps returning to their own time, perhaps continuing their journey, like any traveler.

Qua on Mormonism

Qua

April 17, 1998

I would like to talk tonight just a little bit about my communication with the founder of the Mormon religion.

ETs and Joseph Smith

This person (and I think I'm not revealing church secrets here) had more than one communication with extraterrestrials, who talked to him about Earth's place in the universe, talked about their philosophy and generally spoke of the ways people could be initiated into a philosophy that would support and maintain, ultimately, a world view and then a cosmic view. And many of these initiations have been integrated into the church; some at higher levels, some at day-to-day levels for the average parishioner. I will grant that because of the older times, not all of the philosophy was given with an even hand to all people. Sometimes, you know, when people you admire are talking to you, you will look very much more closely at your common ground—especially if you are nervous around such foreign visitors—and an off-hand remark that one of the ETs once made to this man was that they "cherish and protect their women just the way you do," he said to this man. And what the ET really meant was that cherish, was more that the women were respected and honored and revered, as one might revere a religious leader, for example. But in those days, in those times, the Earth person heard it as cherish, meaning to protect. And while that was done, there was also some things done that were not so good, and that's why the church will, at some point, need to address that so that women are not only equals, but involved in the church hierarchy as ministers and so on. And they'll do that.

My conversations with this man came after his communication with these other ETs, and after some of this was known by other members of the inner circle of that group. Sometimes we would talk in his dreams, and other times when he would go for a step away from everybody else.

We would talk from a distance. I enjoyed my conversations with him because he was a man who was raised very much as a product of his time and place, and from his point of view, he was trying to establish something that was revolutionary in those times: a way of life. He was really attempting literally to create Eden; that was the real intention, to create Eden for his people. So, from that perspective he was really making an effort to do something quite dazzlingly different from the times, and therefore I enjoyed our talks. And these talks would often, as I say, take place in his dreams; in that way it was safe for him. He was a man of great vision, and not unlike most people of today or any time, toward the end of his life he could not communicate quite as well as he once did, and that's why there were some more misunderstandings. But the messages were well taken.

There was a time in your recent time sequence, in the '80s, that there was an arrangement with the original ETs. The original arrangement was that the ETs would return, stand shoulder to shoulder with these church brothers, and reveal the consequence, meaning the intention of ET interaction with the Earth. But because of difficulties in ships penetrating your military web around the planet and so on, they couldn't come. They did send telepathic messages, one of which was received, and because it was a three-stage message, the only one that was received was the message essentially that "We will come when we are able." And since they didn't come, the church didn't reveal anything and basically is in a holding position. [Chuckles.]

So I mention this now because my understanding is that this church, the Mormon church that calls themselves Latter-Day Saints, is really the foundation of the Christian church, and once it integrates women as equals, all right, it will survive. And that's why I've picked them out to talk about them, because they have the greatest potential of surviving with their religion almost intact, with the only changes being the equalization of women and the inclusion of other races and nationalities of human beings in the church as equals as well. Once that is done from the heart—and not just as a discipline [chuckles]—the church will be the most likely candidate, from my historical perspective, to survive and evolve into that benevolent Christian future.

What specific interaction did Joseph Smith, founder of the Mormon religion, have with ETs? They stood in front of him and talked? He channeled them?

They stood in front of him, it was a face-to-face. In those days, bringing a ship and landing was safe.

Yes. And where were they from?

They were from Andromeda, from what I can understand. That was considered a place of great thoughts, and they approached this man on the basis of thought because he was, of course, a thinker. He had to be to have such visions. They also gave some gifts. They gave some knowledge that people might survive, some medical things, some knowledge of herbs. They made an effort to encourage the people to reach out to native peoples in the area, to make friends with them, and alliances—and to keep the alliances sacred, if possible the ETs encouraged the people to support native peoples because the native peoples would be able to support them with a great deal of wisdom that would help them to survive in sometimes hostile situations.

And what year was this, in our time?

Not sure if I can get that, but you can look it up.

Okay. And what the ETs told him, he wrote down, and that is part of what is stored now at the Mormon church?

Yes.

And it's never been revealed publicly.

I don't know if it hasn't been revealed publicly; I think that it's generally not open to the public. There might have been times when outsiders have seen it, but it is not generally known to the vast public.

Few have seen the famous writings. Sometimes writings can be famous without having been published.

The Golden Plates

Who wrote on those golden plates he dug up?

These were gifts. I don't think he dug them up, I think they were given to him.

By the Andromedans?

I think so. That's why they have the symbols. Of course, I don't know about this, but if they said they dug them up, of course it would have been a lot safer to say that than to say that spacemen gave them to him. You wouldn't want to say that, even if it was true. Someday they will, of course, talk about that, when they feel safe.

But do they have them physically now?

These plates are secure, someplace safe. I'd rather say it like this: the plates are safe.

And at a certain time, when they feel it's okay, they will reveal them, they will show them?

When many things have occurred, they will reveal them to the public, but they wisely choose not to at this time, and I support that. I think it would be a mistake to do so now; people are not ready now. But they will be someday.

And that's another reason, I think, that perhaps the people of this religion keep their own counsel, because they're not sure when is the best time. They will receive other telepathic messages, though, more clearly in the future, so I would think within the next five to seven years they'll have a much better grasp of what is the best time and place to do things, and in a way that they will be most safe and protected and supported.

Mormonism is a version of Christianity?

Anyone interested can just obtain their pamphlets from the church. I think I'll just let the writings stand for themselves.

All right.

Sometimes my reason to talk to you is to indicate my interaction with these people.

So, was it only in dreams? You never took a body and actually talked to him?

Oh, yes. On several occasions I had a body and spoke to him; I don't think he realized, though, that I was the person he spoke to in his dreams—and that's to his advantage, you know; I didn't want him to become baffled or confused.

But you had a feeling, sensing interaction with him.

Yes. I wanted to understand the person who was more responsible than any other for the creation of what ultimately becomes the benevolent Christian church. I thought he was important.

Mormonism has the basic tenets of what Jesus tried to teach?

Yes.

But, with how would you say, with what added?

I am shy to put in my words; I'd rather say, with a broader, more modern teaching.

Okay, but the Mormon faith, then, has kept some of the things that Jesus tried to promote that got lost in the early years. Is that a fair thing to say?

I am loathe to talk about it, because it would be so easy for me to say what it is going to be, and unintentionally influence it! I am bending over backwards to avoid influencing it.

And then what about when Smith was gone, did Brigham Young bring a different flavor to it? What is your perspective of that?

I did not talk with this other person, Young, but my perspective is that's where the real patriarchy came in strong. He was not the initiator, he was more of a good manager, but he got too authoritarian, which they're still getting over.

Past Lives, Prominent Players

If you can't answer this, just say so. Did Joseph Smith have a history of other lives in our civilization that we would recognize, if you said what his past lives were?

No one you would know. That is not unusual. People that become prominent practically never have any other prominent lives. That is normally the case; it is very odd. I have not heard of any prominent person going through this world you have here that has another life of prominence. Generally, one life of prominence is more than sufficient for the soul to deal with all of the consequences.

I sometimes wondered if history, you know, had ten souls that had a hundred lives that influenced everything.

No, no, because it's too much for one soul to deal with. Think about it: As an individual, Smith had his own family, so there were consequences there, plus all of these people that he impacted with his vision and wisdom, yes? Plus their succeeding generations, so even though he had passed over long ago.

All of his philosophy is still impacting all of these people, so that's all consequences. It is not burden; sometimes the consequences are benevolent, other times they are a bit of a problem—sometimes from his creation, sometimes from the input from others. So generally speaking, for one soul to have one such prominent and influential life is sometimes even more than that soul can handle on their own, and require assistance.

And as you said about Jesus, people keep pulling on him and he has to stay close to the Earth, right?

Yes, because of his impact. And that a lot of his impact had nothing to do with what he said or did, but what others said about him—or changed, or put words into his mouth, as it were.

The Future of Christianity

Fascinating. So do you feel that the Catholic religion is so structured and so dogmatic that it won't survive on its own? Will it merge into the Mormon religion?

No, I don't think so. I think that it will gradually become more of a philosophical underpinning of the Christian ethic in general. But the discipline aspects of it would have to fall away, and so much of the church ceremonial is built up around discipline. And yet the real purpose of what is now called Christianity is to enrich and nurture, and doesn't have very much to do with discipline at all. Once upon a time, that was very serviceable in different societies, but in the future it won't be. The idea of not doing this on a certain day or the idea of denying yourself something or denying others something that is readily available—that won't have a place in the future.

What a challenge to our belief system! We're brought up to believe that this is the holy way, you know; duty, sacrifice, noble thoughts, and halfway through, it's like, "Well, you have to change."

Well, those principles were good for the time, and in many ways they helped to keep society from doing more extreme things. But as consciousness expands, and as people reach out to others on foreign shores and understand how much alike you all are, this will support being benevolent toward each other. So the age of consciousness has just as much to do with communication as it does with spiritual expansion.

Think about it, if you are a youngster using your computer, talking to a youngster in another country, you will talk about the things that interest you. Often the things that you care about the most, that are the most meaningful to you, are the exact same things that are the most meaningful to a youngster in the other country. And that's a very powerful influence to you growing up now, the youngsters of today, for whom the internet (as you call it) is a fact of life. And when you realize how very similar other people are to you, you cannot either deify them or demonize them. Even if a government says, "These people are evil," you have spoken to individuals over there, and they don't seem very evil to you; they seem just like you. As a matter of fact, you can't wait to meet them. And things like this tend to create more benevolence for the future.

Exciting time to be here, eh?

Yes, and another reason to respect and value the young, and don't believe just the bad things you hear about them [chuckles].

No; they're our future, right?

They are your future, and they are worthy of it.

Is there anything else you'd like to say?

I think I will stop there. I've spoken a lot about various religious leaders that have had some interesting impact with your societies.

Thank you.

THE EXPLORER RACE SERIE

Zoosh through Robert Shapir

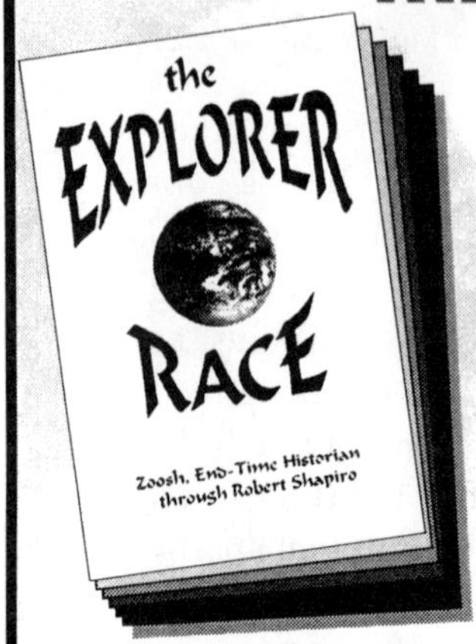

AVAILABLE FROM
LIGHT TECHNOLOGY PUBLISHING
SEE BOOK MARKET ORDER FORM
IN BACK OF THIS ISSUE

The Origin . . .
The Purpose . . .
The Future of Humanity

"After all the words that we put out, ultimately the intention is to persuade people's minds, otherwise known as giving their minds the answers that their minds hunger for so that their minds can get out of the way and let their hearts take them to where they would naturally go anyway."

— Zoosh/Robert Shapiro

THE SERIES

Humans — creators in training — have a purpose and destiny so heartwarmingly, profoundly glorious that it is almost unbelievable from our present dimensional perspective. Humans are great lightbeings from beyond this creation, gaining experience in dense physicality. This truth about the great human genetic experiment of the Explorer Race and the mechanics of creation is being revealed for the first time by Zoosh and his friends through superchannel Robert Shapiro. These books read like adventure stories as we follow the clues from this creation that we live in out to the Council of Creators and beyond.

❶ the EXPLORER RACE

You individuals reading this are truly a result of the genetic experiment c Earth. You are beings who uphold the principles of the Explorer Race. Th information in this book is designed to show you who you are and give you a evolutionary understanding of your past that will help you now. The key empowerment in these days is to not know everything about your past but know what will help you now.

Your souls have been here for a while on Earth and have been trained Earthlike conditions. This education has been designed so that you wou have the ability to explore all levels of responsibility—results, effects ar consequences—and take on more responsibilities.

Your number one function right now is your status of Creator appre tice, which you have achieved through years and lifetimes of sweat. Yo are constantly being given responsibilities by the Creator that would no mally be things that Creator would do. The responsibility and the destin of the Explorer Race is not only to explore, but to create. 574p $25.0

❷ ETs and the EXPLORER RACE

In this book Robert channels Joopah, a Zeta Reticulan now in th ninth dimension, who continues the story of the great experiment – the Explorer Race—from the perspective of his race. The Zetas woul have been humanity's future selves had not humanity re-created th past and changed the future. 237p $14.95

❸ EXPLORER RACE: Origins and the Next 50 Years

This volume has so much information about who we are an where we came from—the source of male and female beings, the wa of the sexes, the beginning of the linear mind, feelings, the origin o souls—it is a treasure trove. In addition, there is a section that relate to our near future—how the rise of global corporations and politic affects our future, how to use benevolent magic as a force of creatior and how we will go out to the stars and affect other civilizations Astounding information. 339p $14.95

❹ EXPLORER RACE: Creators and Friends— the Mechanics of Creation

Now that you have a greater understanding of who you are in the larger sense, it is necessary to remind you of where you came from, the true magnificence of your being, to have some of your true peers talk to you. You must understand that you are creators in training, and yet you were once a portion of Creator. One could certainly say, without being magnanimous, that you are still a portion of Creator, yet you are training for the individual responsibility of being a creator, to give your Creator a coffee break.

This book will give you peer consultation. it will allow you to understand the vaster qualities and help you remember the nature of the desires that drive any creator, the responsibilities to which that creator must answer, the reaction a creator must have to consequences and the ultimate reward of any creator. This book will help you appreciate all of the above and more. 435p $19.95

❺ EXPLORER RACE: Particle Personalities

All around you in every moment you are surrounded by the most magical and mystical beings. They are too small for you to see as single individuals, but in groups you know them as the physical matter of your daily life. Particles who might be considered either atoms or portions of atoms consciously view the vast spectrum of reality, yet also have a sense of personal memory like your own linear memory. These particles remember where they have been and what they have done in their infinitely long lives. Some of the particles we hear from are Gold, Mountain Lion, Liquid Light, Uranium, the Great Pyramid's Capstone, This Orb's Boundary, Ice and Ninth-Dimensional Fire. 237p $14.95

❻ EXPLORER RACE: EXPLORER RACE and BEYOND

With a better idea of how creation works, we go back to the Creator's advisors and receive deeper and more profound explanations of the roots of the Explorer Race. The liquid Domain and the Double Diamond portal share lessons given to the roots on their way to meet the Creator of this Universe and finally the roots speak of their origins and their incomprehensibly long journey here. 360p $14.95

THE EXPLORER RACE SERIES

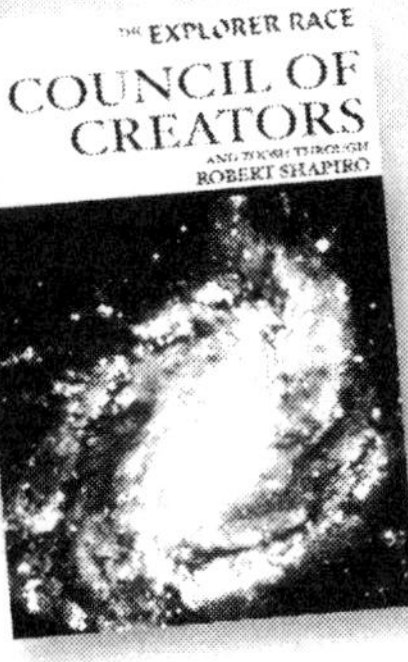

Book 7 of the EXPLORER RACE

THE COUNCIL OF CREATORS

ROBERT SHAPIRO

The thirteen core members of the Council of Creators discuss their adventures in coming to awareness of themselves and their journeys on the way to the Council on this level. They discuss the advice and oversight they offer to all creators, including the creator of this local universe. These beings are wise, witty and joyous, and their stories of Love's Creation creates an expansion of our concepts as we realize that we live in an expanded, multiple-level reality. SOFTCOVER 306P. $14.95 ISBN 1-891824-13-9

Highlights Include

- **Specialist in Colors, Sounds and Consequences of Actions**
- **Specialist in Membranes that Separate and Auditory Mechanics**
- **Specialist in Sound Duration**
- **Explanation from Unknown Member of Council**
- **Specialist in Spatial Reference**
- **Specialist in Gaps and Spaces**
- **Specialist in Divine Intervention**
- **Specialist in Synchronicity and Timing**
- **Specialist in Hope**
- **Specialist in Honor**
- **Specialist in Variety**
- **Specialist in Mystical Connection between Animals and Humans**
- **Specialist in Change**
- **Specialist in the Present Moment**
- **Council Spokesperson and Specialist in Auxiliary Life Forms**

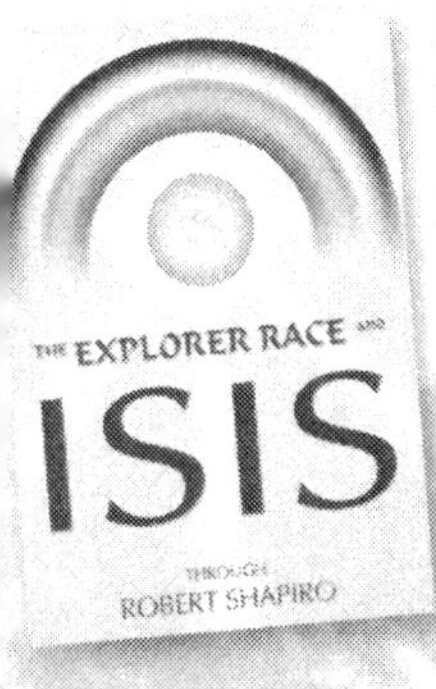

Book 8 of the EXPLORER RACE

THE EXPLORER RACE AND ISIS

ROBERT SHAPIRO

This is an amazing book. It has priestess training, Shamanic training, Isis' adventures with Explorer Race beings—before Earth and on Earth—and an incredibly expanded explanation of the dynamics of the Explorer Race. Isis is the prototypical loving, nurturing, guiding feminine being, the focus of feminine energy. She has the ability to expand limited thinking without making people with limited beliefs feel uncomfortable. She is a fantastic storyteller, and all of her stories are teaching stories. If you care about who you are, why you are here, where you are going and what life is all about—pick up this book. You won't lay it down until you are through, and then you will want more. SOFTCOVER 332P. $14.95 ISBN 1-891824-11-2

Highlights Include

- **The Biography of Isis**
- **The Adventurer**
- **Soul Colors and Shapes**
- **Creation Mechanics**
- **Creation Mechanics and Personal Anecdotes**
- **The Insects' Form and Fairies**
- **Orion and Application to Earth**
- **Goddess Section**
- **Who Is Isis?**
- **Priestess/Feminine Mysteries**

THE EXPLORER RACE SERIE

Book 9 of the EXPLORER RACE

THE EXPLORER RACE AND JESUS

ROBERT SHAPIRO

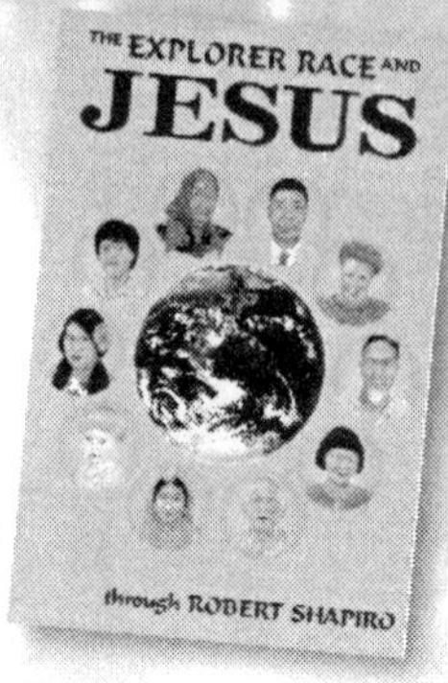

The core personality of that being known on the Earth as Jesus, along with his students and friends, describes with clarity and love his life and teaching 2000 years ago. He states that his teaching is for all people of all races in all countries. Jesus announces here for the first time that he and two others, Buddha and Mohammed, will return to Earth from their place of being in the near future. And a fourth being, a child already born now on Earth, will become a teacher and prepare humanity for their return.

So heartwarming and interesting, you won't want to put it down.
SOFTCOVER 354P. $16.95 ISBN 1-891824-14-7

Highlights Include

- **Jesus' Core Being, His People and the Interest in Earth of Four of Them**
- **Jesus' Life on Earth**
- **Jesus' Home World, Their Love Creations and the Four Who Visited Earth**
- **The "Facts" of Jesus' Life Here, His Future Return**
- **The Teachings and Travels**
- **A Student's Time with Jesus and His Tales of Jesus' Time Travels**
- **The Shamanic Use of the Senses**
- **Other Journeys and the Many Disguises**
- **The Child Student Who Became a Traveling Singer-Healer**
- **Jesus' Autonomous Parts, His Bloodline and His Plans**
- **Learning to Invite Matter to Transform Itself**
- **Inviting Water, Singing Colors**
- **Learning to Teach Usable Skills**
- **Learning about Different Cultures and People**
- **The Role of Mary Magdalene, a Romany**
- **Traveling and Teaching People How to Find Things**

Book 12 of the EXPLORER RACE

TECHNIQUES FOR GENERATING SAFTEY

ROBERT SHAPIRO

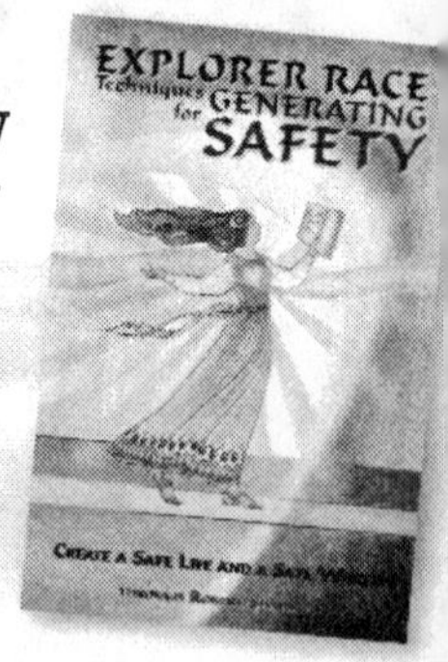

Wouldn't you like to generate safety—so you could go wherever you need to go, do whatever you need to do—in a benevolent, safe and loving way for yourself? Learn safety as a radiated environment which will allow you to gently take the step into the new timeline, into a benevolent future and away from a negative past. SOFTCOVER 175P. $9.95 ISBN 1-891824-26-0

Highlights Include

- **Zero Hour**
- **The Traveler**
- **The Fluid of Time**
- **Ordinator of Souls**
- **Energy Three**
- **The Mother of All Beings**
- **Heart Heat Exercise**
- **Creating Safety in Your Life**
- **Living Prayer**
- **Creator Training and Empowerment Exercises**
- **A Lesson in Benevolent Magic**
- **Mantras of Feeling and Optimistic Vision**
- **Disentanglement**
- **Disentangling Cords of Discomfort**

ORDER NOW TO RECEIVE SPECTACULAR SAVINGS

yes! send me:

	SURFACE	AIR
U.S.	❒ 1 yr. . . .$43	❒ 1 yr. . . .$76
	❒ 2 yrs. . .$69	❒ 2 yrs. . .$139
Canada	❒ 1 yr. . . .$56	❒ 1 yr. . . .$75
	❒ 2 yrs. . .$99	❒ 2 yrs. . .$133
All other countries	❒ 1 yr. . . .$62	❒ 1 yr. . . .$98
	❒ 2 yrs. . .$105	❒ 2 yrs. . .$190
	U.S. FUNDS ONLY	

My Name ______________________

Address ______________________

City ____________ State: ____ Zip: ____________

Phone ______________________

E-mail ______________________

Gift Recipient Name ______________________

Address ______________________

City ____________ State: ____ Zip: ____________

Personalized Gift Card from ______________________

METHOD OF PAYMENT:

❒ CHECK # ❒ M.O.

❒ VISA ❒ MASTERCARD ❒ NOVUS ❒ AMEX

CARD NO. ______________________

EXPIRATION DATE ______________________

SIGNATURE ______________________

Mail to: SEDONA Journal of EMERGENCE!
P.O. BOX 3870, Flagstaff, AZ 86003
Fax to: (800) 393-7017
or order online at:
www.lighttechnology.com

ORDER NOW!

TO RECEIVE
SPECTACULAR SAVINGS
BEFORE SUBSCRIPTION RATES ARE RAISED!

NEW COVER PRICE!
$5.95
SAVE $73.80
OFF THE COVER PRICE!

Easy Order 24 Hours a Day

1. **Order ONLINE!**
   http://www.lighttechnology.com

2. **Order by MAIL**
   Send To:
   Light Technology Publishing
   P.O. Box 3870
   Flagstaff, AZ 86003

3. **Order by PHONE**
   800-450-0985

4. **Order by FAX**
   800-393-7017

CROP CIRCLES REVEALED

LANGUAGE OF THE LIGHT SYMBOLS

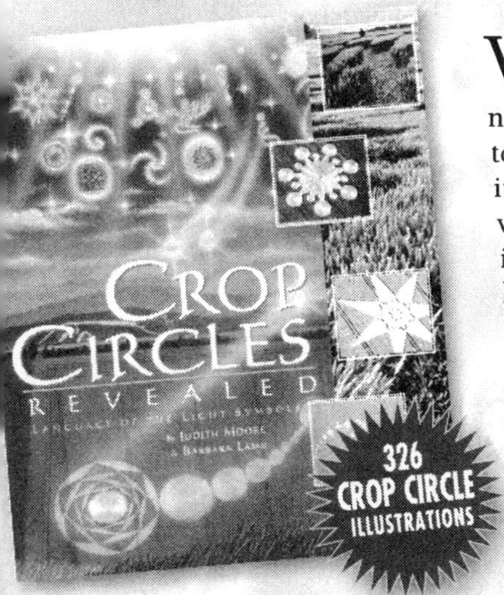

Welcome to the world of crop circles, one of the most TANTALIZING phenomena in our world today. It is difficult not to be captivated by their beauty and complexity and by the questions and issues they provoke, including one that becomes more pressing everyday—what other INTELLIGENT life forms are out there trying to communicate with us? What are their intentions? What is the communication system between them, the Earth and humanity?

Unlock the secret keys for the emergence of a new world of peace, freedom, healing and unconditional love. We are being assisted with energy as never before to REGENERATE ourselves and our ailing planet. Reactivate and discover your invaluable gifts and divine mission. Awaken your DNA and empower yourself!

This comprehensive document reveals the deep mysteries of the crop circle phenomenon. Scientific analysis of the hoaxing controversy and high level spiritual transmissions are combined in one masterful presentation for your use and interpretation. SOFTCOVER 308P. \$25.00 ISBN 1-891824-32-5

Highlights Include:

- **A Comprehensive Look at the Crop Circle Phenomenon**
- **Color Section: 16 pages of Full Color Photos**
- **Laiolin Speaks of the Crop Circles**
- **Exploring the Crop Circles and Star Glyphs**
- **Practical Use of the Crop Circles and Star Glyphs**
- **Transmissions Received on Location in Great Britain, Summer 2000**
- **Essential Channeled Information**
- **Wisdom of the Ages**

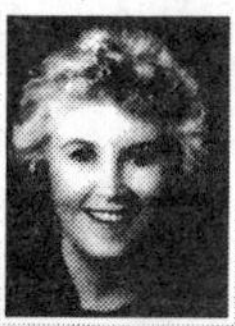

BARBARA LAMB, MS, MFL, has been visiting and researching crop circles in England since 1990. She is one of the leading crop circle researchers and educators in the United States.

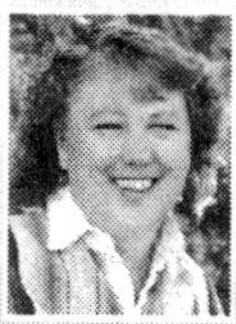

JUDITH K. MOORE has nine years experience as a spiritual interpreter, oracle for the records of Ra and channel for Laiolin, 13th dimensional ambassador of the Central Sun and member of the Council of Abborah.

LIGHT Technology PUBLISHING

LIGHT TECHNOLOGY PUBLISHING
P.O. BOX 3540 • FLAGSTAFF • AZ 86003
PHONE: (928) 526-1345 • 1-800-450-0985 • FAX: (928) 714-1132 • 1-800-393-7017

visit our online bookstore: www.lighttechnology.com